CW01494941

Oracle DBA 7.3 to 8 upgrade

The Cram Sheet

This Cram Sheet contains the distilled, key facts about new Oracle8 features. Review this information last thing before you enter the test room, paying special attention to those areas where you feel you need the most review. You can transfer any of these facts from your head onto a blank sheet of paper before beginning the exam.

MIGRATION FROM ORACLE7 TO ORACLE8

1. Migration utility is provided to speed migration effort.

2. You cannot reverse migration after **ALTER DATABASE CONVERT** command is issued.

3. Basic steps in migration processes:
   - Back up the database.
   - Install the Oracle8 migration utility.
   - Shut down the database (Shutdown Normal).
   - Run the migration utility under Oracle7 software.
   - Restart the database as an Oracle8 database copy files as required.
   - Issue the following commands: **ALTER DATABASE CONVERT, ALTER DATABASE OPEN RESETLOGS**.
   - Run cat8000.sql script and check for any invalid objects in database and revalidate any that are invalid.

4. Valid commands for migration utility are: **CHECK_ONLY, DBNAME, MULTIPLIER, NEW_DBNAME, NLS_NCHAR, NO_SPACE_CHECK, PFILE**, and **SPOOL**.

5. Abandon/cancel migration before **ALTER DATABASE CONVERT** by starting Oracle7 database, dropping the migrate user and running catalog.sql and catproc.sql scripts.

6. Use the utlconst.sql script to check for invalid constraints.

7. **ROWID** conversions might be required in tables that store **ROWID** data types.

ORACLE8 INTERNAL STRUCTURES

8. The large pool is a new memory structure used for MTS session memory, I/O slaves, and backup and recovery memory. Established by setting the **large_pool_size** parameter.

9. The database buffer cache is now referred to as the default buffer pool.

10. Two new buffer pools have been added. Objects need to be specifically assigned to one of these pools in order to use them, or the default buffer pool will be used. Each of these pools is defined in bytes, followed by the number of LRU latches assigned. The new buffer pools are:
    - The **KEEP** buffer pool—Stores database blocks that should not be aged out of memory. Set by using the **buffer_pool_keep** parameter in the init.ora.
    - The **RECYCLE** buffer pool—Stores database blocks that are transitory in nature and will likely not be needed again. Set this by using the **buffer_pool_recycle** parameter.

11. The extended **ROWID** has four different components (ORDR) which are:
    - *Component one*—Data object number that is unique for every database segment.
    - *Component two*—The relative datafile number. This datafile number is relative to the tablespace.
    - *Component three*—The data block the row is in, relative to the datafile the block resides in.
    - *Component four*—The row location in the data block.

12. The datafile number in a restricted **ROWID** is absolute to the entire database.

13. Use the **DBMS_ROWID** package to do **ROWID** conversions and manipulations.

ORACLE8 PARTITIONING

14. Tables and indexes can be partitioned. Bitmap indexes and clustered tables cannot be partitioned.

15. Partitioned tables and indexes are partitioned by the partition key, which can be up to 16 different columns.

16. The partition bounds of a partition is an upper boundary which defines the upper limit of values the partition will store. Partitions are ordered based on their partition bounds.

17. The keyword **MAXVALUE** is used to define a partition with no upper boundary.

18. Partition pruning occurs when Oracle decides not to read data from a partition based on the **WHERE** clause of the query and the partition bounds of that partition.

19. Rows are stored based on the lowest partition bounds as compared to the row being inserted. All partition key columns are compared from left to right until the correct partition is found.

20. Partitions may not contain **LONG**, **LONG RAW**, or Oracle **LOB**s.

21. The partition key columns cannot be updated. Delete the row and recreate.

22. Two different kinds of partitioned indexes: global and local. Possible combinations of indexes on partitioned tables:
    - Nonpartitioned indexes
    - Global prefixed indexes
    - Local prefixed indexes
    - Local nonprefixed indexes

23. Prefixed indexes are built on the same partition boundary as the table and allow for partition pruning to occur. Nonprefixed indexes are not.

24. Global index relationships are not known to Oracle; local index relationships are.

25. Table maintenance operations can cause indexes to become **UNUSABLE**, requiring them to be rebuilt if the affected partitions had data in them:
    - **TRUNCATE**
    - **SPLIT PARTITION**
    - **DELETE PARTITION**
    - Failure of SQL*Loader direct loads

26. To rebuild a local index use the **ALTER TABLE MODIFY PARTITION REBUILD UNUSABLE LOCAL INDEXES** command.

27. To rebuild a global index use the **ALTER INDEX REBUILD PARTITION** command.

28. Important new partitioned object tables: **DBA_PART_TABLES**, **DBA_PART_INDEXES**, **DBA_PART_KEY_COLUMNS**, **DBA_TAB_PARTITIONS**, **DBA_IND_PARTITIONS**.

ORACLE8 OBJECTS

29. An Oracle object consists of attributes and methods.

30. Two new collection types are introduced, **VARRAY** and nested tables. These collection types allow for multiple column values to be stored in a single row.

31. Oracle creates an separate segment to store nested table values out of line with the rest of the row.

32. **VARRAY**s store data that is greater than 4000 bytes out of line, otherwise the data is stored inline with the rest of the row.

33. **VARRAY**s are defined with a limit as to how many values may be stored in one row instance of the **VARRAY** type. Nested tables have no limits as to how many data values can be stored per row.

34. Flattened subquery using the **THE** clause is used to return values from collections.

35. Oracle's Objects option allows for the creation of user-defined data types with the **CREATE OR REPLACE TYPE** command.

36. Created types can be used in other types, relational tables, or object tables.

37. You refer to an attribute of a user-defined type by using dot decimal notation.

38. A row in an object table is a row object reference, and that row is an object itself and is assigned an Object Identifier (OID).

39. **REF**s are used to refer to OID of row objects in either relational tables or other object tables.

40. Methods come in four flavors
    - *Constructor*—Created automatically when the object is created.
    - *MEMBER*—PL/SQL code used to manipulate data within the object. Cannot be used to modify any database state.
    - *MAP*—Used for sorting of the attributes of the object.
    - *ORDER*—Also used for sorting of the attributes of an object.

41. Object cannot contain **LONG**, **LONG RAW**, **NCHAR**, **NCLOB**, **NVARCHAR2**, or **ROWID** data types.

Oracle DBA 7.3 to 8 Upgrade

Robert G. Freeman

Oracle DBA 7.3 to 8 Upgrade Exam Cram

Limits Of Liability And Disclaimer Of Warranty

The author and publisher of this book have used their best efforts in preparing the book and the programs contained in it. These efforts include the development, research, and testing of the theories and programs to determine their effectiveness. The author and publisher make no warranty of any kind, expressed or implied, with regard to these programs or the documentation contained in this book.

The author and publisher shall not be liable in the event of incidental or consequential damages in connection with, or arising out of, the furnishing, performance, or use of the programs, associated instructions, and/or claims of productivity gains.

Trademarks

Trademarked names appear throughout this book. Rather than list the names and entities that own the trademarks or insert a trademark symbol with each mention of the trademarked name, the publisher states that it is using the names for editorial purposes only and to the benefit of the trademark owner, with no intention of infringing upon that trademark.

The Coriolis Group, LLC
14455 N. Hayden Road
Suite 220
Scottsdale, Arizona 85260

480/483-0192
FAX 480/483-0193
http://www.coriolis.com

Library of Congress Cataloging-in-Publication Data
Freeman, Robert
    Oracle DBA 7.3 to 8 upgrade exam cram / by Robert Freeman
      p. cm.
    ISBN 1-57610-543-1
    1. Electronic data processing personnel--Certification.   2. Database management--Examinations--Study guides.   3. Oracle (Computer file) I. Title.
QA76.3.F75   2000
005.75'85--dc21
                                         99-054512
                                          CIP

President, CEO
Keith Weiskamp

Publisher
Steve Sayre

Acquisitions Editor
Jeff Kellum

Marketing Specialist
Cynthia Caldwell

Project Editor
Sharon Sanchez McCarson

Technical Reviewer
Carol Rosenow

Production Coordinator
Wendy Littley

Cover Design
Jesse Dunn

Layout Design
April Nielsen

Printed in the United States of America
10 9 8 7 6 5 4 3 2 1

14455 North Hayden Road • Suite 220 • Scottsdale, Arizona 85260

Coriolis: The Training And Certification Destination™

Thank you for purchasing one of our innovative certification study guides, just one of the many members of the Coriolis family of certification products.

Certification Insider Press™ has long believed that achieving your IT certification is more of a road trip than anything else. This is why most of our readers consider us their *Training And Certification Destination*. By providing a one-stop shop for the most innovative and unique training materials, our readers know we are the first place to look when it comes to achieving their certification. As one reader put it, "I plan on using your books for all of the exams I take."

To help you reach your goals, we've listened to others like you, and we've designed our entire product line around you and the way you like to study, learn, and master challenging subjects. Our approach is *The Smartest Way To Get Certified* ™.

In addition to our highly popular *Exam Cram* and *Exam Prep* guides, we have a number of new products. We recently launched *Exam Cram Audio Reviews*, which are audiotapes based on *Exam Cram* material. We've also developed *Practice Tests Exam Crams* and *Exam Cram Flash Cards*, which are designed to make your studying fun as well as productive.

Our commitment to being the *Training And Certification Destination* does not stop there. We just introduced *Exam Cram Insider*, a biweekly newsletter containing the latest in certification news, study tips, and announcements from Certification Insider Press. (To subscribe, send an email to **eci@coriolis.com** and type "subscribe insider" in the body of the email.) We also recently announced the launch of the Certified Crammer Society and the Coriolis Help Center—two new additions to the Certification Insider Press family.

We'd like to hear from you. Help us continue to provide the very best certification study materials possible. Write us or email us at **cipq@coriolis.com** and let us know how our books have helped you study, or tell us about new features that you'd like us to add. If you send us a story about how we've helped you, and we use it in one of our books, we'll send you an official Coriolis shirt for your efforts.

Good luck with your certification exam and your career. Thank you for allowing us to help you achieve your goals.

Keith Weiskamp

Keith Weiskamp
President and CEO

Look For These Other Books From The Coriolis Group:

Oracle8 DBA: Network Administration Exam Cram
Barbara Ann Pascavage

Oracle8 DBA: SQL and PL/SQL Exam Cram
Michael R. Ault

Oracle8 DBA: Database Administration Exam Cram
Paul Collins

Oracle8 DBA: Backup and Recovery Exam Cram
Debbie Wong

*I dedicate this book to my father, Boyd, and my mother, Jill. May you
ever know of my love for you two.*

⁊⟐

About The Author

Robert G. Freeman is an Oracle7 and Oracle8 Oracle Certified Professional with more than 7 years of Oracle experience and 11 years of IT experience. Currently, he lives in Jacksonville, Florida, with his wife, five kids, and an occasional cat. He works for International Data Services, Inc., and is on fulltime assignment at CSX, Inc., as a senior DBA and project manager. Robert has given numerous presentations and training classes on Oracle.

Acknowledgments

Thanks to the wonderful people at Coriolis: Sharon McCarson, Jeff Kellum, Wendy Littley, Cynthia Caldwell, Jesse Dunn, Wendy Qualls, and April Nielsen. Thanks also to Bonnie Trenga and Mary Millhollon, my copyeditors, and Carol Rosenow, my technical reviewer, who worked hard to make this book happen. To my comrades in arms at CSX, thanks for putting up with my crankiness because of the long hours. Special thanks to Bill, Bill, Charlie, and Tim. Thanks also to Charles Pack for some of your comments and review. Thanks to Norman, who signs my paycheck and bribed me into moving to Florida. (I have yet to dig up any of that pirate treasure you promised was on the beaches, Norman!) Thanks to Glen, who got me going on the Oracle track some years ago; Gary, my Oracle mentor; and Mark B., my original partner in crime in Oracle. Thanks also to Paul from my days at ARIS; what's up, old man? Additionally, thanks to Mike Ault.

Most of all, thanks goes to my wife, Debbie, who is ever my love, and my five kids, Felicia, Sarah, Jacob, Jared, and Elizabeth, who are rays of sunshine in the darkest of nights. Thanks to my dad, who is one of the main reasons why I am where I am today; thanks to Ruth; and thanks to my mother whom I miss greatly. Finally, thanks to God who makes all things possible.

Contents At A Glance

Table Of Contents

Introduction

Welcome to *Oracle DBA 7.3 to 8 Upgrade Exam Cram*. This book will help you get ready to take—and pass—the Oracle8: New Features for Administrators exam (commonly referred to as the Oracle7.3 to 8 upgrade exam). In this Introduction, I talk about Oracle's certification programs in general and how the *Exam Cram* series can help you prepare for the upgrade exam.

Exam Cram books help you understand and appreciate the subjects and materials you need to pass Oracle certification exams. The books are aimed strictly at test preparation and review. They do not teach you everything you need to know about a topic. Instead, I present and dissect the questions and problems that you're likely to encounter on a test.

Nevertheless, to completely prepare yourself for any Oracle test, I recommend that you begin by taking the Self-Assessment included in this book immediately following this Introduction. This tool will help you evaluate your knowledge base against the requirements for an OCP-DBA under both ideal and real circumstances.

Based on what you learn from that exercise, you might decide to begin your studies with some classroom training or by reading one of the many DBA guides available from Oracle and third-party vendors. I also strongly recommend that you install, configure, and fool around with the software or environment that you'll be tested on, because nothing beats hands-on experience and familiarity when it comes to understanding the questions you're likely to encounter on a certification test. Book learning is essential, but hands-on experience is the best teacher of all!

The Oracle Certified Professional (OCP) Program

The OCP program for Oracle7.3 DBA certification includes four separate tests. The Oracle8: New Features for Administrators exam is for those who have achieved their Oracle7.3 certification and want to upgrade to Oracle8. If you do not have your Oracle7.3 certification and want to become an Oracle8 DBA, you need to take five Oracle8 OCP-DBA exams, or you can take the four Oracle7 OCP-DBA exams and then take the Oracle8: New Features for Administrators exam. A brief description of each test in both the Oracle7.3 and Oracle8 tracks follows, and Table 1 shows the required exams for both the Oracle7.3 and Oracle8 OCP certifications.

Oracle7.3 DBA Certification

The following tests are required for Oracle7.3 DBA certification:

➤ *Introduction to Oracle: SQL And PL/SQL (Exam 1Z0-001)*—Test 1 is the base test for the series. Knowledge tested in Test 1 will also be used in all other tests in the DBA series. Besides testing knowledge of SQL and PL/SQL language constructs, syntax, and usage, Test 1 covers Data Definition Language (DDL), Data Manipulation Language (DML), and Data Control Language (DCL). Also covered in Test 1 are basic data modeling and database design.

➤ *Oracle7.3: Database Administration (Exam 1Z0-003)*—Test 2 deals with all levels of database administration in Oracle7 (primarily version 7.3). Topics include architecture, startup and shutdown, database creation, accessing and updating data, managing transaction concurrency, managing the database structure, storage allocation management, managing database internal and external constructs (such as redo logs, rollback segments, and tablespaces), and user and role management. Database auditing and use of SQL*Loader are also covered.

➤ *Oracle7.3: Backup And Recovery (Exam 1Z0-005)*—Test 3 covers one of the most important parts of the Oracle DBA's job: database backup and recovery operations. Test 3 tests knowledge in backup and recovery motives, backup methods, failure scenarios, recovery methodologies, archive logging, minimizing downtime, supporting 24×7 shops, troubleshooting, logical backups, and use of standby database features.

➤ *Oracle7.3: Performance Tuning (Exam 1Z0-004)*—Test 4 covers all aspects of tuning an Oracle7 database. Topics in both application and database tuning are covered. The exam tests knowledge in diagnosing tuning problems, configuring a database, tuning a shared pool and a buffer cache tuning, Oracle block usage, tuning rollback segments and redo mechanisms, monitoring and detecting lock contention, tuning sorts, tuning in OLTP, DSS, and mixed environments, and load optimization.

Note: Oracle is expected to retire its Oracle7.3 DBA exams. It will give Oracle7.3 DBAs six months' notice before it does so.

Table 1   Oracle7.3 And Oracle8 OCP-DBA Requirements*

Oracle7.3

All 4 of these tests are required		
Test 1	Exam 1Z0-001	Introduction to Oracle: SQL and PL/SQL
Test 2	Exam 1Z0-003	Oracle7.3: Database Administration
Test 3	Exam 1Z0-005	Oracle7.3: Backup and Recovery
Test 4	Exam 1Z0-004	Oracle7.3: Performance Tuning

Oracle8

All 5 of these tests are required		
Test 1	Exam 1Z0-001	Introduction to Oracle: SQL and PL/SQL
Test 2	Exam 1Z0-013	Oracle8: Database Administration
Test 3	Exam 1Z0-015	Oracle8: Backup and Recovery
Test 4	Exam 1Z0-014	Oracle8: Performance Tuning
Test 5	Exam 1Z0-016	Oracle8: Network Administration

* If you are currently an OCP certified in Oracle7.3, you need take only the upgrade exam (Oracle8: New Features for Administrators, Exam 1Z0-010) to be certified in Oracle8.

For those who have taken and passed all of these exams and want to become Oracle8 DBA certified, only one test is required:

➤ *Oracle8: New Features for Administrators (1Z0-010)*—This exam covers the new features of Oracle8 and what an Oracle8 DBA should know about Oracle8. The exam covers knowledge of using partitioning, implementing partitioned indexes, supporting commands and guidelines for partitioned tables and indexes, parallelizing **INSERT, UPDATE,** and **DELETE** operations, identifying new **ROWID** structures, defining object relational features, managing large objects, Oracle Advanced Queuing implementation, and using additional features in Oracle8. It also focuses on the Recovery Manager (RMAN), including using catalog commands and reports, using the **RUN** command and executing RMAN backup and recovery scripts, enhancing the network, implementation password management, and using the Migration utility to migrate server and applications.

Oracle8 DBA Certification

The following tests are required for Oracle8 DBA certification:

➤ *Introduction to Oracle: SQL And PL/SQL (Exam 1Z0-001)*—Test 1 is the base test for the series. Knowledge tested in Test 1 will also be used in all other tests in the DBA series. Besides testing knowledge of SQL and PL/SQL language constructs, syntax, and usage, Test 1 covers Data Definition Language (DDL), Data Manipulation Language (DML), and Data Control Language (DCL). Also covered in Test 1 are basic data modeling and database design.

➤ *Oracle8: Database Administration (Exam 1Z0-013)*—Test 2 deals with all levels of database administration in Oracle8 (primarily version 8.0.5 and above). Topics include architecture, startup and shutdown, database creation, managing database internal and external constructs (such as redo logs, rollback segments, and tablespaces), and all other Oracle structures. Database auditing, use of National Language Support (NLS) features, and use of SQL*Loader and other utilities are also covered.

➤ *Oracle8: Backup And Recovery (Exam 1Z0-015)*—Test 3 covers one of the most important parts of the Oracle DBA's job: database backup and recovery operations. Test 3 tests knowledge in backup and recovery motives, architecture as it relates to backup and recovery, backup methods, failure scenarios, recovery methodologies, archive logging, supporting 24×7 shops, troubleshooting, and use of Oracle8's standby database features. The test also covers the use of the Recovery Manager (RMAN) product from Oracle, new in Oracle8.

➤ *Oracle8: Performance Tuning (Exam 1Z0-014)*—Test 4 covers all aspects of tuning an Oracle8 database. Topics in both application and database tuning are covered. The exam tests knowledge in diagnosis of tuning problems, database optimal configuration, shared pool tuning, buffer cache tuning, Oracle block usage, tuning rollback segments and redo mechanisms, monitoring and detection lock contention, tuning sorts, tuning in OLTP, DSS, and mixed environments, and load optimization.

➤ *Oracle8: Network Administration (Exam 1Z0-016)*—Test 5 covers all parts of the Net8 product: Net8, Oracle Names Server, the listener process, lsnrctl (the listener control utility), and the Net8 configuration files sqlnet.ora, tnsnames.ora, and listener.ora.

For those who have taken and passed all of the Oracle7.3 exams and want to become Oracle8 DBA certified, only one test is required:

➤ *Oracle8: New Features for Administrators (1Z0-010)*—This exam covers the new features of Oracle8, and what an Oracle8 DBA should know about Oracle8. The exam covers knowledge of using partitioning, implementing partitioned indexes, supporting commands and guidelines for partitioned tables and indexes, parallelizing **INSERT, UPDATE**, and **DELETE** operations, identifying new **ROWID** structures, defining object relational features, managing large objects, Oracle Advanced Queuing implementation, and using additional features in Oracle8. It also focusing on the Recovery Manager, including using catalog commands and reports, using **RUN** commands and scripts, enhancing the network, implementation password management, and using the Migration utility to migrate server and applications.

Becoming An OCP-DBA

To obtain an OCP certificate in database administration, an individual must pass all four or five exams, depending on what track you are pursuing. You do not have to take the tests in any particular order. However, it is usually better to take the examinations in order because the knowledge tested builds from each exam. The core exams require individuals to demonstrate competence with all phases of an Oracle database's lifetime activities.

It's not uncommon for the entire process to take a year or so, and many individuals find that they must take a test more than once to pass. The primary goal of the *Exam Cram* series is to make it possible, given proper study and preparation, to pass the OCP-DBA tests on the first try.

Finally, certification is an ongoing activity. Once an Oracle version becomes obsolete, OCP-DBAs (and other OCPs) typically have a six-month time frame in which they can become recertified on current product versions. (If an individual does not get recertified within the specified time period, his certification becomes invalid.) Because technology keeps changing and new products continually supplant old ones, this should come as no surprise.

The best place to keep tabs on the OCP program and its various certifications is on the Oracle Web site. The current root URL for the OCP program is at **http:// education.oracle.com/certification**. Oracle's certification Web site changes frequently, so if this URL doesn't work, try using the Search tool on Oracle's site (**www.oracle.com**) with either "OCP" or the quoted phrase "Oracle Certified Professional Program" as the search string. This will help you find the latest and most accurate information about the company's certification programs.

Taking A Certification Exam

Alas, testing is not free. You'll be charged $125 for each test you take, whether you pass or fail. In the United States and Canada, tests are administered by Sylvan Prometric. Sylvan Prometric can be reached at 1-800-891-3926, any time from 7:00 A.M. to 6:00 P.M., Central Time, Monday through Friday. If you can't get through at this number, try 1-612-896-7000 or1-612-820-5707.

To schedule an exam, call at least one day in advance. To cancel or reschedule an exam, you must call at least one day before the scheduled test time (or you may be charged the $125 fee). When calling Sylvan Prometric, please have the following information ready for the telesales staffer who handles your call:

➤ Your name, organization, and mailing address.

➤ The name of the exam you want to take.

➤ A method of payment. (The most convenient approach is to supply a valid credit card number with sufficient available credit. Otherwise, payments by check, money order, or purchase order must be received before a test can be scheduled. If the latter methods are required, ask your order-taker for more details.)

An appointment confirmation will be sent to you by mail if you register more than five days before an exam, or will be sent by fax if less than five days before the exam. A Candidate Agreement letter, which you must sign to take the examination, will also be provided.

On the day of the test, try to arrive at least 15 minutes before the scheduled time slot. You must bring and supply two forms of identification, one of which must be a photo ID.

All exams are completely closed book. In fact, you will not be permitted to take anything with you into the testing area. I suggest that you review the most critical information about the test you're taking just before the test. (*Exam Cram* books provide a brief reference—The Cram Sheet, located inside the front of this book—that lists the essential information from the book in distilled form.) You will have some time to compose yourself, to mentally review this critical information, and even to take a sample orientation exam before you begin the real thing. I suggest you take the orientation test before taking your first exam; they're all more or less identical in layout, behavior, and controls, so you probably won't need to do this more than once.

When you complete a certification exam, the testing software will tell you whether you've passed or failed. Results are broken into several topical areas. Whether you pass or fail, I suggest you ask for—and keep—the detailed report that the test administrator prints for you. You can use the report to help you prepare for another go-round, if necessary, and even if you pass, the report shows areas you may need to review to keep your edge. If you need to retake an exam, you'll have to call Sylvan Prometric, schedule a new test date, and pay another $125.

Tracking OCP Status

Oracle generates transcripts that indicate the exams you have passed and your corresponding test scores. After you pass the necessary set of exams, you'll be certified as an Oracle DBA. (Obviously, if you are taking the upgrade exam, there is only one exam to take.) Official certification normally takes anywhere from four to six weeks (generally within 30 days), so don't expect to get your credentials overnight. Once certified, you will receive a package with a Welcome Kit that contains a number of elements:

➤ An OCP-DBA certificate, suitable for framing.

➤ A license agreement to use the OCP logo. Once it is sent into Oracle and your packet of logo information is received, the license agreement allows you to use the logo for advertisements, promotions, documents, letterhead, business cards, and so on. An OCP logo sheet, which includes camera-ready artwork, comes with the license.

Many people believe that the benefits of OCP certification go well beyond the perks that Oracle provides to newly anointed members of this elite group. I am starting to see more job listings that request or require applicants to have an OCP-DBA certification, and many individuals who complete the program can qualify for increases in pay and/or responsibility. As an official recognition of hard work and broad knowledge, OCP certification is a badge of honor in many IT organizations.

How To Prepare For An Exam

At a minimum, preparing for OCP-DBA exams requires that you obtain and study the following materials:

➤ The Oracle8 Server version 8.0.5 Documentation Set on CD-ROM.

➤ The exam prep materials, practice tests, and self-assessment exams on the Oracle certification page (**http://education.oracle.com/certification**). Find the materials, download them, and use them!

➤ This *Exam Cram* book. It's the first and last thing you should read before taking the exam.

In addition, you'll probably find any or all of the following materials useful in your quest for Oracle8 DBA expertise:

➤ *OCP Resource Kits*—Oracle Corporation has a CD-ROM with example questions and materials to help with the exam; generally, these are provided free by requesting them from your Oracle representative. They have also been offered free for the taking at most Oracle conventions, such as IOUGA-Alive! and Oracle Open World.

➤ *Classroom Training*—Oracle, TUSC, LearningTree, and many others offer classroom and computer based training-type material that you will find useful to help you prepare for the exam. But a word of warning: these classes are fairly expensive (in the range of $300 per day of training). However, they do offer a condensed form of learning to help you "brush up" on your Oracle knowledge. The tests are closely tied to the classroom training provided by Oracle, so I would suggest at least taking the introductory classes to get the Oracle-specific (and classroom-specific) terminology under your belt.

➤ *Other Publications*—You'll find direct references to other publications and resources in this book, and there's no shortage of materials available about Oracle8 DBA topics. To help you sift through some of the publications out there, I end each chapter with a "Need To Know More?" section that provides pointers to more complete and exhaustive resources covering the chapter's subject matter. This section tells you where to look for further details.

➤ *The Oracle Support CD-ROM*—Oracle provides a Support CD-ROM on a quarterly basis. This CD-ROM contains useful white papers, bug reports, technical bulletins, and information about release-specific bugs, fixes, and new features. Contact your Oracle representative for a copy.

➤ *The Oracle Administrator and PL/SQL Developer*—These are online references from RevealNet, Inc., an Oracle and database online reference provider. These online references provide instant lookup on thousands of database and developmental topics and are an invaluable resource for study and learning about Oracle. Demo copies can be downloaded from **www.revealnet.com/**. Also available at the RevealNet Web site are the DBA and PL/SQL Pipelines, online discussion groups where you can obtain expert information from Oracle DBAs worldwide. The costs of these applications run about $400 each (current pricing is available on the Web site) and are worth every cent.

These required and recommended materials represent a nonpareil collection of sources and resources for Oracle8 DBA topics and software. In the section that follows, I explain how this book works and give you some good reasons why this book should also be on your required and recommended materials list.

About This Book

Each topical *Exam Cram* chapter follows a regular structure, along with graphical cues about especially important or useful material. Here's the structure of a typical chapter:

➤ *Opening Hotlists*—Each chapter begins with lists of the terms, tools, and techniques that you must learn and understand before you can be fully conversant with the chapter's subject matter. I follow the hotlists with one or two introductory paragraphs to set the stage for the rest of the chapter.

➤ *Topical Coverage*—After the opening hotlists, each chapter covers a series of topics related to the chapter's subject. Throughout this section, I highlight material most likely to appear on a test using a special Exam Alert layout, like this:

This is what an Exam Alert looks like. Normally, an Exam Alert stresses concepts, terms, software, or activities that will most likely appear in one or more certification test questions. For that reason, any information found offset in Exam Alert format is worthy of unusual attentiveness on your part. Indeed, most of the facts appearing in The Cram Sheet appear as Exam Alerts within the text.

Occasionally in *Exam Crams*, you'll see tables called "Vital Statistics." The contents of Vital Statistics tables are worthy of an extra once-over. These tables contain informational tidbits that might show up in a test question.

Even if material isn't flagged as an Exam Alert or included in a Vital Statistics table, *all* the contents of this book are associated, at least tangentially, to something test-related. This book is tightly focused for quick test preparation, so you'll find that what appears in the meat of each chapter is critical knowledge.

I have also provided tips that will help build a better foundation of data administration knowledge. Although the information may not be on the exam, it is highly relevant and will help you become a better test-taker.

This is how tips are formatted. Keep your eyes open for these, and you'll become a test guru in no time!

➤ *Practice Questions*—This section presents a series of mock test questions and explanations of both correct and incorrect answers. I also try to point out especially tricky questions by using a special icon, like this:

Ordinarily, this icon flags the presence of an especially devious question, if not an outright trick question. Trick questions are calculated to "trap" you if you don't read them carefully, and more than once at that. Although they're not ubiquitous, such questions make regular appearances in the Oracle exams. That's why exam questions are as much about reading comprehension as they are about knowing DBA material inside out and backward.

➤ *Details And Resources*—Every chapter ends with a section titled "Need To Know More?". This section provides direct pointers to Oracle and third-party resources that offer further details on the chapter's subject matter. In addition, this section tries to rate the quality and thoroughness of each topic's coverage. If you find a resource you like in this collection, use it; but don't feel compelled to use all these resources. On the other hand, I recommend only resources I use on a regular basis, so none of my recommendations will be a waste of your time or money.

The bulk of the book follows this chapter structure slavishly, but there are a few other elements that I would like to point out. Chapter 12 includes a sample test that provides a good review of the material presented throughout the book to ensure you're ready for the exam. Chapter 13 provides an answer key to the sample test. Additionally, you'll find the Glossary, which explains terms, and an index that you can use to track down terms as they appear in the text.

Finally, look for The Cram Sheet, which appears inside the front of this *Exam Cram* book. It is a valuable tool that represents a condensed and compiled collection of facts, figures, and tips that I think you should memorize before taking the test. Because you can dump this information out of your head onto a piece of paper before answering any exam questions, you can master this information by brute force—you need to remember it only long enough to write it down when you walk into the test room. You might even want to look at it in the car or in the lobby of the testing center just before you walk in to take the test.

How To Use This Book

If you're prepping for a first-time test, I've structured the topics in this book to build on one another. Therefore, some topics in later chapters make more sense after you've read earlier chapters. That's why I suggest you read this book from front to back for your initial test preparation.

If you need to brush up on a topic or you have to bone up for a second try, use the index or table of contents to go straight to the topics and questions that you need to study. Beyond the tests, I think you'll find this book useful as a tightly focused reference to some of the most important aspects of topics associated with being a DBA, as implemented under Oracle8.

Given all the book's elements and its specialized focus, I've tried to create a tool that you can use to prepare for—and pass—the Oracle OCP-DBA set of examinations. Please share your feedback on the book with me, especially if you have ideas about how I can improve it for future test-takers. I'll consider everything you say carefully, and I try to respond to all suggestions. You can reach me via email at **dbaoracle@aol.com**. Or you can send your questions or comments to **cipq@coriolis.com**. Please remember to include the title of the book in your message; otherwise, I'll be forced to guess which book of mine you're making a suggestion about.

For up-to-date information on certification, online discussion forums, sample tests, content updates, and more, visit the Certification Insider Press Web site at **www.certificationinsider.com**.

Thanks, and enjoy the book!

Self-Assessment

I've included a Self-Assessment in this Exam Cram to help you evaluate your readiness to tackle Oracle Certified Professional-Oracle8 Certified Database Administrator (OCP-DBA) certification. It should also help you understand what you need to master the topic of this book—namely, Exam 1Z0-010 (upgrade exam), "Oracle8: New Features for Administrators." But before you tackle this Self-Assessment, let's talk about the concerns you may face when pursuing an Oracle8 OCP-DBA certification, and what an ideal Oracle8 OCP-DBA candidate might look like.

Oracle8 OCP-DBAs In The Real World

In the next section, I describe an ideal Oracle8 OCP-DBA candidate, knowing full well that only a few actual candidates meet this ideal. In fact, my description of that ideal candidate might seem downright scary. But take heart, because, although the requirements to obtain an Oracle8 OCP-DBA may seem pretty formidable, they are by no means impossible to meet. However, you should be keenly aware that it does take time, requires some expense, and consumes a substantial effort.

You can get all the real-world motivation you need from knowing that many others have gone before you. You can follow in their footsteps. If you're willing to tackle the process seriously and do what it takes to obtain the necessary experience and knowledge, you can take—and pass—the certification tests. In fact, these Exam Crams—and the companion Exam Preps—are designed to make it as easy as possible for you to prepare for these exams. But prepare you must!

The same, of course, is true for other Oracle certifications, including:

➤ Oracle7.3 OCP-DBA, which is like the Oracle8 OCP-DBA certification but requires only four core exams.

➤ Application Developer, Oracle Developer Rel 1 OCP, which is aimed at software developers and requires five exams.

➤ Application Developer, Oracle Developer Rel 2 OCP, which is aimed at software developers and requires five exams.

➤ Oracle Database Operators OCP, which is aimed at database operators and requires only one exam.

➤ Oracle Java Technology Certification OCP, which is aimed at Java developers and requires five exams.

The Ideal Oracle8 OCP-DBA Candidate

Just to give you some idea of what an ideal Oracle8 OCP-DBA candidate is like, here are some relevant statistics about the background and experience such an individual might have. Don't worry if you don't meet these qualifications (or, indeed, if you don't even come close), because this world is far from ideal, and where you fall short is simply where you'll have more work to do. The ideal candidate will have:

➤ Academic or professional training in relational databases, Structured Query Language (SQL), performance tuning, backup and recovery, and Net8 administration.

➤ Three-plus years of professional database administration experience, including experience installing and upgrading Oracle executables, creating and tuning databases, troubleshooting connection problems, creating users, and managing backup and recovery scenarios.

I believe that well under half of all certification candidates meet these requirements. In fact, most probably meet less than half of these requirements (that is, at least when they begin the certification process). But, because all those who have their certifications already survived this ordeal, you can survive it, too—especially if you heed what this Self-Assessment can tell you about what you already know and what you need to learn.

Put Yourself To The Test

The following series of questions and observations is designed to help you figure out how much work you'll face in pursuing Oracle certification and what kinds of resources you may consult on your quest. Be absolutely honest in your answers, or you'll end up wasting money on exams you're not ready to take. There are no right or wrong answers, only steps along the path to certification. Only you can decide where you really belong in the broad spectrum of aspiring candidates.

Two things should be clear from the outset, however:

➤ Even a modest background in computer science will be helpful.

➤ Hands-on experience with Oracle products and technologies is an essential ingredient to certification success.

Educational Background

1. Have you ever taken any computer-related classes? [Yes or No]

   If yes, proceed to question 2; if no, proceed to question 4.

2. Have you taken any classes on relational databases? [Yes or No]

   If yes, you will probably be able to handle Oracle's architecture and network administration discussions. If you're rusty, brush up on the basic concepts of databases and networks. If the answer is no, consider some basic reading in this area. I strongly recommend a good Oracle database administration book such as *Oracle8 Administration and Management* by Michael Ault (Wiley, 1998). Or, if this title doesn't appeal to you, check out reviews for other, similar titles at your favorite online bookstore.

3. Have you taken any networking concepts or technologies classes? [Yes or No]

   If yes, you will probably be able to handle Oracle's networking terminology, concepts, and technologies (but brace yourself for frequent departures from normal usage). If you're rusty, brush up on basic networking concepts and terminology. If your answer is no, you might want to check out the Oracle technet web site (**http://technet.oracle.com**) and read some of the white papers on Net8. If you have access to the Oracle MetaLink website, download the Oracle Net8 Administration manual.

4. Have you done any reading on relational databases or networks? [Yes or No]

   If yes, review the requirements from questions 2 and 3. If you meet those, move to the next section, "Hands-On Experience." If you answered no, consult the recommended reading for both topics. This kind of strong background will be of great help in preparing you for the Oracle exams.

Hands-On Experience

Another important key to success on all of the Oracle tests is hands-on experience, especially with Net8 Assistant. If I leave you with only one realization after taking this Self-Assessment, it should be that there's no substitute for time spent installing, configuring, and using the various Oracle products upon which you'll be tested repeatedly and in depth.

5. Have you installed, configured, and worked with Net8? [Yes or No]

If yes, make sure you understand basic concepts as covered in Exam 1Z0-013, "Oracle8: Database Administration" (Test 2) and advanced concepts as covered in Exam 1Z0-014, "Oracle8: Performance Tuning" (Test 4). You should also study the Net8 configuration and administration for Exam 1Z0-010 (upgrade exam), "Oracle8: New Features for Administrators."

You can download the candidate certification guide, objectives, practice exams, and other information about Oracle exams from the company's Training and Certification page on the Web at **http://education.oracle.com/certification**.

If you haven't worked with Oracle, you must obtain a copy of Oracle8 or Personal Oracle8. Then, learn about the database and Net8.

For any and all of these Oracle exams, the candidate guides for the topics involved are a good study resource. You can download them free from the Oracle Web site (**http://education. oracle.com**). You can also download information on purchasing additional exam practice tests ($99 per exam).

If you have the funds or your employer will pay your way, consider taking a class at an Oracle training and education center.

Before you even think about taking any Oracle exam, make sure you've spent enough time with Net8 to understand how it may be installed and configured, how to maintain such an installation, and how to troubleshoot that software when things go wrong. This will help you in the exam—as well as in real life.

Testing Your Exam-Readiness

Whether you attend a formal class on a specific topic to get ready for an exam or use written materials to study on your own, some preparation for the Oracle certification exams is essential. At $125 a try, pass or fail, you want to do everything you can to pass on your first try. That's where studying comes in.

I have included in this book several practice exam questions for each chapter and a sample test, so if you don't score well on the chapter questions, you can study more and then tackle the sample test at the end of the book. If you don't earn a score of at least 70 percent after this test, you'll want to investigate the other practice test resources I mention in this section.

For any given subject, consider taking a class if you've tackled self-study materials, taken the test, and failed anyway. If you can afford the privilege, the opportunity to interact with an instructor and fellow students can make all the difference in the world. For information about Oracle classes, visit the Training and Certification page at **http://education.oracle.com**.

If you can't afford to take a class, visit the Training and Certification page anyway, because it also includes free practice exams that you can download. Even if you can't afford to spend much at all, you should still invest in some low-cost practice exams from commercial vendors, because they can help you assess your readiness to pass a test better than any other tool. All of the following companies offer practice exams on their Web sites for less than $100 apiece (and some for significantly less than that):

➤ Selftest Software at **www.selftestsoftware.com**

➤ CramSession at **www.cramsession.com**

6. Have you taken a practice exam on your chosen test subject? [Yes or No]

   If yes—and you scored 70 percent or better—you're probably ready to tackle the real thing. If your score isn't above that crucial threshold, keep at it until you break that barrier. If you answered no, obtain all the free and low-budget practice tests you can find (or afford) and get to work. Keep at it until you can comfortably break the passing threshold.

There is no better way to assess your test readiness than to take a good-quality practice exam and pass with a score of 70 percent or better. When I'm preparing, I shoot for 80-plus percent, just to leave room for the "weirdness factor" that sometimes shows up on Oracle exams.

Assessing Your Readiness For Exam 1Z0-010 (Upgrade Exam)

In addition to the general exam-readiness information in the previous section, other resources are available to help you prepare for the Oracle8: New Features for Administrators exam. For starters, visit the Revealnet pipeline (**www.revealnet.com**)

or **technet.oracle.com.** These are great places to ask questions and get good answers, or simply to observe the questions that others ask (along with the answers, of course).

Oracle exam mavens also recommend checking the Oracle Knowledge Base from Revealnet. You can get information on purchasing the Revealnet software at **www.revealnet.com.**

For Introduction to Oracle: SQL and PL/SQL preparation in particular, I'd also like to recommend that you check out one or more of these books as you prepare to take the exam:

➤ Ault, Michael. *Oracle8 Administration and Management.* Wiley, 1998.

➤ Loney, Kevin. *Oracle8 DBA Handbook.* Oracle Press, 1998.

➤ Kreines, David C., and Laskey, Brian. *Oracle Database Administration.* O'Reilly, 1999.

➤ Toledo, Hugo. *Oracle Networking.* Oracle Press, 1996.

Stop by your favorite bookstore or online bookseller to check out one or more of these books. The first two are—in my opinion—the best general all-around references on Oracle8 available, and the third complements the contents of this *Exam Cram* very nicely. The fourth book provides excellent basic information on networking.

One last note: Hopefully, it makes sense to stress the importance of hands-on experience in the context of the Oracle8: New Features for Administrators exam. As you review the material for that exam, you'll realize that hands-on experience with Oracle8 commands, tools, and utilities is invaluable.

Onward, Through The Fog!

Once you've assessed your readiness, undertaken the right background studies, obtained the hands-on experience that will help you understand the products and technologies at work, and reviewed the many sources of information to help you prepare for a test, you'll be ready to take a round of practice tests. When your scores come back positive enough to get you through the exam, you're ready to go after the real thing. If you follow my assessment regime, you'll not only know what you need to study, but when you're ready to make a test date at Sylvan. Good luck!

Oracle OCP
Certification Exams

Terms you'll need to understand:

√ Radio button

√ Checkbox

√ Exhibit

√ Multiple-choice question formats

√ Careful reading

√ Process of elimination

Techniques you'll need to master:

√ Assessing your exam-readiness

√ Preparing to take a certification exam

√ Practicing (to make perfect)

√ Making the best use of the testing software

√ Budgeting your time

√ Saving the hardest questions until last

√ Guessing (as a last resort)

As experiences go, test-taking is not something that most people anticipate eagerly, no matter how well they're prepared. In most cases, familiarity helps ameliorate test anxiety. In plain English, this means you probably won't be as nervous when you take your fourth or fifth Oracle certification exam as you will be when you take your first one.

But no matter whether it's your first test or your tenth, understanding the exam-taking particulars (how much time to spend on questions, the setting you'll be in, and so on) and the testing software will help you concentrate on the material rather than on the environment. Likewise, mastering a few basic test-taking skills should help you recognize—and perhaps even outfox—some of the tricks and gotchas you're bound to find in some of the Oracle test questions.

In this chapter, I'll explain the testing environment and software, as well as describe some proven test-taking strategies you should be able to use to your advantage.

Assessing Exam-Readiness

Before you take any Oracle exam, I strongly recommend that you read through and take the Self-Assessment included with this book (it appears just before this chapter, in fact). This will help you compare your knowledge base to the requirements for obtaining an OCP, and it will also help you identify parts of your background or experience that may be in need of improvement, enhancement, or further learning. If you get the right set of basics under your belt, obtaining Oracle certification will be that much easier.

Once you've gone through the Self-Assessment, you can remedy those topical areas where your background or experience may not measure up to an ideal certification candidate. But you can also tackle subject matter for individual tests at the same time, so you can continue making progress while you're catching up in some areas.

Once you've worked through an *Exam Cram*, have read the supplementary materials, and have taken the practice test at the end of the book, you'll have a pretty clear idea of when you should be ready to take the real exam. Although I strongly recommend that you keep practicing until your scores top the 80 percent mark, 85 percent would be a good goal to give yourself some margin for error in a real exam situation (where stress will play more of a role than when you practice). Once you hit that point, you should be ready to go. But if you get through the practice exam in this book without attaining that score, you should keep taking practice tests and studying the materials until you get there. You'll find more information about other practice test vendors in the Self-Assessment, along with even more pointers on how to study and prepare. But now, on to the exam itself!

The Testing Situation

When you arrive at the Sylvan Prometric Testing Center where you scheduled your test, you'll need to sign in with a test coordinator. He or she will ask you to produce two forms of identification, one of which must be a photo ID. Once you've signed in and your time slot arrives, you'll be asked to leave any books, bags, or other items you brought with you, and you'll be escorted into a closed room. Typically, that room will be furnished with anywhere from one to half a dozen computers, and each workstation is separated from the others by dividers designed to keep you from seeing what's happening on someone else's computer.

You'll be furnished with a pen or pencil and a blank sheet of paper, or in some cases, an erasable plastic sheet and an erasable felt-tip pen. You're allowed to write down any information you want on this sheet, and you can write stuff on both sides of the page. I suggest that you memorize as much as possible of the material that appears on The Cram Sheet (inside the front of this book), and then write that information down on the blank sheet as soon as you sit down in front of the test machine. You can refer to the sheet any time you like during the test, but you'll have to surrender it when you leave the room.

Most test rooms feature a wall with a large window. This allows the test coordinator to monitor the room, to prevent test-takers from talking to one another, and to observe anything out of the ordinary that might go on. The test coordinator will have preloaded the Oracle certification test you've signed up for, and you'll be permitted to start as soon as you're seated in front of the machine.

All Oracle certification exams permit you to take up to a certain maximum amount of time (usually 90 minutes) to complete the test (the test itself will tell you, and it maintains an on-screen counter/clock so that you can check the time remaining any time you like). Each exam consists of between 60 and 70 questions, randomly selected from a pool of questions.

The passing score varies per exam and the questions selected. For Exam 1Z0-010, the passing score is 78 percent.

All Oracle certification exams are computer generated and use a multiple-choice format. Although this might sound easy, the questions are constructed not just to check your mastery of basic facts and figures about Oracle8 DBA topics, but also require you to evaluate one or more sets of circumstances or requirements. Often, you'll be asked to give more than one answer to a question; likewise, you may be asked to select the best or most effective solution to a problem from a range of choices, all of which technically are correct. The tests are quite an adventure, and they involve real thinking. This book will show you what to expect and how to deal with the problems, puzzles, and predicaments you're likely to find on the tests—in particular, Exam 1Z0-010, "Oracle8: New Features for Administrators."

Test Layout And Design

A typical test question is depicted in Question 1. It's a multiple-choice question that requires you to select a single correct answer. Following the question is a brief summary of each potential answer and why it was either right or wrong.

Question 1

What is the purpose of the **BFILENAME()** function?

○ a. To insert a **LOB** into a **BFILE**

○ b. To create a file in the operating file system so that you can later insert data into the file in subsequent operations

○ c. To define the file name and directory alias for the file that the **bfile** column in a row will point to

○ d. To create the **LOB** segment for out-of-line storage

○ e. None of the above

Answer c is correct. The **BFILENAME()** function, when used with an **INSERT** statement, creates the pointer in the **bfile** column of a row in a table to an external operating system data file. Answer a is incorrect because **BFILE LOB**s are read only, and you cannot insert data into them. Answer b is incorrect because the **BFILE LOB**s do not create data files and are read only. Answer d is incorrect because the **BFILENAME()** function has no relationship to out-of-line storage of **LOB**s. Answer e is incorrect because a correct answer is given.

This sample question corresponds closely to those you'll see on Oracle certification tests. To select the correct answer during the test, you would position the cursor over the radio button next to answer c and click the mouse to select that particular choice. The only difference between the certification test and this question is that the real questions are not immediately followed by the answers.

Next, I'll examine a question where one or more answers are possible. This type of question provides checkboxes, rather than radio buttons, for marking all appropriate selections.

Question 2

What types of categories of subprograms are there in **DBMS_LOB**? [Choose two]

- ❑ a. Mutator
- ❑ b. **LOB** locator
- ❑ c. Originator
- ❑ d. Destructor
- ❑ e. Observer

Answers a and e are correct. The two types of subprograms are mutators, which manipulate data, and observers, which simply display data read from a **LOB**. Answer b is incorrect because a **LOB** locator is a pointer to data that is stored out of line in the row; it not a type of subprogram in **DBMS_LOB**. Answers c and d are incorrect because neither has any relationship to the **DBMS_LOB** package.

For this type of question, one or more answers must be selected to answer the question correctly. For Question 2, you would have to position the cursor over the checkboxes next to items a, and e to obtain credit for a correct answer.

These two basic types of questions can appear in many forms. They constitute the foundation on which all the Oracle certification exam questions rest. More complex questions may include so-called "exhibits," which are usually tables or data-content layouts of one form or another. You'll be expected to use the information displayed in the exhibit to guide your answer to the question.

Other questions involving exhibits may use charts or diagrams to help document a workplace scenario that you'll be asked to troubleshoot or configure. Paying careful attention to such exhibits is the key to success—be prepared to toggle between the picture and the question as you work. Often, both are complex enough that you might not be able to remember all of either one.

Using Oracle's Test Software Effectively

A well-known test-taking principle is to first read over the entire test from start to finish, but to answer only those questions that you feel absolutely sure of on the first pass. On subsequent passes, you can dive into more complex questions, knowing how many such questions you have to deal with.

Fortunately, Oracle test software makes this approach easy to implement. At the bottom of each question, you'll find a checkbox that permits you to mark that question for a later visit. (Note that marking questions makes review easier, but you can return to any question by clicking the Forward and Back buttons repeatedly until you get to the question.) As you read each question, if you answer only those you're sure of and mark for review those that you're not, you can keep going through a decreasing list of open questions as you knock the trickier ones off in order.

There's at least one potential benefit to reading the test over completely before answering the trickier questions: Sometimes, you find information in later questions that sheds more light on earlier ones. Other times, information you read in later questions might jog your memory about Oracle8 DBA facts, figures, or behavior that also will help with earlier questions. Either way, you'll come out ahead if you defer those questions about which you're not absolutely sure of the answer(s).

Keep working on the questions until you are absolutely sure of all your answers or until you know you'll run out of time. If there are still unanswered questions, you'll want to zip through them and guess. No answer guarantees no credit for a question, but a guess has at least a chance of being correct. (Oracle scores blank answers and incorrect answers as equally wrong.)

At the very end of your test period, you're better off guessing than leaving questions blank or unanswered.

Taking Testing Seriously

The most important advice I can give you about taking any Oracle test is this: Read each question carefully. Some questions are deliberately ambiguous; some use double negatives; others use terminology in incredibly precise ways. I've taken numerous practice tests and real tests myself, and in nearly every test I've missed at least one question because I didn't read it closely or carefully enough.

Here are some suggestions on how to deal with the tendency to jump to an answer too quickly:

➤ Make sure you read every word in the question. If you find yourself jumping ahead impatiently, go back and start over.

➤ As you read, try to restate the question in your own terms. If you can do this, you should be able to pick the correct answer(s) much more easily.

➤ When returning to a question after your initial read-through, reread every word again—otherwise, the mind falls quickly into a rut. Sometimes seeing a question afresh after turning your attention elsewhere lets you see something you missed before, but the strong tendency is to see what you've seen before. Try to avoid that tendency at all costs.

➤ If you return to a question more than twice, try to articulate to yourself what you don't understand about the question, why the answers don't appear to make sense, or what appears to be missing. If you chew on the subject for a while, your subconscious might provide the details that are lacking, or you may notice a "trick" that will point to the right answer.

Above all, try to deal with each question by thinking through what you know about being an Oracle8 DBA—the utilities, characteristics, behaviors, facts, and figures involved. By reviewing what you know (and what you've written down on your information sheet), you'll often recall or understand things sufficiently to determine the answer to the question.

Question-Handling Strategies

Based on the tests I've taken, a couple of interesting trends in the answers have become apparent. For those questions that take only a single answer, usually two or three of the answers will be obviously incorrect, and two of the answers will be plausible. But, of course, only one can be correct. Unless the answer leaps out at you (and if it does, reread the question to look for a trick; sometimes those are the ones you're most likely to get wrong), begin the process of answering by eliminating those answers that are obviously wrong.

Things to look for in the "obviously wrong" category include spurious command choices or table or view names, nonexistent software or command options, and terminology you've never seen before. If you've done your homework for a test, no valid information should be completely new to you. In that case, unfamiliar or bizarre terminology probably indicates a totally bogus answer. As long as you're sure what's right, it's easy to eliminate what's wrong.

Numerous questions assume that the default behavior of a particular Oracle utility (such as SQL*Plus or SQL*Loader) is in effect. It's essential, therefore, to know and understand the default settings for SQL*Plus, SQL*Loader, and Server Manager utilities. If you know the defaults and understand what they mean, this knowledge will help you cut through many Gordian knots.

Likewise, when dealing with questions that require multiple answers, you must know and select all of the correct options to get credit. This, too, qualifies as an example of why careful reading is so important.

As you work your way through the test, another counter that Oracle thankfully provides will come in handy—the number of questions completed and questions outstanding. Budget your time by making sure that you've completed one-fourth of the questions one-quarter of the way through the test period (between 13 and 17 questions in the first 22 or 23 minutes). Check again three-quarters of the way through (between 39 and 51 questions in the first 66 to 69 minutes).

If you're not through after 85 minutes, use the last five minutes to guess your way through the remaining questions. Remember, guesses are potentially more valuable than blank answers, because blanks are always wrong, but a guess might turn out to be right. If you haven't a clue with any of the remaining questions, pick answers at random, or choose all a's, b's, and so on. The important thing is to submit a test for scoring that has an answer for every question.

Mastering The Inner Game

In the final analysis, knowledge breeds confidence, and confidence breeds success. If you study the materials in this book carefully and review all of the questions at the end of each chapter, you should be aware of those areas where additional studying is required.

Next, follow up by reading some or all of the materials recommended in the "Need To Know More?" section at the end of each chapter. The idea is to become familiar enough with the concepts and situations that you find in the sample questions to be able to reason your way through similar situations on a real test. If you know the material, you have every right to be confident that you can pass the test.

Once you've worked your way through the book, take the practice test in Chapter 12. The test will provide a reality check and will help you identify areas you need to study further. Make sure you follow up and review materials related to the questions you miss before scheduling a real test. Only when you've covered all the ground and feel comfortable with the whole scope of the practice test, should you take a real test.

If you take the practice test (Chapter 12) and don't score at least 80 percent correct, you'll want to practice further. At a minimum, download the practice tests and the self-assessment tests from the Oracle Education Web site's download page (its location appears in the next section). If you're more ambitious or better funded, you might want to purchase a practice test from one of the third-party vendors that offers them. I've had good luck with tests from Self Test Software (the vendor who supplies the practice tests). See the next section in this chapter for contact information.

Armed with the information in this book and with the determination to augment your knowledge, you should be able to pass the certification exam. But if you don't work at it, you'll spend the test fee more than once before you finally do pass. If you prepare seriously, the execution should go flawlessly. Good luck!

Additional Resources

By far, the best source of information about Oracle certification tests comes from Oracle itself. Because its products and technologies—and the tests that go with them—change frequently, the best place to go for exam-related information is online.

If you haven't already visited the Oracle certification pages, do so right now. As I'm writing this chapter, the certification home page resides at **http:// education.oracle.com/certification/** (see Figure 1.1).

Note: It might not be there by the time you read this, or it may have been replaced by something new and different, because things change regularly on the Oracle site. Should this happen, please read the section titled "Coping With Change On The Web," later in this chapter.

Figure 1.1 The Oracle certification page should be your starting point for further investigation of the most current exam and preparation information.

The menu options in the left column of the page point to the most important sources of information in the certification pages. Here's what to check out:

➤ *FAQs*—Frequently Asked Questions, yours may get answered here.

➤ *What's New*—Any new tests will be described here.

➤ *Test Information*—This is a detailed section that provides many jump points to detailed test descriptions for the several OCP certifications.

➤ *Assessment Tests*—This section provides a download of the latest copy of the assessment test after you fill out an online questionnaire.

➤ *Test Registration*—This section provides information for phone registration and a link to the Prometric Web page for online registration. Also, this section provides a list of testing sites outside of the USA.

➤ *Candidate Agreements*—Just what are you agreeing to be by becoming Oracle certified?

➤ *Oracle Partners*—This link provides information about test discounts and other offers for Oracle Partner companies.

Of course, these are just the high points of what's available in the Oracle certification pages. As you browse through them—and I strongly recommend that you do—you'll probably find other things I didn't mention here that are every bit as interesting and compelling.

Coping With Change On The Web

Sooner or later, all the specifics I've shared with you about the Oracle certification pages, and all the other Web-based resources I mention throughout the rest of this book, will go stale or be replaced by newer information. In some cases, the URLs you find here might lead you to their replacements; in other cases, the URLs will go nowhere, leaving you with the dreaded "404 File not found" error message.

When that happens, please don't give up. There's always a way to find what you want on the Web—if you're willing to invest some time and energy. To begin with, most large or complex Web sites—and Oracle's qualifies on both counts—offer a search engine. As long as you can get to Oracle's home page (and I'm sure that it will stay at **www.oracle.com** for a long while yet), you can use this tool to help you find what you need.

The more particular or focused you can make a search request, the more likely it is that the results will include information you can use. For instance, you can search the string "training and certification" to produce a lot of data about the subject in general, but if you're looking for the Preparation Guide for the Oracle DBA tests, you'll be more likely to get there quickly if you use a search string such as this:

```
"DBA" AND "preparation guide"
```

Likewise, if you want to find the training and certification downloads, try a search string such as this one:

```
"training and certification" AND "download page"
```

Finally, don't be afraid to use general search tools such as **www.search.com**, **www.altavista.com**, or **www.excite.com** to search for related information. Even though Oracle offers the best information about its certification exams online, there are plenty of third-party sources of information, training, and assistance in this area that do not have to follow a party line like Oracle does. The bottom line is this: If you can't find something where the book says it lives, start looking around. If worse comes to worse, you can always email me! I just might have a clue. My email address is **dbaoracle@aol.com**.

Third-Party Test Providers

There are third-party companies that provide example assessment tests. I suggest obtaining and taking as many of these as you can so that you become completely familiar and confident with test taking. Among these third-party providers are:

➤ *RevealNet, Inc.*—In the Oracle Administrator program, there is a complete review section for the DBA examination with example test questions. A fully functional 15-day demo can be downloaded from the Web site free of charge. The company is reached through its Web site at **www.revealnet.com/**. You can also call RevealNet at 1-800-738-3254 or 202-234-8557. RevealNet's address is: RevealNet, Inc., PO Box 5560, Rockville, MD 20855.

➤ *Self Test Software*—Self Test also offers sample Oracle tests for all four of the Oracle7 OCP-DBA tests and the Oracle8 New Features For Administrators test. Self Test is located at 4651 Woodstock Road, Suite 203-384, Roswell, GA, 30075. The company can be reached by phone at 770-641-9719 or 1-800-200-6446, and by fax at 770-641-1489. Visit Self Test's Web site at **www.selftestsoftware.com**; you can even order the software online.

➤ *DBDomain*—Formerly ORAWorld, the Web site is at **www.dbdomain.com/** and provides study guides for the OCP exams. The company can be called at 1-800-235-3030 or faxed at 805-929-8906, and is associated with Animated Learning, Incorporated. The address is: PO Box 239, Arroyo Grande, CA, 93421-0239.

Oracle7 Migration To Oracle8

Terms you'll need to understand:

√ Migration

√ Upgrading

√ Source database

√ Target database

√ **ROWID**

Techniques you'll need to master:

√ Installing the Oracle Migration utility with the Oracle installer

√ Using the Oracle installer to install the Oracle8 Migration product

√ Starting the Migration utility from the command line or the installer

√ Using Import/Export to migrate an Oracle7 database to Oracle8

√ Using SQL*Plus **COPY** commands and **CREATE TABLE AS SELECT** commands to migrate an Oracle7 database to Oracle8

√ Recovering from or canceling a failed migration

This chapter, and the Oracle Certified Professional (OCP) exam, is concerned with the migration process from a pre-Oracle8 database to an Oracle8 database. This chapter looks at how to prepare for the Oracle7 migration and how to do the migration. The chapter also covers the migration tool and post-migration steps. Finally, we look at using Import/Export and SQL*Plus to perform migrations to Oracle8 from versions of Oracle that the Migration utility does not support. I will spend a great deal of time discussing the Migration utility and its use. I will not, however, discuss Import/Export and SQL*Plus in much detail because as an experienced database administrator (DBA), you should already have some working knowledge of them.

The examples in this chapter deal primarily with Oracle on the Unix platform and the migration of Oracle on that platform. Oracle currently supports many platforms, including Unix, NT, OS/2, NetWare, and Vax. The migration process is generally the same on each platform, although there are differences on certain platforms. The OCP exam questions are platform-neutral, so you should not be concerned about platform-specific issues when preparing for the exam.

 You must clearly understand the migration process as well as the Migration program.

The Migration Process

The significant changes present in Oracle8 requires a rather involved migration process from previous versions of Oracle. *Migration* is moving from one major release of Oracle to another. *Upgrading* is moving from one revision within the same release to another. For example, making an Oracle7.3 database an Oracle8.0.5 database is a migration. Making an Oracle8.0.4 database into an Oracle8.0.5 database is an upgrade.

The migration process, using the Migration utility, consists of several basic steps, which are outlined in this section. These steps are:

➤ Preparing for the migration

➤ Determining your migration strategy

➤ Installing the Migration utility

➤ Backing up the database before the migration begins

➤ Migrating the Oracle7 data dictionary to Oracle8

➤ Backing up the Oracle7 database again before the final Oracle8 migration

➤ Finishing the Oracle8 migration

➤ Executing tasks to be performed after the migration

Preparing For The Migration

Preparation is the hallmark of any successful database migration. As a DBA, you can never prepare too much for any action you are performing on a critical production database. You can therefore do a lot to prepare so that the migration process runs smoothly. Oracle8 includes new reserved words, new **ROWID** formats, new configuration parameters, and other changes that can trip up the unprepared DBA during the migration to Oracle8—as well as on the exam.

 Before you start your migration planning, always review the current Oracle migration guide for the version of the Oracle8 database you are migrating to. The migration seems to change slightly with each new Oracle version. The guide will also provide you with insight into platform-specific issues.

When you are upgrading from Oracle7 to Oracle8, it is always a good idea to have a checklist prepared. Although some of the details (i.e., names of the migration-executable files) may differ among the various platforms, the steps you take during the migration are similar regardless of the platform. Oracle provides checklists online on the Metalink forum, and you can create your own checklist by referring to the Migration documentation. If you are using an Oracle-supplied checklist, ensure that you are using a checklist prepared for the version of Oracle8 to which you are migrating.

This checklist is the one I use to ensure that I remember everything during the task-intensive migration process. You can use this checklist for your own migration, though it is specific to a Unix environment. Feel free to add or remove items from it as your environment requires.

1. Review the Oracle documentation about changes in the migration process.

2. Prepare a test plan for the migration.

3. Install the Oracle8 software.

4. Check the status of the last backup and ensure it was successful.

5. Install the Oracle7 to Oracle8 Migration utility into the source Oracle7 **ORACLE_HOME** from the Oracle8 CD-ROM.

6. Ensure that enough space is available for the growth of control files.

7. Check that all tablespaces and datafiles are **ONLINE, OFFLINE NORMAL,** or **AVAILABLE**.

8. Check all schema names and ensure that none is called **MIGRATE**.

9. Check the **SYSTEM** tablespace to ensure that there is sufficient room to double its size.

10. Check the size of the **SYSTEM** rollback segment, and ensure that it is not near **MAXEXTENTS**.

11. Resolve all pending transactions with users (for example, sessions that have not committed their transactions yet).

12. Check **DBA_2PC_TRANSACTIONS** for any possible unresolved distributed transactions.

13. Make sure **TWO_TASK** is or is not set as required by your operating system (OS).

14. Check that the ORA_NLS33 environment is set to $ORACLE_HOME/ocommon/nls/admin/data if you are not using the US7ASCII character set.

15. Shut down the database normally. Do *not* use **SHUTDOWN ABORT**.

16. Run the Migration utility to check space: **mig check_only = true**. Review the log from this run for errors.

17. Run the Migration utility: **mig spool=\"/tmp/oracle/migrate/migrate_001.lst\"** (note the \ {escape} before the quotation marks).

18. Check the spool file for any errors.

19. Make sure the convert file in $ORACLE_HOME/dbs called convSID.dbf was created.

20. If time allows, perform another backup before finishing the migration to Oracle8.

21. Change the /etc/oratab file to reflect the new environment.

22. Change the environment for the new Oracle8 home (oraenv), and make sure the **LD_LIBRARY_PATH** is set properly.

23. Copy and adjust the init.ora file for version 8. Change the compatible parameter and other parameters as needed.

24. Rename the existing control files for the old Oracle7 database. New ones will be created.

25. Copy the convert DBF file from the Oracle7 **$ORACLE_HOME** to the Oracle8 **ORACLE_HOME.**

26. If you have a password file, move it to the Oracle8 environment.

27. Start Server Manager, and issue the **CONNECT INTERNAL** and **STARTUP NOMOUNT** commands. *Do not start the database in any other mode.*

28. Convert the database. Issue the **ALTER DATABASE CONVERT** command.

29. Open the new Oracle8 database. Issue the **ALTER DATABASE OPEN RESETLOGS** command.

30. Spool the output to a text file and run the cat8000.sql script. This is the version 8 conversion script.

31. If you are running advanced replication, run catrep8m.sql.

32. **SHUTDOWN** the database using the **NORMAL** or **IMMEDIATE** option. Do not perform a **SHUTDOWN ABORT** at this point or corruption may occur.

33. **STARTUP** the database again.

34. Change any backup and administration scripts to reflect the new Oracle8 database.

35. Recompile any objects that might have been invalidated by the migration.

36. Back up the new Oracle8 database.

37. Run your test plan and validate the results.

38. If time permits, use the Export command (**EXP**) and redirect the output file to /dev/null. This will force full tablescans on all tables to update the file and block headers to Oracle8 format.

39. Change the listener.ora file to reflect the new **ORACLE_HOME.** Shut down or reload the listener that the old Oracle7 database was on and then restart the database under the Oracle8 listener.

40. Check the SQL*Net net connection with the client.

41. Run the utlconst.sql script to check for bad date constraints. Run the test plan and then validate the results.

 One problem that has been reported is a compatibility problem with the SQL*Net listener between version 7 and 8. Generally, if a version 8 database will need to communicate with a version 7 database, you should run the version 7 database using the version 8 SQL*Net listener.

Defining The Source And Target Database Of The Migration

During the migration process, you may see references to the *source* database and the *target* database. The source database is the Oracle7 database that you are going to convert. The target database is the Oracle8 database that you are converting to. These could be the same database (with *source* referring to the Oracle7 version of that database, and *target* referring to the Oracle8 version of that same database). Alternately, in the case of the Import/Export or SQL*Plus data move methodologies, the source and target databases can be two completely different databases. These databases may even reside on different hardware.

Installing The Oracle8 Software

Your first act towards migrating an Oracle7 database is to install the Oracle8 software. Carefully review the Oracle8 installation guide, and follow the platform-specific instructions to install the database software on your system. Pay close attention to operating system requirements, including current patch levels, as you plan for the software install. A good Oracle8 install will go a long way to a successful migration.

 Check to make sure you have the most current patch level of your Oracle software. There are often bugs in the original ship code. If you have an Oracle Metalink account, you can sign on there and check for the most current patch level and the known bugs that it corrects. Also, check for known bugs in other products, such as SQL*Net, that might relate to the migration.

In some cases, multiple versions of software may be available to load, and you should take care as to which version you load. In the case of an NT conversion, the version of the Oracle8 SQL*Net you install highly depends on the version of the Oracle7 database you wish to migrate. Again, always check the documentation before you attempt a migration or software install.

Dealing With The New Oracle **ROWID** Formats

One change in Oracle8 is the new **ROWID** format. The **ROWID** is a data type that corresponds to the physical address in a table of a row. It is similar to a street address, but only identifies the address of a row in the database itself. With this **ROWID**, the database can easily find a specific row very quickly.

The **ROWID** format changes in Oracle8 may require that you modify existing code or convert existing column data in your database. A database migration to Oracle8 may require application code changes, which are changes to SQL code called by various processes. In addition, you may need to modify DBA SQL code used for tuning and administration. You may also need to write conversion code to convert stored **ROWID**s in tables to Oracle8 **ROWID**s. Circumstances that will require you to modify code or objects in the database include:

➤ Any code that manipulates part of the Oracle7 **ROWID**. This may include code that breaks apart the **ROWID** into its individual parts: the block, the row, and the file number.

➤ Any tables that may contain a column that stores the Oracle7 **ROWID**. Oracle converts the column specifications during the conversion. However, Oracle does not convert the data in these columns, so you must convert it yourself.

Conversions of existing code may require you to use the **DBMS_ROWID** package provided with Oracle8, if that code is going to access tables that have been previously populated with old Oracle7 restricted **ROWID**s. Otherwise, you do not need to modify code as long as it does not attempt to assemble and disassemble **ROWID**s. For further discussion on **ROWID**s, the new **DBMS_ROWID** package, and examples of its use, see Chapter 3.

You should become familiar with the changes in the Oracle8 **ROWID** formats. Review this topic in Chapter 3 carefully.

Using New Oracle8 Reserved Words

Oracle8 has many new reserved words. As a part of your pre-migration checklist, you should ensure that these reserved words are not used in column definitions, object names, and PL/SQL code. Table 2.1 lists the new Oracle8 reserved words.

Table 2.1 New Oracle8 reserved words.

ACCOUNT	ARRAY	BFILE
BLOB	CAST	CFILE
CHAR_CS	CHUMK	CLOB
CLONE	DANGLING	DATAOBJNO
DEFERRABLE	DEFERRED	DEREF
DIRECTORY	ENFORCE	EXCHANGE
EXPIRE	EXTENT	FLOB
GLOBALLY	HASH	HASHKEYS
HEAP	IDGENERATORS	INITIALLY
LIBRARY	LOCKED	LOGGING
LOGICAL_READS_PER_CALL	LOGICAL_READS_PER_SESSION	MASTER
NATIONAL	NCHAR	NCHAR_CS
NCLOB	NESTED	NOLOGGING
NOPARALLEL	NOREVERSE	NORMAL
NVARCHAR2	OBJECT	OBJNO_REUSE
OID	OIDINDEX	ORGANIZATIONOVERFLOW
PASSWORD	PCTHRESHOLD	PCTVERSION
PRESERVE	PURGE	QUEUE
REF	REPLACE	RETURN
RETURNING	REVERSE	SCOPE
SEG_BLOCK	SEG_FILE	SKIP
SYS_OP_NTCIMG	THAN	THE
TOPLEVEL	UNLOCK	USAGE
VALUE (Reserved Word)	VARYING	

Examining New, Obsolete, And Renamed Oracle Initialization Parameters

New Oracle initialization parameters have been added in Oracle8. Other parameters have become made obsolete and are no longer supported. Finally, some parameters have had their names changed. Table 2.2 lists new initialization parameters, Table 2.3 lists obsolete parameters, and Table 2.4 lists parameters whose names have been changed. Refer to Chapter 3 for a more detailed description of the new parameters, their default values, descriptions, and purpose in Oracle8.

Table 2.2   New init.ora parameters in Oracle8.

o7_dictionary_accessibility	allow_partial_sn_results
always_semi_join	aq_tm_processes
arch_io_slaves	uadit_file_det
b_tree_bitmap_plans	background_core_dump
backup_disk_io_slaves	backup_tape_io_slaves
bitmap_merge_area_size	buffer_pool_keep
buffer_pool_recycle	complex_view_merging
control_file_record_keep_time	core_dump_dest
create_bitmap_area_size	db_block_max_dirty_target
db_file_name_convert	db_writer_processes
dbwr_io_slaves	disk_asynch_io
fast_full_scan_enabled	freeze_db_for_fast_instance_recovery
gc_defer_time	gc_files_to_lock
gc_latches	hi_shared_memory_address
instance_groups	large_pool_min_alloc
large_pool_size	lgwr_io_slaves
lm_locks	lm_procs
lm_ress	local_listener
lock_name_space	lock_sga
lock_sga_areas	log_archive_duplex_dest
log_archive_min_succeed_dest	log_file_name_convert
mts_rate_log_size	mts_rate_scale
object_cache_max_size_percent	object_cache_optimal_size
ogms_home	open_links_per_instance
ops_admin_group	optimizer_features_enable
optimizer_search_limit	parallel_adaptive_multi_user
parallel_broadcast_enabled	parallel_execution_message_size

(continued)

Table 2.2   New init.ora parameters in Oracle8 *(continued)*.

parallel_instance_group	parallel_min_message_pool
parallel_server	parallel_transaction_resource_timeout
plsql_v2_compatibility	push_join_predicate
read_only_open_delayed	reduce_alarm
replication_dependency_tracking	serial_reuse
session_max_open_files	shadow_core_dump
shared_memory_address	spion_count
star_transformation_enabled	tape_asynch_io
text_enable	timed_os_statistics
transaction_auditing	use_indirect_data_buffers

Table2.3   Obsolete init.ora parameters in Oracle8.

ccf_io_size	checkpoing_process
gc_db_locks	gc_freelist_groups
gc_rollback_segments	gc_save_rollback_locks
gc_segments	gc_tablespaces
io_timeout	init_sql_files
ipq_address	ipq_net
lm_domains	lm_non_fault_tolerant
optimizer_parallel_pass	parallel_default_max_scans
parallel_default_scan_size	sequence_cache_hash_buckets
serializable	session_cached_cursors
unlimited_rollback_segments	use_ipq
use_readv	use_sigio
v733plans_enabled	

Table 2.4 Changed parameters in Oracle8.	
Pre-Oracle8 Name	**Version 8 Name**
asynch_read	disk_asynch_io
asynch_write	disk_asynch_io
db_file_standby_name_convert	db_file_name_convert
db_writers	db_writer_process
log_file_standby_name_convert	log_file_name_convert
snapshot_refresh_interval	job_queue_interval
snapshot_refresh_process	job_queue_processes
use_asynch_io	disk_asynch_io

You should review your init.ora initialization file before you migrate to Oracle8 to determine if you must modify any of the parameters you have set. In addition, you should review any undocumented parameters you have set as well, and determine if Oracle8 still supports them.

Checking Software Certification For Oracle8

Oracle recommends you ensure that all the Oracle product versions, OS versions, and third-party software versions are certified for the version of the Oracle Relational Database Management System (RDBMS) you are installing. You should review this information in the Oracle installation guide specific to your operating platform. It is important to ensure that you are working on supported version levels of hardware and software and that the latest patch levels are installed so that the migration will go smoothly.

Creating A Test Plan To Validate The Oracle8 Database

You should always create a plan to exercise the newly migrated Oracle8 database. The plan should ensure that the applications still work properly, that load scripts still work properly, and that PL/SQL objects still have the expected functionality. This ensures that there were no problems during the migration, such as objects becoming invalid (PL/SQL objects that use new reserved words that were not discovered before the migration, for instance). Create this test plan in concert with the application development team and make sure you run it after the migration is complete.

You should also design the test plan to validate the performance of the new Oracle8 database to ensure that it is performing at least as well as the Oracle7 database.

Another task you should always perform is testing your migration strategy on a development or test database before attempting to migrate a mission-critical database. Always test the results of your migration and ensure that it went as you expected before moving on to migrate the production environment.

 Your migration will go a lot more smoothly if you plan first. Migration by the seat of the pants can be a dangerous thing.

Determining Your Migration Strategy

Oracle supports three methods of migrating to Oracle8:

➤ Using the Oracle8 Migration utility

➤ Using the Import/Export facility

➤ Using the SQL*Plus **COPY** command

You should determine which method you will use to migrate the existing Oracle7 database to Oracle8. The Oracle8 Migration utility is the most common method used to migrate an Oracle7 database to Oracle8. You cannot use this method for a pre-Oracle7.x database, and in these cases, Import/Export is the likely candidate for migration. In the case of pre-Oracle6 databases, they generally have to be migrated to Oracle6 before they can be migrated to Oracle8 via Import/Export.

 Oracle provides a graphical interface called the Migration Assistant for use on NT. This product appears automatically when new Oracle8 software is installed on NT if an Oracle7 database is installed on the box. You may use this Graphical User Interface (GUI) to migrate the existing database if you wish. Refer to the Oracle8 for NT *Getting Started Guide* for further information on this utility.

You should review the platform-specific documentation for the Migration utility. There are some Oracle database platforms that the Migration utility can not be used on to migrate pre-7.1.x databases to Oracle8. In these cases, you must use one of the other migration options. In all cases, if you are migrating a pre-Oracle7 database, you cannot use the Migration utility unless you have first upgraded the database to Oracle7.

Your Oracle8 upgrade exam will likely contain questions on the migration utility and the other migration processes.

Tables 2.5 and 2.6 provide a list of the advantages and disadvantages of the various migration methods, respectively. Use these tables to assist you in selecting your migration methodology.

As always, you should print and read the latest Oracle8 migration document because the migration process may have changed.

Table 2.5	Advantages of Oracle-supported migration methodologies.
Migration utility	Is generally faster than other methods
	Requires fewer system resources than other methods
	Moves the entire database with relative ease
	Migration time is generally not affected by database size
	Migration time is reduced significantly; useful for 24×7 operations to reduce outage for Oracle8 migration to a minimum
Import/Export	Conversion of Oracle6 and Oracle7 databases permitted
	Allows more selective migration of objects
	The old Oracle7 database remains available
	Can be used to defragment existing database objects
SQL*Plus **COPY** or **CREATE TABLE AS SELECT**	Allows conversion of Oracle6 and Oracle7 databases
	Allows more selective migration of objects
	The old Oracle7 database remains available
	Can be used to defragment existing database objects

Table 2.6	Disadvantages of Oracle-supported migration methodologies.
Method Used	**Factors To Consider Against Use**
Migration utility	Will not migrate pre-Oracle7.x databases
	Cannot migrate specific objects
	Does not allow you to maintain the old Oracle7 database
Import/Export	Requires more system resources to run two databases
	Requires much more time and disk space generally than does the Migration utility
SQL*Plus **COPY** or **CREATE TABLE AS SELECT**	Requires more system resources to run two databases
	Requires much more time and disk space generally than does the Migration utility

The migration process described is the one that Oracle supplies with Oracle8.0.5.

Checking Other Resource Requirements Of The Oracle8 Server And Databases

The Oracle8 server has increased disk and memory requirements. Review the installation guide for your platform to determine if you have adequate resources for the Oracle8 install. The Oracle8 database control files are larger than those in Oracle7, so sufficient disk space should be available for these to grow. Oracle8 database data dictionaries are also larger. You should also use the **CHECK_ ONLY** option of the Migration tool, discussed later in this chapter, to ensure that sufficient data dictionary space is available for your database to grow during the migration.

The Oracle8 Migration Utility

Installing and running the migration is an involved process. The following sections review processes such as installation and using the Migration utility, and how to revert back a failed migration and cancel a migration.

Installing The Migration Utility

Before you can begin the migration process, you must install the Migration utility in the Oracle7 **ORACLE_HOME** of the database you are going to migrate. To do so, follow these steps:

1. Set your **ORACLE_HOME** environment for the Oracle7 **ORACLE_HOME**. Doing so ensures that the software gets copied to the correct place.

2. Start the Oracle8 installer from CD-ROM or CD staging area.

   Note: You cannot load the migration software from an already existing Oracle8 installation.

3. Once the installer has started, select Custom Install on the Install Type screen.

4. Select Install, Upgrade, or De-Install Software at the Select The Installer Activity window.

5. Select Migrate From ORACLE7 To ORACLE8 on the Select The Installer Option window.

6. Respond to the prompt for the **ORACLE_HOME** and then the log file locations window.

7. Select Install Migration Utility on the Select Oracle7 To Oracle8 Migration Action window.

8. Respond to the prompt for the **ORACLE_SID**.

9. Select Migration Utility: Oracle7 To Oracle8 on the Software Asset Manager window and then press Install.

10. Respond to the Migrate Sid window by entering the SID of the database you are migrating. The Migration utility then begins to migrate that database.

Using The Command-Line Migration Utility

The Migration utility (mig in Unix, and mig80 in NT) is a stand-alone executable used to migrate the Oracle7 database data dictionary to Oracle8. You execute the Migration utility with the environment pointing to the Oracle7 environment for the database you wish to migrate. The Migration utility creates a schema in the database called **MIGRATE**. The utility then creates an Oracle8 data dictionary based on the Oracle7 data dictionary, making the appropriate dictionary conversions in your database. The Migration utility creates a file called convSID.dbf in the ORACLE_HOME/dbs directory as a part of the migration. Lots of output is generated during this process, and you should spool it out for later reference.

You can run the Migration utility as many times as you wish and still be able to return to the Oracle7 version of the database. You do, however, need to perform some steps to successfully return to Oracle7 after the Migration utility has been run. The reason is that the Migration utility removes the version 7 catalog views that catalog and catproc create. Later in this chapter (in the section "Reverting To Oracle7 After a Failed Migration Utility Run") is information on how to return to Oracle7 after an Oracle8 migration has started.

The Migration utility (**mig**) has several command-line parameters that you can use:

➤ *check_only*—When this is set to TRUE, the Migration utility performs space-usage calculations without performing a migration. When this is set to False, the Migration utility performs both space-usage calculations and the migration. This command-line option is mutually exclusive with **NO_SPACE_CHECK**. If no **CHECK_ONLY** command line option is specified, the Migration utility sets it to False by default.

➤ *dbname*—This specifies the name of the database to migrate (**DB_NAME** in init.ora).

➤ *multiplier*—This specifies the **INITIAL** size of the version 8 i_file#_block# index relative to that of version 7. For example, **MULTIPLIER=30** triples the **INITIAL** size when the index is created. If no **MULTIPLIER** command-line option is specified, the Migration utility uses the i_file#_block# value of 15, creating an index for version 8 that is 1.5 times larger than that of version 7.

➤ *new_dbname*—This specifies a new name for the migrated database. Do not use the default name, "DEFAULT"; choose a more meaningful name.

➤ *nls_nchar*—This specifies the National Language Standard (NLS) NCHAR character set in props$ for the version 8 database, W52DEC or US7ASCII, for example. If no **NLS_NCHAR** command line option is specified, the Migration utility uses the version 7 database character set.

➤ *no_space_check*—When this is set to TRUE, the Migration utility does not perform a space-usage check before the migration. When it is set to FALSE, the Migration utility performs a space-usage check before migration. When this command-line option is not specified, the Migration utility uses **FALSE** by default.

➤ *pfile*—This specifies the name of the parameter file. If no **PFILE** command-line option is specified, the Migration utility uses the default init.ora file.

Note: On Unix, the **PFILE** *pathname must be enclosed by double
quotation marks masked by a backslash, for example:*

```
mig PFILE=\"/tmp/mig/pfile\"
```

➤ *spool*— This specifies the file name for the spool output.

Note: On Unix, the **SPOOL** *pathname must be enclosed by double
quotation marks masked by a backslash, for example:*

```
mig SPOOL=\"/tmp/mig/spool\"
```

➤ *cfile*—When set, this identifies the database control file to Oracle (not
available in Oracle8.0.5).

➤ *cnvfile*—When used, this identifies the convert.ora file if the standard
name is not used (not available in Oracle8.0.5).

 It is important to know the Migration utility's command-line
parameters well. The OCP exam may ask you what one of the
parameters is used for, or may ask which is valid when used
with the Migration utility.

Using The Installation Utility To Do A Migration

The Oracle8 installation utility (Orainst on Unix) allows you to do the Oracle7
to Oracle8 migration from it, but it does not allow you to use command line
arguments. As a result, you cannot do the space checking independent of the
migration as the command-line Migration utility allows. Follow these steps to
migrate the Oracle7 database:

1. Start the Oracle installer.

2. Once the installer has started, select Default Or Customer Install on the
   Install Type screen.

3. Select Install, Upgrade or De-Install Software at the Select The Installer
   Activity window.

4. Select the Migrate From ORACLE7 To ORACLE8 on the Select The
   Installer Option window.

5. Respond to the prompt for the **ORACLE_HOME** and then the log file
   locations window.

6. Select Run Migration Utility on the Select Oracle7 To Oracle8 Migration Action window.

7. Respond to the prompt for the **ORACLE_SID**.

8. Select Migration Utility: Oracle7 To Oracle8 on the Software Asset Manager window and then press Install.

9. Respond to the Migrate Sid window by entering the SID of the database you are migrating. The Migration utility then begins to migrate that database.

Making Final Checks And Notes Before Starting The Migration

Before the final migration process begins, you need to check a couple things. First, the Migration utility will fail if any tablespace is not in **ONLINE** or **OFFLINE NORMAL** status and if the datafiles are not in Available status. Any tablespace that is not **ONLINE** or **OFFLINE NORMAL** cannot be brought **ONLINE** after the Oracle8 database migration. Tablespaces that are **OFFLINE NORMAL** at the time of the Oracle8 migration remain in Oracle7 format until you bring them online after the migration. At that time, the Oracle8 software upgrades the datafile headers of the tablespaces.

 You can migrate the Oracle7 database to Oracle8 with all tablespaces in **OFFLINE NORMAL** status except the **SYSTEM** tablespace and tablespaces with rollback segments.

Before continuing to the backup and the migration process, check these final items:

➤ If you have an Oracle7 database on which you never installed the procedural option, you must install this option before you attempt to migrate the database to Oracle8.

➤ Check that your database does not have a user or role called **MIGRATE**. The Migration utility creates a schema by this name and overwrites any pre-existing schema called this. It drops the schema upon completion of the upgrade.

➤ Make sure you check the status of the **SYSTEM** rollback segment. Make sure it is not near running out of extents (**MAXEXTENTS**) because this will cause the Migration program to fail.

➤ Make sure there is enough room in the **SYSTEM** tablespace for the addition of the Oracle8 data dictionary along with the Oracle7 dictionary, and sufficient room for growth of the **SYSTEM** rollback segment (if that is required).

➤ If you are running the distributed option, ensure that there are no pending in-doubt transactions in the **DBA_2PC_PENDING** table. If there are some, resolve them before attempting to do the upgrade.

➤ Check the platform-specific documentation to determine if the **TWO_ TASK** environment is to be set. In Unix, it is generally not set, whereas on NT, it generally is.

➤ Do not allow others to sign onto the database while the migration is running.

➤ If you customized the Oracle7 sql.bsq file, make similar changes to a file called migrate.bsq. Doing so allows the Oracle8 data dictionary to be created in a similar fashion. Changes you might make to this file include changing the **INITIAL** and **NEXT** extent settings of data dictionary objects so they are sized more correctly for your environment. If your environment is rich in PL/SQL, you might particularly need to be concerned with this issue.

➤ Make sure you check the character set you used when you created the Oracle7 database. If it is not US7ASCII, you must make sure the proper NLS environment variables are set and that you apply the correct parameters to the Migration program that indicates the NLS character set.

You can modify the storage parameters of database data dictionary objects by modifying the migrate.bsq script. If your current Oracle7 data dictionary is fragmented badly, consider resizing the objects in Oracle8. Oracle supports changes to several storage parameters of these tables, including **INITIAL** and **NEXT**. See your Oracle manuals for more information on this.

Backing Up The Oracle Database

Before migrating the Oracle8 database, you should back it up. You should perform three backups:

➤ Before you begin the migration process

➤ After the Migration utility has completed its work but before you begin the new Oracle8 instance

➤ After the completion of the Oracle8 upgrade

You should always do a backup before you begin the Oracle8 migration process. Archive the first backup until you are sure the new Oracle8 database has been exercised and you are confident that you will not need to revert to Oracle7. If the migration has serious problems, you might want to return the database to how it was before, until you can correct the problems you discovered. The first backup allows you to do this.

Once the initial Oracle migration is complete and before you open the database, you should perform a second backup of the database. This second backup allows you to recover the database to the point immediately after the migration utility was executed on it. The first and second backups allow you to recover the database back to the previous version or back to the point after you ran the migration utility.

 Consider this when doing the second backup after the migration process has completed: Make all tablespaces **OFFLINE NORMAL** except the **SYSTEM** tablespace and any tablespace with rollback segments. Then back up only the **SYSTEM** tablespace and rollback segment tablespaces. This allows for faster recovery. In addition, the backup itself should take significantly less time. All you need to do to recover the database is restore the **SYSTEM** tablespace datafiles as well as the rollback tablespaces datafiles, and then recover them. The other datafiles are not affected by the migration utility and do not need to be backed up. You should then make the tablespaces **ONLINE** after the migration is complete. As always, you should test any backup and recovery strategy before using it in a production environment.

After the second backup, you change to the Oracle8 environment for the database. You rename the control files, start Server Manager, and issue an **ALTER DATABASE CONVERT** command to have the Oracle8 software complete the migration. After you **CONVERT** the database, you open it with the **RESETLOGS** option. If any of this process fails, you can recover to the second backup and not have to rerun the migration utility again.

As the instructions indicate, back up the new Oracle8 database immediately after the migration is complete.

Migrating The Oracle7 Database To Oracle8

Checking for available space to create the Oracle8 data dictionary and creation of the Oracle8 data dictionary is the next step that we will cover.

Check For Available Space In The Data Dictionary

When you are ready to migrate the database, your first step should be to use the migration utility with the **check_size=true** parameter. Listing 2.1 shows a snippet of the output from the execution of this utility.

Listing 2.1   Using the **mig** utility with **check_size** parameter.

```
oracle@sunbox>$ mig CHECK_ONLY=TRUE

starting up database ...mounting database ...opening  database
...#^ connect (internal)

... SNIP EXTRANEOUS OUTPUT  ...

#^ space_fb(
estimated space requirement for c_file#_block# is 88 blocks
estimated space requirement for i_file#_block# is 15 blocks
)
#^ connect (migrate, migrate)
#^ create_cluster_fb()
#^ connect (internal)
#^ space_ts(
estimated space requirement for c_ts# is 10 blocks
estimated space requirement for i_ts# is 10 blocks
)
#^ connect (migrate, migrate)
#^ create_cluster_ts()
#^ connect (internal)
#^ space_out(
estimated space requirement for V8 version of V7 catalog objects is
14287 blocks
estimated space requirement for new V8 catalog objects is 395
blocks
estimated space requirement for total V8 catalog is 14802 blocks
free space found in system tablespace is 5681 blocks
insufficient space for new dictionaries, 30314496 bytes needed,
11634688 found
) v8 catalog space requirement:  30314496
free space found:  11634688
```

The main things to review are the report of available space and the space that the report suggests is required to create the Oracle8 data dictionary. If there is not enough space or if remaining available space is very slim, you should add space to the **SYSTEM** tablespace before running the migration utility. Doing so ensures that the migration will not fail due to space constraints within the database data dictionary.

Running the Migration utility with the **check_size** parameter does not migrate the database. Running the Migration utility with **check_size** is important because the migration you are about to execute temporarily expands the size of the data dictionary. When the Migration utility is done, copies of the Oracle7 and the Oracle8 data dictionaries are contained within the database's **SYSTEM** tablespace. The **check_size** parameter ensures that there is sufficient space within the database for this operation.

Migrating The Database With The Migration Utility

The next step is to actually migrate the database with the Migration utility. Make sure you check that the environment is set correctly. You must shut down the database before you can start the Migration utility. If you do not (and the Migration utility does not do this for you when you run it with the **check_size** parameter set to True), the migration will have an error and fail. You should not do a shutdown abort, unless you restart the database and then do a shutdown normal immediately afterwards. Do not migrate the database after doing a shutdown abort; doing so may corrupt the database after the Oracle8 migration.

Start the Migration utility with the command-line parameters you have selected to use. Don't forget that if you are running an NLS character set other than US7ASCII, you need to make sure that the NLS parameter is set properly. Doing so ensures the migration is successful.

It is a good practice to have the Migration utility create a spool file using the **spool** parameter. This is so you can review the results of the migration after it is complete. Also add the command line parameter **no_space_check** (you already checked the space and there is no sense in doing so again). Finally, use the Unix **TEE** command to send the output to a file at the same time to record the screen output of the migration command to an output file as well.

The output from an Oracle7 to Oracle8 Migration utility run is shown in Listing 2.2. Remember that if the Migration utility fails while it is running, you can resolve the problem and rerun the utility without any problem.

Listing 2.2   Sample run of the Migration utility, including the screen output and the spool file results.

```
oracle@sunbox>$mig spool=\"log.txt\"
starting up database ...
mounting database ...
opening  database ...

#^ connect (internal)

drop table grant_mig_priv$;
... SNIP EXTRANEOUS OUTPUT  ...
drop user migrate cascade;

grant connect, resource, dba to migrate identified by migrate;
alter user migrate default tablespace system;
drop table dual;
drop public synonym dual;
drop table v8_objects;

/* pl/sql's standard pckg requires dual. */
create table dual
/* note, the optimizer knows sys.dual is single row */
  (dummy varchar2(1)) storage (initial 1)
/
insert into dual values('X')
/
create public synonym dual for dual
/
grant select on dual to public with grant option
/

commit;

update seg$ s set s.maxexts = 2147483645
  where (s.file#, s.block#) =
     (select u.file#, u.block# from undo$ u
          where us# = 0);
... SNIP EXTRANEOUS OUTPUT  ...
commit;

update ts$ set inc# = (select inc# from sys.ts$ where
  name = 'SYSTEM')
where name = 'SYSTEM';
#^ connect (internal)

shutting down database ...
```

Reverting To Oracle7 After A Failed Migration Utility Run

If the migration utility fails and you determine after looking at the problem that you need to revert back to Oracle7, you can do so without recovering the database any time during the migration process. You can back out of the migration at any point up until you issue the **ALTER DATABASE CONVERT** command in Server Manager (reviewed in a moment). Oracle calls this abandoning the migration, leaving me with visions of mice fleeing the sinking ship.

To abandon/cancel the migration, follow these steps:

1. Start the Oracle7 database using Server Manager.

2. You will want to drop the user **MIGRATE** in your database, using the cascade option (**DROP USER MIGRATE CASCADE**). This will remove the schema called **MIGRATE** that Oracle creates when the migration utility runs.

3. Run the catalog.sql and catproc.sql scripts. Run other scripts as required by your environment to rebuild the Oracle7 data dictionary (catrep.sql, catexp.sql, catparr.sql, and so on).

You should then have removed all hints of the migration and be able to continue with business as normal. Another backup at this point is a good idea. (Can you tell I'm backup happy?)

Finishing The Oracle8 Migration

Now that you have completed running the Migration utility, you are not quite done migrating your database to Oracle8, and several steps remain. These steps include such things as switching the database's environment from Oracle7 to Oracle8, opening the migrated database for the first time under Oracle8, and running the internal upgrade processes required once the database is running on the Oracle8 software.

Preparing Your Database Environment For The New Oracle8 Database

Once the Oracle migration has completed, you have finished with the Oracle7 environment for that database, and it is ready to become a full-fledged Oracle8 database. Modify the environment for your database so that it reflects its new Oracle8 nature. You should modify the following settings, among others:

➤ Change the oratab file entry for the database to reflect the new **ORACLE_HOME** location.

➤ Reset the current environmental variables **PATH, ORACLE_HOME, ORACLE_SID, LD_LIBRARY_PATH,** and any others that might be used (such as **ORA_NLS33, NLS_LANG,ORACLE_BASE**).

➤ Modify any automatically executing scripts that might set your environment when you sign onto the system (such as .profile, .login, and so on).

 If you are not already aware, the Oracle-supplied oraenv script (in Unix, this hint also applies to coraenv script for cshell), which allows you to move among different Oracle databases, does not change the Unix environment variable **LD_LIBRARY_ PATH**. If this is the first time that you are using Oracle8, be careful that you properly set this environment variable.

Changing init.ora

To make sure that your database comes up the first time under Oracle8, you might need to make a few changes to init.ora. Probably the most important one of these for the migration is the compatibility parameter, which you should set to the version of Oracle8 you are migrating to. See Chapter 3 for a more detailed discussion of the changes to the Oracle7 init.ora parameters.

Tying Up The Loose Ends Before Starting Up The Database Again

Copy the convSID.dbf file that was created by the Oracle Migration utility from the Oracle7 ORACLE_HOME/dbs directory to the Oracle8 ORACLE_HOME directory. It is possible to change the SID when you are using the Migration utility, and multiple conversion files may exist in the directory, so make sure you are copying the correct conversion file. If you have a password file for your database, move it now to the correct location for the Oracle8 database you are preparing to migrate.

Final Conversion To Oracle8

Now we approach the point of no return. It is time to open the database under Oracle8. To avoid database corruption, it is important that you follow the conversion steps in the proper order. The first step is to start the Oracle8 instance **(STARTUP NOMOUNT)** in preparation for the conversion. Once the instance has started, issue the conversion command from Server Manager: **ALTER DATABASE CONVERT.**

You have now dropped the Oracle7 data dictionary, and the control files have been recreated, reflecting the new Oracle8 structure changes that make them so big. Now, open the database and reset the redo logs (**ALTER DATABASE OPEN RESETLOGS**). Then, run a script that makes some additional final updates to the data dictionary. From Server Manager, after opening a spool file, run the cat8000.sql script. There are other scripts to run if you also use a parallel server (catparr.sql) or advanced replication (catrep8m.sql). Review the migration guide for the most current information.

Some publications tell you that you have to run catalog.sql and catproc.sql after running cat8000.sql. This is, in fact, not required in the 8.0.5 migration from Oracle7. The cat8000.sql script runs catalog.sql and catproc.sql scripts when it is executed from Server Manager.

At this point, the database has been converted and is now an Oracle8 database. You should shut down the database normally the first time to avoid any corruption, and then back up the database as quickly as possible.

Note: Recovery to a point in time, based on the Oracle7 backup, is not possible at this point. Therefore, do not delay in getting a backup of the database, particularly if the database is a mission-critical database and you do hot backups.

After The Migration To Oracle8

After you back up your new Oracle8 database for the first time, you may want to do a few more things. These are tasks designed to exercise the database to validate that the Oracle8 migration was successful, to force the Oracle8 database to go ahead and update the **ROWID**s in the tables to Oracle8 **ROWID**s, and to validate certain types of constraints and indexes.

Checking For Bad Data Constraints

It is possible to have constraints set up in the database that are invalid for Y2K date checking. You may use invalid date manipulation in your constraints, or if you fall victim to an interesting Oracle date-conversion bug that was fixed in Oracle8. For example, in Oracle7, you were allowed to create a table using a two-digit year as the constraint, as shown in Listing 2.3. Notice also in that

Oracle8 no longer permits this kind of operation (unless you set a specific event in the init.ora, which is not recommended) because of its potential as a Y2K bug. Listing 2.3 shows the correct way to create a table with a date constraint that is acceptable with Oracle8.

Listing 2.3   Example of an invalid Oracle8 date constraint that is valid in Oracle7.

```
ATTEMPT TO CREATE TABLE IN ORACLE7 DATABASE

create table test
(dot date check(dot < '01-JAN-00'));

Table created.

SAME ATTEMPT TO CREATE TABLE IN ORACLE8 DATABASE
create table test
(dot date check(dot < '01-JAN-00'))

(dot date check(dot < '01-JAN-00'))
                  *
ERROR at line 2:
ORA-02436: date or system variable wrongly specified
in CHECK constraint
```

To prevent these invalid constraints from affecting your database, you should run the SQL script utlconst.sql. This script searches for illegal date constraints and invalidates them. It then produces a report that indicates which constraints were invalidated. You should review the report and correct the constraints that have problems.

 As an Oracle7 DBA, you should already be aware of how to rebuild invalidated bitmap indexes, check for invalid PL/SQL modules, and run your test plan. This is why these topics are covered only briefly here.

Rebuilding Invalidated Bitmap Indexes

During the Oracle migration, some bitmap indexes may become invalid. Check in **DBA_INDEXES** for these invalid indexes and then rebuild these indexes again.

Checking For Invalid PL/SQL Modules

Run the ORACLE_HOME/rdbms/admin/utlrp.sql script to check the status of the PL/SQL objects in your database. Doing so ensures that any PL/SQL packages invalidated during the migration are revalidated.

Running Your Test Plan

Make sure performance is as you expected. During the migration, most of your database objects become invalid. Oracle provides a script to recompile the invalidated objects. Refer to the platform-specific migration documentation for the script name on your platform.

Migrating To Oracle8 With Import/Export

In some cases, you cannot use the Oracle7 to Oracle8 Migration utility to migrate your Oracle database, or you may wish to migrate your data between an existing Oracle7 database and a newly created Oracle8 database. There may be many reasons for this, including:

➤ The Migration utility will not work on the version of Oracle your database is currently on (for example, Oracle version 6).

➤ You want to migrate only part of an existing database structure to Oracle8.

➤ You want to leave the existing Oracle7 database in place for the time being.

➤ Migration using the Import/Export utility can double as a database defragmentation at the same time you migrate it.

➤ Migration using the Import/Export utility will allow you to restructure the database with modified or new tablespaces.

➤ While using the Import/Export utility to migrate a database, you can move other logical database objects associated with the database over at the same time (constraints, foreign keys, PL/SQL, and so on).

➤ Migration using the Import/Export utility will let you restructure the database, allowing you to partition tables as a part of the migration.

There are some negative factors to consider as well, including:

➤ The Import/Export process can be very slow.

➤ The process is even slower if long data types are used frequently in tables.

➤ The process takes large amounts of disk space to copy the data to the target database. File system space limitations might impose additional problems when trying to export the database.

➤ Import/Export imposes additional resource constraints associated with two databases running at the same time.

Oracle supports migration using the Import/Export methodology for migrating to Oracle8. DBAs should fully understand the Import/Export facility before attempting this type of migration. The basic steps of an Oracle7 to Oracle8 migration using Import/Export are:

1. Export the data from the Oracle7 source database that you wish to migrate

2. Create the Oracle8 database into which you will migrate the source database data

3. Import the data exported from the source database into the new Oracle8 target database

DBAs who have worked in Oracle7 and passed the Oracle7 OCP exam should be well versed in using Export and Import to create/re-create a database.

Migrating To Oracle8 Using SQL*Plus To Copy Data

In some situations, it might be preferable to use SQL*Plus to actually migrate the data from Oracle7 to Oracle8, as opposed to using the Migration utility. You typically use SQL*Plus when there is little data to move because it can take significantly less time to move data through SQL*Plus than to use the Import/Export method. You may want to use the SQL*Plus method for these reasons:

➤ The Migration utility will not work on the version of Oracle your database is currently on (such as Oracle version 6).

➤ You want to migrate only part of an existing database structure to Oracle8.

➤ You want to leave the existing Oracle7 database in place for the time being.

➤ Use of the SQL*Plus migration method can double as a database defragmentation at the same time you move the data.

➤ Using the SQL*Plus migration method, you can restructure the database with a modified design, taking advantage of new Oracle8 features such as partitioning.

➤ The SQL*Plus method of migrating to Oracle8 lets you restructure the database, allowing you to partition tables as a part of the migration.

The negative factors to using SQL*Plus include:

➤ The movement of data through Net8/SQL*Net can be very slow.

➤ The process is even slower if long data types are used frequently in tables.

➤ The process takes large amounts of disk space to copy the data to the new database.

➤ There are additional resource constraints associated with two databases running at the same time.

➤ Objects associated with the data are not created. You must therefore make sure that all objects are created: constraints, indexes, Foreign keys, and so on. It would be easy for a database to get out of sync using this method of migration.

Oracle supports using SQL*Plus and the SQL*Plus **COPY** or **CREATE TABLE AS SELECT** command for migrating to Oracle8. DBAs should fully understand the SQL*Plus methods of moving data—including using the **CREATE TABLE AS SELECT** command and the SQL*Plus **COPY** command—before attempting a migration using the SQL*Plus **COPY** command. If you use the SQL*Plus **COPY** command, you must create the table on the Oracle8 server before you can copy the data. If you use the **CREATE TABLE AS SELECT** command, you are pulling the data from the Oracle7 server. On the other hand, the SQL*Plus **COPY** command pushes the data to the Oracle8 server.

The basic steps of an Oracle7 to Oracle8 migration using SQL*Plus are:

1. Create the Oracle8 database that you are copying data into. You must also set up the new database in Net8.

2. If you are going to use the **CREATE TABLE AS SELECT** command, sign into the Oracle8 database.

3. Set up a link to the Oracle7 database.

4. Once the link is set up, create the table using the **CREATE TABLE AS SELECT** command. Doing so creates the table and pulls the data from

Oracle7. Don't forget to create any foreign keys, constraints, indexes, and the like on the table so that the table is logically the same as the one in Oracle7.

5. If you are going to use the SQL*Plus **COPY** command, you must create the table on the Oracle8 database. You must then create a link to the Oracle8 database from the Oracle7 database that contains the data you intend to migrate. Once the link is created, use the **COPY** command to move the data.

Practice Questions

Question 1

> What are the most critical steps to performing a good Oracle8 migration? [Choose two]
>
> ❑ a. Back up the database before the migration
>
> ❑ b. Properly plan the migration
>
> ❑ c. Revalidate objects
>
> ❑ d. Run the migration utility with the **CHECK_ONLY** option
>
> ❑ e. Tune the new Oracle8 database parameters in init.ora

Answers a and b are correct. You should always back up the database before the migration as well as make sure you properly plan the migration process before executing it. Answer c is incorrect because even if you don't revalidate the objects, they will revalidate themselves over time—although doing so may cause performance problems at first. Answer d is incorrect because the **CHECK_ ONLY** option is used only to verify the availability of space in the **SYSTEM** tablespace for the new Oracle8 data dictionary objects. The Oracle Migration utility, by default, checks for sufficient space when doing the migration anyway, so this step is optional. Answer e is incorrect because although tuning the database itself is important, it is not critical for successful migration of the database.

Question 2

> Which command-line option is not available in the Migration utility?
>
> ○ a. **DBNAME**
>
> ○ b. **NO_SPACE_CHECK**
>
> ○ c. **CHECK**
>
> ○ d. **SPOOL**
>
> ○ e. **NEW_DBNAME**

Answer c is correct, there is no **CHECK** option to the Migration utility. Answer a is incorrect because **DBNAME** specifies the name of the database to migrate to. Answer b is incorrect because it specifies that the Migration utility should not check for adequate space in the data dictionary. Answer d is incorrect because it specifies where the spool file should be sent to. Answer e is incorrect because it specifies a new name for the migrated database.

Question 3

Which step is performed first during a migration from Oracle7 to Oracle8?

- O a. Back up the Oracle7 database
- O b. Run the Migration utility
- O c. Start the database with the Oracle8 software
- O d. Create a plan for the migration
- O e. Issue the **ALTER DATABASE CONVERT** command from Server Manager

Answer d is correct. You should always plan the conversion before you set out to do it. This step includes getting the application developers involved so they can review their code for new reserved words. It should also include a review of the database to make sure there are no migration issues. Answer a is incorrect because although it is among the first steps and is almost as important as planning, it is not the first step. Answers b, c, and e are incorrect because they are several steps along in the migration process.

Question 4

Which method of migrating data from Oracle7 to Oracle8 does Oracle not support?

- O a. Using the Oracle Migration utility
- O b. Using the **COPY** command in SQL*Plus
- O c. Starting up the Oracle7 database with the Oracle8 software and running catalog.sql and catproc.sql to migrate
- O d. Using Import and Export to migrate the database
- O e. Using the SQL*Plus command **CREATE TABLE AS SELECT**

Answer c is correct. Oracle does not support just starting an Oracle7 database under Oracle8 and running the data dictionary scripts to migrate the database to an Oracle8 database. Answers a, b, d, and e are all incorrect because they are Oracle-supported options that allow you to migrate Oracle7 data to an Oracle8 database.

Question 5

What are the benefits of using the Migration utility to convert an Oracle7 database to Oracle8 over using Import/Export or using the SQL*Plus **COPY** command? [Choose three]

- ❏ a. Use of the Migration utility requires fewer system resources.
- ❏ b. Use of the Migration utility allows you to copy individual data from the Oracle7 database into the Oracle8 database.
- ❏ c. Use of the Migration utility generally is the fastest method to migrate an entire database.
- ❏ d. Use of the Migration utility allows you to revert the database back to Oracle7 at any time.
- ❏ e. Use of the Migration utility imposes no limit on the size of the database you wish to migrate.
- ❏ f. Use of the Migration utility allows you to migrate from any version of Oracle to Oracle8.

Answers a, c, and e are correct. Answer a is correct because you don't have to have two Oracle databases up in order to migrate the database; therefore, fewer system resources are required. Answer c is correct because the Migration utility is generally faster than Import/Export or copying data through SQL*Plus. Answer e is correct because the Migration utility has no requirements for space for storage of data, unlike with the Import/Export method. Answer b is incorrect because there is no provision in the Migration utility to migrate specific data into an Oracle8 database. Answer d is incorrect because you cannot revert to Oracle7 after you have issued the **ALTER DATABASE CONVERT** command in Oracle8; to return to an Oracle7 database, you must recover the database with the Oracle7 backup. Answer f is incorrect because you cannot use the Migration utility to migrate from an Oracle database version of earlier than 7.x.

Question 6

Migration from Oracle7 to Oracle8 increases disk space requirements in which area?

○ a. SGA

○ b. Sort area

○ c. Data dictionary

○ d. Sort extent pool

○ e. Database buffer cache

Answer c is correct. Additional space in the **SYSTEM** tablespace is required to accommodate the increase in size of the Oracle8 data dictionary. Answer a is incorrect because the SGA size is controlled by init.ora, and there are no disk space requirements associated with it as far as the upgrade. Answer b is incorrect for the same reason that answer a is incorrect. Answer d is incorrect because the sort extent pool is not affected by the migration. Answer e is incorrect because the database buffer cache is a memory area and is not stored on disk.

Question 7

Which part of the migration can you run and still revert to the Oracle7 database without restoring the Oracle7 backup? [Choose two]

❏ a. The final backup

❏ b. The running of the Migration utility

❏ c. Execution of the **ALTER DATABASE CONVERT** command

❏ d. Execution of the **ALTER DATABASE OPEN RESETLOGS** command

❏ e. The first backup

Answers b and e are correct. Answer b is correct because you can revert to Oracle7 with a minimum of effort after running the Oracle Migration utility. Answer e is correct because the migration process has not even occurred yet. Answer a is incorrect because the entire migration has already taken place by this time. You would have to restore the first or second backup to return to Oracle7 at this point. Answer c is incorrect because this step actually marks the point of no return. After this step, you can return to Oracle7 only by recovering from the first or second backup. Answer d is incorrect because it is executed after the point of no return.

Question 8

Which Oracle script is supplied with the Oracle8 product to check for bad constraints that may have been created in the Oracle7 database because of a bug in Oracle7?

○ a. catalog.sql

○ b. utlbstat.sql

○ c. utlcons.sql

○ d. chkconst.sql

○ e. utlconst.sql

Answer e is correct. utlconst.sql is provided by Oracle to check all constraints and make sure the date checking in them is valid. Answer a is incorrect because it is used to create catalog views when you create a database. Answer b is incorrect because that script is used to generate performance statistics for tuning a database. Answers c and d are incorrect because they do not exist.

Question 9

When you start the Oracle8 database for the first time after the Migration utility has been executed, what command do you issue to start up the Oracle8 instance?

○ a. **STARTUP**

○ b. **STARTUP MOUNT**

○ c. **STARTUP NOMOUNT**

○ d. **STARTUP FORCE**

○ e. **SHUTDOWN ABORT**

Answer c is correct When starting the instance the first time under Oracle8, after the Migration utility has executed, you will always do a startup nomount. Answers a and b are incorrect because you never want to open an Oracle8 migrated database without first issuing the **ALTER DATABASE CONVERT** command. Answer d is incorrect because this command attempts to open the database as well. Answer e is incorrect because you want to start the instance, not shut it down.

Question 10

> After you migrate the database to Oracle8, a stored procedure doesn't run
> any longer. What might be the problem?
>
> ○ a. Oracle8 no longer supports PL/SQL.
>
> ○ b. The stored procedure may be attempting to manipulate a **ROWID** in
>   the Oracle7 format and might need to be modified.
>
> ○ c. The stored procedure was not specified in the parameter file for the
>   Migration utility and was therefore not migrated properly.
>
> ○ d. You must manually recompile all procedures after an Oracle8
>   migration.
>
> ○ e. All stored procedures must have their headers changed and then be
>   recompiled in Oracle8.

Answer b is correct. This is because if the stored procedure is modifying a
ROWID and is expecting the **ROWID** to be in ORACLE7 restricted **ROWID**
format, it will require modification. Answer a is incorrect because Oracle8 defi-
nitely supports PL/SQL. Answer c is incorrect because there is no parameter
file in which to list stored procedures for the Migration utility. Answer d is
incorrect because you do not have to manually recompile all the procedures after
an Oracle8 migration. Answer e is incorrect because you do not have to modify
PL/SQL headers after a migration to Oracle8.

Question 11

> Which part of the migration processes modifies the **ROWID**s stored in the
> Oracle data dictionary?
>
> ○ a. The **ALTER DATABASE CONVERT** command
>
> ○ b. The **ALTER DATABASE OPEN RESETLOGS** command
>
> ○ c. The Migration utility
>
> ○ d. The utilconst.sql scrip
>
> ○ e. None of the above

Answer e is correct. Remember that the **ROWID** is a derived column and is
not stored in the Oracle database data dictionary. Answers a, b, c, and d are all
incorrect for this reason.

Need To Know More?

Review the Oracle8 Migration utility documentation included with your version of Oracle8.

Review the *Oracle8 Install* manual and the *Oracle8 New Features For The Administrators* manual.

Review the Oracle8 *Getting Started Guide* for your specific platform.

Curtis, Mike and King, Jacqueline: *Oracle8 & Windows NT Black Book*. The Coriolis Group, 1998. ISBN 1-57610-248-3.

Oracle's Metalink Web site is a wonderful resource if you have Oracle Metals Support. Go to **www.support.com**.

Oracle8 Internal Structures

Terms you'll need to understand:

√ Large pool

√ Default buffer pool

√ **KEEP** buffer pool

√ **RECYCLE** buffer pool

√ CKPT process

√ Chained rows

√ Restricted **ROWID**

√ Extended **ROWID**

Techniques you'll need to master:

√ Understanding what the large pool is

√ Understanding how multiple buffer pools are config-ured, and their purpose

√ Understanding the new dynamically changeable system configuration settings and how to use them

√ Understanding changes in the Oracle processes

√ Understanding National Language Support (NLS) enhancements in Oracle

√ Understanding changes in the Oracle **ROWID** format

√ Understanding and being able to use the **DBMS_ ROWID** package

Oracle has made several changes to the internal structures of the Oracle database. In addition, new processes have been added, and Oracle has made one previously optional process mandatory. This chapter addresses these changes as well as the changes to the initialization parameters that were touched on in Chapter 2. This chapter then looks at enhancements to NLS data types. Finally, the chapter reviews the changes to the **ROWID** structure, and reviews the new **DBMS_ROWID** package.

Changes To The Oracle8 SGA

In Oracle8, Oracle has introduced changes to the SGA (Shared Global Area) in an attempt to improve the performance of the SGA structures. This section looks at some of these changes, including the large pool and the multiple buffer pool structures introduced in Oracle8.

The Large Pool

Oracle has modified the SGA in Oracle8, particularly where MTS (multi-threaded server) is concerned. As an Oracle7 certified professional, you should already be acquainted with Oracle's MTS option, which allows you to have one process manage several user connections. Oracle has added a new optional structure, called the *large pool*, to the SGA. When the large pool is configured, it is used for two main purposes:

➤ Contains the User Global Area (UGA) when sessions are connected using MTS

➤ Buffers for sequential file I/O

Before Oracle8, Oracle stored MTS user connection information in the UGA structure of the shared pool. As the number of users would increase, it was possible for the SGA to run out of space. This additional memory requirement imposed by the use of MTS would reduce the shared pool memory available for the data dictionary cache and the library cache. Oracle now uses the large pool for the session's UGA if the DBA has configured it. The large pool is protected by the shared pool latch and does not use any LRU (least recently used) algorithm to manage space. Therefore, memory must be allocated and freed by each session. An ORA-4031 message will occur if the large pool runs out of memory. You can see the space usage of the large pool by querying the **V$SGASTAT** view, as shown in Listing 3.1.

 You should understand the large pool and its purpose before taking the OCP exam.

Listing 3.1   A sample query of the **V$SGASTAT** view that shows the large pool allocations.

```
SVRMGR> SELECT * FROM v$sgastat;
POOL         NAME                          BYTES
-----------------------------------------------
             fixed_sga                     48656
             db_block_buffers            1638400
             log_buffer                    65536
shared pool  free memory                 2138560
shared pool  miscellaneous                151620
shared pool  table columns                 15232
shared pool  PLS non-lib hp                 2096
shared pool  KGK heap                       3220
shared pool  DML locks                     30624
shared pool  PL/SQL DIANA                 205396
shared pool  Checkpoint queue              15420
shared pool  latch nowait fails or sle     25664
shared pool  fixed allocation callback      1248
shared pool  network connections           16720
shared pool  ktlbk state objects           28248
shared pool  kcb where/why stats array     10752
shared pool  transaction_branches          11776
shared pool  SYSTEM PARAMETERS             48288
shared pool  state objects                 13072
shared pool  transactions                  56496
shared pool  State objects                 59228
shared pool  db_files                      66344
shared pool  node map                      16384
shared pool  KQLS heap                     99104
shared pool  file # translation table       8252
shared pool  dictionary cache             151036
shared pool  db_block_buffers              41600
shared pool  PL/SQL MPCODE                 23824
shared pool  character set memory          23456
shared pool  enqueue_resources             20448
shared pool  library cache                335672
shared pool  branches                      16080
shared pool  sql area                     336416
shared pool  processes                     37600
shared pool  sessions                     125520
shared pool  KGFF heap                      3152
shared pool  event statistics per sess    151680
shared pool  VIRTUAL CIRCUITS              82356
shared pool  db_handles                    21000
shared pool  LRMPD SGA Table               20216
large pool   free memory                99967760  ← Total left in
   large pool
```

```
large pool  session heap                      32240  ← Space used by
   one session
42 rows selected.
SVRMGR>
```

Another use of the large pool is as a memory buffering area for slaved DB writers. You use the writers to attempt to mimic asynchronous I/O on various systems that do not provide this feature. Check your system's specific documentation to determine if you might benefit from multiple DB writers.

Multiple Buffer Pools

The way objects use blocks in the SGA depends on the nature of the object (table, index, and so forth) and the way the object is used (for example, an object may be a small, static, but constantly used lookup table, or a large, static, but rarely used data warehouse table). The different usage characteristics of these objects often demand different types of storage. Some objects should be kept in memory as long as possible and others should be cleared out of memory soon after use. To deal with these types of situations, Oracle8 provides a method of allowing more granular control over the SGA storage of database blocks and how long blocks are maintained in memory. Oracle now provides three pools for database data block storage:

➤ Default buffer cache

➤ **KEEP** buffer pool

➤ **RECYCLE** buffer pool

Each of these pools allows you to assign specific database objects to them and to retain the blocks from those objects using different retention criteria. The **KEEP** buffer pool and the **RECYCLE** buffer pool segment memory from the default buffer pool, so be careful that you do not leave the default buffer pool short of memory. DBAs may use the **V$BUFFER_POOL** view to monitor the various buffer pool settings currently in use.

The Default Buffer Pool

The *default buffer pool* (still referred to as the database buffer cache) is always allocated in an Oracle8 database. To allocate memory to the default buffer pool, set the number of database buffer blocks you want the cache to be and do so by setting the **DB_BUFFER_BLOCKS** setting in the init.ora parameter file. The total size of this cache then is calculated as **DB_BUFFER_BLOCKS** *****DB_BLOCK_SIZE**. As with Oracle7, the LRU algorithm manages the data blocks in the default buffer pool.

The **KEEP** Buffer Pool

In later versions of Oracle7, a **CACHE** option was available on database tables. This caused the database blocks that were read in from a table during a full table scan to be put onto the MRU (most recently used) end of the LRU (least recently used) list, as opposed to the LRU end. Thus, the data blocks associated with that table remained in the database buffer cache for a longer period of time before being aged out. The idea was to allow for as close to a 100 percent cache hit ratio as possible on these often-hit, smaller tables. Although this option is still available in Oracle8, the new *KEEP buffer pool* gives you a dedicated segment of database buffer cache memory in which to load the blocks of these tables. Typically, these are smaller tables, such as lookup tables.

You can set the **buffer_pool_keep** parameter in init.ora to reserve part of the database buffer cache for pinned data blocks. Once the **KEEP** buffer pool is created, you can assign objects to this pool, and if the pool is sized properly, the data blocks from these objects will remain in memory. You must exercise caution when setting up the **KEEP** buffer pool. Ensure that you allocate only enough memory to store the blocks you wish kept in the buffer pool, and yet not over-allocate to the pool memory that will go unused. You determine how much memory to allocate to the pool by adding up the sizes of all the objects you intend to assign to the pool. Keep in mind that as you allocate memory to the pool, you reduce the amount of memory available in the database buffer cache to the default pool. If you undersize the pool, objects will be aged out using the LRU algorithm, as with the default buffer pool. Refer to Chapter 6 for more information on assigning objects to the **KEEP** buffer pool. An example of assigning a table to the **KEEP** buffer pool is shown below.

```
CREATE TABLE small_table
(pk_id    NUMBER    NOT NULL    PRIMARY KEY,
table_info    VARCHAR2    NOT NULL)
STORAGE (INITIAL 1M, NEXT 1M, BUFFER_POOL_KEEP)
```

The **RECYCLE** Buffer Pool

The *RECYCLE buffer pool*'s purpose is to store memory blocks that are not likely to be reused again soon. In the case of very large objects, access to individual blocks may be very random and scattered. In these circumstances, you may wish to assign such objects to the **RECYCLE** buffer pool.

It is important not to size the **RECYCLE** buffer pool too small. Doing so may cause blocks to age out of the pool before an application or SQL statement uses them completely. If the block is aged out before the transaction is done with it, it needs to be re-read, causing more I/O. You can determine if this is happening by using one of the trace methods (for example, turning on trace and using tkprof to format the output trace file). To do so, compare disk accesses that occur in the default pool to disk access occurring in the **RECYCLE** buffer pool. In both cases, disk accesses should be the same. If the statement that ran and that was using the **RECYCLE** buffer pool has more disk accesses, you may conclude that the pool is too small. Another method of monitoring the pool is to monitor the free buffer waits and log file sync statistics. If either of these starts to grow after you allocate the **RECYCLE** buffer pool, it may mean that you have not allocated enough memory to the pool.

How does one determine which objects should fit in the **RECYCLE** buffer pool? Oracle supplies the following as a guide:

➤ A good candidate for a segment to put into the **RECYCLE** buffer pool is one that is at least twice the size of the default buffer pool and has incurred at least a few percent of the total I/Os in the system.

➤ A good candidate for a segment to put into the **KEEP** pool is one that is smaller than 10 percent of the size of the default buffer pool and has incurred at least 1 percent of the total I/Os in the system.

➤ Calculate the ratio of blocks for a segment of the object in question that is used frequently to those used rarely. For that object, count the number of blocks that exist in the hot half of the cache (the MRU end) to the number of blocks in the cold half (the LRU end). If the ratio for a segment is close to 1, the segment may be a good candidate for the **RECYCLE** cache. If the ratio is high (perhaps 3), the segment might be a good candidate for the **KEEP** cache.

An example of assigning a table to the **RECYCLE** buffer pool is shown below.

```
CREATE TABLE small_table
(pk_id     NUMBER  NOT NULL    PRIMARY KEY,
table_info   VARCHAR2    NOT NULL)
STORAGE (INITIAL 1M, NEXT 1M, BUFFER_POOL_KEEP)
```

Sizing The New Buffer Pools

Each of the new buffer pools is configured in the init.ora. Once you configure them, you have to **SHUTDOWN** the database for the new settings to take effect. To configure the large pool in the init.ora, use the **large_pool_size** and **large_pool_min_alloc** parameters. The values can be expressed in kilobytes (KB) or megabytes (MB). Keep in mind that in allocating these structures, you are allocating additional memory to the SGA. Be careful that you do not allocate the large pool so that memory starts paging out to disk, because this can have serious performance impacts.

To configure the **KEEP** pool or the **RECYCLE** pool, set the parameters **buffer_pool_keep** and **buffer_pool_recycle**, respectively, in the init.ora. The format of the parameters is the same. When setting the parameter, you define the number of database buffer blocks for the pool and then the number of LRU latches to be allocated to the pool, each parameter separated by a comma. The number of latches you allocate to each pool is subtracted from the total number of latches allocated to the instance. Thus, you may need to increase the **db_block_lru_latches** parameter to allocate more latches to the buffer cache. The default value of this parameter is half the number of CPUs in your machine, and the maximum value is the total number of CPUs in your machine. Finally, the minimum number of buffers that Oracle allows you to allocate to each buffer pool is 50 times the number of LRU latches. Listing 3.2 shows an example of an init.ora where these values are configured.

Listing 3.2   init.ora in which the various buffer pools are configured.

```
# Configure the pool cache.
DB_BLOCK_BUFFERS = 2000
# Configure the number of LRU latches. The Default is
# CPU_COUNT / 2 and the maximum is CPU_COUNT.
DB_BLOCK_LRU_LATCHES = 6
# Configure the keep buffer pool. Assign 100 blocks to it from the
# Cacheand 2 LRU latches.
BUFFER_POOL_KEEP = '100,2'
# Configure the recycle buffer pool. Assign 100 blocks to it from
the Cache and # 2 LRU Latches.
BUFFER_POOL_RECYCLE = '50,1'
```

Make sure you understand the different buffer pools and how they are used and allocated before taking the OCP exam.

Changes To Oracle8 Processes

Oracle has made several changes to the processes that run when the database is up. This section highlights those changes, which include adding the CKPT process as a required process, the new advanced queuing processes, and changing to the DBWR processes.

The CKPT Process

Along with the other minimum required Oracle processes—the process monitor (PMON), the system monitor (SMON), the database (or dirty block) writer (DBWR), and the log writer (LGWR)—the previously optional checkpoint

(CKPT) process is now required. In Oracle7, a checkpoint required that the LGWR process stop writing data from the redo log buffer to the redo logs, and instead update sequence numbers on the datafile headers and the control file. In very heavy-volume systems, this could cause performance problems. Oracle provided an optional process in Oracle7, the *CKPT process*, to relieve LGWR of this responsibility, allowing LGWR to continue to write redo log entries. The CKPT process is no longer optional in Oracle8.

The QMN*nn* Process

Associated with Oracle's advanced queuing is a new process called the queue manager process. To enable this optional process, set the init.ora parameter **aq_tm_processes**. This parameter can be set to only 0 or 1. The process monitors the Oracle advanced queuing message queues. For more information on Oracle advanced queuing, see Chapter 9.

On certain platforms, there are problems enabling the QMN process. Oracle has created a workaround document to deal with this issue. Reference Oracle bug 638191 if you have a problem starting this process. Some Oracle documentation reports that you can start up to 10 of these processes, but this is not the case in Oracle8.0.5, where only one process may be started.

The DBW*n* Process

Oracle has changed the naming format of the DBWR process to DBW*n*, where *n* can be a number from 0 through 9. If you use multiple DB writer processes, you should note that the **db_writers** parameter has changed to **db_writer_processes**.

Also new to Oracle8 is the **dbwr_io_slaves** parameter. This parameter allows for one or more **DBWR_IO_SLAVES** processes to be started by the database. These **DBWR_IO_SLAVES** processes can be used to write to the Oracle datafiles. When the **dbwr_io_slaves** parameter is set, you set **db_writer_processes=1** in the init.ora parameter file. You can then set up multiple **DBWR_IO_SLAVES** processes. **DBWR_IO_SLAVES** processes are designed to simulate asynchronous I/O on platforms that do not support it. I/O slaves may also be used on platforms that have asynchronous I/O. **DBWR_IO_SLAVES** processes can be identified in Unix as S*nnn* processes, where *nnn* is the number of the process assigned by Oracle. One DBW0 process will always be running regardless of whether you are running **DBWR_IO_SLAVE** processes. It is still possible in Oracle8 to run multiple DBW*n* processes, but you can not run both multiple DBW*n* processes and **DBWR_IO_SLAVES** processes at the same time.

One difference between running multiple DBWR processes and multiple **IO_SLAVES** is that the **IO_SLAVES** processes can fail without the failure of these processes taking the instance down. If the DBWR processes fail, they fail the instance. In addition to the **DBWR_IO_SLAVES** processes, Oracle has other **IO_SLAVE** processes you can use to simulate asynchronous I/O: LGWR_IO_SLAVES, BACKUP_DISK_IO_SLAVES, and BACKUP_TAPE_IO_SLAVES.

Configuration Parameters In Oracle8

Chapter 2 listed several init.ora parameter changes between Oracle7 and Oracle8. Many have been added, some are no longer supported, and some have had their names changed. This section discusses some of the more important changes you should be aware of.

Dynamically Changeable init.ora Parameters

There are times when it's inconvenient to have to bounce the database to change a parameter. In version 7, Oracle allowed you to dynamically change a limited set of parameters without needing to shut down and restart the database. In version 8, Oracle has added to the number of dynamically changeable parameters. To change a parameter, you use the **ALTER SYSTEM** or **ALTER SESSION** command.

You can refer to the **V$PARAMETER** table to determine if a parameter is changeable at either the session or database wide level. The columns of primary interest are **isses_modifiable** and **issys_modifiable**. The **isses_modifiable** column indicates if a user who has the **ALTER SESSION** privilege can change the init.ora parameter for his or her session. If this column is **TRUE**, then the user can do so; otherwise, the column is **FALSE**.

The **issys_modifiable** column indicates if someone with **ALTER SYSTEM** privileges can change a parameter. It has three statuses:

➤ *IMMEDIATE*—Indicates that the parameter is changeable and that the change takes effect immediately

➤ *FALSE*—Means that the parameter is not changeable dynamically

➤ *DEFERRED*—Indicates that the parameter is changeable but that it will not take effect until your next session

In order to take advantage of dynamically settable parameters, the user must have the **ALTER SESSION** privilege (which changes session-level settings) and the **ALTER SYSTEM** privilege (which changes system-level settings). Take care before you issue these privileges; some of the settings allow the user to change memory allocations for the user's current session. Having multiple users changing their memory settings can significantly impact performance and how much memory is used on the database. In addition, once you change a setting with the **ALTER SYSTEM** command, that setting remains constant even if you shut down and restart the database. Thus, the init.ora settings for a parameter may be totally incorrect.

Never assume that the parameter settings in the init.ora correctly represent the settings of the database. Many of them can be modified dynamically, and can take on new settings. These new settings do not reset when the database is restarted.

Listing 3.3 shows the parameters that Oracle8 allows you to change dynamically at either the system or session level. It also shows an example of how to use the **ALTER SYSTEM** and **ALTER SESSION** commands to change a database parameter dynamically.

Listing 3.3 Dynamically modifiable system and session parameters.

```
COLUMN isses_modifiable HEADING 'Sess|Mod|Param'
COLUMN issys_modifiable HEADING 'Sys|Mod|Param'
COLUMN name FORMAT a20 WRAP
COLUMN value FORMAT a20 WRAP
SQL> SELECT name,value,isses_modifiable
, issys_modifiable
FROM v$parameter
WHERE isses_modifiable <> 'FALSE'
OR issys_modifiable <> 'FALSE'
ORDER BY name;
```

NAME	VALUE	Sess Mod Param	Sys Mod Param
allow_partial_sn_results	FALSE	TRUE	DEFERRED
aq_tm_processes	0	FALSE	IMMEDIATE
b_tree_bitmap_plans	FALSE	TRUE	FALSE
background_dump_dest	/ora01/oracle/admin/ testo8/bdump	FALSE	IMMEDIATE

backup_disk_io_slaves	0	FALSE	DEFERRED
backup_tape_io_slaves	FALSE	FALSE	DEFERRED
close_cached_open_cursors	FALSE	TRUE	FALSE
complex_view_merging	FALSE	TRUE	FALSE
control_file_record_keep_ time	7	FALSE	IMMEDIATE
core_dump_dest	/ora01/oracle/admin/ testo8/cdump	FALSE	IMMEDIATE
db_block_checkpoint_batch	8	FALSE	IMMEDIATE
db_block_checksum	FALSE	FALSE	IMMEDIATE
db_block_max_dirty_target	4294967294	FALSE	IMMEDIATE
db_file_direct_io_count	64	FALSE	DEFERRED
db_file_multiblock_read_c ount	8	TRUE	IMMEDIATE
fixed_date		FALSE	IMMEDIATE
freeze_DB_for_fast_instan ce_recovery	FALSE	FALSE	IMMEDIATE
gc_defer_time	10	FALSE	IMMEDIATE
global_names	FALSE	TRUE	IMMEDIATE
hash_area_size	0	TRUE	FALSE
hash_join_enabled	TRUE	TRUE	FALSE
hash_multiblock_io_count	1	TRUE	IMMEDIATE
job_queue_processes	0	FALSE	IMMEDIATE
license_max_sessions	0	FALSE	IMMEDIATE
license_max_users	0	FALSE	IMMEDIATE
license_sessions_warning	0	FALSE	IMMEDIATE
log_archive_duplex_dest		FALSE	IMMEDIATE
log_archive_min_succeed_d est	1	FALSE	IMMEDIATE
log_checkpoint_interval	4294967294	FALSE	IMMEDIATE
log_checkpoint_timeout	0	FALSE	IMMEDIATE
log_small_entry_max_size	80	FALSE	IMMEDIATE
max_dump_file_size	204800	TRUE	IMMEDIATE
mts_dispatchers		FALSE	IMMEDIATE
mts_servers	0	FALSE	IMMEDIATE
nls_calendar		TRUE	FALSE
nls_currency		TRUE	FALSE
nls_date_format		TRUE	FALSE
nls_date_language		TRUE	FALSE
nls_iso_currency		TRUE	FALSE
nls_language	AMERICAN	TRUE	FALSE
nls_numeric_characters		TRUE	FALSE
nls_sort		TRUE	FALSE
nls_territory	AMERICA	TRUE	FALSE
object_cache_max_size_per cent	10	TRUE	DEFERRED
object_cache_optimal_size	102400	TRUE	DEFERRED

```
ops_admin_group                                   TRUE   IMMEDIATE
optimizer_index_caching   0                        TRUE   FALSE
optimizer_index_cost_adj  100                      TRUE   FALSE
optimizer_max_permutation 80000                    TRUE   FALSE
s
optimizer_mode            CHOOSE                   TRUE   FALSE
optimizer_percent_paralle 0                        TRUE   FALSE
l
optimizer_search_limit    12                       TRUE   FALSE
parallel_adaptive_multi_u FALSE                    TRUE   FALSE
ser
parallel_broadcast_enable FALSE                    TRUE   FALSE
d
parallel_instance_group                           TRUE   IMMEDIATE
parallel_min_percent      0                        TRUE   FALSE
parallel_transaction_reso 300                      FALSE  IMMEDIATE
urce_timeout
partition_view_enabled    FALSE                    TRUE   FALSE
plsql_v2_compatibility    FALSE                    TRUE   IMMEDIATE
push_join_predicate       FALSE                    TRUE   FALSE
remote_dependencies_mode  TIMESTAMP                TRUE   IMMEDIATE
resource_limit            FALSE                    FALSE  IMMEDIATE
session_cached_cursors    0                        TRUE   FALSE
sort_area_retained_size   0                        TRUE   DEFERRED
sort_area_size            65536                    TRUE   DEFERRED
sort_direct_writes        AUTO                     TRUE   DEFERRED
sort_read_fac             5                        TRUE   DEFERRED
sort_write_buffer_size    32768                    TRUE   DEFERRED
sort_write_buffers        2                        TRUE   DEFERRED
spin_count                2000                     FALSE  IMMEDIATE
star_transformation_enabl FALSE                    TRUE   FALSE
ed
text_enable               FALSE                    TRUE   IMMEDIATE
timed_os_statistics       0                        FALSE  IMMEDIATE
timed_statistics          FALSE                    TRUE   IMMEDIATE
transaction_auditing      TRUE                     FALSE  DEFERRED
user_dump_dest            /ora01/oracle/admin/ FALSE  IMMEDIATE
                          testo8/udump

76 rows selected.

--Changing the session parameter value for TIMED_STATISTICS.
SQL> ALTER SESSION SET timed_statistics = FALSE;

Session altered.
--Changing the system-wide parameter value for TIMED_STATISTICS.
SQL> ALTER SESSION SET TIMED_STATISTICS = FALSE;

System altered.
```

Oracle8 NLS Enhancements

Oracle8 had added new data types in support of various NLS (National Language Support) formats: **NCHAR** and **NVARCHAR2**. In this section, we will review what these new data types are and how to use them.

NCHAR Data Type

The **NCHAR** data type is similar to the Oracle **CHAR** data type. It is either defined in character size, in the case of a fixed-width NLS format (e.g., **US7ASCII**), or in number of bytes, in the case of a variable-width NLS format (e.g., **JA16EUCFIXED**). The NLS character set of the database is determined when you create the database. **NCHAR** is blank padded to the right. **NCHAR** data types are limited to 2,000 characters or bytes, depending on the NLS character set you are using. You cannot insert a **CHAR** type into a **NCHAR** type.

Listing 3.4 shows an example of creating a table with an **NCHAR** value, inserting a row into an **NCHAR** value, and selecting this row from a table with an **NCHAR** value.

> *Note: When referring to a value to be inserted, or queried on, you prefix it with an N. This is true for both **NCHAR** and **NVARCHAR2**.*

Listing 3.4   Using the **NCHAR** data type in Oracle8.

```
Oracle8 Enterprise Edition Release 8.0.5.1.0 - Production
PL/SQL Release 8.0.5.1.0 - Production
--We create the table with an NCHAR type.
SQL> CREATE TABLE emp
  2  (emp_id      NUMBER,
  3  emp_name     NCHAR(30));

Table created.
--Next we insert a row into the table. Note the N in front of
--the 'Robert Freeman'.
--This indicates that this is inserting into an NLS variable
--type.
SQL> INSERT INTO emp
  2  (emp_id, emp_name)
  3  VALUES
  4  (1,N'Robert Freeman');

1 row created.
--Just checking to see that the row was really there.
SQL> SELECT * FROM emp;
```

```
   EMP_ID EMP_NAME
-------------------------------------
       1 Robert Freeman
--We can query on the table as normal.
SQL> SELECT emp_id,emp_name FROM emp;

   EMP_ID EMP_NAME
-------------------------------------
       1 Robert Freeman
--Unfortunately, we can't do WHERE clauses quite like normal.
SQL> SELECT * FROM emp WHERE emp_name LIKE 'Robert Freeman';
SELECT * FROM emp WHERE emp_name LIKE 'Robert Freeman'
                                          *
ERROR at line 1:
ORA-12704: character set mismatch
--The error above was generated because we did not prefix the
--'Robert Freeman' literal with an N as we should have. The
--correct way to do this is listed below.

1* SELECT * FROM emp WHERE emp_name LIKE N'Robert Freeman%'
SQL> /

   EMP_ID EMP_NAME
-------------------------------------
       1 Robert Freeman

--Finally, note that with NCHAR, the statement below fails,
--because of blank padding.
1* SELECT * FROM emp WHERE emp_name LIKE N'Robert Freeman'
SQL> /

no rows selected
SQL> DESC emp
 Name                              Null?    Type
 --------------------------------------------------
 EMP_ID                                     NUMBER
 EMP_NAME                                   NCHAR(30)
```

NVARCHAR2 Data Type

The **NVARCHAR2** data type is similar to Oracle's **VARCHAR2** data type. Like **NCHAR**, **NVARCHAR2** is defined in terms of character size or in terms of bytes, depending on the NLS character set with which the database was created. **NVARCHAR2** can be a maximum of either 4,000 characters (this is a new limit beginning in Oracle8 for **VARCHAR2** data types; see the "Oracle8 Increased Capacity" section later in this chapter for more information) or 4,000 bytes. Oracle does not blank pad characters stored in **NVARCHAR2** data types, like the **VARCHAR2** data type. Listing 3.5 shows an example of creating a table, inserting a row into it, and selecting an **NVARCHAR2** data type from it.

Listing 3.5   Using the **NVARCHAR2** data type in Oracle8.

```
SQL> CREATE TABLE emp
  2  (emp_id       NUMBER,
  3  emp_name      NVARCHAR2(30));

Table created.
--Next we insert a value into it. Note the N in front of
--the 'Robert Freeman'.
--This indicates that this is inserting into an NLS variable type.
SQL>  INSERT INTO emp
  2  (emp_id, emp_name)
  3  VALUES
  4  (1,N'Robert Freeman');

1 row created.
--Just checking to see that the row was really there.
SQL> SELECT * FROM emp;

    EMP_ID EMP_NAME
----------------------------------------
         1 Robert Freeman
--We can query on the table as normal.
SQL> SELECT emp_id,emp_name FROM emp;

    EMP_ID EMP_NAME
----------------------------------------
         1 Robert Freeman
--Unfortunately, we can't do WHERE clauses quite like normal.
SQL> SELECT * FROM emp WHERE emp_name LIKE 'Robert Freeman';
SELECT * FROM emp WHERE emp_name LIKE 'Robert Freeman%'
                                        *
ERROR at line 1:
ORA-12704: character set mismatch
--The error above was generated because we did not prefix the
--'Robert Freeman' literal with an N as we should have. The correct
--way to do this is listed below.
1* SELECT * FROM emp WHERE emp_name LIKE N'Robert Freeman%'
SQL> /
    EMP_ID EMP_NAME
----------------------------------------
         1 Robert Freeman
--Finally, note that where NCHAR failed, NVARCHAR2 succeeds. The
--statement below would fail, because of
```

```
--blank padding if using an NCHAR.
SQL> SELECT * FROM emp WHERE emp_name LIKE N'Robert Freeman';

   EMP_ID EMP_NAME
---------------------------------------
        1 Robert Freeman
SQL> desc emp
 Name                              Null?    Type
-------------------------------------------
 EMP_ID                                     NUMBER
 EMP_NAME                                   NVARCHAR2(30)
```

Oracle8 Increased Capacity

In release 8, Oracle has increased the capacity of the database significantly. These changes allow for much larger databases and storage of larger objects. Some of the capacity changes you should be familiar with are:

➤ Total database size is 512 Petabytes.

➤ The maximum number of data files per tablespace is 1,022.

➤ The maximum number of tablespaces is 2 billion+.

➤ The maximum number of columns in a table has been increased to 1,000.

➤ The **CHAR** data type storage has been increased to 2,000 bytes.

➤ The **VARCHAR2** data type storage has been increased to 4,000 bytes.

➤ Indexes (including primary key indexes) can contain up to 32 columns, except for bitmap indexes, which are limited at 30 columns.

The Oracle8.0.5 documentation is confusing in regards to the limitations on the number of columns allowed in a primary key index. In some places, it indicates that only 16 columns are allowed, whereas in others, it indicates that 32 columns are allowed. In fact, Oracle allows a primary key index to be 32 columns in length. Discussions with Oracle indicate that if this issue comes up on the test, 32 would be the correct value.

Oracle8's New ROWID Format

As discussed in Chapter 2, Oracle has significantly changed the **ROWID** format for Oracle8. This is a result, in part, of the move to a more object-oriented database and providing for larger databases. These new Oracle features required a change to the **ROWID** format. We will discuss the new **ROWID** format, and **ROWID**s in general in this section.

ROWIDs: A Primer

This section will examine the **ROWID** in Oracle. We will look at what a **ROWID** is and where it is used in the database. We will review how a **ROWID** was formatted in Oracle7 and then look at the new **ROWID** format in Oracle8.

The **ROWID** In Oracle

The purpose of the **ROWID** is to provide a unique address for every row in the database. Using a **ROWID** is the quickest way to find a single row of data and is the method that Oracle uses to address a specific row in the database. The **ROWID** represents the physical address of a row's row piece or the initial row piece if the row is chained into multiple row pieces. Clustered tables are an exception. In this case, rows in different tables but in the same block can have the same **ROWID**. **ROWIDs** are not stored internally in the Oracle database, except in indexes.

Each table has a pseudocolumn called **ROWID**, which represents the **ROWID** of the row being returned. You cannot set this value by insert or updates statements, nor can you delete a **ROWID**. Oracle does not store **ROWIDs** in the database, so **ROWIDs** are not database data either. **ROWIDs** are instead dynamically generated when requested. Thus, when you issue this query:

```
SELECT part_no, ROWID FROM parts;
```

Oracle dynamically creates the **ROWID** for each of the rows returned. It is possible to create tables that contain columns with the **ROWID** data type, but there is no method of guaranteeing the validity of these **ROWIDs**.

ROWIDs Stored In The Oracle Database

Oracle uses **ROWIDs** when building indexes. Each index key is associated with a **ROWID** that belongs to the data being indexed. Oracle uses the restricted format of the **ROWID** in indexes, even in Oracle8. The reason for this is that the restricted format **ROWID** requires less space (6 bytes for restricted **ROWIDs** vs. 10 bytes for extended **ROWIDs**) than an extended **ROWID**. Remember that **ROWIDs** are displayed as a **CHAR(18)**, but that they are stored internally in 6- and 10-byte datum. There is an exception to using restricted format **ROWIDs** in indexes, in the case of global indexes on partitioned tables. In the case of a global index on a partitioned table, Oracle stores the extended **ROWID** in the index. For more information on global indexes and partitioned tables, see Chapter 4.

Why do **ROWIDs** need to be stored in an index? First, remember that the quickest way to retrieve a row is always by a **ROWID** lookup. Therefore, when

you create an index on a table, columns being indexed are stored along with the
ROWID that identifies those columns. If a row in a table has a **NULL** value
for the indexed column, that column is not stored in the index, nor is the
ROWID. Thus, when you execute a query, and the optimizer decides to do an
index read (or scan), Oracle retrieves the **ROWID** from the index for the
value(s) in the index that you have selected in your **WHERE** clause. Oracle
will then do a table lookup using that **ROWID** to access the row you require.
ROWIDs and their relationship to a specific row of data do not change unless
the data is exported and imported. Of course, if you delete data from a row,
that **ROWID** may be used by another row inserted in a later transaction.

ROWIDs are also stored in the database when you have *chained rows*. Chained
rows occur if a user performs an update on an existing row and that row does
not have room to expand. In this case, the row is chained to another block; that
is, part of the row's content is physically stored in a new row in a new block
where space is available. A **ROWID** is then inserted into the first row, pointing (chaining) to the second row. You can have many chains in a row, which
can cause performance problems. You should review the use of **PCTUSED**
and particularly **PCTFREE** to relieve row chaining if it occurs.

Finally, if you use replication, **ROWID**s may be stored internally, depending
on if you replicate by **ROWID** (the only option in Oracle7) or by primary key
(PK). The **ROWID**s are not stored in the data dictionary, but Oracle manages
the storage of the tables in which they are maintained. If you replicate by PK,
Oracle does not store the **ROWID** of the snapshot data.

Given a **ROWID**, you can discover a variety of information about that row,
such as which database data file the data resides in, what row in the block the
object resides in, and so on. Developers may use the **ROWID**s in other tables
to refer to the **ROWID** of the object, or perhaps because the **ROWID** makes
the rows in a table unique. DBAs might use the **ROWID**s for tuning, monitoring, or just to determine how many rows in a particular table exist in a
particular tablespace datafile.

ROWID Format In Oracle7

In Oracle7, the **ROWID** was represented by three groupings of numbers separated by a period that could be found in a pseudo-column in each table called
ROWID. Each group of numbers was a hexadecimal string. The groups are:

➤ *Group One*—Represents the block number of the row.

➤ *Group Two*—Represents the row number. A 0 always denotes the first row.

➤ *Group Three*—Represents the absolute file number of the database data
file that the row/block resided in. The first data file has a number 1.

The **ROWID** format has changed in Oracle8 (as you'll see in the "Format Of The **ROWID** In Oracle8" section later in this chapter). However, you can still convert to the old Oracle7 **ROWID** format and back using an Oracle-supplied package, **DBMS_ROWID** (see the "The **DBMS_ROWID** Package" section later in this chapter). Oracle calls the Oracle7 version of the **ROWID** a *restricted ROWID*. Listing 3.6 shows an example of an Oracle7 **ROWID** and how it can be used to identify the data file in which the row resides.

Listing 3.6 Using the Oracle7 **ROWID** to identify the datafile a
row resides in.

```
--Describe the table we will be selecting from.
--PRICE_I and CREATION_TS
--are the primary keys in this case.
SQL> DESC price
 Name                               Null?    Type
 ----------------------------------------------
 PRICE_I                            NOT NULL NUMBER
 CREATION_TS                        NOT NULL DATE
 LAST_UPDATE_TS                     NOT NULL DATE
 ACTIVE_D                                    DATE
 EFFECTIVE_D                        NOT NULL DATE
 EXPIRATION_D                                DATE
--Now SELECT one unique row FROM PRICE.
SQL> SELECT price_i,creation_ts,ROWID FROM price
  2  WHERE rownum < 2;

  PRICE_I CREATION_ ROWID
 -----------------------------------
    20090 03-JUN-96 00000003.0000.0004

1 row selected.

--Now determine the datafile this row exists in.
SQL> SELECT file_name,file_id FROM dba_data_files
  2   WHERE file_id = 4;

FILE_NAME
  FILE_ID
----------------------------------------------------------------
-
/ora01/oracle/admin/prmx/link/prm_data02.dbf
4

1 row selected.
```

Format Of The **ROWID** In Oracle8

Oracle has changed the **ROWID** format in Oracle8 significantly, and the old Oracle7 **ROWID**s are no longer valid. Oracle calls the Oracle8 version of the **ROWID** an *extended ROWID*. Every row in a non-clustered table in Oracle is assigned an Oracle8-extended **ROWID**. This now includes addresses of rows in partitioned and non-partitioned tables and indexes (see Chapter 4 for more information on partitioning). You can convert extended Oracle8 **ROWID**s back to restricted Oracle7 **ROWID**s and the reverse by using the **DBMS_ROWID** package.

The Oracle8 **ROWID** is now a base 64-encoded physical address and looks significantly different from the Oracle7 **ROWID** format. It has a four-piece format:

```
OOOOOOFFFBBBBBBRRR
```

Here is a breakdown of the format of the Oracle8 extended **ROWID**:

➤ *Component One (OOOOOO)*—This is a six-character piece that represents the data object number. It is a base 64 encoding of the 32-bit data object number. (The data object number was introduced in Oracle8 to trace versions of the same segment. Certain database operations can change the version. The data object number is used to discover stale **ROWID**s and stale undo records.) This number identifies the database segment, and objects that reside in the same segment, such as a cluster of tables having the same object number. This is a tablespace-relative number. We will discuss this component in more detail later in this section.

➤ *Component Two (FFF)*—This is three characters that represent the base 64 representation of the relative datafile that the row is assigned to. Datafile file numbers are unique. This is a tablespace-relative number. We will discuss this component in more detail later in this section.

➤ *Component Three (BBBBBB)*—This is a six-character piece that represents the data block that the row is in. Block numbers are relative to the datafile they reside in, not relative to the tablespace. For example, two rows may have the same block number in the same tablespace if they are in two different datafiles.

➤ *Component Four (RRR)*—This is a three-character piece that represents the row in the block represented by piece three.

You should be well versed on the Oracle8 **ROWID** format when preparing for the Oracle8 upgrade exam. Most likely, there will be several questions revolving around the new **ROWID** format.

I like to use the acronym ORDR (Order) to remember the ROWID structure in Oracle8 and its order. It stands for **O**bject number, **R**elative-datafile number, **D**ata block number, and **R**ow number.

The primary changes to the **ROWID** in Oracle8 are the first two pieces of the **ROWID**, the data object number, and the relative file number.

The *data object number* is a unique identifier for an object created in Oracle. Each time the object is changed, this number changes as well. Operations that can cause this number to change include table truncates or movement of a partition.

The *relative file number* is a tablespace-relative file number. This being the case, different files belonging to different tablespaces can have the same relative file number. This change to the **ROWID** format was required to allow for the capacity increases that Oracle wanted to make to the database. This change to the **ROWID** format was also required to implement partitioning, and for the addition of the object-based structures Oracle wished to implement in Oracle8.

One of the main differences between an extended **ROWID** and a restricted **ROWID** is that the Oracle8 extended **ROWID** is relative only to the tablespace the data is in. The new Oracle8 extended **ROWID** is not unique across the database, as was the Oracle7 restricted **ROWID** format. As a result of this, you will often need an absolute file number to perform certain operations such as a block dump, since the Oracle7 **ROWID** is an absolute row number and is absolute to the whole system. A final issue to be aware of is that if you wish to enforce an index range scan in Oracle8, you can do so with only an extended **ROWID**.

Make sure you remember that the file number contained in the Oracle7 **ROWID** (restricted) is absolute to the database and that the file number contained in the Oracle8 **ROWID** format (extended) is relative to the tablespace. You must clearly understand what the differences are between a relative and absolute **ROWID**.

Figure 3.1 shows the breakout of the Oracle8 **ROWID** and represents the relationship of the **ROWID** to the various physical and logical parts of the Oracle8 database.

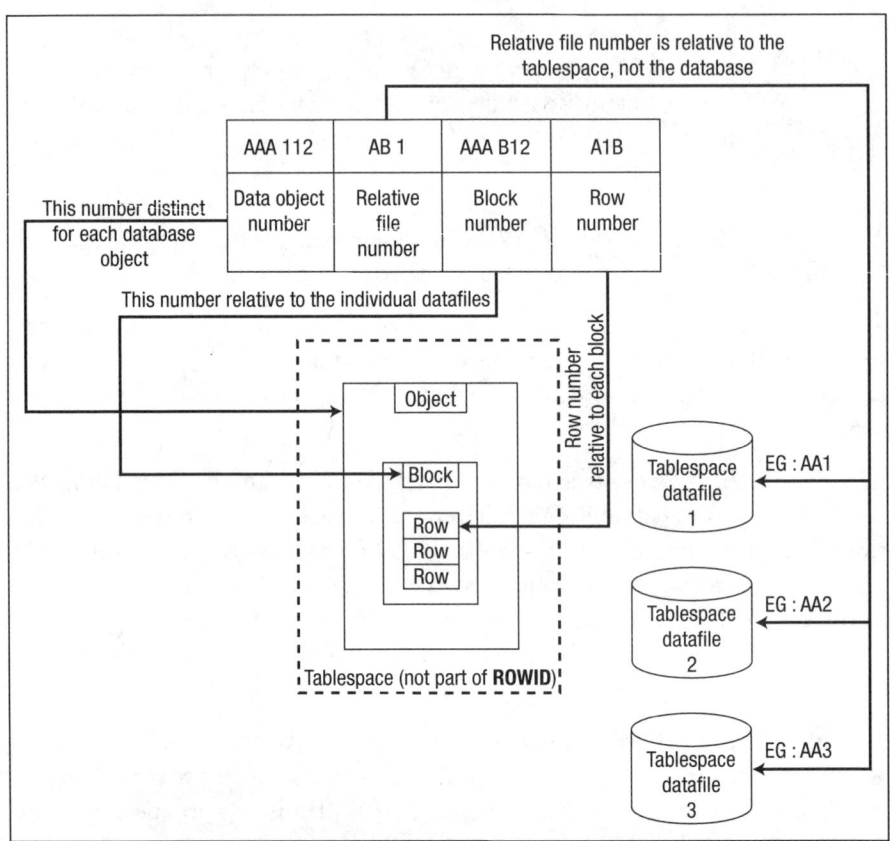

Figure 3.1 Diagram of the Oracle8 extended **ROWID** and its relationship to Oracle physical and logical structures.

The **DBMS_ROWID** Package

In Oracle7, a function, **ROWIDTOCHAR**, converted an Oracle7 **ROWID** into a character value. You could then strip it apart and perform any other operations on the **ROWID**. The **CHARTOROWID** conversion function provided the reverse function. With it, you could convert a text-generated **ROWID** into the Oracle **ROWID** format and query as if it were a **ROWID**.

These restricted **ROWID** conversion functions are still available in Oracle8. However, in order for you to manipulate a **ROWID** with these functions, it must be in the restricted form. It is also possible that a table in a database may be designed to store **ROWIDs** and that these were stored in an Oracle7 restricted format. As a part of the conversion process, it may be necessary to convert Oracle7 restricted-format **ROWIDs** into Oracle8 extended **ROWIDs**.

Oracle provides the **DBMS_ROWID** package to assist in dealing with the mix of restricted **ROWID**s and extended **ROWID**s. The **DBMS_ROWID** package's functionality includes:

➤ Conversion of extended **ROWID**s to restricted **ROWID**s

➤ Conversion of restricted **ROWID**s to extended **ROWID**s

➤ Procedures and functions to strip out the various components of the different **ROWID** formats

The Oracle code for **DBMS_ROWID** is contained in a script called dbmsutil.sql. This script is automatically run by catproc.sql, which you run at the time you create the database.

DBMS_ROWID Exceptions

DBMS_ROWID has two named exceptions associated with it. The first is ROWID_INVALID, exception number −1410. This exception is returned if the **ROWID** format is invalid. The second exception is **ROWID_BAD_ BLOCK**, which is error −28516. This error is returned if the **ROWID** requested is beyond the end of the block.

DBMS_ROWID Constants

DBMS_ROWID defines the following constants for use with the package:

➤ *ROWID_CONVERT_EXTERNAL*—Assigned a value of 1. Is a **ROWID** conversion type.

➤ *ROWID_CONVERT_INTERNAL*—Assigned a value of 0. Is a **ROWID** conversion type.

➤ *ROWID_IS_VALID*—Assigned a value of 0.

➤ *ROWID_IS_INVALID*—Assigned a value of 1.

➤ *ROWID_OBJECT_UNDEFINED*—Assigned a value of 0. Indicates that an object number is undefined. Generally returned with restricted **ROWID**s because they do not have object numbers associated with them.

➤ *ROWID_TYPE_EXTENDED*—Assigned a value of 1.

➤ *ROWID_TYPE_RESTRICTED*—Assigned a value of 0.

DBMS_ROWID Functions And Procedures

The Oracle **DBMS_ROWID** package has several functions and procedures associated with it. These are:

➤ DBMS_ROWID.ROWID_CREATE

➤ DBMS_ROWID.ROWID_INFO

➤ DBMS_ROWID.ROWID_TYPE

➤ DBMS_ROWID.ROWID_OBJECT

➤ DBMS_ROWID.ROWID_RELATIVE_FNO

➤ DBMS_ROWID.ROWID_BLOCK_NUMBER

➤ DBMS_ROWID.ROWID_ROW_NUMBER

➤ DBMS_ROWID.ROWID_TO_ABSOLUTE_FNO

➤ DBMS_ROWID.ROWID_TO_EXTENDED

➤ DBMS_ROWID.ROWID_TO_RESTRICTED

➤ DBMS_ROWID.ROWID_VERIFY

Let's look at these in more detail.

DBMS_ROWID.ROWID_CREATE

The **DBMS_ROWID.ROWID_CREATE** function returns a **ROWID** (restricted or extended) based on parameters sent to it. The function takes five parameters, as shown below:

```
FUNCTION DBMS_ROWID.ROWID_CREATE(rowid_type IN NUMBER,
object_number IN NUMBER,
relative_fno IN NUMBER,
block_number IN NUMBER,
row_number IN NUMBER),
RETURN ROWID;
```

The descriptions of the parameters for this function are as follows:

➤ *rowid_type*—The type of **ROWID** you wish to be returned either an extended or restricted ROWID. Use 0=restricted **ROWID** and 1=Extended **ROWID**.

➤ *object_number*—The object number that you wish to be represented in the created **ROWID**. Not used in creating the extended **ROWID**, but you must still supply a number.

➤ *relative_fno*—This is the relative file number component of the **ROWID** you wish to create.

➤ *block_number*—This is the block number component of the **ROWID** you wish to create.

➤ *row_number*—The row number of the **ROWID** you wish to create.

Listing 3.7 below gives an example of a call to **DBMS_ROWID.ROWID_ CREATE**.

Listing 3.7   A sample call to the **DBMS_ROWID.ROWID_CREATE** function.

```
--This will give us a restricted ROWID.
SQL> SELECT DBMS_ROWID.ROWID_create(0,25,50,75,100) FROM dual;


DBMS_ROWID.ROWID_C
------------------
0000004B.0064.0032

--And an extended ROWID.
SQL> SELECT DBMS_ROWID.ROWID_create(1,25,50,75,100) FROM dual;
DBMS_ROWID.ROWID_C
------------------
AAAAAZAAyAAAABLABk
```

DBMS_ROWID.ROWID_INFO

The **DBMS_ROWID.ROWID_INFO** procedure breaks a **ROWID** into its component parts and returns the parts through the **out** parameters for further work. The function takes six parameters, as shown below.

```
PROCEDURE DBMS_ROWID.ROWID_INFO(rowid_in_IN IN ROWID,
rowid_type OUT number,
object_number OUT number,
relative_fno OUT number,
block_number OUT number,
row_number OUT number);
```

The descriptions of the parameters for this function are as follows:

➤ *rowid_in*—The **ROWID** you wish to dissect.

➤ *rowid_type*—The type of **ROWID** you wish to be returned, either an extended or restricted **ROWID**. Use 0 for a restricted **ROWID** or 1 for an extended **ROWID**.

➤ *object_number*—The **object_number** of the **ROWID**.

➤ *relative_fno*—The relative file number component of the **ROWID** you wish to create.

➤ *block_number*—The block number component of the **ROWID** you wish to create.

➤ *row_number*—The row number of the **ROWID** you wish to create.

Listing 3.8 below gives an example of a call to **DBMS_ROWID.ROWID_ INFO**.

Listing 3.8   A sample call to the **DBMS_ROWID.ROWID_INFO** procedure.

```
--Create PL/SQL code to retrieve the ROWID_INFO for a
--given ROWID.
--Could also do this using SQL*Plus variables.
CREATE OR REPLACE PROCEDURE get_ROWID_info
(p_row_id    ROWID)
AS
v_row_id_type    NUMBER;
v_object_number NUMBER;
v_relative_fno  NUMBER;
v_block_number  NUMBER;
v_row_number    NUMBER;

BEGIN
DBMS_ROWID.ROWID_info(p_row_id,v_row_id_type,v_object_number,v_relative_fno,
                      v_block_number, v_row_number);

DBMS_OUTPUT.PUT_LINE('Information returned on the ROWID sent: ');
DBMS_OUTPUT.PUT_LINE('row_id_type '||v_row_id_type);
DBMS_OUTPUT.PUT_LINE('object_number '||v_object_number);
DBMS_OUTPUT.PUT_LINE('relative_fno '||v_relative_fno);
DBMS_OUTPUT.PUT_LINE('block_number '||v_block_number);
DBMS_OUTPUT.PUT_LINE('row_number '||v_row_number);
END;
/
Procedure created.

--Now run the code for a ROWID! SET SERVEROUTPUT on first!
SQL> SET SERVEROUTPUT ON
SQL> EXEC GET_ROWID_INFO('00000003.0000.0004');
Information returned on the ROWID sent:
row_id_type 0
```

```
object_number 0
relative_fno 4
block_number 3
row_number 0

PL/SQL procedure successfully completed.
--Now for an extended ROWID.
SQL> EXEC GET_ROWID_INFO('AAAAitAAEAAAAADAAA');
Information returned on the ROWID sent:
row_id_type 1
object_number 2221
relative_fno 4
block_number 3
row_number 0

PL/SQL procedure successfully completed.
```

DBMS_ROWID.ROWID_TYPE

The **DBMS_ROWID.ROWID_TYPE** function takes a **ROWID** and returns a 0 or 1 depending on the **ROWID** type. In this function a return code
of 0 means the **ROWID** was a restricted **ROWID** and a 1 return code indicates an extended **ROWID**.

```
FUNCTION DBMS_ROWID.ROWID_TYPE(row_id IN ROWID)
RETURN NUMBER;
```

The description of the parameter for this function is:

➤ *rowid_in*—This is the **ROWID** you wish to know the format of.

Listing 3.9 shows a sample call to this function.

Listing 3.9   A sample call to the **DBMS_ROW.ROWID_TYPE** procedure.

```
--Find the type for a restricted ROWID - 0 = restricted
--ROWID.
SQL> SELECT DBMS_ROWID.ROWID_type('0000004B.0064.0032')
  FROM dual;

DBMS_ROWID.ROWID_TYPE('0000004B.0064.0032')
-------------------------------------------
                                          0
--Find the type for an extended ROWID - 1 = extended ROWID.
SQL> SELECT DBMS_ROWID.ROWID_type('AAAAAZAAyAAAABLABk')
  FROM dual;
```

```
DBMS_ROWID.ROWID_TYPE('AAAAAZAAYAAAABLABK')
-------------------------------------------
                                          1
```

DBMS_ROWID.ROWID_OBJECT

The **DBMS_ROWID.ROWID_OBJECT** function returns the object number if the **ROWID** passed is an extended **ROWID**, and returns a 0 if the object passed is a restricted **ROWID**, which has no object component to it.

```
FUNCTION DBMS_ROWID.ROWID_OBJECT(row_id IN ROWID)
RETURN NUMBER;
```

The description of the parameter for this function is:

➤ *rowid_in*—This is the **ROWID** you wish to know the format of.

Listing 3.10 shows a sample call to this function.

Listing 3.10   A sample call to the **DBMS_ROW.ROWID_OBJECT** function.

```
--Get the object for an extended ROWID.
SQL> SELECT DBMS_ROWID.ROWID_OBJECT('AAAAAZAAyAAAABLABk') FROM
dual;

DBMS_ROWID.ROWID_OBJECT('AAAAAZAAYAAAABLABK')
---------------------------------------------
                                           25

--Get the object for a restricted ROWID.
SQL> SELECT DBMS_ROWID.ROWID_OBJECT('0000004B.0064.0032') FROM
dual;

DBMS_ROWID.ROWID_OBJECT('0000004B.0064.0032')
---------------------------------------------
                                            0
--This is another example of how an object id relates to a
--created table and dba_objects table.
--Create a table.
CREATE TABLE parts
(part_no NUMBER,
quantity NUMBER);

Table created.
--Insert a value into the table.
SQL> insert into parts values (1,5);
1 row created.
```

```
--Now, SELECT the value and get the object_id of the table using --
--DBMS_ROWID.ROWID_OBJECT.
SQL> SELECT part_no,quantity,ROWID,DBMS_ROWID.ROWID_object(ROWID)
  2  FROM parts;

 PART_NO   QUANTITY ROWID
DBMS_ROWID.ROWID_OBJECT(ROWID)
-------- -------- ------------------ ------------------------------
       1        5 AAAAiiAABAAAAoxAAA
2210

--Now, find out the object name based on the object number re-
turned.
SQL> SELECT owner, object_name,object_id FROM dba_objects WHERE
object_id=2210;

OWNER                          OBJECT_NAME                 OBJECT_ID
------------------------------ --------------------------- ---------
SYSTEM                         PARTS                            2210
```

DBMS_ROWID.ROWID_RELATIVE_FNO

The **DBMS_ROWID.ROWID_RELATIVE_FNO** function takes a
ROWID and returns the relative file number associated with the **ROWID**.
This file number relates to the **dba_data_files file_id**column.

```
FUNCTION DBMS_ROWID.ROWID_RELATIVE_FNO(row_id IN ROWID)
RETURN NUMBER;
```

The description of the parameter for this function is:

➤ *rowid_in*—This is the **ROWID** you wish to know the format of.

Listing 3.11 shows a sample call to this function.

Listing 3.11   A sample call to the **DBMS_ROWID.ROWID_ RELATIVE_FNO** function.

```
--We have a table that is sitting on multiple datafiles.
--Let's find out how many rows are in each datafile.

SQL> SELECT distinct DBMS_ROWID.ROWID_relative_fno(ROWID) "FILE
NUMBER", count(*)
  2  FROM test.condition_group
  3  group by DBMS_ROWID.ROWID_relative_fno(ROWID);
```

```
FILE NUMBER  COUNT(*)
---------- --------
         3     246
         4     230
```
--We can see that the rows are evenly distributed among data files.
--File number references the file_id column in dba_data_files, so
--now we can determine
--what files the rows are in!
```
SQL> SELECT file_name,file_id
  2  FROM dba_data_files
  3  WHERE file_id in (3,4);
```

```
FILE_NAME
  FILE_ID
--------------------------------------------------------------------
--- --------
/ora01/oracle/admin/testo8/link/testo8_payroll_data_02.dbf
4
/ora01/oracle/admin/testo8/link/testo8_payroll_data_01.dbf
3
```

DBMS_ROWID.ROWID_BLOCK_NUMBER

The **DBMS_ROWID.ROWID_BLOCK_NUMBER** function takes a **ROWID** and returns the block number that the row resides in. This can be very useful in a variety of tuning situations.

```
FUNCTION DBMS_ROWID.ROWID_BLOCK_NUMBER(row_id IN ROWID)
RETURN NUMBER;
```

The description of the parameter for this function is:

➤ *rowid_in*—This is the **ROWID** you wish to know the format of.

Listing 3.12 shows a sample call to this function.

Listing 3.12   A sample call to the **DBMS_ROW.ROWID_ BLOCK_NUMBER** function.

--Let's determine how many rows there are per block.
```
SQL> SELECT distinct DBMS_ROWID.ROWID_block_number(ROWID)
  2  "BLOCK NUMBER", count(*)
  3  FROM test.condition_group
  4  group by DBMS_ROWID.ROWID_block_number(ROWID);
```

```
BLOCK NUMBER  COUNT(*)
```

```
- - - - - - - - - - - - -  - - - - - - - -
      2          23
      3          56
      4          55
      5          59
      6          61
      7          53
      8          61
      9          54
     10          54
```

DBMS_ROWID.ROWID_ROW_NUMBER

The **DBMS_ROWID.ROWID_ROW_NUMBER** function takes a **ROWID** and returns the row number that the row resides in.

```
DBMS_ROWID.ROWID_ROW_NUMBER (row_id IN ROWID)
RETURN NUMBER;
```

The description of the parameters for this function is:

➤ *rowid_in*—This is the **ROWID** you wish to know the format of.

Listing 3.13 shows a sample call to this function.

Listing 3.13 A sample call to the **DBMS_ROWID.ROWID_ ROW_NUMBER** function.

```
--Notice this interesting bit of code. rownum in SQL*PLUS
--starts with 1 but
--ROWID row numbers start with 0!!
SQL> SELECT DBMS_ROWID.ROWID_row_number(ROWID) FROM
  test.condition_group
  2  WHERE rownum < 5;


DBMS_ROWID.ROWID_ROW_NUMBER(ROWID)
----------------------------------
                                 0
                                 1
                                 2
                                 3
```

DBMS_ROWID.ROWID_TO_ABSOLUTE_FNO

The DBMS_ROWID.ROWID_TO_ABSOLUTE_FNO function takes a
ROWID, object name, and schema name, and returns the relative file number
for that combination. This file number relates to the **dba_data_files file_id**
column.

```
DBMS_ROWID.ROWID_TO_ABSOLUTE_FNO (row_id IN ROWID,
schema_name IN VARCHAR2,
object_name IN VARCHAR2)
RETURN NUMBER;
```

The descriptions of the parameters for this function are as follows:

➤ *rowid_in*—The **ROWID** you wish to know the format of.

➤ *schema_name*—The name of the schema that contains the table.

➤ *object_anme*—The name of the table associated with the **ROWID**.

Listing 3.14 shows a sample call to this function.

Listing 3.14 A sample call to the **DBMS_ROWID.ROWID_
TO_ABSOLUTE_FNO** function.

```
SQL> SELECT DBMS_ROWID.ROWID_to_absolute_fno(ROWID,'TEST',
  'CONDITION_GROUP')
  2  "ABSOLUTE FILE NUMBER",count(*)
  3  FROM test.condition_group
  4  group by DBMS_ROWID.ROWID_to_absolute_fno(ROWID,'TEST',
  'CONDITION_GROUP');

ABSOLUTE FILE NUMBER  COUNT(*)
--------------------  --------
                   3       246
                   4       230
```

DBMS_ROWID.ROWID_TO_EXTENDED

The **DBMS_ROWID.ROWID_TO_EXTENDED** function takes a
ROWID and a conversion type, and optionally the schema name and object
name. It returns the extended **ROWID**.

```
FUNCTON DBMS_ROWID.ROWID_TO_EXTENDED(old_rowid IN ROWID,
Schema_name IN VARCHAR2,
object_name IN VARCHAR2,
conversion_type IN INTEGER)
RETURN ROWID;
```

The descriptions of the parameters for this function are as follows:

➤ *rowid_in*—The **ROWID** you wish to know the format of.

➤ *schema_name*—This is the name of the schema that contains the table.
(Optional)

➤ *object_name*—The name of the table associated with the **ROWID**.
(Optional)

➤ *conversion_type*—This parameter defines if the **ROWID_IN** is in a
column of **ROWID** type or a character type. Use either a 0 or 1
(0=**ROWID** and 1=**CHAR**)

Listing 3.15 shows a sample call to this function.

Listing 3.15   A sample call to the **DBMS_ROWID.ROWID_
TO_EXTENDED** function.

```
--We have a table called OLD_ROWID. It contains a restricted
--ROWID format and a unique identifier for a value
--in another table. We wish to convert the ROWIDs from
--restricted to extended ROWIDs and move the table into
--the NEW_ROWID table.
--Description of OLD_ROWID . . .
SQL> desc old_ROWID
 Name                             Null?    Type
 ------------------------------- -------- ----
 OLD_ROWID                                CHAR(20)
 VALUE                                    NUMBER

--A sample of the data in old_ROWID . . .
SQL> SELECT * FROM old_ROWID WHERE rownum < 5 order by value;

OLD_ROWID                 VALUE
-------------------- --------
0000000A.000F.0004       217
0000000A.0010.0004       218
0000000A.0011.0004       219
0000000A.0018.0003       476

--Create the new_ROWID table.
SQL> create table new_ROWID
  2  (new_ROWID char(20), value number);

Table created.
--Make the conversion.
SQL> insert into new_ROWID
  2  (SELECT DBMS_ROWID.ROWID_to_extended(ROWID,NULL,NULL,1),value
```

```
FROM
  3  old_ROWID);

476 rows created.

SQL> SELECT * FROM new_ROWID WHERE rownum < 5 order by value;

NEW_ROWID                   VALUE
------------------          --------
AAAAi2AABAAAAZOAAA          217
AAAAi2AABAAAAZOAAB          218
AAAAi2AABAAAAZOAAC          219
AAAAi2AABAAAAo1AD7          476
```

DBMS_ROWID.ROWID_TO_RESTRICTED

The **DBMS_ROWID.ROWID_TO_RESTRICTED** function takes a **ROWID** and a conversion type and returns the restricted **ROWID**.

```
FUNCTION DBMS_ROWID.ROWID_TO_RESTRICTED(old_rowid IN ROWID,
Conversion_type IN INTEGER),
RETURN ROWID;
```

The descriptions of the parameters for this function are as follows:

➤ *old_rowid*—The **ROWID** you wish to know the format of.

➤ *conversion_type*—This is the **ROWID** type to be returned. Use a 0 or 1 to determine the type of **ROWID** passed in. (**0=ROWID** and **1=CHAR**)

Listing 3.16 shows a sample call to this function.

Listing 3.16   A sample call to the **DBMS_ROWID.ROWID_TO_RESTRICTED** function.

```
--Converts the extended ROWID returned into a restricted
--ROWID format.
SQL> SELECT DBMS_ROWID.ROWID_to_restricted(ROWID,0) FROM
test.condition_group
  2  WHERE rownum < 5;

DBMS_ROWID.ROWID_T
------------------
00000003.0000.0004
00000003.0001.0004
00000003.0002.0004
00000003.0003.0004
```

DBMS_ROWID.ROWID_VERIFY

The **DBMS_ROWID.ROWID_VERIFY** function takes a **ROWID** and a conversion type and optionally the schema name and object name, and returns a value as to the validity of that **ROWID**. The return value will be 0 if the **ROWID** is valid and 1 if the **ROWID** is not valid.

```
DBMS_ROWID.ROWID_VERIFY(old_rowid IN ROWID,
schema_name IN VARCHAR2,
object_name IN VARCHAR2,
conversion_type IN INTEGER)
RETURNS NUMBER;
```

The descriptions of the parameters for this function are as follows:

➤ *old_rowid*—The **ROWID** you wish to know the format of.

➤ *schema_name*—The name of the schema that contains the table. (Optional)

➤ *object_name*—The name of the table associated with the **ROWID**. (Optional)

➤ *conversion_type*—Was the **ROWID** in a column of **ROWID** type or as a character string.

Listing 3.17 shows a sample call to this function.

Listing 3.17   A sample call to the **DBMS_ROWID.ROWID_VERIFY** function.

```
--First send through an invalid ID.
SQL> SELECT DBMS_ROWID.ROWID_verify('44',NULL,NULL,0)
  FROM dual;

DBMS_ROWID.ROWID_VERIFY('44',NULL,NULL,0)
-----------------------------------------
                                        1


--Next, let's send it a valid ROWID.
SQL>  SELECT DBMS_ROWID.ROWID_verify(ROWID,NULL,NULL,0)
  FROM dual;

DBMS_ROWID.ROWID_VERIFY(ROWID,NULL,NULL,0)
------------------------------------------
                                        0
```

Practice Questions

Question 1

Which Oracle process was optional in Oracle7 but is no longer optional in Oracle8?

○ a. DBWR

○ b. CKPT

○ c. ARCH

○ d. LGWR

○ e. SMON

Answer b is correct. The CKPT process was an option in Oracle7 that you enabled in init.ora. In Oracle8, this process is no longer optional. Answers a, d, and e are incorrect because DBWR, LGWR, and SMON have always been required. Answer c is incorrect because the ARCH process is still optional. Answer e is incorrect because a correct answer is given.

Question 2

Which one structure listed is *not* part of the SGA in Oracle8?

○ a. Large pool

○ b. PGA

○ c. **KEEP** buffer pool

○ d. **RECYCLE** buffer pool

○ e. Default buffer cache

Answer b is correct. The PGA is not stored in the SGA of an Oracle database. Answers a, c, d, and e are incorrect because they are parts of the SGA in Oracle8.

Question 3

What is the proper order and format of the extended **ROWID** in Oracle8?

- ○ a. Relative datafile number, object number, data block, row number
- ○ b. Object number, data block, row number
- ○ c. Data block number, datafile address, row number, relative row number
- ○ d. Data object number, relative datafile number, data block number, row number
- ○ e. Extended datafile, extended block address, relative row number, relative data block address

Answer d is correct. The correct order is data object number, relative datafile number, data block number, and row number. Answer a is incorrect because the position of the elements is incorrect. Answer b is incorrect because only three elements of the **ROWID** are listed. Answer c is incorrect because the elements are in the incorrect order. Answer d does not include a datafile address, but rather a relative datafile number, and there is not a relative row number but rather just a row number. Answer e is incorrect because even the terms being used are not correct.

Question 4

What is the purpose of the **DBMS_ROWID** package?

- ○ a. As part of the migration process, to convert existing internally stored Oracle7 **ROWIDs** into Oracle8 **ROWIDs**
- ○ b. To allow conversion between extended and restricted **ROWIDs**
- ○ c. To allow DBAs to change the **ROWIDs** assigned by Oracle to a row in a table
- ○ d. To allow DBAs to manage the **ROWIDs** stored in the data dictionary efficiently
- ○ e. To allow the DBA to create and store **ROWIDs** for future use by rows

Answer b is correct. The **DBMS_ROWID** package is provided in Oracle8 to allow conversions from extended **ROWIDs** and restricted **ROWIDs**. Answer a is incorrect because Oracle does not store **ROWIDs** internally except in limited cases (e.g., indexes). Oracle converts these **ROWIDs** after the migration to Oracle8. Answer c is incorrect because DBAs cannot change the

ROWID of a row in a table with the **DBMS_ROWID** package. Answer d is incorrect because **ROWID**s are not stored in the data dictionary, and DBAs cannot directly change a **ROWID** anyway. Answer e is incorrect because the DBMS_ROWID package does not allow creation of **ROWID**s for later "use."

Question 5

What is the purpose of the **KEEP** buffer pool?

○ a. It allows DBAs to configure an area outside the SGA for memory storage of blocks.

○ b. It allows DBAs to configure an area in the database buffer cache for blocks of data that typically should not be aged out.

○ c. It increases the size of the database buffer cache for storage of blocks that should not typically be aged out by the LRU algorithm.

○ d. It manages empty database buffer block allocations.

○ e. It provides an audit trail of all users work.

Answer b is correct. The **KEEP** pool allows you to configure an area in the SGA for blocks that you would like to see remain in the SGA and not be aged out. Answer a is incorrect because the **KEEP** pool is allocated as a part of the existing SGA. It is defined within the already allocated memory that belongs to the database buffer cache. Answer c is incorrect because allocating the **KEEP** pool does not increase the size of the SGA. Answer d is incorrect because the **KEEP** pool does not manage empty database buffer block allocations. Answer e is incorrect because the **KEEP** buffer pool has no relationship to auditing in Oracle.

Question 6

If a parameter reads as **false** in the **issys_modifiable** column of the **V$PARAMETERS** table, how do you dynamically change this database value so it will be changed system wide?

○ a. Make the change in the init.ora.

○ b. Use the **ALTER SYSTEM** command to make the change.

○ c. Use the **ALTER DATABASE** command to make the change.

○ d. Use the **ALTER CHECKPOINT** command to make the change.

○ e. The **false** parameter indicates that you cannot make the dynamic change.

Answer e is correct. If **issys_modifiable** is **false**, then you cannot change that database parameter dynamically. This is a trick question because the question actually leads you to believe that you can, in fact, change the parameter. Answers a, b, c, and d are incorrect because it is not possible to use any command to change a parameter systemwide where **issys_modifiable = false**.

Question 7

What table can you use to determine if a parameter is dynamically changeable?

○ a. **V$CHANGE_PARAM**

○ b. **V$PARAMETER**

○ c. **V$PROCESS**

○ d. **V$PARAMETER_STATUS**

○ e. **DBA_PARAMETERS**

Answer b is correct. The **V$PARAMETER** table provides information on the dynamic nature of parameters in Oracle. In particular, the **isses_modifiable** and **issys_modifiable** columns define the changability of parameters at both the system and session levels. Answers a and d are incorrect because they are not views available in Oracle8. Answer c is incorrect because **V$PROCESS** reports process-level information, not parameter information. Answer e is incorrect because there is no **DBA_PARAMETERS** table in Oracle.

Question 8

The Oracle8 extended **ROWID** datafile number is relative to what?

○ a. The object that the **ROWID** is associated with

○ b. The tablespace that the object resides in

○ c. The object identifier (**OID**) of the table

○ d. The instance that the **ROWID** is associated with

○ e. The database datafiles

Answer b is correct. The datafile number in an extended **ROWID** is relative to the tablespace that the object resides in. Answer a is incorrect because the file number is not relative to the object that the **ROWID** belongs to. Answer c is incorrect because the **ROWID** and the **OID** (which is discussed in Chapter 5) are not related. Answer d is incorrect because the **ROWID** file number is not relative to the instance. Answer e is incorrect because the **ROWID** is relative to a tablespace, not a datafile.

Question 9

Select the types of **ROWID**s used in Oracle8. [Choose two]

❑ a. Extended

❑ b. Selective

❑ c. Terminal

❑ d. Descriptive

❑ e. Restricted

Answers a and e are correct. Answer a is correct because an extended **ROWID** is the new type of **ROWID** provided in Oracle8. Answer e is correct because a restricted **ROWID** is the old type of **ROWID** available in Oracle7. You can use the **DBMS_ROWID** package to convert extended **ROWID**s to restricted **ROWID**s and back again. While only extended **ROWID**s are returned in the **ROWID** pseudocolumn, it is still possible to use restricted **ROWID**s by converting them to or from the extended **ROWID**. Answers b, c, and d are incorrect because they are not names of **ROWID** types.

Question 10

Select the purposes for the large pool. [Choose two]

❑ a. It provides an area for the UGA when sessions are connected using MTS.

❑ b. It provides an additional memory area for large SQL transactions instead of the database buffer cache.

❑ c. It provides buffering for sequential file I/O.

❑ d. It creates a memory area for large packages to be pinned, saving space in the shared pool area.

❑ e. None of the above.

Answers a and c are correct. Answer a is correct because the large pool provides an area of memory for the UGA when MTS is enabled. Answer c is correct because sequential file I/O buffering is provided through the large pool. Answer b is incorrect because the large pool has nothing to do with the database buffer cache or blocks retrieved in a SQL transaction. Answer d is incorrect because the large pool has nothing to do with pinning PL/SQL packages. Answer e is incorrect because a correct answer is given.

Need To Know More?

 Review the *Oracle8 Install* manual, and the *Oracle8 New Features For Administrators* manual. All the Oracle documentation on the server is a good resource.

 The Oracle8 *Concepts* guide and Oracle8 *Tuning* are good resources.

 Ault, Michael R.: *Oracle8 Black Book.* The Coriolis Group, 1998. ISBN 1-57610-187-8. This is a great reference guide to Oracle8. The book covers the topics covered in this chapter in depth.

 Feuerstein, Steven, et al.: *Oracle Built-in Packages.* O'Reilly & Associates, 1998. ISBN 1-56592-375-8. This book is the definitive guide on the built-in Oracle-supplied PL/SQL packages. Highly recommended.

 Niemiec, Richard K.: *Oracle Performance Tuning Tips & Techniques.* Oracle Press, 1999. ISBN 0-07-882434-6. Niemiec has written a useful book on tuning a database that contains lots of Oracle8 specific information.

 **www.support.com** is Oracle's Metalink Web site. It is a wonderful resource if you have Oracle Metals Support.

Oracle8 Partitioning

Terms you'll need to understand:

√ Partitioning

√ Partitioned tables

√ Partitioned indexes

√ Partition key

√ Partition pruning

√ Partition bounds

√ Prefixed indexes

√ Nonprefixed indexes

√ Global indexes

√ Local indexes

Techniques you'll need to master:

√ Understanding what the benefits of partitioning are

√ Understanding how to partition a table correctly

√ Understanding how to partition an index correctly

√ Understanding the difference between a global and a local index

√ Understanding the various views available to database administrators (DBAs) to maintain partitioned objects

A significant part of the Oracle8 upgrade exam includes questions on a new feature in Oracle8: object partitioning. This chapter explores partitioning and what you need to know about it to successfully answer questions on this topic, including partitioning concepts, partitioning of tables, and the different kinds of partitioned indexes that are available in Oracle8. We will also look at the commands used to support these new partitioning features. Further, we will examine various data dictionary views that help the DBA to manage partitions, and explore how to use new SQL syntax relating to partitions. The chapter concludes with a review of changes to utility programs such as Import/Export and SQL*Loader to enable them to support partitioning.

Oracle8 Partitioning Concepts

Partitioning is a method of splitting an object (table or index) into separate parts (*partitions*) based on some criterion that is assigned to the partition. The criterion might be a date range, a number range, or any other possible value.

As time goes on, certain objects tend to grow quickly, some becoming very large indeed. This can lead to several problems:

➤ As a nonpartitioned table grows larger, queries start to take longer and longer to run.

➤ As a nonpartitioned table grows larger, it takes longer to back up the tablespace in which the nonpartitioned table resides.

➤ As a nonpartitioned table grows larger, the time required to recover a tablespace will increase.

➤ As a nonpartitioned table grows larger, it becomes harder to manage. Object management issues such as storage parameters and defragmentation become more complicated as an object gets bigger.

➤ As a nonpartitioned table grows larger, you cannot assign different parts of the nonpartitioned table to other tablespaces. This ability might make for better performance and faster backup and recovery.

Partitioning is one method of effectively dealing with these problems. It is a particularly effective strategy with certain types of Very Large Databases (VLDBs). Partitioning can be used with Decision Support System (DSS) databases, which typically store and process large amounts of data using complex queries. Partitioning may also assist with VLDB that are of an Online Transaction Processing (OLTP) nature. These databases may store large amounts of data, have high concurrent activity rates, and have relatively noncomplex queries processing a small amount of data.

Prior to Oracle7.3, Oracle did not provide a method of partitioning data from within the database. If you wished to partition data, you had to do so by striping data on different disks or through an application programmatically. This was an imprecise, complex methodology at best. Often, as datafiles were added, and in the rush of fixing problems and adding space, the balanced I/O load, initially carefully established, could become unbalanced. Unfortunately, DBAs couldn't effectively deal with the data at a granular level until Oracle7.3.

Oracle7.3 Partitioned Views

In version 7.3, Oracle gave us a taste of things to come with the introduction of partitioned views. Partitioned views allowed DBAs to create views based on underlying tables. These underlying tables would have check constraints added for particular columns that constrained those columns' values. A view was then created on these tables and if all went well, the Oracle optimizer would recognize that the view was a partitioned view and select execution paths that would only access the tables that needed to be accessed.

In this chapter, I will be using a table called **SALES_DETAIL_DATA** as an example. Listing 4.1 shows a description of this table.

Listing 4.1   A sample sales table.

```
SQL> DESC sales_detail_data
 Name                                   Null?    Type
 -------------------------------------  -------- ----
 date_of_sale                           NOT NULL DATE
 INVOICE_NUMBER                         NOT NULL NUMBER
 ITEM_LINE_NO                           NOT NULL NUMBER
 item_sku                               NOT NULL CHAR(20)
 QTY_SOLD                               NOT NULL NUMBER
```

Taking the **SALES_DETAIL_DATA** table as the example, in Oracle7.3, you might have split this data into 12 tables. You would use the **date_of_sale** column of the table and split it into 12 tables based on the month. The DBA would have defined a check constraint, such as

```
CHECK(TO_CHAR(date_of_sale,'MON')='JAN')
```

and then created an index on this column. The DBA would then have created a view on these tables, joining them together into one partitioned view. The developer then could issue a query, and include in the **WHERE** clause:

```
sales_date='21-JUN-99'
```

In this case, the optimizer should recognize that the partition view is being used and access the only table where the **sales_date** matches.

There were problems with partitioned views in 7.3. One of the larger issues was updating values within the views. In version 7.3, the rules regarding views and changes to objects underlying the views significantly restricted the effectiveness of partitioned views. Other difficulties included some performance problems because the optimizer would not always take advantage of all the underlying base indexes and because of severe load restrictions (you cannot directly load into a **UNION ALL** view). See the "Need To Know More?" section at the end of this chapter for materials about views, partitioned views, and view restrictions. Oracle8 maintains the availability of partitioned views for backward compatibility, but Oracle suggests using partitions in ongoing development efforts. For more information on how to convert partitioned views to partitioned tables, see the "Converting Partitioned Views To Partitioned Tables" section later in this chapter.

Object Partitioning In Oracle8

In version 8, Oracle has provided the next step in partitioning data with the advent of *partitioned tables* and *partitioned indexes*. Now, rather than just striping extents, or creating a partitioned view, DBAs can partition based on data values across multiple tablespaces. Oracle supports very large partitioning schemes, allowing you to create up to 64,000 partitions for a single object. In addition, Oracle has added new SQL syntax to help you deal with partitioning. Let's look at partitioning of tables in Oracle8 in more detail.

 You can partition tables and indexes. You cannot partition clusters, their associated indexes, or snapshots.

Partitioned Tables And Their Benefits

Using the sample table **SALES_DETAIL_DATA**, you might want to partition by the **sales_date** column, with one quarter's worth of data in each partition. Having done this, you would make the **sales_date** column the partition key. The *partition key* is a column or series of up to 16 columns that contains a range of values by which you wish to partition an object. You choose the partition key of a table based on a number of factors, including the nature of the data, its volume, and its volatility. See the "Partitioning Tables" section later in this chapter for more details on how to actually do the partitioning.

The benefits of partitioning include:

➤ Each partition can correspond to a range of values in a given column or columns called the partition key. Thus, you can segment your data in different tablespaces and also on different devices. For example, if you had two sets of disks to choose from—slow ones and very fast ones—you might choose to partition your general ledger data differently. You might partition the most current (and most commonly accessed) dates in your General Ledger table into tablespaces sitting on the faster disks, because they will be accessed more often. You might also partition the older (and less frequently accessed) dates into different tablespaces created on the slower disks.

➤ You can create multiple partitions on separate tablespaces (and thus on different physical devices), which potentially reduces the scope of an outage if a disk device fails.

➤ A partitioned object can now reside in more than one tablespace. A single partition is limited to one tablespace, however.

➤ Partitions are easy for DBAs to control. Each can have its own storage parameters, and you can control where each partition is created.

➤ A partitioned object can span tablespaces, so it has become easier to manage backing up the database. You can now back up just one partition of a large table rather than being forced to back up the entire table.

➤ Tablespaces for partitions can be read-only if that partition is not going to be modified. This relieves backup requirements completely for that partition. Because you can define tablespaces as read-only, you can force parts of a partitioned object to be read-only and other parts to be read-write. This can reduce backup requirements and reduce time of backups, since read-only tablespaces do not need to be constantly backed up.

➤ Partitioning aids DBAs during the recovery process. The partitioned object can reside in multiple tablespaces, so DBAs can recover individual partitions in the event of media failure. At the same time, the other partitions remain available for use. The object is spread over several disks, so the impact of the failure of one disk or tablespace is less severe than if the object existed all in one tablespace. The user encounters an error only if he or she attempts to access the offline partitioned object.

➤ Partitions are independent. DBAs can maintain a particular partition's data (e.g., perform a data load that locks the partition) while the other partitions remain available to the user population, though in some cases indexes may be unavailable for the duration of the load. Also, DBAs can load into multiple partitions at the same time.

➤ There are significant potential performance gains from queries executed against partitioned tables. The optimizer in Oracle8 removes partitions that do not need to be accessed during a query in an action known as *partition pruning*. If the rows in the partition are not needed, based on the partition range that the partition was created with, then Oracle will "prune" that partition from the query and Oracle will not scan that partition, while it will scan the needed partitions of the same table. This reduces the total I/O required to execute a query, thus reducing the time to execute the query.

➤ By using partitioned tables, you are further able to expand on Oracle8's parallel DML and DDL capabilities. These offer even greater potential performance gains.

 You should understand the benefits of partitioning before you take the OCP exam.

Equipartitioned And Nonequipartitioned Objects

You can create *equipartitioned* objects or *nonequipartitioned* objects. Two tables or indexes are said to be equipartitioned if they have identical logical partitioning attributes. However, objects don't have to be of the same type to be equipartitioned; a table and an index can be equipartitioned if they have identical logical partitioning attributes.

The benefits of equipartitioning include:

➤ Offering possible performance increases in SQL operations. Equipartitioning table partitions and index partitions can reduce the number of sorts and joins that the statement requires.

➤ Making tablespace recovery much easier. For example, you may equijoin a parent and child table, placing them in the same tablespace. Thus, you could recover corresponding table and index partitions to a point in time using tablespace point in time recovery available with Oracle8 (see Chapter 10 for issues relating to tablespace point in time recovery).

Equipartitioning might also make development platforms easier to use if you often have to recover certain large tables because of data-destructive testing. If you can partition the data that is being changed into its own partition and its own tablespace, recovery back to the point in time before the destructive testing might be quicker. For an example of the difference between equipartitioning and nonequipartitioning of objects, see Figure 4.1.

➤ Creation and maintenance of equipartitioned indexes on a partitioned table is generally easier than creation and maintenance on nonequipartitioned indexes. We will cover this in more detail later in the chapter in the sction "Partitioning Indexes."

Make sure you understand the difference between equipartitioned objects and nonequipartitioned objects.

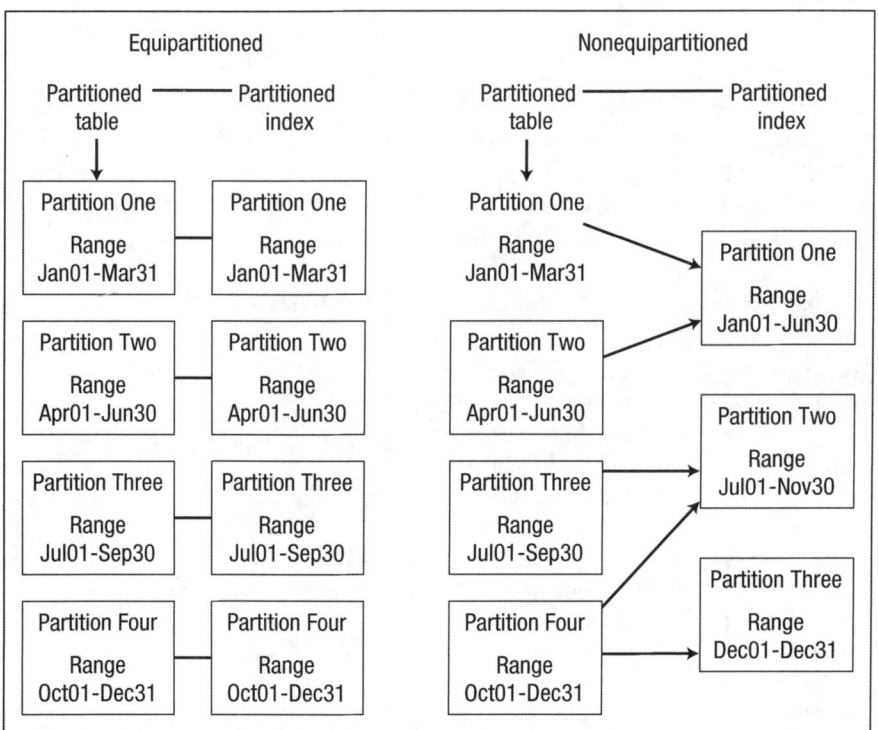

Figure 4.1   Example of equipartitioned and nonequipartitioned objects.

Partitioning Tables

We are now into the meat of partitioning. This section examines how to actually set up a partitioned table as well as alter one. This includes how to define the partition keys and how to create multiple keyed partitions. We will look at how Oracle assigns rows to partitions and then, we will review the restrictions that exist when you are partitioning tables.

How To Partition A Table

It's time for you to take the **SALES_DETAIL_DATA** table and create it as a partitioned table with four partitions (each partition will store one quarter's worth of data). You will store each of these partitions in four separate tablespaces (named **QUARTER_ONE, QUARTER_TWO, QUARTER_THREE,** and **QUARTER_FOUR**).

 Carefully study how to create partitioned tables. The OCP exam may ask you questions about partitioned tables and how to create them.

Creating The Partitioned Table

To create the partitioned table, you will use the Oracle **CREATE TABLE** command. The syntax of this command has changed quite a bit in Oracle8. Without further ado, let's create the **SALES_DETAIL_DATA** partitioned table. Listing 4.2 shows the DDL for this creation.

Listing 4.2 Creating the **SALES_DETAIL_DATA** table.

```
CREATE TABLE sales_detail_data
(date_of_sale      DATE      NOT NULL,
invoice_number     NUMBER    NOT NULL,
item_line_no       NUMBER    NOT NULL,
item_sku           NUMBER    NOT NULL,
qty_sold           NUMBER    NOT NULL
)
/* Below are the default partition storage
   attributes. Partitions without any defined attributes take
   on the attributes defined on these lines. */
PCTFREE 10
PCTUSED 60
STORAGE (INITIAL 10K NEXT 10K)
```

```
/* The table partition clause and the whole rest of the
   syntax make up the partition specification. */
/* date_of_sale is the partition key. */
PARTITION BY RANGE (date_of_sale)
(
   /* Now the partition description clauses: */
   /* The name of the first partition is sales_q1_99. It
      contains values for all */
   /* dates inserted that are earlier than  Feb 02 1999. */
   /* This partition is assigned to the quarter_one
      tablespace. */
   /* Note that we have now added storage clauses to
      the partitions, so they are created as we define. */
   PARTITION sales_q1_99 VALUES LESS THAN
   (TO_DATE('1999-02-01','YYYY-MM-DD') )
   PCTFREE 10
   PCTUSED 60
   TABLESPACE quarter_one
   STORAGE (INITIAL 10K NEXT 10K),
   PARTITION sales_q2_99 VALUES LESS THAN
   (TO_DATE('1999-07-01','YYYY-MM-DD') )
   PCTFREE 10
   PCTUSED 60
   TABLESPACE quarter_two
   STORAGE (INITIAL 10K NEXT 10K ),
   PARTITION sales_q3_99 VALUES LESS THAN
   (TO_DATE('1999-10-01','YYYY-MM-DD') )
   PCTFREE 10
   PCTUSED 60
   TABLESPACE quarter_three
   STORAGE (INITIAL 20K NEXT 20K ),
   PARTITION sales_q4_99 VALUES LESS THAN
   (TO_DATE('2000-01-01','YYYY-MM-DD') )
   PCTFREE 10
   PCTUSED 60
   TABLESPACE quarter_four
   STORAGE (INITIAL 40K NEXT 40K ) );
CREATE TABLE sales_detail_data
*
ERROR at line 1:
ORA-00439: feature not enabled: Partitioning
```

Note the unfortunate error that occurred when I tried to create the partitioned table. This is because partitioning is an option you have to install when you install the Oracle database software; it is not part of the base install of the

Oracle8 RDBMS. If you do not install the partitioning option, you cannot partition the object. After I installed the partitioning option, the partitioned table was created successfully.

Details On Partitioning Tables.

Let's look at the **CREATE TABLE** statement above in a bit of detail. I have included comments in Listing 4.2 to describe each section of the statement. The first seven lines look like the old **CREATE TABLE** syntax. Next, you can include default partition physical attributes. Any partition not given specific physical storage attributes derives its attributes from the default attributes defined. The next section of code involves some new syntax known as the *partition specification*. This consists of the:

➤ *PARTITION BY RANGE clause*—This specifies that the table is partitioned based on columns listed in the **column_list** that is enclosed in parentheses. The **column_list** (**date_of_sale**, in the example) defines the column(s) (known as the partition key, as described shortly) that the partitions will be keyed on. This clause is also known as the *TABLE PARTITION clause*.

➤ *List of partition descriptions*—These clauses define the partitions, what data they hold, the storage characteristics of the storage, and so on. Each partition is assigned a unique name, and this name must remain unique within the partitioned table.

The Partition Key Of A Partitioned Table

The **date_of_sale** column listed in the table partition clause is known as the partition key. A partition key may consist of up to 16 columns and is an ordered list of the values for the partitioning columns. A partition key may not contain the **LEVEL, ROWID,** or **MLSLABEL** pseudocolumns or any column that is of type **ROWID**. The partition key is sorted by its binary value.

 Make sure you are clear on what the partition key is and how many columns it can be.

Note in Listing 4.2 that the partitions are created with different storage size values. Partitioning allows you to size each partition as you wish. Controlling the size of each partition is handy in cases where the data is cyclical: Large volumes come in during well-defined times, and smaller volumes come in during others. You can then more effectively manage your disk space, allocating a smaller amount of space to one partition and allocating a larger amount to another.

 It is always a good idea to carefully analyze the data you intend to partition. Carefully look at the data, and size the partitions relative to the partition key(s) and the volume and nature of data related to that key. Look at historical volumes and how they might fluctuate over time, and determine how you split the partitions based on the key you select.

Let's look at different elements of the **PARTITION BY RANGE** clause for a moment. It starts with the keyword **PARTITION** followed by the name of the partition. Each partition has a name, and this name must conform to Oracle naming rules for objects. In addition, each partition name that belongs to the same table must be unique.

The next section is the *partition bounds*. Every partition has a noninclusive upper bound that is represented by the **VALUES LESS THAN** clause. All partitions but the first have an inclusive lower bound. This bound is specified by the **VALUES LESS THAN** clause of the partition before it. These partition bounds define the order of the partitions in the table (and also the partition that rows will be stored in). The first partition has the lowest **VALUES LESS THAN** value. Each subsequent partition is ordered based on the relationship of its partition bounds to those of the others. The partition with the highest partition bound value becomes the highest partition in the table.

In the **SALES_DETAIL_DATA** table, the order of the partitions is **sales_q1_99, sales_q2_99, sales_q3_99,** and then **sales_q4_99.** As stated above, the ordering is defined by the **VALUES LESS THAN** clauses associated with these partitions. The date range in **sales_q1_99** is less than that of **sales_q2_99,** so **sales_q1_99** is ordered first, then **sales_q2_99.**

Remember that the values stored in each partition are less than the partition bounds defined for a specific partition. Thus, if you create a partition with a partition key of the letters A through Z and then make "Z" the last partition's **VALUES LESS THAN,** you cannot store any value with a Z in that partition. In this case, a Z is an ASCII value of 90. In order to store the value Z, you need to define the partition's **VALUES LESS THAN** as ASCII character 91, which is a "[".

Note: Partition boundary limits have implications with lowercase values as well, because they start at ASCII values of 97 and up. When partitioning a table, take care that you do not inadvertently prevent yourself from inserting the data you wish to store, such as lowercase letters.

Creating Multiple Partition Key Partitions

As mentioned in the "Partitioned Tables and Their Benefits" section, you can choose to partition a table based on multiple columns. Returning to the example of the **SALES_DETAIL_DATA**, assume that you wish to partition not only on the date of sale, but perhaps also on what was sold (the **item_sku** in this example). It might be that in the environment that our demonstration tables were created, it would be determined that further partitioning of the table would allow partitioning of sales by what date and what was being sold (jeans, shoes, and other items). See Listing 4.3 in the next section for an example of a multiple partitioned table.

Partition Boundaries And **MAXVALUE**

You can attempt to insert into a partitioned table a value that does not conform to the partition bounds defined for that table. In this case, the insert will fail. For example, in **SALES_DETAIL_DATA** (refer back to Listing 4.2), if I tried to insert sales data for March 1, 2001, the insert would fail because no partition is defined that would include the date being inserted within its partition bounds. If you will need to insert partition key values into a partitioned table greater than the maximum partitioned boundary, then you will need to include the **MAXVALUE** clause when you create the partitioned table. The **MAXVALUE** clause represents all values possible that are higher than the greatest partition boundary in a partitioned table. Thus, in our sample **sales_detail_data** table, if we wish to be able to enter any dates greater than December 31, 1999, we would add a new partition using the **MAXVALUE** clause instead of a specific date. Listing 4.3 shows an example of this changed code. The listing includes multiple partitions and uses the **MAXVALUE** clause.

Make sure you understand what **MAXVALUE** is and how to use it when creating partitioned tables. Make sure you understand why you need to use it.

Listing 4.3   Using the **MAXVALUE** clause and multiple partition keys.

```
CREATE TABLE sales_detail_data
(date_of_sale     DATE      NOT NULL,
invoice_number    NUMBER    NOT NULL,
item_line_no      NUMBER    NOT NULL,
item_sku          NUMBER    NOT NULL,
qty_sold          NUMBER    NOT NULL
)
/* Below are the Default partition storage attributes. Partitions
   without any defined attributes take on the attributes defined
   on these lines. */
PCTFREE 10
PCTUSED 60
STORAGE (INITIAL 10K NEXT 10K)
/* Now the table Partition clause and the whole rest of the syntax
   make up the partition specification. */
PARTITION BY RANGE (date_of_sale,item_sku)
(
    /* Now the partition description clauses: */
    /* The name of the first partition is sales_q1_99. It
       contains values for all */
    /* dates inserted less than Feb 02 1999. */
    /* This partition is assigned to the quarter_one
       tablespace. */
    /* Note that we have added storage clauses to the
       partitions,
       so they are created as we define. */
PARTITION sales_q1_99_jeans VALUES LESS THAN
(TO_DATE('1999-04-01','YYYY-MM-DD'),100000 )
  PCTFREE 10
  PCTUSED 60
  TABLESPACE quarter_one
  STORAGE (INITIAL 10K NEXT 10K ),
PARTITION sales_q1_99_shirts VALUES LESS THAN
(TO_DATE('1999-04-01','YYYY-MM-DD'),200000 )
  PCTFREE 10
  PCTUSED 60
  TABLESPACE quarter_one
  STORAGE (INITIAL 10k NEXT 10k ),
PARTITION sales_q1_99_allelse VALUES LESS THAN
(TO_DATE('1999-04-01','YYYY-MM-DD'),MAXVALUE )
  PCTFREE 10
  PCTUSED 60
  TABLESPACE quarter_one
  STORAGE (INITIAL 10k NEXT 10k ),
```

```
PARTITION sales_q2_99_jeans VALUES LESS THAN
(TO_DATE('1999-07-01','YYYY-MM-DD'),100000 )
  PCTFREE 10
  PCTUSED 60
  TABLESPACE quarter_two
  STORAGE (INITIAL 10k NEXT 10k ),
PARTITION sales_q2_99_shirts VALUES LESS THAN
(TO_DATE('1999-07-01','YYYY-MM-DD'),200000 )
  PCTFREE 10
  PCTUSED 60
  TABLESPACE quarter_two
  STORAGE (INITIAL 10k NEXT 10k ),
PARTITION sales_q2_99_allelse VALUES LESS THAN
(TO_DATE('1999-07-01','YYYY-MM-DD'),MAXVALUE )
  PCTFREE 10
  PCTUSED 60
  TABLESPACE quarter_two
  STORAGE (INITIAL 10k NEXT 10k ),
PARTITION sales_q3_99_jeans VALUES LESS THAN
(TO_DATE('1999-10-01','YYYY-MM-DD'),100000 )
  PCTFREE 10
  PCTUSED 60
  TABLESPACE quarter_three
  STORAGE (INITIAL 10k NEXT 10k ),
PARTITION sales_q3_99_shirts VALUES LESS THAN
(TO_DATE('1999-10-01','YYYY-MM-DD'),200000 )
  PCTFREE 10
  PCTUSED 60
  TABLESPACE quarter_three
  STORAGE (INITIAL 10k NEXT 10k ),
PARTITION sales_q3_99_allelse VALUES LESS THAN
(TO_DATE('1999-10-01','YYYY MM DD'),MAXVALUE )
  PCTFREE 10
  PCTUSED 60
  TABLESPACE quarter_three
  STORAGE (INITIAL 10k NEXT 10k ),
PARTITION sales_q4_99_jeans VALUES LESS THAN
(TO_DATE('2000-01-01','YYYY-MM-DD'),100000 )
  PCTFREE 10
  PCTUSED 60
  TABLESPACE quarter_four
  STORAGE (INITIAL 30k NEXT 30k ),
PARTITION sales_q4_99_shirts VALUES LESS THAN
(TO_DATE('2000-01-01','YYYY-MM-DD'),200000 )
  PCTFREE 10
  PCTUSED 60
  TABLESPACE quarter_four
  STORAGE (INITIAL 20k NEXT 20k ),
```

```
PARTITION sales_q4_99_allelse VALUES LESS THAN
(TO_DATE('2000-01-01','YYYY-MM-DD'),MAXVALUE )
  PCTFREE 10
  PCTUSED 60
  TABLESPACE quarter_four
  STORAGE (INITIAL 10k NEXT 10k ) );
```

 Although Oracle allows you to use two-digit years, it is always good practice to use four-digit years when creating partition boundaries.

Row Partition Assignments

In a partitioned table with a single partition key, the order of the partitions starts with the lowest sorted partition based on the partition key. A new row is inserted into the partition based on its relationship to the partition key. If the value of the partition key column being inserted is less than the value of the partition bound for that partition, then the row is in that partition. For example, if the partition bounds are 5, 10, and 15, and the value being inserted into the partitioned table is 7, the insert would occur in the partition bounded by 10. Rows with partition key inserts equal to the range boundary end up in the next-higher partition. Therefore, an attempt to insert a value of 10 causes the row to be inserted into the partition bounded by 15. An attempt to insert a value outside valid partition boundaries results in an error.

Placement of a row in a multicolumn partition keyed table is a bit more complex than single column partition keyed tables are. Here are the rules:

➤ Oracle looks at the range values from left to right to determine on which partition the row belongs.

➤ Oracle looks at the left most partition key column value in the row to be inserted. If that value is less than the first partition key range boundary of the partitioned table, Oracle will move to the next partition key column. Oracle will continue to move left to right, through the partition column keys of the row, comparing them to the partition range values of the tables key columns, until it finds the correct partition to insert the row into.

➤ If all the columns are equal to the range boundaries, then the row is assigned to the next-higher partition.

How Rows Are Assigned To Partitions

This section offers some examples that might make it easier for you to understand how a row is assigned to a partition. In addition, Figure 4.2 shows a graphical depiction of what is happening. For these examples, review the table created by Listing 4.3.

➤ *Example One*—The user inserts a row with a partition key value for **date_of_sale** of **1999-01-01** with an **item_sku** of '99000'. Which partition will this be assigned to? Remember that the rules say you must start from left to right. Look for the first value that is less than the range value and that is the partition to which the row is assigned. So, look at the first partition, **sales_q1_99_jeans** (remember that partitions are ordered based on the ordering of the partition keys). The **date_of_sale** column is the first in the partition key, so start comparing its value in the inserted row with the partition bound value of the first partition. The first partition's partition bound range starts with a **date_of_sale** earlier than **01-APR-1999**. Next, compare the **item_sku**. The **item_sku** is less than the partition range of the partition for **item_sku**, so the row is inserted into the first partition, **sales_q1_99_jeans**.

➤ *Example Two*—Assume the next row to be inserted has a value of **1999-04-01** for the **date_of_sale** and an **item_sku** of '954333'. Starting with the first partition, **sales_q1_99_jeans**, compare the **date_of_sale** to the range value allowed by the first partition for this column. The two values should be equal so you must move to the next range defined in the partition key. You actually skip the next two partitions (**sales_q1_99_shirts** and **sales_q1_99_allelse**) for the same reason. Then, you compare the **item_sku** to the range allowed in the fourth partition (**sales_q2_99_jeans**). Comparing the **date_of_sale**, you find it is now less than the range of the **date_of_sale** for the partition. Next, start comparing the next key, **item_sku**. The **item_sku** range in the fourth partition is '100000'. The item_sku value you wish to insert is higher than that range, so you must go to the next (fifth) partition in order, **sales_q2_99_shirts**. This partition has the **date_of_sale** range of greater than your date, again, so look at the **item_sku** value, which is now '200000'. Again, your inserted value is higher than this. Your next move is to the next (sixth) partition, **sales_q2_99_allelse**. Here again, you find the two **date_of_sale** values to be equal, and therefore you have to move to the **item_sku** range defined in the partition key. You find the next **item_sku** range to be **MAXVALUE**, which allows you an unlimited ceiling for row values. The insert of the **item_sku** is—and will always be— less than **MAXVALUE**, so insert the row in the sixth partition, **sales_q2_99_allelse**.

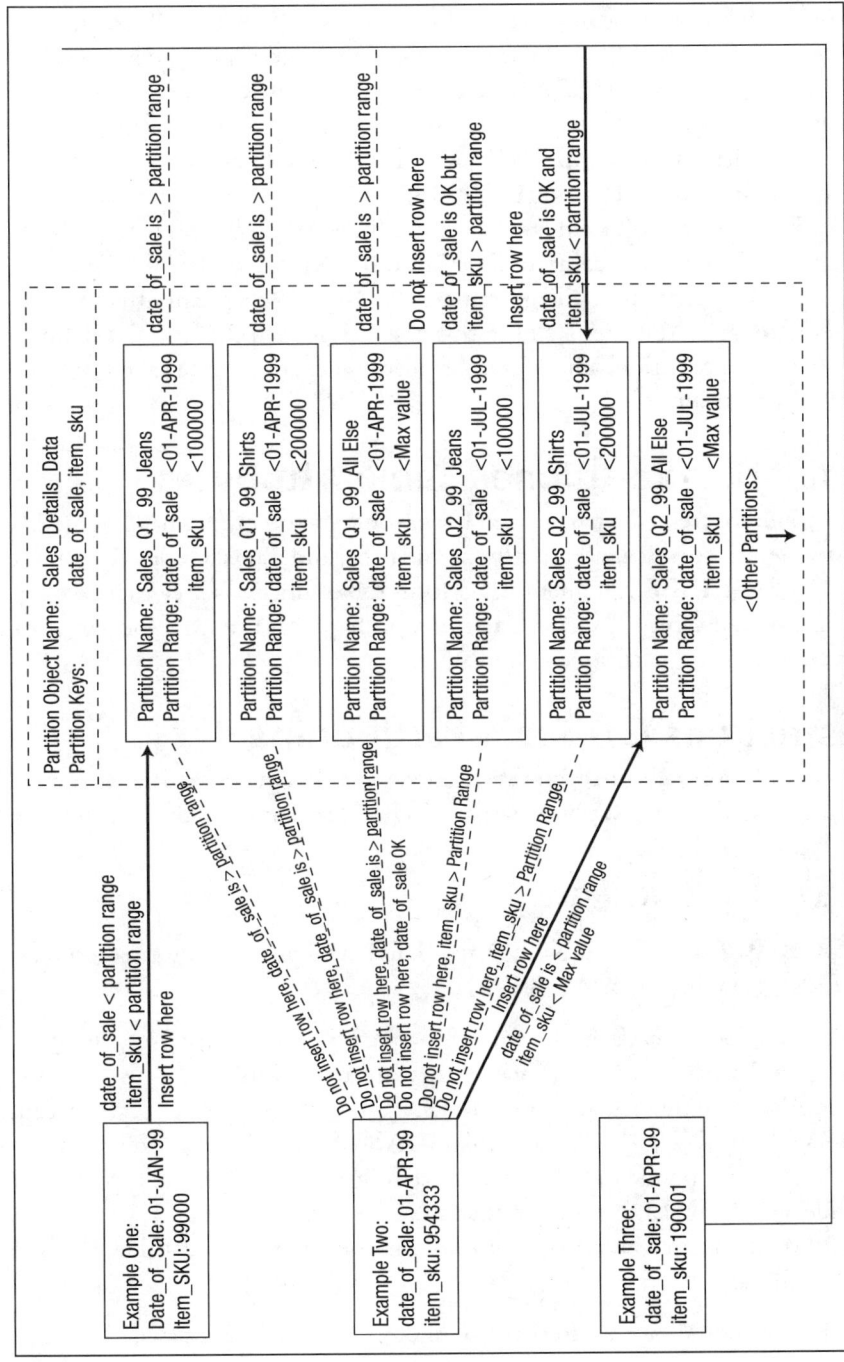

Figure 4.2 Deciding which partition a row belongs to in a partitioned table.

➤ *Example Three*—Assume that a **date_of_sale** of **1999-04-04** and an **item_sku** of '190001' are being inserted. In this example, you again skip the first three partitions because the first partition boundary of each is less than the **date_of_sale** value of **04-APR-1999**. You then arrive at the fourth partition, **sales_q2_99_jeans**, where the **date_of_sale** is less than the partition boundary of **01-JUL-1999**. Comparing the **item_sku**, you find that your row's **item_sku** is greater than the partition range of that partition's **item_sku** column. Proceed to the **NEXT** partition. There, again, the partition boundary remains **01-JUL-1999**, greater than your **date_of_sale**. Your **item_sku** in this case is less than the '200000' boundary for the partition. Therefore, this insert goes into the **sales_q2_99_ shirts** partition.

Modifying Partitioned Table Attributes

After you have created a partitioned table, you may sometimes need to modify its parameters, as well as add partitions and other functions. Generally, you use the **ALTER TABLE** statement to perform these functions. See the "Managing Partitioned Objects" section later in this chapter for more information on managing existing partitioned objects.

Restrictions On Table Partitioning

You should be aware of several restrictions in relation to partitioned tables. First, Oracle does not support partitioning tables that contain the following data types:

➤ **LONG** or **LONG RAW**.

➤ **LOB** (**BLOB**, **CLOB**, **NCLOB**, or **BFILE**). For more information on **LOB**, see Chapter 5.

You cannot specify **NULL** as a value for a partition boundary. Nor can blank strings be defined as values, because they are treated as **NULLs** within the server. Also note that Oracle sorts **NULLs** higher than all other values except **MAXVALUE**. **NULLs** sort less than **MAXVALUE**. This means that if a table's partition bounds are defined on a column that is nullable, you must include a **MAXVALUE** clause in the table's creation statement. If you do not, any **NULLs** inserted will map above the highest partitioned value, and the insert will fail.

Oracle does not allow you to partition index organized tables (see Chapter 6 for more information), nor can a partitioned table be part of a cluster. You cannot update the partition key column. Doing so causes an error. If you need to change the value of a row's partition key column, such that it would move the row into another partition, you must delete the column and reinsert it because Oracle does not let you move a row between partitions.

Note the use of the **TO_DATE** format mask used in the example in Listing 4.3. The use of the format mask is required. If you do not use the **TO_DATE** format mask, partition pruning will not be possible.

Other restrictions include the inability to define a synonym that points to a partition of a table, and the inability to use the new SQL syntax to access partitions directly in PL/SQL code.

You may be able to circumvent the inability of PL/SQL code to directly refer to a partition. You can try to create a view that contains the hints and references you need and then refer to the view in the PL/SQL code. You may also reference partitions in dynamic SQL, using the dbms_sql package.

Converting Partitioned Views To Partitioned Tables

Oracle has provided a method to move partitioned views into partitioned tables. Through a combination of the **CREATE TABLE** statement and the **ALTER TABLE** statement, you may convert the old partitioned views to partitioned tables. Follow these steps to perform this operation (assuming that in Oracle7.3 you used a partitioned view called **SALES_VIEW** that joined four tables called **SALES_Q1** through **SALES_Q4** together):

1. First, define a partitioned table. As in Listing 4.2, define the partitions that are represented in the partition view.

2. Next, exchange the tables that are underlying the view for the partitions. You do this with an **ALTER TABLE** statement:

```
ALTER TABLE sales_detail_data
EXCHANGE PARTITION sales_q1_99 WITH TABLE SALES_Q1;
```

3. Perform Step 2 for each table in the partitioned view. Once this is complete, the data that was in the tables underlying the partitioned view will reside in the partitions of the table. You may drop the tables and the view.

Partitioning Indexes

This section looks at the different kinds of partitioned indexes and how you actually create them. You will then look at the **ALTER INDEX** command and the options it provides to maintain the partitioned indexes. Finally, this section reviews the restrictions that exist when you are partitioning indexes.

In Oracle, there are four general types of indexes:

➤ Nonpartitioned indexes

➤ Global prefixed indexes

➤ Local prefixed indexes

➤ Local nonprefixed indexes

As with tables, indexes have to have a partition key that is used to separate the values into different partitions based on the range defined for the key. An index is *prefixed* if the left-most column (leading edge) of the index is the same as the left-most column on which the table is partitioned. If this is not the case, the index is *nonprefixed*. For example, if we were to create a multicolumn index on the partitioned table created above in Listing 4.3, and we created the index on the **date_of_sale** column, then that index would be considered prefixed. This is because the index has the partition key as its leading or only key. If, however, you created an index on **item_sku**, it would not be prefixed because **item_sku** is not the leading edge of the partition key. In a multicolumn index, as long as **date_of_sale** was the left-most value that the index was created on, it would be a prefixed index. Unique prefixed indexes can have performance advantages over nonprefixed indexes by allowing the database to access only one index partition to find the data it requires. As with any index, the contents of the **WHERE** clause in a select statement can control the efficiency of the index lookup. Take care to index properly.

 Make sure you are clear on what a prefixed and nonprefixed index is.

The benefits of using partitioned indexes are:

➤ Only one partition of an index is searched if the index is a unique prefixed partitioned index and the **WHERE** clause specifies the value(s) of the column(s) in the index.

➤ Only one partition of an index is searched if the index is a prefixed non-unique index and if the **WHERE** clause specifies a value for all the columns in the index. If this is not the case, all the index's partitions are scanned.

➤ If the index is a unique nonprefixed index, you may still be able to scan only one partition. If the **WHERE** clause of the select statement contains the partition key, Oracle uses only the partition that contains the data requested.

➤ If the index is nonunique and nonprefixed, Oracle must search all the partitions of that index to get the data queried.

 There are a couple restrictions regarding index partitioning. You cannot partition indexes that are part of an index cluster, nor can you partition a bitmap index.

Global Indexes

Global indexes allow you to define the partitions of the index differently than the partition of the table. This means that the partitioned index can contain partition key range values different from those of the associated table. A global index is how you create a nonequipartitioned index with a partitioned table.

If you create a global index, Oracle does not maintain the relationship between the table and the index as it does with a local index. Execution of DDL on the table associated with the global index can cause the index to become invalid.

 Make sure you understand global indexes—what they are, what can cause them to go invalid, and that they are not maintained by Oracle.

To rebuild a global index, DBAs can use the **ALTER INDEX REBUILD PARTITION** statement. For more information on rebuilding partitioned indexes, see the "Managing Partitioned Indexes" section later in this chapter.

Note: All global indexes must be prefixed.

Listing 4.4 shows an example of creating a global index on **SALES_DETAIL_DATA**. Note that the index is partitioned differently than the **SALES_DETAIL_DATA** table. Also note that if you did not use the **MAXVALUE** clause and you attempted to insert a value out of the range of the index partition defined in Listing 4.2, the statement would fail. In addition, you explicitly name the partitions when creating the index. Naming the partitions is not required, though it is good practice; Oracle assigns default partition names if they are not explicitly defined. Finally, note that the partition definition syntax for a global index is essentially the same as that for partitioning a table.

 Generally, local prefixed indexes are preferable to global indexes. They are less of a maintenance burden and generally provide better performance than global indexes do.

Listing 4.4   Creating a global index.

```
CREATE INDEX ix_sales_dos_01 ON sales_detail_data(date_of_sale)
    global
PARTITION BY RANGE(date_of_sale)
(PARTITION par1 VALUES LESS THAN
(TO_DATE('01-APR-1999','DD-MON-YYYY') )
 TABLESPACE quarter_one
 STORAGE (INITIAL 10k NEXT 10k),
 PARTITION par2 VALUES LESS THAN
(TO_DATE('01-JUL-1999','DD-MON-YYYY') )
 TABLESPACE quarter_three
STORAGE (INITIAL 20k NEXT 10k),
 PARTITION par3 VALUES LESS THAN (MAXVALUE)
 TABLESPACE quarter_four
STORAGE (INITIAL 10k NEXT 10k) );
```

 Always name your partitions explicitly. Doing so makes administration much easier down the road.

Local Indexes

Local indexes, when created, automatically inherit both the same number of partitions as the referenced partitioned table and the names of those partitions. Oracle can even provide the storage specifications for the partitions. When created, the partitions are automatically equipartitioned. Oracle maintains local indexes so that changes to the associated table structure (e.g., adding a new partition) do not require significant DBA involvement to revalidate the indexes. Local prefixed indexes generally offer more advantages to DBAs from both a performance and a maintenance standpoint than global indexes do. In addition, you can create a local nonprefixed index for columns that aren't members of the partition key.

Some operations may require you to rebuild a local index. These include moving a partition and truncating a partition. DBAs use the **ALTER TABLE MODIFY PARTITION REBUILD UNUSABLE LOCAL INDEXES** statement to rebuild the invalidated index. See the "Managing Partitioned Indexes" section later in this chapter for more information on maintaining local indexes.

Listing 4.5 shows an example of creating a prefixed local index on **SALES_DETAIL_DATA**. Note how much less work is required to create the local index as opposed to creating global indexes. You can still include storage requirements, if you desire, but you don't need to define the key on which to partition or the partition range values.

Listing 4.5 Creating a prefixed and nonprefixed local index.

```
/* A very simple local index creation. Oracle provides all the
partition information and storage. */
CREATE INDEX test_id ON sales_detail_data
(date_of_sale, item_sku) LOCAL;
/* Prefixed index creation. */
CREATE INDEX ix_sales_dos_01 ON sales_detail_data(date_of_sale)
LOCAL
(PARTITION ix_sales_dos_q1_jeans_99 TABLESPACE quarter_one,
PARTITION ix_sales_dos_q1_shirt_99 TABLESPACE quarter_one,
PARTITION ix_sales_dos_q1_allelse_99 TABLESPACE quarter_one,
PARTITION ix_sales_dos_q2_jeans_99 TABLESPACE quarter_two,
PARTITION ix_sales_dos_q2_shirt_99 TABLESPACE quarter_two,
PARTITION ix_sales_dos_q2_allelse_99 TABLESPACE quarter_two,
PARTITION ix_sales_dos_q3_jeans_99 TABLESPACE quarter_three,
PARTITION ix_sales_dos_q3_shirt_99 TABLESPACE quarter_three,
PARTITION ix_sales_dos_q3_allelse_99 TABLESPACE quarter_three,
PARTITION ix_sales_dos_q4_jeans_99 TABLESPACE quarter_four,
PARTITION ix_sales_dos_q4_shirt_99 TABLESPACE quarter_four,
PARTITION ix_sales_dos_q4_allelse_99 TABLESPACE quarter_four);

/* Nonprefixed index creation. */
CREATE INDEX ix_sales_sku_01 ON sales_detail_data(item_sku)
LOCAL
(PARTITION ix_sales_dos_q1_jean_99 TABLESPACE quarter_one,
PARTITION ix_sales_dos_q1_shirt_99 TABLESPACE quarter_one,
PARTITION ix_sales_dos_q1_allelse_99 TABLESPACE quarter_one,
PARTITION ix_sales_dos_q2_jeans_99 TABLESPACE quarter_two,
PARTITION ix_sales_dos_q2_shirt_99 TABLESPACE quarter_two,
PARTITION ix_sales_dos_q2_allelse_99 TABLESPACE quarter_two,
PARTITION ix_sales_dos_q3_jeans_99 TABLESPACE quarter_three,
PARTITION ix_sales_dos_q3_shirt_99 TABLESPACE quarter_three,
PARTITION ix_sales_dos_q3_allelse_99 TABLESPACE quarter_three,
```

```
PARTITION ix_sales_dos_q4_jeans_99 TABLESPACE quarter_four,
PARTITION ix_sales_dos_q4_shirt_99 TABLESPACE quarter_four,
PARTITION ix_sales_dos_q4_allelse_99 TABLESPACE quarter_four);
```

Modifying Partitioned Index Attributes

Having created partitioned indexes, you may sometimes need to modify the indexes' parameters, add partitions, and perform other functions. Generally, you use the **ALTER INDEX** statement to perform these functions. See the "Managing Partitioned Indexes" section later in this chapter for more information on managing existing partitioned objects.

Managing Partitioned Objects

Once you have created partitioned objects, there will be occasions when you will need to change some attribute of the object. You may need to rebuild an existing index or add a partition to a table. In this section, we will cover management of existing partitioned objects.

Managing Partitioned Tables

Once a partitioned table is created, several management issues arise from time to time. You may sometimes need to modify the partition table's storage parameters, or add, drop, or split partitions and other functions. In this section, we will address managing partitioned tables.

The **ALTER TABLE** Command

Generally, you use the **ALTER TABLE** statement to perform these functions. Its syntax has changed significantly since Oracle7.3.

You can perform several functions with the **ALTER TABLE** command that should already seem like second nature. These functions include:

➤ Altering the default and partition storage clauses.

➤ Adding a partition to the table (this can be done only at the end of a partitioned table's partition range).

➤ Dropping a partition.

➤ Moving a partition (this allows you to move a table partition to another tablespace).

➤ Renaming a partition.

➤ Splitting a partition (this allows you to take one partition of a partitioned table and split it into two partitions).

Using The **ALTER TABLE** Command To Modify Partitioned Tables

When you are adding partitions, be aware that you cannot add a partition to the middle of a table's partition order. You must add the partition onto the high end of the partition order. If you find you must have an additional partition in the middle or at the beginning of the table, you may split an existing partition.

Beware of partition splitting and the effects it may have on indexes associated with that partition. If you split an empty partition, there will be no impact on the indexes. If you split a partition with data, indexes will be invalidated and you must rebuild them. This rule also applies if you truncate a partition. If it was empty, the indexes will not be affected; otherwise, you will need to rebuild them.

As with a regular table, you can truncate a partition's data. If you do so and there was data in the partition, you will render global indexes invalid. This problem does not occur with local indexes. As with the **TRUNCATE TABLE** command, there are options to **REUSE STORAGE** or **DROP STORAGE**. Listing 4.6 shows examples of these operations.

Listing 4.6   Using the **ALTER TABLE** command.

```
/* Change the default storage for a partitioned table. */
ALTER TABLE sales_detail_data MODIFY
DEFAULT ATTRIBUTES STORAGE (INITIAL 10M NEXT 10M);

/* Change the storage parameters for a specific partition. */
ALTER TABLE sales_detail_data modify
PARTITION sales_q1_99 STORAGE (NEXT 10m);

/* Drop a partition in a partitioned table. */
ALTER TABLE sales_detail_data
DROP PARTITION sales_q1_99_jeans;

/* Move a partition in a partitioned table to another tablespace. */
ALTER TABLE sales_detail_data
MOVE PARTITION sales_q1_99_shirts TABLESPACE quarter_one;

ALTER TABLE sales_detail_data
RENAME PARTITION sales_q1_99 TO sales_q1_1999;
```

```
ALTER TABLE sales_detail_data
TRUNCATE PARTITIONsales_q1_99 DROP STORAGE;

ALTER TABLE sales_detail_data ADD PARTITION sales_q1_00
VALUES LESS THAN(TO_DATE('2000-04-01','YYYY-MM-DD'),100000)
PCTFREE 10
PCTUSED 60
TABLESPACE quarter_one
STORAGE (INITIAL 10K NEXT 10K);
/* Drop a partition in an index. This operation
   CANNOT be done in a local index. */

ALTER TABLE sales_detail_data SPLIT PARTITION sales_q1_99_jeans
AT (TO_DATE('1999-04-01','YYYY-MM-DD'),5000) INTO
( PARTITION sales_q1_99_bluejean STORAGE (INITIAL 10k NEXT 10k),
PARTITION sales_q1_99_blackjean STORAGE (INITIAL 10k NEXT 10k) );
```

 You can speed up certain partition management processes by using the Oracle **NOLOGGING** option, which causes your actions to be performed with a minimum of redo logging, saving you time. Of course, a backup should be performed after any **NOLOGGING** operation, if it will be important to recover the final product of the **NOLOGGING** transaction.

The **ALTER TABLE EXCHANGE** Command

The **ALTER TABLE EXCHANGE** command is used to move partitioned data into a separate table or to move data from a separate table into a partitioned object. Certain restrictions apply to moving a table into a partitioned table:

➤ The columns and constraints must be identical.

➤ The table coming into the partitioned table must not be clustered.

An option of the **ALTER TABLE EXCHANGE** command is the **EXCLUDING INDEXES** clause, which leaves indexes intact or excludes them when creating tables out of partitions. Listing 4.7 shows an example of moving tables in and out of a partition.

Listing 4.7   Using the **ALTER TABLE EXCHANGE** command.

```
ALTER TABLE sales_detail_data EXCHANGE PARTITION sales_q1_99
WITH TABLE sales_quarter_99 EXCLUDING INDEXES;
```

Managing Partitioned Indexes

Managing partitioned indexes is similar in some respects to managing partitions of tables. You can perform the following operations on indexes:

➤ Alter the default and partition storage clauses.

➤ Drop a partition (this cannot be done to a local index).

➤ Rebuild a partition (this allows you to move an index partition to another tablespace).

➤ Rename a partition.

➤ Split a partition (this allows you to take one partition of a global index and split it into two partitions).

A rule about index partitions: You cannot add a partition to an index. If you add a partition to a table that has local indexes associated with it, Oracle adds a partition to those indexes for you. With a global index, you may want to split a partition, drop and rebuild the index, or do nothing. Listing 4.8 shows examples of each of these operations.

Listing 4.8   Variations on the ALTER INDEX clause.

```
/* Change the default storage for a partitioned index. */
ALTER INDEX ix_sales_isku_01
MODIFY DEFAULT ATTRIBUTES STORAGE (NEXT 10M);

/* Change the storage parameters for a specific partition. */
ALTER INDEX ix_sales_dos_01
MODIFY PARTITION PAR1 STORAGE (NEXT 10M);

/* Drop a partition in an index. This operation cannot be done in a
local index. */
ALTER INDEX ix_sales_dos_01 DROP PARTITION par1;
/* Rebuild the index partition in another tablespace. */

ALTER INDEX ix_sales_dos_01
REBUILD PARTITION par2 TABLESPACE quarter_two;

ALTER INDEX ix_sales_dos_01
RENAME PARTITION par2 TO ix_sales_q1_1999;

ALTER INDEX sales_detail_data
SPLIT PARTITION sales_q1_99_jeans
AT (TO_DATE('1999-04-01','YYYY-MM-DD'),5000) INTO
( PARTITION sales_q1_99_bluejean STORAGE (INITIAL 10k NEXT 10k),
PARTITION sales_q1_99_blackjean STORAGE (INITIAL 10k NEXT 10k) );
```

Indexes In **UNUSABLE** State

Several operations may put an index into a **UNUSABLE** state. They include:

➤ In certain cases, import can cause this if it is set to bypass updates on the partitioned index (e.g., the **skip_unusable_indexes** parameter in the import utility).

➤ If the DBA moves a table partition to another tablespace.

➤ If the DBA truncates a partition (if the underlying partition had data in it).

➤ If the DBA splits a partition (if data exists in one of the new ranges, that partitioned index will be invalidated).

➤ If the DBA drops a partition (if the underlying partition had data in it).

➤ You use SQL*Loader to do a direct path load.

If an index on a partitioned table shows a status of **UNUSABLE** in **DBA_INDEXES**, or the DBA knows that an operation to be performed will set the status of the indexes to such a state, the DBA must plan to rebuild the indexes accordingly. The command to rebuild partitioned indexes depends on the type of index that needs to be rebuilt. Local prefixed (equipartitioned) indexes are rebuilt with the **ALTER TABLE MODIFY PARTITION REBUILD UNUSABLE LOCAL INDEXES** command. Therefore, for a single partitioned table, if it has only local indexes, you need issue only one command. The DBA can also cause all indexes to become unusable by issuing the **ALTER TABLE MODIFY PARTITION UNUSABLE LOCAL INDEXES** statement.

For global indexes or local nonprefixed indexes, you must instead use the **ALTER INDEX REBUILD PARTITION** statement.

Administrative Views

Several views that already existed in Oracle7.3, and some new views, assist DBAs in managing partitioned tables. The primary views that DBAs will use are:

➤ *DBA_IND_PARTITIONS*—Provides information on all index partitions in the database.

➤ *DBA_INDEXES*—Shows the name, tablespace, associated table, and other statistics for all indexes in the database.

➤ *DBA_OBJECTS*—Provides information on all objects within the database.

➤ *DBA_PART_COL_STATISTICS*—Provides a view to review the statistics collected by the cost-based optimizer for partitioned tables.

➤ *DBA_PART_HISTOGRAMS*—Displays the distribution of data in partitions, for all analyzed partitions in the database.

➤ *DBA_PART_INDEXES*—Provides information on indexes and how they are partitioned for the tables in the database.

➤ *DBA_PART_KEY_COLUMNS*—Identifies partition keys used for all tables and indexes.

➤ *DBA_PART_TABLES*—Provides information on partitioned tables in the database, including partition keys.

➤ *DBA_SEGMENTS*—Shows segment-level information. Each partition is a segment, so each partition appears in the **DBA_SEGMENTS** view along with the partitioned table.

➤ *DBA_TAB_COL_STATISTICS*—Provides a view to review the statistics collected by the cost-based optimizer for partitioned indexes.

➤ *DBA_TAB_PARTITIONS*—Provides information on all table partitions in the database.

➤ *DBA_TABLES*—Shows the name, tablespace, and statistics on all tables in the database.

The following sections examine these views in more detail and show you what information they can provide.

Note: The DBA_TAB_COLUMNS, DBA_TAB_COL_STATIS-TICS, DBA_TAB_HISTOGRAMS, and DBA_IND_COLUMNS views have not changed significantly for partitioning in Oracle8, so they are not addressed in this chapter.

As already mentioned, **SALES_DETAIL_DATA** has been created as an example. In addition, I have created two indexes on **SALES_DETAIL_DATA**:

➤ A global equipartitioned prefixed index based on the **SALES_DE-TAIL_DATA** column **sales_date**.

➤ A local non-prefixed index based on the **item_sku** column.

DBA_IND_PARTITIONS View

The **DBA_IND_PARTITIONS** view is a new view that provides granular partition-level information for all partitions of an object. Many of the columns are similar to those in the **DBA_TAB_PARTITIONS** table. Here, you can find a variety of information on specific partitions, including the tablespace the partitions are assigned to, partition storage parameters, and various statistics gathered for each partition by the **ANALYZE** command. Many of the columns are similar to the columns you already use in **DBA_INDEXES**.

*Note: If you are looking for indexes with an **UNUSABLE** status, this is the table you query.*

DBA_IND_PARTITIONS is a rather large view. Listing 4.9 shows a description of the table and a sample query against the table.

Listing 4.9   Description and sample query of the DBA_IND_ PARTITIONS view.

```
SQL> desc dba_ind_partitions
 Name                                 Null?     Type
 -----------------------------------  --------  ------------
 INDEX_OWNER                          NOT NULL  VARCHAR2(30)
 INDEX_NAME                           NOT NULL  VARCHAR2(30)
 PARTITION_NAME                                 VARCHAR2(30)
 HIGH_VALUE                                     LONG
 HIGH_VALUE_LENGTH                    NOT NULL  NUMBER
 PARTITION_POSITION                   NOT NULL  NUMBER
 STATUS                               NOT NULL  VARCHAR2(8)
 /* The previous column reports an index status UNUSABLE */
 TABLESPACE_NAME                      NOT NULL  VARCHAR2(30)
 PCT_FREE                             NOT NULL  NUMBER
 INI_TRANS                            NOT NULL  NUMBER
 MAX_TRANS                            NOT NULL  NUMBER
 INITIAL_EXTENT                       NOT NULL  NUMBER
 NEXT_EXTENT                          NOT NULL  NUMBER
 MIN_EXTENT                           NOT NULL  NUMBER
 MAX_EXTENT                           NOT NULL  NUMBER
 PCT_INCREASE                         NOT NULL  NUMBER
 FREELISTS                                      NUMBER
 FREELIST_GROUPS                                NUMBER
 LOGGING                              NOT NULL  VARCHAR2(3)
 BLEVEL                                         NUMBER
 LEAF_BLOCKS                                    NUMBER
```

```
DISTINCT_KEYS                              NUMBER
AVG_LEAF_BLOCKS_PER_KEY                     NUMBER
AVG_DATA_BLOCKS_PER_KEY                     NUMBER
CLUSTERING_FACTOR                          NUMBER
NUM_ROWS                                   NUMBER
SAMPLE_SIZE                                NUMBER
LAST_ANALYZED                              DATE
BUFFER_POOL                 NOT NULL VARCHAR2(7)
```

```
SQL> SELECT index_owner,index_name,partition_name,tablespace_name,
  2  initial_extent, next_extent
  3  FROM dba_ind_partitions;
```

INDEX_ OWNER	INDEX_NAME	PARTITION_ OWNER	TABLESPACE_ NAME	INITIAL_ EXTENT	NEXT_ EXTENT
OBJOWN	IX_SALES_DOS_01	SYS_P13	QUARTER_ONE	16384	16384
OBJOWN	IX_SALES_DOS_01	SYS_P14	QUARTER_THREE	24576	16384
OBJOWN	IX_SALES_DOS_01	SYS_P15	QUARTER_FOUR	16384	16384
OBJOWN	IX_SALES_ISKU_01	IX_SALES_ Q2_ISKU_99	QUARTER_TWO	40960	40960
OBJOWN	IX_SALES_ISKU_01	IX_SALES_ Q3_ISKU_99	QUARTER_THREE	40960	40960
OBJOWN	IX_SALES_ISKU_01	IX_SALES_ Q4_ISKU_99	QUARTER_FOUR	40960	40960
OBJOWN	IX_SALES_ISKU_01	IX_SALES_ Q1_ISKU_99	QUARTER_ONE	40960	40960

DBA_INDEXES View

There have been similar changes to the **DBA_INDEXES** view for partition indexes. The tablespace names for the partitions of indexes are in the **DBA_PART_INDEXES** view. Listing 4.10 shows a description of the **DBA_INDEXES** table with selected comments and a sample query of the **DBA_INDEXES** view.

Listing 4.10 Partitioned indexes on a partitioned table using **DBA_INDEXES**.

```
SQL> DESC dba_indexes
  Name                              Null?    Type
  -------------------------------   -------- ------------
  OWNER                             NOT NULL VARCHAR2(30)
  INDEX_NAME                        NOT NULL VARCHAR2(30)
  INDEX_TYPE                        NOT NULL VARCHAR2(12)
  /* The INDEX_TYPE column defines the index as partitioned or not.
  */
```

```
TABLE_OWNER                      NOT NULL VARCHAR2(30)
TABLE_NAME                       NOT NULL VARCHAR2(30)
TABLE_TYPE                       NOT NULL VARCHAR2(11)
/* The TABLE_TYPE shows if the associated table is partitioned or
   not. */
UNIQUENESS                       NOT NULL VARCHAR2(9)
TABLESPACE_NAME                  NOT NULL VARCHAR2(30)
INI_TRANS                        NOT NULL NUMBER
MAX_TRANS                        NOT NULL NUMBER
INITIAL_EXTENT                            NUMBER
NEXT_EXTENT                               NUMBER
MIN_EXTENTS                               NUMBER
MAX_EXTENTS                               NUMBER
PCT_INCREASE                              NUMBER
PCT_THRESHOLD                             NUMBER
INCLUDE_COLUMN                            NUMBER
/* INCLUDE_COLUMN is for index-organized tables. See Chapter 6. */
FREELISTS                                 NUMBER
FREELIST_GROUPS                           NUMBER
PCT_FREE                         NOT NULL NUMBER
LOGGING                          NOT NULL VARCHAR2(3)
/* LOGGING reports if logging is enabled on the object. */
BLEVEL                                    NUMBER
LEAF_BLOCKS                               NUMBER
DISTINCT_KEYS                             NUMBER
AVG_LEAF_BLOCKS_PER_KEY                   NUMBER
AVG_DATA_BLOCKS_PER_KEY                   NUMBER
CLUSTERING_FACTOR                         NUMBER
STATUS                           NOT NULL VARCHAR2(8)
NUM_ROWS                                  NUMBER
SAMPLE_SIZE                               NUMBER
LAST_ANALYZED                             DATE
DEGREE                                    VARCHAR2(40)
INSTANCES                                 VARCHAR2(40)
PARTITIONED                      NOT NULL VARCHAR2(3)
/* PARTITIONED defines if the index is partitioned.
   This column has a YES or NO Value. */
TEMPORARY                                 VARCHAR2(1)
GENERATED                                 VARCHAR2(1)
/* GENERATED indicates if the index name generated by the
   system. */
BUFFER_POOL                               VARCHAR2(7)
/* BUFFER_POOL displays the buffer pool assignment of the
   object. */
```

```
SQL> SELECT owner, index_name, index_type,
  2    status, partitioned
  3    FROM dba_indexes where TABLE_NAME
  4    = 'SALES_DETAIL_DATA';
OWNER   INDEX_NAME          INDEX_TYPE   STATUS   PARTITIONED
------  ----------------    ----------   ------   -----------
OBJOWN  IX_SALES_DOS_01     NORMAL       N/A      YES
OBJOWN  IX_SALES_ISKU_01    NORMAL       N/A      YES
```

DBA_OBJECTS View

The **DBA_OBJECTS** view appears slightly different than in Oracle7 because now, for a single partitioned table, it lists each partition as a separate object. For a partitioned object, the **object_name** column contains the name of the partitioned table, and the **subobject_name** column contains an entry for each partition of the object. Listing 4.11 shows an example of the pertinent output from this view. The object type **TABLE PARTITION** is new for Oracle8.

Listing 4.11 Sample query of the **DBA_OBJECTS** view for a partitioned table.

```
SQL> DESC dba_objects
 Name                               Null?      Type
 ---------------------------------  --------   -------------
 OWNER                                         VARCHAR2(30)
 object_name                                   VARCHAR2(128)
 subobject_name                                VARCHAR2(30)
 /* The SUBOBJECT_NAME is the Name of the subobject */
 /* (e.g., the name of the partition.)*/
 OBJECT_ID                                     NUMBER
 DATA_OBJECT_ID                                NUMBER
 OBJECT_TYPE                                   VARCHAR2(15)
 CREATED                                       DATE
 LAST_DDL_TIME                                 DATE
 TIMESTAMP                                     VARCHAR2(19)
 STATUS                                        VARCHAR2(7)
 TEMPORARY                                     VARCHAR2(1)
 GENERATED                                     VARCHAR2(1)

SQL> SELECT owner, subobject_name, object_id, data_object_id,
  2    object_type, status
  3    FROM dba_objects
  4    WHERE object_name = 'SALES_DETAIL_DATA';
```

```
OWNER  SUBOBJECT_N OBJECT_ID DATA_OBJECT_ID OBJECT_TYPE      STATUS
------ ----------- --------- -------------- ---------------- ------
OBJOWN SALES_Q1_99 2578      2578           TABLE PARTITION  VALID
OBJOWN SALES_Q2_99 2579      2579           TABLE PARTITION  VALID
OBJOWN SALES_Q3_99 2580      2580           TABLE PARTITION  VALID
OBJOWN SALES_Q4_99 2581      2581           TABLE PARTITION  VALID
OBJOWN             2577                     TABLE            VALID
```

DBA_PART_COL_STATISTICS View

The **DBA_PART_COL_STATISTICS** view is a new view that provides granular partition-level column information for all columns of an object. This includes statistical and histogram information that is populated after an **ANALYZE** is executed on the table. Listing 4.12 shows a description of the table and a sample query against the table.

Listing 4.12   Description and sample query of the **DBA_PART_ COL_STATISTICS** view.

```
SQL> DESC dba_part_col_statistics
 Name                              Null?    Type
 --------------------------------- -------- ------------
 OWNER                             NOT NULL VARCHAR2(30)
 TABLE_NAME                        NOT NULL VARCHAR2(30)
 PARTITION_NAME                             VARCHAR2(30)
 COLUMN_NAME                       NOT NULL VARCHAR2(30)
 NUM_DISTINCT                               NUMBER
 LOW_VALUE                                  RAW(32)
 HIGH_VALUE                                 RAW(32)
 DENSITY                                    NUMBER
 NUM_NULLS                                  NUMBER
 NUM_BUCKETS                                NUMBER
 SAMPLE_SIZE                                NUMBER
 LAST_ANALYZED                              DATE

SQL> SELECT owner, partition_name, column_name, num_distinct
  2    FROM dba_part_col_statistics
  3   WHERE table_name = 'SALES_DETAIL_DATA';

OWNER  PARTITION_NAME COLUMN_NAME     NUM_DISTINCT
------ -------------- --------------- ------------
SYSTEM SALES_Q1_99    date_of_sale               1
SYSTEM SALES_Q1_99    INVOICE_NUMBER             2
SYSTEM SALES_Q1_99    ITEM_LINE_NO               2
SYSTEM SALES_Q1_99    item_sku                   1
SYSTEM SALES_Q1_99    QTY_SOLD                   1
SYSTEM SALES_Q2_99    date_of_sale               2
```

```
SYSTEM  SALES_Q2_99      INVOICE_NUMBER                 2
SYSTEM  SALES_Q2_99      ITEM_LINE_NO                   2
SYSTEM  SALES_Q2_99      item_sku                       3
SYSTEM  SALES_Q2_99      QTY_SOLD                       2
SYSTEM  SALES_Q3_99      date_of_sale                   2
SYSTEM  SALES_Q3_99      INVOICE_NUMBER                 2
SYSTEM  SALES_Q3_99      ITEM_LINE_NO                   1
SYSTEM  SALES_Q3_99      item_sku                       2
SYSTEM  SALES_Q3_99      QTY_SOLD                       1
SYSTEM  SALES_Q4_99      date_of_sale                   1
SYSTEM  SALES_Q4_99      INVOICE_NUMBER                 1
SYSTEM  SALES_Q4_99      ITEM_LINE_NO                   1
SYSTEM  SALES_Q4_99      item_sku                       1
SYSTEM  SALES_Q4_99      QTY_SOLD                       1
```

DBA_PART_HISTOGRAM View

The **DBA_PART_HISTOGRAM** view is a new view that provides histogram data for all partitions of a table. Listing 4.13 shows a description of the table and a sample query against the table, looking at columnar distinct values.

Listing 4.13   Description and sample query of the **DBA_PART_HISTOGRAM** view.

```
SQL> DESC dba_part_histograms
 Name                            Null?    Type
 -------------------------------  --------  ------------

 OWNER                                     VARCHAR2(30)
 TABLE_NAME                                VARCHAR2(30)
 PARTITION_NAME                            VARCHAR2(30)
 COLUMN_NAME                               VARCHAR2(30)
 BUCKET_NUMBER                             NUMBER
 ENDPOINT_VALUE                            NUMBER


SQL> SELECT owner, partition_name, column_name,
  2  bucket_number, endpoint_value from dba_part_histograms
  2  WHERE table_name LIKE 'SALES_DETAIL_DATA' AND
  3  partition_name LIKE 'SALES_Q3_99';


                                              BUCKET
 OWNER   PARTITION_NAME        COLUMN_NAME    NUMBER ENDPOINT_VALUE
 ------  --------------------  -------------  ------ --------------
 SYSTEM  SALES_Q3_99           date_of_sale        0        2451361
 SYSTEM  SALES_Q3_99           date_of_sale        1        2451423
 SYSTEM  SALES_Q3_99           INVOICE_NUMBER      0              4
 SYSTEM  SALES_Q3_99           INVOICE_NUMBER      1              5
 SYSTEM  SALES_Q3_99           ITEM_LINE_NO        0              1
 SYSTEM  SALES_Q3_99           ITEM_LINE_NO        1              1
 SYSTEM  SALES_Q3_99           item_sku            0        2000000
```

```
SYSTEM   SALES_Q3_99            item_sku            1         4000000
SYSTEM   SALES_Q3_99            QTY_SOLD            0               1
SYSTEM   SALES_Q3_99            QTY_SOLD            1               1
```

DBA_PART_INDEXES View

The **DBA_PART_INDEXES** view is a new view that provides partitioning information for all partitioned indexes. Listing 4.14 shows a description of the view and a sample query against the view. In the query, you see the owner and name of the index. No table information is provided, so you have to join this view with **DBA_INDEXES** to get the table information. The **partitioning_type** column defines that this is a **RANGE** partitioned index. Of course, because a partitioning on a range of values is currently the only method of building partitions, **RANGE** is the only allowable value in the **partitioning_type** column. The **partitioning_count** returns the number of partitions (four), and the **partitioning_key_count** returns the number of columns that make up the partition key (1 equals **sales_date**). You also discover from the **locality** column if this is a **LOCAL** or **GLOBAL** index and from the **alignment** column if it is **PREFIXED** or **NON_PREFIXED**. This view also contains the partition default value settings used if you add new partitions.

Listing 4.14   Description and sample query of the **DBA_PART_INDEXES** view.

```
SQL> DESC dba_part_indexes
Name                                   Null?     Type
-----------------------------------    --------  ------------
OWNER                                  NOT NULL VARCHAR2(30)
INDEX_NAME                             NOT NULL VARCHAR2(30)
partitioning_type                      NOT NULL VARCHAR2(7)
/* The value of the column above is always RANGE. */
partition_count                        NOT NULL NUMBER
/* The column above is the number of partitions in the index. */
partitioning_key_count                 NOT NULL NUMBER
/* The column above is the number of columns in partition key. */
locality                                        VARCHAR2(6)
/* The column above defines the index as Local or global. */
alignment                                       VARCHAR2(12)
/* The column above is PREFIXED or NON-PREFIXED depending
   on the type of index. */
DEF_TABLESPACE_NAME                             VARCHAR2(30)
/* The NEXT several storage parms are defaults. */
DEF_PCT_FREE                           NOT NULL NUMBER
DEF_INI_TRANS                          NOT NULL NUMBER
DEF_MAX_TRANS                          NOT NULL NUMBER
DEF_INITIAL_EXTENT                     NOT NULL VARCHAR2(40)
```

```
DEF_NEXT_EXTENT                     NOT NULL VARCHAR2(40)
DEF_MIN_EXTENTS                     NOT NULL VARCHAR2(40)
DEF_MAX_EXTENTS                     NOT NULL VARCHAR2(40)
DEF_PCT_INCREASE                    NOT NULL VARCHAR2(40)
DEF_FREELISTS                       NOT NULL NUMBER
DEF_FREELIST_GROUPS                 NOT NULL NUMBER
DEF_LOGGING                         NOT NULL VARCHAR2(7)
DEF_BUFFER_POOL                              VARCHAR2(7)


SQL> SELECT owner, partitioning_type,partition_count,
  2  partitioning_key_count,locality, alignment FROM dba_part_indexes
  3  WHERE index_name LIKE 'IX_SALES_ISKU_01';


OWNER  PART    PARTITION PARTITIONING LOCALITY ALIGNMENT
       RANGE   COUNT     KEY_COUNT
------ ------- --------- ------------ -------- --------
OBJOWN RANGE           4            1 LOCAL    NON_PREFIXED


SQL> SELECT owner, partitioning_type, partition_count,
  2  partitioning_key_count, locality, alignment FROM
     dba_part_indexes
  3  WHERE index_name LIKE 'IX_SALES_DOS_01';


OWNER  PART    PARTITION PARTITIONING LOCALITY ALIGNMENT
       RANGE   COUNT     KEY_COUNT
------ ------- --------- ------------ -------- --------
OBJOWN RANGE           3            1 GLOBAL   PREFIXED
```

DBA_PART_KEY_COLUMNS View

Another new view, **DBA_PART_KEY_COLUMNS**, provides partitioning information for all partitioned indexes. Listing 4.15 shows a description of the view and a sample query against the view. The view provides information about which columns a partitioned object is keyed on. The **owner** and **name** columns are the owner and name of the object. The **OBJECT_TYPE** is either **TABLE** or **INDEX**. The **COLUMN_NAME** displays the name of the column(s) that the object is keyed on, and the order of that column in the composite key is displayed in the **column_position** column.

Listing 4.15   Description and sample query of the **DBA_PART_ KEY_COLUMNS** view.

```
SQL> DESC dba_part_key_columns
 Name                               Null?    Type
 ---------------------------------- -------- ----
 OWNER                                       VARCHAR2(30)
 NAME                                        VARCHAR2(30)
```

```
OBJECT_TYPE                              VARCHAR2(11)
COLUMN_NAME                              VARCHAR2(30)
COLUMN_POSITION                          NUMBER

SQL> SELECT * FROM dba_part_key_columns;

OWNER  NAME                 OBJECT_TYPE COLUMN_NAME    COLUMN_POS
------ -------------------- ----------- -------------- ----------
OBJOWN IX_SALES_DOS_01      INDEX       date_of_sale            1
OBJOWN IX_SALES_ISKU_01     INDEX       date_of_sale            1
OBJOWN SALES_DETAIL_DATA    TABLE       date_of_sale            1
```

DBA_PART_TABLES View

The **DBA_PART_TABLES** view is a new view that provides partitioning information for all partitioned tables. Listing 4.16 shows a description of the view and a sample query against the view. In the query, you see:

➤ The name of the table returned in the **table_name** column.

➤ What type of partitioning is being used (**RANGE** is currently the only valid method) in the **partitioning_type** column.

➤ The number of partitions (four) in the **partition_count** column.

➤ The number of columns that make up the partition key in the **partition_key_count** column.

In addition, the partition default value settings used (if you are adding a new partition) are contained in this view.

Listing 4.16   Description and sample query of the **DBA_PART_TABLES** view.

```
SQL> DESC dba_part_tables
Name                              Null?    Type
------------------------------    -------- ------------
OWNER                             NOT NULL VARCHAR2(30)
table_name                        NOT NULL VARCHAR2(30)
partitioning_type                 NOT NULL VARCHAR2(7)
/* The value of the PARTITIONING_TYPE column is always  RANGE. */
partition_count                   NOT NULL NUMBER
/* The value of the PARTITION_COUNT is the number of
   partitions in table. */
partitioning_key_count            NOT NULL NUMBER
/* The value of the PARTITIONING_KEY_COUNT represents the
   Number of columns */
/* in the partition key. */
```

```
/* Next several columns are defaults for the partitions. */
DEF_TABLESPACE_NAME               NOT NULL VARCHAR2(30)
DEF_PCT_FREE                      NOT NULL NUMBER
DEF_PCT_USED                      NOT NULL NUMBER
DEF_INI_TRANS                     NOT NULL NUMBER
DEF_MAX_TRANS                     NOT NULL NUMBER
DEF_INITIAL_EXTENT                NOT NULL VARCHAR2(40)
DEF_NEXT_EXTENT                   NOT NULL VARCHAR2(40)
DEF_MIN_EXTENTS                   NOT NULL VARCHAR2(40)
DEF_MAX_EXTENTS                   NOT NULL VARCHAR2(40)
DEF_PCT_INCREASE                  NOT NULL VARCHAR2(40)
DEF_FREELISTS                     NOT NULL NUMBER
DEF_FREELIST_GROUPS               NOT NULL NUMBER
DEF_LOGGING                       NOT NULL VARCHAR2(7)
DEF_BUFFER_POOL                            VARCHAR2(7)


SQL> SELECT owner,partitioning_type, partition_count,
  2  partitioning_key_count
  3  FROM dba_part_tables
  4  WHERE table_name LIKE 'SALES_DETAIL_DATA';


OWNER   PART     PARTITION_COUNT PARTITIONING_KEY_COUNT
        RANGE
-------------------------------------------------------
OBJOWN RANGE            4                       1
```

DBA_SEGMENTS View

The **DBA_SEGMENTS** view is slightly different than the version in Oracle7, as you might expect. It is different because each partition is a segment and the partitioned table is a segment, so each appears in the view. For a partitioned object, the **segment_name** column contains the name of the partitioned table as well as that of each partition. the **partition_name** column defines the partitioned table that each partition belongs to. Listing 4.17 shows an example of the pertinent output from this view.

Listing 4.17   Sample query of the DBA_SEGMENTS view for a partitioned table.

```
SQL> desc dba_segments
 Name                             Null?   Type
 --------------------------------------------------
 OWNER                                    VARCHAR2(30)
 SEGMENT_NAME                             VARCHAR2(81)
 PARTITION_NAME                           VARCHAR2(30)
 SEGMENT_TYPE                             VARCHAR2(17)
 TABLESPACE_NAME                          VARCHAR2(30)
```

```
HEADER_FILE                              NUMBER
HEADER_BLOCK                             NUMBER
BYTES                                    NUMBER
BLOCKS                                   NUMBER
EXTENTS                                  NUMBER
INITIAL_EXTENT                           NUMBER
NEXT_EXTENT                              NUMBER
MIN_EXTENTS                              NUMBER
MAX_EXTENTS                              NUMBER
PCT_INCREASE                             NUMBER
FREELISTS                                NUMBER
FREELIST_GROUPS                          NUMBER
RELATIVE_FNO                             NUMBER
BUFFER_POOL                              VARCHAR2(7)


SQL> SELECT owner, segment_name,
  2    partition_name, segment_type,
  3    tablespace_name
  4    FROM dba_segments
  5    WHERE segment_type = 'TABLE PARTITION';
```

OWNER	SEGMENT_NAME	PARTITION _NAME	SEGMENT_TYPE	TABLESPACE _NAME
SYSTEM	SALES_DETAIL_DATA	SALES_Q1_99_SHIRTS	TABLE PARTITION	QUARTER_ONE
SYSTEM	SALES_DETAIL_DATA	SALES_Q1_99_ALLELSE	TABLE PARTITION	QUARTER_ONE
SYSTEM	SALES_DETAIL_DATA	SALES_Q2_99_JEANS	TABLE PARTITION	QUARTER_TWO
SYSTEM	SALES_DETAIL_DATA	SALES_Q2_99_SHIRTS	TABLE PARTITION	QUARTER_TWO
SYSTEM	SALES_DETAIL_DATA	SALES_Q2_99_ALLELSE	TABLE PARTITION	QUARTER_TWO
SYSTEM	SALES_DETAIL_DATA	SALES_Q3_99_JEANS	TABLE PARTITION	QUARTER_THREE
SYSTEM	SALES_DETAIL_DATA	SALES_Q3_99_SHIRTS	TABLE PARTITION	QUARTER_THREE
SYSTEM	SALES_DETAIL_DATA	SALES_Q3_99_ALLELSE	TABLE PARTITION	QUARTER_THREE
SYSTEM	SALES_DETAIL_DATA	SALES_Q4_99_JEANS	TABLE PARTITION	QUARTER_FOUR
SYSTEM	SALES_DETAIL_DATA	SALES_Q4_99_SHIRTS	TABLE PARTITION	QUARTER_FOUR
SYSTEM	SALES_DETAIL_DATA	SALES_Q4_99_ALLELSE	TABLE PARTITION	QUARTER_FOUR

```
SYSTEM  SALES_DETAIL_DATA  SALES_Q1_    TABLE PARTITION  QUARTER_ONE
                           99_BLUEJEAN
SYSTEM  SALES_DETAIL_DATA  SALES_Q1_    TABLE PARTITION  QUARTER_ONE
                           99_BLACKJEAN
```

DBA_TAB_PARTITIONS View

The **DBA_TAB_PARTITIONS** view is a new view that provides granular partition-level information for all partitions of a table. Here, you can find a variety of information on specific partitions, including the tablespace that the partitions are assigned to, partition storage parameters, and various statistics gathered for each partition by the **ANALYZE** command. Many of the columns are similar to the columns you already use in **DBA_TABLES**. Listing 4.18 shows a description of the table and a sample query against the table.

Listing 4.18   Description and sample query of the **DBA_TAB_ PARTITIONS** view.

```
SQL> desc dba_tab_partitions
 Name                           Null?    Type
 ------------------------------ -------- -----------
 TABLE_OWNER                    NOT NULL VARCHAR2(30)
 TABLE_NAME                     NOT NULL VARCHAR2(30)
 PARTITION_NAME                          VARCHAR2(30)
 HIGH_VALUE                              LONG
 /* The HIGH_VALUE column is the Partition bound expression. */
 HIGH_VALUE_LENGTH              NOT NULL NUMBER
 /* The HIGH_VALUE_LENGTH column is the Length of HIGH_VALUE
    expression. */
 PARTITION_POSITION             NOT NULL NUMBER
 /* The PARTITION POSITION column is the position of partition
    based on its boundary setting. */
 TABLESPACE_NAME                NOT NULL VARCHAR2(30)
 PCT_FREE                       NOT NULL NUMBER
 PCT_USED                       NOT NULL NUMBER
 INI_TRANS                      NOT NULL NUMBER
 MAX_TRANS                      NOT NULL NUMBER
 INITIAL_EXTENT                 NOT NULL NUMBER
 NEXT_EXTENT                    NOT NULL NUMBER
 MIN_EXTENT                     NOT NULL NUMBER
 MAX_EXTENT                     NOT NULL NUMBER
 PCT_INCREASE                   NOT NULL NUMBER
 FREELISTS                               NUMBER
 FREELIST_GROUPS                         NUMBER
 LOGGING                        NOT NULL VARCHAR2(3)
```

```
NUM_ROWS                              NUMBER
BLOCKS                                NUMBER
EMPTY_BLOCKS                          NUMBER
AVG_SPACE                             NUMBER
CHAIN_CNT                             NUMBER
AVG_ROW_LEN                           NUMBER
SAMPLE_SIZE                           NUMBER
LAST_ANALYZED                         DATE
BUFFER_POOL                  NOT NULL VARCHAR2(7)

SQL> SELECT table_owner "owner",table_name,partition_name,
       partition_position,tablespace_name
  2  FROM dba_tab_partitions;
                                             PARTITION
OWNER   TABLE_NAME           PARTITION_NAME  POSITION  TABLESPACE_NAME
------  -------------------  --------------  --------  ---------------
OBJOWN  SALES_DETAIL_DATA    SALES_Q1_99            1  QUARTER_ONE
OBJOWN  SALES_DETAIL_DATA    SALES_Q2_99            2  QUARTER_TWO
OBJOWN  SALES_DETAIL_DATA    SALES_Q3_99            3  QUARTER_THREE
OBJOWN  SALES_DETAIL_DATA    SALES_Q4_99            4  QUARTER_FOUR
```

DBA_TABLES View

Listing 4.19 shows the **DBA_TABLES** view. I have affixed comments to the end of certain columns in the view if the columns are new or if their use has changed in Oracle8. In the query, you see the owner of the table, and the name of the table. Note that the tablespace column is blank, which is because it is a partitioned table. The tablespace names for each partition appear in the **DBA_PART_TABLES** view, which is described shortly. Nothing substantial has changed with this view, and most partition-specific information is contained in the new **DBA_PART%** views.

Note the **table_lock** column. It indicates if DML table locks are allowed on this table (in this case, they are not). The **table_lock** column is set via the **ALTER TABLE DISABLE TABLE LOCK** command. Issuing this command can aid in performance tuning of a parallel server because it reduces the number of locks the distributed lock manager process needs to deal with when issuing DML statements against the table. When the **table_lock** column is set to **DISABLED**, Oracle does not attempt to get a table-level or partition-level lock when querying the table. As a result, you cannot issue DDL commands against the object; you must re-enable locking on the table to modify it. The partitioned column indicates if the table is partitioned or not.

Listing 4.19   The pertinent **DBA_TABLES** view columns.

```
SQL> DESC dba_tables
 Name                            Null?    Type
 ------------------------------  -------- ------------
 OWNER                           NOT NULL VARCHAR2(30)
 TABLE_NAME                      NOT NULL VARCHAR2(30)
 TABLESPACE_NAME                 NOT NULL VARCHAR2(30)
 CLUSTER_NAME                    NOT NULL VARCHAR2(30)
 IOT_NAME                        NOT NULL VARCHAR2(30)
 /* The IOT_NAME column is the name of if the table is an an */
 /* index organized tables. See Chapter 6. */
 PCT_FREE                        NOT NULL NUMBER
 PCT_USED                        NOT NULL NUMBER
 INI_TRANS                       NOT NULL NUMBER
 MAX_TRANS                       NOT NULL NUMBER
 INITIAL_EXTENT                           NUMBER
 NEXT_EXTENT                              NUMBER
 MIN_EXTENTS                              NUMBER
 MAX_EXTENTS                              NUMBER
 PCT_INCREASE                             NUMBER
 FREELISTS                                NUMBER
 FREELIST_GROUPS                          NUMBER
 LOGGING                         NOT NULL VARCHAR2(3)
 /* LOGGING column value (YES or NO) set if table is in the */
 /* NOLOGGING mode. */
 BACKED_UP                       NOT NULL VARCHAR2(1)
 /* BACKED_UP records table backup status since last
    modification. */
 NUM_ROWS                                 NUMBER
 BLOCKS                                   NUMBER
 EMPTY_BLOCKS                             NUMBER
 AVG_SPACE                                NUMBER
 CHAIN_CNT                                NUMBER
 AVG_ROW_LEN                              NUMBER
 AVG_SPACE_FREELIST_BLOCKS                NUMBER
 NUM_FREELIST_BLOCKS                      NUMBER
 DEGREE                                   VARCHAR2(10)
 INSTANCES                                VARCHAR2(10)
 CACHE                           NOT NULL VARCHAR2(5)
 /* TABLE_LOCK defines if DML table and partition locking
    is enabled. */
 TABLE_LOCK                      NOT NULL VARCHAR2(8)
 /* The SAMPLE_SIZE column is and LAST_ANALYED columns used
    when table is ANALYZED. */
```

```
SAMPLE_SIZE                              NUMBER
LAST_ANALYZED                            DATE
/* The PARTITIONED column shows if the table is partitioned
   (Value YES/NO). */
PARTITIONED                    NOT NULL VARCHAR2(3)
IOT_TYPE                       NOT NULL VARCHAR2(12)
TEMPORARY                               VARCHAR2(1)
NESTED                         NOT NULL VARCHAR2(3)
BUFFER_POOL                             VARCHAR2(7)
/* BUFFER_POOL displays the table's buffer pool assignment. */

SQL> SELECT owner,table_name, tablespace_name, table_lock,
     partitioned
   2 FROM dba_tables WHERE table_name LIKE 'SALES_DETAIL_DATA';

OWNER  TABLE_NAME           TABLESPACE_NAME     TABLE   PARTITION
                                                LOCK    LOCK
------ -------------------- ------------------- ------  ---------
SYSTEM SALES_DETAIL_DATA                        DISABLED YES
```

Using Partitions

Finally, it's time to review some last bits of information regarding partitioning and other changes Oracle has made to SQL as well as various utilities so that they can support this new feature. We will examine how to address a partition explicitly through SQL statements. In addition, we will review the process required to analyze partitioned objects and how using partitioned objects can change the output of the **EXPLAIN PLAN** command and its associated **PLAN_TABLE** table. In closing, we will look at import and export issues revolving around partitioned objects and finally SQL*Loader issues.

Accessing Partitions Directly In SQL

Oracle has added new syntax to SQL to allow you to manipulate partitions directly. In the **FROM** clause of a select statement, you may now directly refer to a partition that you wish to query. You do so by appending the keyword **PARTITION** after the **FROM** clause, and then in parentheses, you list the partition name you wish to restrict the search to. The positive benefit of this is that you can direct Oracle where to look for the data if you know where it is. The negative aspect of this is that if you instruct Oracle to look at only one specific partition, if the partition is incorrect and the data actually resides in another partition, the results that you expect to be returned will be incorrect.

It bears noting again that the SQL syntax, allowing direct access to partitions, is not yet supported in PL/SQL currently. Some parallel operations—including parallel updates and deletes—can be used only on partitioned tables. Certain hints have been added to Oracle to accommodate the new partitioning features in combination with the new parallel processing features of Oracle8. See Chapter 6 for more information on this topic. Listing 4.20 shows an example of selecting a row from a specific partition.

Listing 4.20 Selecting a row from a specific partition of the **SALES_DETAIL_DATA** table.

```
--First look at all of the data.
SQL> SELECT * FROM sales_detail_data;

date_of_s INVOICE_NUMBER ITEM_LINE_NO  item_sku  QTY_SOLD
--------- -------------- ------------  --------  --------
01-JAN-99              1            1  1000000         1
01-JAN-99              2            1  1000000         1
01-JAN-99              2            2  1000000         1
01-APR-99              2            1  2000000         1
01-APR-99              2            2  9000000         5
30-JUN-99              3            1  1000000         1
01-JUL-99              4            1  2000000         1
01-SEP-99              5            1  4000000         1
31-DEC-99              6            1  1000000         2

--Now just the data in the SALES_Q1_99 partition.
SQL> SELECT * FROM sales_detail_data partition (sales_q1_99);

DATE_OF_S INVOICE_NUMBER ITEM_LINE_NO  item_sku  QTY_SOLD
--------- -------------- ------------  --------  --------
01-JAN-99              1            1  1000000         1
01-JAN-99              2            1  1000000         1
01-JAN-99              2            2  1000000         1
--Note the problem if we are looking for specific data in the wrong
partition.
--This query works fine.
SQL> SELECT * FROM sales_detail_data PARTITION (sales_q1_99)
  2  WHERE TO_CHAR(date_of_sale,'DD-MON-YY')=
  3  TO_DATE('01-JAN-99','DD-MON-YY');

DATE_OF_S INVOICE_NUMBER ITEM_LINE_NO  item_sku  QTY_SOLD
--------- -------------- ------------  --------  --------
01-JAN-99              1            1  1000000         1
01-JAN-99              2            1  1000000         1
01-JAN-99              2            2  1000000         1
```

```
--This query fails because the wrong partition is selected.
SQL> SELECT * FROM sales_detail_data PARTITION (sales_q2_99)
  2   WHERE TO_CHAR(date_of_sale,'DD-MON-YY')=
  3   TO_DATE('01-JAN-99','DD-MON-YY');
no rows selected
```

Analyzing The Partitioned Object

Oracle uses cost-based optimization only when dealing with partitioned tables. (If you are using rule-based optimization, you will derive little benefit from partitioning. Rule-based optimization is not designed to take advantage of partitioned objects.) Therefore, it is important to create statistics on the partitioned tables. Oracle provides the **ANALYZE** command to facilitate statistics collection on both partitioned tables and indexes.

You can analyze the entire partitioned object or just specific partitions. Analyzing the partitioned table, by default, also causes the associated index to be analyzed. Listing 4.21 shows examples of analyzing a partitioned table and a partitioned index, and specific partitions of both.

Listing 4.21   Analysis of a partitioned table and a partitioned index.

```
SQL> ANALYZE TABLE sales_detail_data COMPUTE STATISTICS;
Table analyzed.
SQL> ANALYZE TABLE sales_detail_data PARTITION (sales_q1_99)
     COMPUTE STATISTICS;
Table analyzed.
SQL> ANALYZE index IX_SALES_ISKU_01 COMPUTE STATISTICS;
Index analyzed.
SQL> ANALYZE TABLE sales_detail_data ESTIMATE STATISTICS
     SAMPLE 30 PERCENT;
Table analyzed.
SQL> ANALYZE TABLE sales_detail_data PARTITION (sales_q1_99)
     ESTIMATE STATISTICS SAMPLE 20 PERCENT;
```

Oracle has also added functionality to its packages to allow DBAs to use them to analyze partitioned tables. The new **DBMS_UTILITY.ANALYZE_PART_OBJECT** package allows DBAs to analyze a partition in a partitioned object. Note that this new procedure can only be used to analyze partitioned object. The call to the **DBMS_UTILITY.ANALYZE_PART_OBJECT** takes this format:

```
PROCEUDRE DBMS_UTILITY.ANALYZE_PART_OBJECT
(schema IN VARCHAR2 DEFAULT NULL,
 object_name IN VARCHAR2 DEFAULT NULL,
```

```
object_type IN CHAR DEFAULT 'T',
command_type IN CHAR DEFAULT 'E',
command_opt  IN  VARCHAR2 DEFAULT NULL,
sample_clause IN VARCHAR2 DEFAULT 'SAMPLE 5 PERCENT');
```

The description of the parameters for **DBMS_UTILITY.ANALYZE_ PART_OBJECT** are as follows:

➤ *SCHEMA*—The schema that owns the object to be analyzed.

➤ *OBJECT_NAME*—The name of the object to be analyzed.

➤ *OBJECT_TYPE*—The type of object being analyzed (T = Table and I = Index).

➤ *COMMAND_TYPE*—Indicates type of analysis to be performed. Valid codes are C = Compute statistics, E = Estimate statistics, D = Delete statistics, and V = Validate structure.

➤ *COMMAND_OPT*—Indicates options for different command types. If the **COMMAND_TYPE** code is a C or an E, then valid **COMMAND_OPT** values are: **FOR TALLE, FOR ALL LOCAL INDEXES**, and **FOR ALL COLUMNS**. Also valid are combinations of the **FOR** options for the **ANALYZE STATISTICS** command. If the **COMMAND_TYPE** code is a V and the **OBJECT_TYPE** is T (Table), then **CASCADE** is a valid **COMMAND_OPT** entry.

➤ *SAMPLE_CLAUSE*—Contains the sample clause for estimating statistics.

See Listing 4.22 for an example of using this package.

Listing 4.22   Using DBMS_UTILITY.ANALYZE_PART_OBJECT.
```
EXEC DBMS_UTILITY.ANALYZE_PART_OBJECT('ACCT_OWN',
'GENERAL_LEDGER_DETAIL','T','E',NULL,'SAMPLE 20 PERCENT');
```

EXPLAIN PLAN

The **PLAN_TABLE** table has changed somewhat. The **partition_start**, **partition_stop**, and **partition_id** columns have been added. They indicate, respectively, the starting partition of the partitioned range of access, the ending partition in the range of accessed partitions, and the step that determines the values for these partitions.

Explain plans look somewhat different with partitioning, as you might expect, from previous Oracle7 explain plans, which contained no partitioning operations. You now have partition operations, such as the partition concatenation operation, as shown in the explain plan in Listing 4.23. Using **AUTOTRACE**, if you access a partition directly, nothing is displayed in the plan to indicate that a specific partition is being used. The only sure way to tell is the difference in the block gets and consistent gets, or you can run a manual **EXPLAIN PLAN** and look at the **PLAN_TABLE** table results for more information.

Listing 4.23 Sample **EXPLAIN PLAN**s for queries on partitioned tables.

```
SQL> SELECT * FROM sales_detail_data;

date_of_s INVOICE_NUMBER ITEM_LINE_NO  item_sku QTY_SOLD
--------- -------------- ------------  -------- --------
01-JAN-99              1            1  1000000         1
01-JAN-99              2            1  1000000         1
01-JAN-99              2            2  1000000         1
01-APR-99              2            1  2000000         1
01-APR-99              2            2  9000000         5
30-JUN-99              3            1  1000000         1
01-JUL-99              4            1  2000000         1
01-SEP-99              5            1  4000000         1
31-DEC-99              6            1  1000000         2

Execution Plan
----------------------------------------------------------
   0      SELECT STATEMENT Optimizer=CHOOSE (Cost=1 Card=9 Bytes=207)
   1    0   PARTITION (CONCATENATED)
   2    1     TABLE ACCESS (FULL) OF 'SALES_DETAIL_DATA' (Cost=1
Card=
          9 Bytes=207)
Statistics
----------------------------------------------------------
        0  recursive calls
       12  db block gets
        9  consistent gets
        0  physical reads
        0  redo size
      977  bytes sent via SQL*Net to client
      291  bytes received via SQL*Net from client
       13  SQL*Net roundtrips to/from client
        0  sorts (memory)
        0  sorts (disk)
        9  rows processed

SQL> select * from sales_detail_data
  2  where date_of_sale < TO_DATE('01-APR-1999','DD-MON-YYYY');
```

```
DATE_OF_SALE INVOICE_NUMBER ITEM_LINE_NO  item_sku  QTY_SOLD
--------     --------------  ------------  --------  --------

01-JAN-99              1            1  1000000         1

01-JAN-99              2            1  1000000         1

01-JAN-99              2            2  1000000         1
Execution Plan
----------------------------------------------------------------
    0      SELECT STATEMENT Optimizer=CHOOSE (Cost=1 Card=3 Bytes=69)
    1    0   PARTITION (CONCATENATED)
    2    1     TABLE ACCESS (FULL) OF 'SALES_DETAIL_DATA' (Cost=1
Card=
           3 Bytes=69)
Statistics
----------------------------------------------------------------
      0   recursive calls
      6   db block gets
      4   consistent gets
      0   physical reads
      0   redo size
    573   bytes sent via SQL*Net to client
    307   bytes received via SQL*Net from client
      7   SQL*Net roundtrips to/from client
      0   sorts (memory)
      0   sorts (disk)
      3   rows processed
```

Importing/Exporting Partitions

You can use the Oracle Import/Export utility to export data from a specific partition rather than the entire partitioned table. You can export a partitioned table in table, user, and full modes. There are restrictions, though, on exporting individual partitions, and these can be exported in table mode only. To export a partition, use the **tables** = syntax and refer to the partition as **table_name: partition**. Listing 4.24 shows an example of an export of a partition.

Listing 4.24   Sample export of a partitioned table and a partition in a partitioned table.

```
oracle@sun002>$ exp system file=test.dmp tables=sales_detail_data
Export: Release 8.0.5.1.0 - Production on Tue Aug 10 13:18:53 1999
(c) Copyright 1998 Oracle Corporation.  All rights reserved.
Password:
Connected to: Oracle8 Enterprise Edition Release
8.0.5.1.0 - Production
```

```
With the Partitioning and Objects options
PL/SQL Release 8.0.5.1.0 - Production
Export done in US7ASCII character set and US7ASCII NCHAR character
set
About to export specified tables via Conventional Path ...
. . exporting table               SALES_DETAIL_DATA
. . exporting partition           SALES_Q1_99    3 rows exported
. . exporting partition           SALES_Q2_99    3 rows exported
. . exporting partition           SALES_Q3_99    2 rows exported
. . exporting partition           SALES_Q4_99    1 rows exported
Export terminated successfully without warnings.
oracle@sun002>$ exp system file=test_part.dmp
tables=sales_detail_data:sales_q1_99
Export: Release 8.0.5.1.0 - Production on Tue Aug 10 13:19:37 1999
(c) Copyright 1998 Oracle Corporation.  All rights reserved.
Password:
Connected to: Oracle8 Enterprise Edition Release
8.0.5.1.0 - Production
With the Partitioning and Objects options
PL/SQL Release 8.0.5.1.0 - Production
Export done in US7ASCII character set and US7ASCII NCHAR character
set
About to export specified tables via Conventional Path ...
. . exporting table               SALES_DETAIL_DATA
. . exporting partition              SALES_Q1_99   3 rows exported
Export terminated successfully without warnings.
```

The importing of partitions is also supported. When you import an entire partitioned table or even specific partitions exported from a partitioned table, Import creates a partitioned table, the partitions you import, and its associated indexes. You can also use the **SKIP_UNUSABLE_INDEXES** clause to have Import not create indexes that were in an **UNUSABLE** status when you did the export. Chapter 9 discusses the other changes to the Export/Import utilities in Oracle8. Listing 4.25 shows an example of an export of a partition.

Listing 4.25 Sample import of a partitioned table and a partition in a partitioned table.

```
# Sample import of an entire partitioned table
oracle@sun002>$ imp system file=test.dmp full=y
Import: Release 8.0.5.1.0 - Production on Tue Aug 10 13:28:10 1999
(c) Copyright 1998 Oracle Corporation.  All rights reserved.
Password:
Connected to: Oracle8 Enterprise Edition Release 8.0.5.1.0 - Pro-
duction
```

```
With the Partitioning and Objects options
PL/SQL Release 8.0.5.1.0 - Production
Export file created by EXPORT:V08.00.05 via conventional path
. importing SYSTEM's objects into SYSTEM
. . importing partition "SALES_DETAIL_DATA":"SALES_Q1_99"
   3 rows imported
. . importing partition "SALES_DETAIL_DATA":"SALES_Q2_99"
   3 rows imported
. . importing partition "SALES_DETAIL_DATA":"SALES_Q3_99"
   2 rows imported
. . importing partition "SALES_DETAIL_DATA":"SALES_Q4_99"
   1 rows imported
Import terminated successfully without warnings.

# Sample import of a single partition
oracle@sun002>$ imp system file=test_part.dmp full=y
Import: Release 8.0.5.1.0 - Production on Tue Aug 10 13:30:10 1999
(c) Copyright 1998 Oracle Corporation.  All rights reserved.
Password:
Connected to: Oracle8 Enterprise Edition Release 8.0.5.1.0 - Pro-
duction
With the Partitioning and Objects options
PL/SQL Release 8.0.5.1.0 - Production
Export file created by EXPORT:V08.00.05 via conventional path
. importing SYSTEM's objects into SYSTEM
. . importing partition "SALES_DETAIL_DATA":"SALES_Q1_99"
   3 rows imported
IMP-00057: Warning: Dump file may not contain data of all
   partitions of this table
Import terminated successfully with warnings.
```

Using SQL*Loader With Partitions

Several changes to SQL*Loader have occurred so that they work smoothly with partitioned tables. Changes to the conventional path are:

➤ DBAs can run multiple loads into different partitions of the same table at the same time.

➤ DBAs can load data into specific partitions. They do so by changing the control file to indicate into which partition to load the data.

➤ When any user is loading data using SQL*Loader, row data that does not meet the partition criterion is dumped into the bad file for DBAs to review. Be careful and mindful of the data you are trying to load into a partition. Its key values may lie outside the partition key range boundaries for the partition into which you are trying to load.

Changes to the direct path are:

➤ DBAs can run multiple loads into different partitions of the same table at the same time, in parallel (parallel direct path).

➤ Only one direct path load to a partitioned table (as opposed to a specific partition) may occur at one time.

➤ A direct path can be used to load into a single partition.

Practice Questions

Question 1

What are the different kinds of partitioned indexes that you can build?
[Choose two]

❑ a. Bitmap

❑ b. Local

❑ c. Temporary

❑ d. Index organized table

❑ e. Global

Answers b and e are correct. Answer a is incorrect because you cannot partition a bitmap index. Answer c is incorrect; there are no temporary indexes in Oracle. Answer d is not correct because you cannot partition an index-organized table.

Question 2

Which of the following is *not* a benefit of a partitioned table?

○ a. Partitioned tables permit selective backup and recovery of a partitioned object.

○ b. Partition pruning can improve performance.

○ c. You can partition a clustered table to make performance of inserts faster.

○ d. Maintenance operations on partitions do not make the entire table unavailable.

○ e. SQL*Loader and Import can work with specific partitions or the whole table.

Answer c is correct. You cannot partition a clustered table. Answer a is incorrect because being able to selectively back up a partition is a benefit of partitioned tables. Answer b is incorrect because partition pruning can improve performance by reducing the numbers of rows read from the table. Answer d is incorrect because maintenance operations on partitions can be performed on specific partitions and not affect others. Answer e is incorrect because both utilities can work with specific partitions.

Question 3

What is one rule in regards to global indexes?

- O a. The global index must be equipartitioned.
- O b. The global index must be prefixed.
- O c. The global index is maintained by Oracle when DDL changes are made to the associated partitioned table.
- O d. A global index cannot be partitioned.
- O e. A global index must be associated with a local index.

Answer b is correct. A global index must be prefixed with the partition key of the partitioned table off which it is built. Answer a is incorrect because a global index is not required to be equipartitioned. Answer c is incorrect because Oracle does not maintain global indexes when structure (DDL) changes are made to the associated table, and the global index may in fact have to be rebuilt. Answer d is incorrect because a global index is partitioned. Answer e is incorrect because a global index is not associated with another index.

Question 4

When exporting a partition from a table, what is the proper format of referring to a partition?

- O a. `table = table name:partition name`
- O b. `partition = table name:partition name`
- O c. `partition = partition name`
- O d. `table = table name.partition name`
- O e. `table.partition = table.partition`

Answer a is correct. With Export, the table name and the partition name is separated with a colon, using the **table** keyword. Answer b is incorrect because **partition** is not an available keyword in export. Answer c is incorrect because **partition** is not a valid keyword with export, and just the partition name should not be used. Answer d is incorrect because a colon, not a period, is used to separate the table name and the partition name. Answer e is incorrect because the partition is listed only on either side of the = sign, and a colon is used instead of a period.

Question 5

Which of the following is *not* an option when you are maintaining global indexes?

○ a. Split a partition

○ b. Add a partition

○ c. Drop a partition

○ d. Move a partition

○ e. None of the above

Answer b is correct. You cannot add a partition to a global index. Answers a, c, and d are incorrect because you can perform those actions. Answer e is incorrect because a correct answer is given.

Question 6

Given the SQL statement shown below (options a, b, c, and d together represent the statement), which line will cause an error when trying to create a partitioned table?

○ a. **CREATETABLE SALES TABLE (date_of_sale date, item_number number)**

○ b. **PARTITION (date_of_sale)**

○ c. **(PARTITION sales_partition_one values less than (TO_DATE ('1999-06-01','YYYY-MM-DD')),**

○ d. **PARTITION sales_partition_two values less than (TO_DATE ('2000-01-01','YYYY-MM-DD')));**

○ e. None of the above; this statement will execute without error.

Answer b is correct. The line that reads **PARTITION(date_of_sale)** is not the correct syntax. It should read **PARTITION BY RANGE**(date_of_sale).

Question 7

Which clauses are valid when you are creating the partition bounds?

○ a. **VALUES LESS THAN, VALUES EQUAL TO**

○ b. **VALUES LESS THAN, VALUES EQUAL TO, VALUES GREATER THAN**

○ c. **VALUES LESS THAN**

○ d. **VALUES BOUNDED BY**

○ e. **VALUES ASSOCIATED WITH**

Answer c is correct. The **VALUES LESS THAN** clause is the only valid clause when you are defining the partition bounds. Answers a, b, d and e are incorrect because they are not valid options.

Question 8

How many columns can the partition key have?

○ a. 8

○ b. 26

○ c. 16

○ d. 1,024

○ e. 128

Answer c is correct. You can create a partition key with up to 16 columns. The other options are incorrect.

Question 9

> If a partitioned table (global or local) and its associated index are said to be equipartitioned, what can be said about these two objects?
>
> O a. The table and the index are both maintained by the Oracle database server.
>
> O b. The table and the index have the same number and range of values for their partitions.
>
> O c. The index has one partition that contains data for all the partitions of the table.
>
> O d. The index is logically contained within the table that it's associated with.
>
> O e. The index will never become invalid.

Answer b is correct. An equipartitioned table and index have the same numbers of partitions, and the partition ranges are the same. Answer a is incorrect because a global index can be equipartitioned, and it is not maintained by the Oracle server. Answer c is incorrect because by definition, the index and the table have the same number of partitions. Answer d is incorrect because the index is stored separately from the equijoined partitioned table. Answer e is incorrect as indexes on equipartitioned indexes can become invalid for various reasons.

Question 10

> Given the results of the SQL statement below, how many different partitions does the **IX_SALES_DOS_01** index have?
>
> ```
> SQL> select index_owner,index_name,partition_name,
> tablespace_name,
>   2   INITIAL_extent, NEXT_extent
>   3   from dba_ind_partitions;
>
> INDEX_OWNER       INDEX_NAME PARTITION_NAME  TABLESPACE_NAME
> - - - - - - - - - - - - - - - - - - - - - - - - - - - - - - - - - - -
> IX_SALES_DOS_01  SYS_P13    QUARTER_ONE     OBJOWN
> IX_SALES-DOS-01  SYS_P14    QUARTER_THREE   OBJOWN
> IX_SALES_DOS_01  SYS_P15    QUARTER_FOUR    OBJOWN
> ```
>
> O a. 3
>
> O b. 2
>
> O c. 1
>
> O d. 0
>
> O e. You cannot tell from this output.

Answer a is correct. Three partitions are associated with the **IX_SALES_DOS_01** index. These three partitions are shown as three different rows in the output. Note that the index name is the same, but that the partition names are different. Because the index name is the same, each of the partitions belong to that index.

Question 11

> What is the maximum number of partitions you can define in a local index?
>
> O a. 255
>
> O b. 512
>
> O c. 1,024
>
> O d. The answer depends on the block size of the database.
>
> O e. The number of partitions depends on the number of partitions in the related table.

Answer e is correct. A local index is equipartitioned and therefore contains the same number of partitions as the table it is built on. Answers a, b, and c are incorrect because these are not limits on the number of partitions in a partitioned local index, which is why this is a trick question. Answer d is incorrect because the number of partitions in a local index has no relationship to the block size.

Question 12

> Refer to Exhibit A to answer this question. If a ticket number of 2,500,000 is sold, which partition will it be assigned to?
>
> Exhibit A
> ```
> CREATE TABLE TICKET_SALES
> (ticket_number    NUMBER  NOT NULL,
>  date_of_sale     DATE    NOT NULL,
>  sales_price      NUMBER  NOT NULL)
> PCTFREE 10
> PCTUSED 60
> STORAGE (INITIAL 10M  NEXT 10M)
> PARTITION BY RANGE (ticket_number)
> (
> ```

(continued)

Question 12 *(continued)*

```
PARTITION westside_tickets VALUES LESS THAN (1000000)
PCTFREE 10
PCTUSED 60
TABLESPACE westside_data
STORAGE (INITIAL 10M NEXT 10M)
PARTITION eastside_tickets VALUES LESS THAN (2000000)
 PCTFREE 10
 PCTUSED 60
 TABLESPACE eastside_data
STORAGE (INITIAL 10M NEXT 10M)
 PARTITION northside_tickets VALUES LESS THAN (3000000)
 PCTFREE 10
 PCTUSED 60
 TABLESPACE northside_data
 STORAGE (INITIAL 10M NEXT 10M)
 PARTITION southside_tickets VALUES LESS THAN (4000000)
  PCTFREE 10
  PCTUSED 60
  TABLESPACE southside_data
 STORAGE (INITIAL 10M NEXT 10M) )
```

○ a. **southside_tickets**

○ b. **northside_tickets**

○ c. **eastside_tickets**

○ d. **westside_tickets**

○ e. The insert will fail because there is no valid partition.

Answer b is correct. The data will be put in the **northside_tickets** partition. Because the number, 2,500,000 is larger than 2,000,000 it will not fall within the partition range of either the **westside_tickets** partition (making answer d wrong) or the **eastside_tickets** partition (making answer c wrong). Because the next partition in the partition order is **northside_tickets**, it will get put there. Since the order of **northside_tickets** partition comes before the **southside_tickets** partition, the row doesn't get inserted into the **southside_tickets** partition, making answer a wrong. Answer e is incorrect because the insert was successful.

Question 13

Refer to Exhibit A to answer this question. If a ticket number of 5,000,000 is sold, which partition will it be assigned to?

Exhibit A

```
CREATE TABLE TICKET_SALES
(ticket_number    NUMBER  NOT NULL,
 date_of_sale     DATE    NOT NULL,
 sales_price      NUMBER  NOT NULL)
PCTFREE 10
PCTUSED 60
STORAGE (INITIAL 10M  NEXT 10M)
PARTITION BY RANGE (ticket_number)
(
PARTITION westside_tickets VALUES LESS THAN (1000000)
PCTFREE 10
PCTUSED 60
TABLESPACE westside_data
STORAGE (INITIAL 10M NEXT 10M)
PARTITION eastside_tickets VALUES LESS THAN (2000000)
 PCTFREE 10
 PCTUSED 60
 TABLESPACE eastside_data
STORAGE (INITIAL 10M NEXT 10M)
 PARTITION northside_tickets VALUES LESS THAN (3000000)
 PCTFREE 10
 PCTUSED 60
 TABLESPACE northside_data
 STORAGE (INITIAL 10M NEXT 10M)
 PARTITION southside_tickets VALUES LESS THAN (4000000)
 PCTFREE 10
 PCTUSED 60
 TABLESPACE southside_data
 STORAGE (INITIAL 10M NEXT 10M) )
```

○ a. **southside_tickets**

○ b. **northside_tickets**

○ c. **eastside_tickets**

○ d. **westside_tickets**

○ e. The insert will fail because there is no valid partition.

Answer e is correct; the insert will fail. Because only values of less than 4,000,000 are valid in any of the partition ranges, the value of 5,000,000 will fail to insert. Because the **MAXVALUE** keyword was not used, there are upper limits to the partitions. Answers a, b, c and d are all incorrect then because their partition boundaries are less than that of the value being inserted.

Need To Know More?

 Ault, Michael R.:*Oracle7 DBA Test 1 and Test 2 Exam Cram.* The Coriolis Group, 1998. ISBN 1-57610-262-9. A thorough introduction to the first two Oracle7 OCP exams. A good general Oracle7 reference as well.

 Ault, Michael R.: *Oracle8 Black Book.* The Coriolis Group, 1998. ISBN 1-57610-187-8. This book deals in great depth with several new Oracle8 features including partitioning.

 Curtis, King: *Oracle8 and Windows NT Black Book.* The Coriolis Group, 1998. ISBN 1-57610-248-3. Another good book that addresses the topic of partitioning in Oracle8.

 Feuerstein, Steven, et al.: *Oracle Built-in Packages.* O'Reilly & Associates, 1998. ISBN 1-56592-375-8. A good guide to Oracle packages.

 Niemiec, Richard K.: *Oracle Performance Tuning, Tips & Techniques.* Oracle Press, 1999. ISBN 0-07-882434-6. A good Oracle reference.

 Oracle's online documentation, including *Oracle8 Concepts, Oracle8 Administrators Guide,* and *Oracle8 Tuning* are all on CDs supplied with the Oracle database server product. This is a principle source of information for any Oracle feature you wish to make use of.

 **www.support.com** is Oracle's Metalink Web site. It is a wonderful resource if you have Oracle Metals Support.

5

Oracle8 Objects

Terms you'll need to understand:

√ Object

√ Attribute

√ Method

√ Constructor method

√ Collection

√ Nested table

√ **VARRAY**

√ Flattened subquery

√ Object table

Techniques you'll need to master:

√ Creating user-defined object types

√ Creating nested tables and **VARRAY**s

√ Creating methods associated with objects

√ Creating object tables

√ Creating object views

Oracle8 introduces the concept of objects into the Oracle world. The Oracle Certified Professional (OCP) exam does have some questions that revolve around this new feature and although Oracle doesn't expect you to be an object design expert when taking the test, it does expect you to understand how to create and administer objects. This chapter discusses what an object relational database is and looks at Oracle's use of objects and how to implement them.

Object Concepts

Oracle8 introduces object-oriented concepts with the addition of the Objects option. The Objects option is an optional extension to Oracle8. It is not loaded with the RDBMS code when you install Oracle unless you specifically select to install it from the Oracle install medium. You can tell if the Objects option of Oracle is installed by looking at the **V$OPTIONS** table in the database, or by looking at the header of SQL*Plus when you connect to the database.

As of this writing, the Objects option is a separately licensed product, so you may not have access to it in the Oracle8 database you are using to prepare for the exam. Thus, you may not be able to run any of the examples you see in this chapter. Don't worry, though. The exam questions on the Objects option are likely to be general enough that you should be able to derive what information you need from this chapter and the examples contained in it.

Before delving into the practical side of creating objects in Oracle using the Objects option, let's review some terms that relate to object-oriented development and specifically how they relate to Oracle.

> *Note: The definitions of the object-oriented design terms that are reviewed in this chapter in general relate to all object-oriented development. However, if a term has a specific meaning as it relates to Oracle, that will be the meaning used here.*

Object-Oriented Development

Object-oriented programming (OOP) is a design concept that has been around for some time. It is common in the development environment in the forms of languages such as C++ and smalltalk. Some databases even claimed to be object-oriented before Oracle introduced the Objects option.

Oracle has introduced several new terms to be added to the DBA's vocabulary with the introduction of objects. Many DBAs may already be familiar with some of these terms, as they are common to object-oriented programming. An *object* is a collection of related data types (*attributes*) and programs associated with those data types (*methods*). An object can be *persistent*, meaning it remains until removed by the DBA (such as an object table), or it might be *transient* and disappear after use (such as a PL/SQL table). Therefore, an object in an Oracle database may simply represent an employee, a part, or a building. Another word for an object type is a *class*, for example, an HR database.

When you are going to use an object type in the database, you define an object type first and then you create instances of that object. Before you can use an object, you must first create its *type*. The type of an object assigns the attributes (similar to columns in a table) to the object and any methods (PL/SQL code associated with the object) that might be associated with that object. Object types do not take any storage in the database, and they are much like a template to be used later when creating instances of that object. An *instance* of an object is created when you use the object type subsequently as part of the creation of another object (for example, a table). The instance of an object can actually store data and will take up database space as data is inserted into the instance of the object within the table it is an attribute of.

As an example of the differences between a type and an instance, assume we are developing an employee table in an HR database. You might well create an object table; this object type might be called **employee_info**. The **employee_info** type might contain such *attributes* as the employee's last name, first name, and address. All objects have attributes, which describe the individual data columns in the object. After you create the **employee_info** object type, you would then create an instance of that object when creating the employee table in the HR database. This table will contain an instance of the **employee_info** object type as one of its attributes. The use of the **employee_info** type would also be known as a *column object*.

Also associated with objects are *methods*. Methods are programmatic interfaces to the object that allow you to define specific actions. Until Oracle8 and the object extensions available in Oracle8, if you created an **employee_info** object, developers had to design their own code to work with the attributes within the object. If the developers manage their code well, they might be able to share code. However, this often does not happen due to time, location, and poor communication. Oracle provided stored packages or procedures, but these were never directly associated with the data. They were therefore quasi-methods at best and did not represent a true object-oriented paradigm.

Having designed the **employee_info** object, the development staff can then define methods that will work on that object. For example, you would perhaps design a method to report on total salaries paid to new employees over a given time frame, or report on average employee sales. Now, all that developers need do is code to interface with the methods available to the given object, within certain restrictions. Generally, methods are *encapsulated* within the object; that is to say, the methods are the only processes available to manipulate the data within the object. In Oracle, because you can deal with objects through object SQL, the methods and data are not truly encapsulated.

An object can have four types of methods: constructor, member, map, and order. Each object type can have multiple types of methods. I talk more about methods—and the significant potential improvements they offer—later in this chapter.

Figure 5.1 relates the elements of an object and its attributes and methods.

Oracle's Objects

How you use the object-oriented features of Oracle8 is wholly up to you. Oracle doesn't require you to use them, and in fact, unless you install the object option, Oracle does not let you use any of the new object features. Still, object support does provide many powerful features. Among other things, it allows you to:

➤ Create user-defined data types

➤ Create object tables and use an object-oriented approach to database design (instead of using a relational approach)

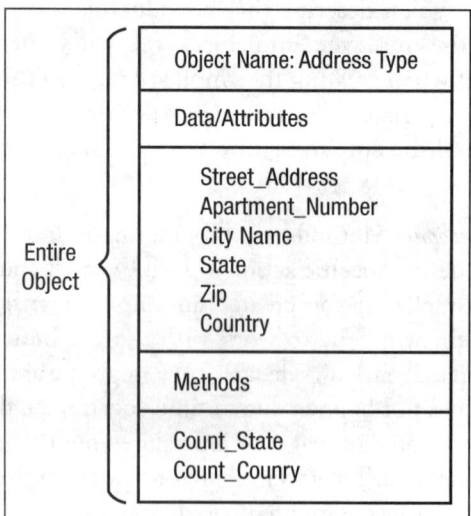

Figure 5.1   An Oracle object with its attributes and methods.

➤ Create database tables that contain nested tables and/or **VARRAY** types (which are much like arrays)

➤ Associate data and methods together

The next section covers each of these options in much more detail.

Using Oracle8 Objects

There is a significant learning curve associated with using Oracle objects. Oracle has added some complex new functionality with the introduction of the Objects option. In this section, we will try to remove some of the fogginess surrounding Oracle objects. We will look closely at user-defined data types and collection objects and how they are used in Oracle8.

User-Defined Data Types

Creating custom data types is probably how database administrators (DBAs) will first use objects. Until now, Oracle provided only internal fixed data types (also known as *scalar data types*). The inability to define data types within the database can force programmers, especially those in object-oriented environments, to create additional code within their programs in order to move the data from the programs to the database. This is because object-oriented developers normally create classes that may not directly map into a relational Oracle model. Developers must therefore convert the data structures into SQL syntax statements to read data from the database or to write it to the database. After that, they must create code to move it into their object-oriented structures. With the advent of user-defined data types, and the ability to use them in relational and object tables, developers can interact with the database more easily. Another benefit is that they have to use much less code.

New for Oracle8, user-defined data types allow developers to add and use custom data types to the database. The attributes of these objects appear in the data dictionary (as you'll see shortly), providing developers with a repository to refer to when they are trying to determine if a custom data type already exists.

Using **CREATE OR REPLACE TYPE** To Create A Type

User-defined data types are created with the **CREATE OR REPLACE TYPE** command.

Of all the information in this chapter, creating a user-defined data type is probably the most important concept to understand for the OCP exam. Be sure that you clearly understand how to create a user-defined data type.

Let's assume you need to create a data type object in the HR database called **address_type**. In this case, you want to include attributes that describe an address. These might include the street address, apartment number, city name, state, zip code, and perhaps the country. Listing 5.1 shows how the statement to create the object might look.

Listing 5.1   Creating the **address_type** custom data type.

```
CREATE OR REPLACE TYPE objects.address_type AS OBJECT
(
     street_address      VARCHAR2(40),
     apartment_number    VARCHAR2(10),
     city_name           VARCHAR2(30),
     state               VARCHAR2(2),
     zip                 VARCHAR2(10),
     country             VARCHAR2(20)
);
```

Creating An Instance Of The Type

Once you have defined the user-defined data type object **address_type**, you can create a relational table with an instance of this type in it. For example, to create the employee table with the **address_type** type in it, format the Data Definition Language (DDL), as shown in Listing 5.2. (Of course, you would add **tablespace** and other parameters as required; they are omitted here for brevity's sake.)

Listing 5.2   Creating the employee table.

```
CREATE TABLE objects.employee
(
     employee_number   NUMBER,
     last_name         VARCHAR2 (20),
     first_name        VARCHAR2(20),
     middle_initial    CHAR,
     address_info      OBJECTS.ADDRESS_TYPE
);
```

Accessing User-Defined Objects Through SQL

Now that you have created a table with this user-defined type, you may want to interface with the column object created in the table through SQL. To do so, refer to a column object's attribute(s) through some new SQL syntax introduced in Oracle8. When referring to a user defined type, you will use dot decimal notation. *Dot decimal notation* allows you to refer to the attribute within the specific data type you wish to access. For example, in the employee table above, you would refer to the **employee_number** in a SQL statement as simply

employee_number. When referring to a user-defined type, you must refer first to the name of the object you defined (in the case of the employees table, you would refer to column object name, **address_info**). Then you would refer to the data type attribute name of the type, using a dot as a delimiter between the two values. Thus, you would refer to the **street_address** attribute of the **address_info** column attribute as **address_info.street_address**.

Also when accessing user-defined data types from SQL, you must alias the table that contains the user-defined data type you wish to have returned. If you don't, an error occurs. Listing 5.3 shows an example of SQL syntax that addresses our new object.

Listing 5.3   Accessing objects through SQL.

```
--Selecting from a column object. Remember
--you refer to it using the column name and then the
--data type attribute name with a period in between.
--Note the alias on the object.employee table. It is
--required, or the SQL will fail.
SELECT employee_number, first_name, last_name,
s.address_info.street_address
FROM objects.employee s
WHERE
(employee_number > 1200000 AND employee_number < 1500000)
AND s.address_info.zip like '32246%';

--Updating a value in the item table...
--Again note the alias on the employee table.
UPDATE objects.employee s
 SET s.address_info.street_address='1201 Canyon Lake Drive'
 Where s.employee_number=1499999;
```

You might have noticed that Listing 5.3 did not include an **INSERT** statement. That's because inserting a row into an table that has a column that consists of a user-defined data type is slightly different than inserting it into a scalar column type. Inserting into user-defined data types requires you to use the *constructor method*, one of the four types of methods (you'll learn more about the other methods later in this chapter). The constructor method is created automatically when you create an object. The constructor method and the object associated with it have the same name. For example, the constructor name for the **address_type** object would be **address_type**. Listing 5.4 shows an example of an insert into the item table using the constructor method.

Listing 5.4 Inserting a row into an object using the constructor method.

```
--Insert row into the employee object.
INSERT INTO objects.employee
VALUES
(1499999,'FREEMAN','ROBERT',NULL,objects.address_type
('12200 W. 8th','Apt. 11',
 'Seattle','WA','32246','US') );
```

You can also use user-defined data types in PL/SQL, and you can pass them in to PL/SQL code. To refer to the data type in the PL/SQL code, use the syntax shown in Listing 5.5.

Listing 5.5 Using a user-defined data type in PL/SQL.

```
--Here we define item_info datatype as a parameter and a variable
--called new_item_info
--in this PL/SQL code.
CREATE OR REPLACE PROCEDURE objects.show_employee
(
    employee_number  IN  NUMBER,
    address_info     IN  objects.address_type
)
IS
BEGIN
    dbms_output.put_line(employee_number);
    dbms_output.put_line(address_info.street_address);
END;
--A sample call to this procedure would be...
exec objects.show_employee (12345,objects.address_type
('12200 W. 8th','Apt. 11',
'Seattle','WA','32246','US') );
```

Collection Objects

In Oracle8, objects are not limited to user-defined data types. Oracle allows you to use collections as well. *Collections* allow you to store related embedded multiple rows of the same type of data. They are ordered groups of elements within an Oracle table that are all the same type (such as the dependents of an employee). Much like arrays in a programming language, collections have a single dimensional subscript that determines their position within the collection.

Collections can add another dimension to your tables (no pun intended), allowing you to store header- and detail-related information in the same table. Doing so allows you to reduce joins and can aid developers in developing clearer and even better performing code by reducing the joins that are required. In concept, the two types of collection types (nested table and the **VARRAY**) perform the same general function: They allow you to store and access data related to a master table without having to use a join to a second related table. However, the two collection types differ in how they store the data and how the data is retrieved (you'll learn about these differences in a moment). Figure 5.2 shows an example of the master/detail relationship of a nested table or a **VARRAY**.

Nested Tables

A *nested table* allows you to represent a one-to-many relationship in a single object rather than two (or more) objects. In creating a nested table, Oracle maintains the referential integrity of the relationship automatically. Nested tables can remove the need for certain types of joins, and can make application development easier.

An example of a nested table would be an employee master table and its associated dependents detail table. Each table has a direct relationship to the other, where each employee row may have one or more dependents associated with it.

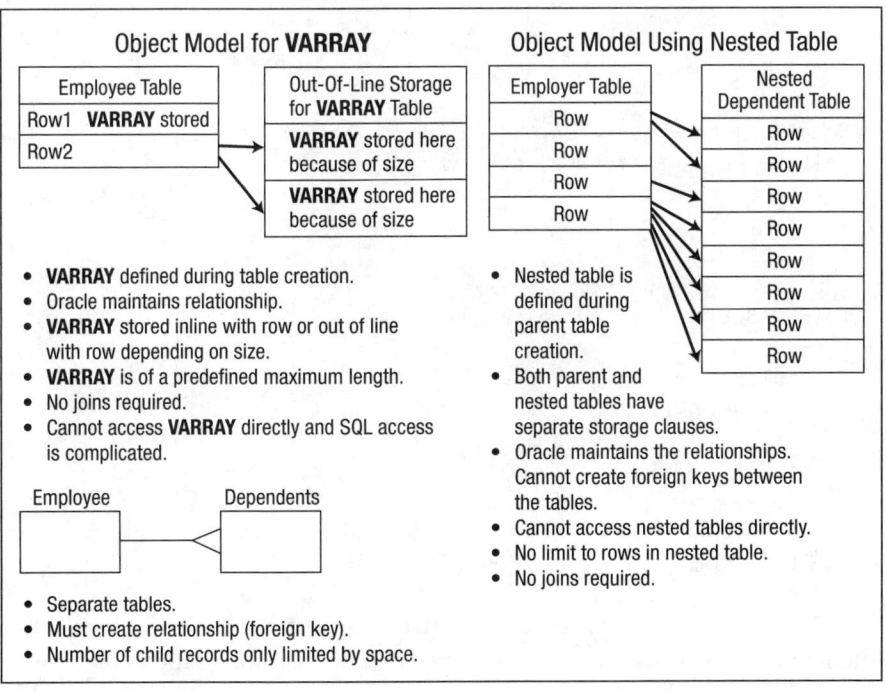

Figure 5.2   Master/detail relationships of nested tables and **VARRAY** collection objects.

Creating a nested table is generally a three-step process. These steps are:

1. Creating the object type for the nested table (such as the order_detail table type).

2. Defining an object as a type of **TABLE**, using the type created in Step 1.

3. Creating the master table, including the nested table defined in Step 2.

Look at the relation of the employee table to the employee dependents table mentioned earlier. These two tables might be good candidates for a nested table structure. Listing 5.6 shows an example of how nested tables are used.

Listing 5.6   Creating nested tables.

```
--Create a custom datatype object with attributes of the
--nested table you wish to create.
CREATE OR REPLACE TYPE objects.type_dependents AS OBJECT
(
      dependent_no      number,
      last_name         varchar2(20),
      first_name        varchar2(20),
      sex               varchar2(1)
)
/
--Create a table type for the custom object created above.
CREATE OR REPLACE TYPE objects.type_dependents_table
AS TABLE OF objects.type_dependents
/

--Now create the nested table!
CREATE TABLE objects.employee
(
      employee_number   NUMBER,
      last_name         varchar2(20),
      first_name        varchar2(20),
      middle_initial    char,
      address_info      objects.ADDRESS_TYPE,
      dependents        objects.type_dependents_table
) NESTED TABLE dependents STORE AS dependents_table;
```

Oracle appears to store the data in one data segment; however, within the data dictionary, two tables are actually recorded: **employee** and **dependents_table**. You define the name of this second table (the **dependents_table**) in the last line when you include the **STORE AS** statement.

There are a few issues to note about nested tables. First is that the nested table entries are unlimited. Therefore, when you create the **dependents_table** and nest it in the employee table, the employee can have as many dependents as he or she wishes (assuming the spouse agrees!). Secondly, data for a nested table is kept out of line with the associated row, in its own segment. In addition, the nested tables can have their own storage clauses and can reside in separate tablespaces. As you'll see in the "VARRAYs" section later in this chapter, VARRAYs store information differently. The last point to note about nested tables is that in the **dependents_table** example, you cannot address the **dependents_table** segment directly; an attempt to do so results in an error.

Of course, creating nested tables is one thing; actually using them is quite another. You must deal with all sorts of new SQL syntax in these cases. Oracle has added a lot of new SQL syntax that you need to know about in order to allow you to deal with nested tables.

Using SQL On Nested Tables

In Oracle8, SQL syntax changes have been made to accommodate nested tables. **INSERT** statements that are to populate a row in the master table and associated rows in the nested table at the same time require you to use the constructor for the nested table object. Recall that the constructor method for an object is created automatically when the object is created and takes the name of the type for itself automatically. This constructor method's parameters are the attributes of the table. You'll use the constructor method quite a bit in the examples to come.

When you issue **SELECT** queries, which use the * operator, these queries return the rows and the nested table rows associated with the row. The returned rows look a bit odd, however, because the result set returns the rows based on a user-defined type using the constructor syntax. For example, the SQL statement **SELECT * FROM employee;** returns a row that looks something like this after you strip the header off:

```
20000  FREEMAN    ROBERT    G    ADDRESS_TYPE
('12200 W. 8th', 'Apt. 11', 'Seattle', 'WA', '32246', 'US')
```

Note the use of **address_type** followed by the address information (street, apartment, state, and so on). **address_type** is the constructor of the **type_address** type that was defined before the table was created.

To get specific data values in columnar format and without the presence of the constructor name, you use a *flattened subquery*. You do a flattened subquery by using the new SQL **THE** keyword. A flattened subquery defines the nested table to be used during the query and must return only one row from the main table (though the flattened subquery itself might return several rows from the nested table in the row). For example, I can use a flattened subquery to return one employee from the employee table and at the same time, all of the dependents associated with that employee.

A new keyword for Oracle8, **THE** has been added to do the following:

➤ Allow **SELECT, UPDATE,** and **DELETE** queries against nested tables

➤ Allow the use of the **INSERT** statement to insert rows into just the nested table when the master row already exists

➤ Permit the use of flattened subqueries

Listing 5.7 shows an example of various types of operations on the employee nested table, including those that use the **THE** syntax.

Listing 5.7   Creating SQL queries on the employee table.

```
--Insert values into the table.
--Note that we have the address_type user-defined data type we
--insert data into using its constructor and then we insert two
--records into the nested table type_dependents.
INSERT INTO objects.employee VALUES
(20000,'FREEMAN','ROBERT',NULL,objects.address_type
   ('12200 W. 8th',   'Apt. 11','Seattle','WA','32246','US'),
   objects.type_dependents_table(objects.type_dependents
   (1,'Freeman',  'Jared','M'),
   objects.type_dependents(1,'Freeman','Elizabeth','F') ) );

--Selecting from a nested table, not using a flattened subquery.
SELECT * FROM objects.employee;

EMPLOYEE_NUMBER ADDRESS_INFO(STREET_ADDRESS, APARTMENT_NUMBER,
CITY_NAME, STATE, ZIP, COUNTRY)
-------------------------------------------------------------------
DEPENDENTS(DEPENDENT_NO, LAST_NAME, FIRST_NAME, SEX)
-------------------------------------------------------------------
        20000 ADDRESS_TYPE('12200 W. 8th', 'Apt. 11',
'Seattle', 'WA', '32246', 'US')
TYPE_DEPENDENTS_TABLE(TYPE_DEPENDENTS(1, 'Freeman', 'Jared',
'M'), TYPE_DEPENDENTS(1, 'Freeman', 'Elizabeth', 'F'))

--Using a flattened subquery in a select to return a nested
--table for employee 12200.
--Note that the THE query limits the employee row to a single
--row.
SELECT first_name,last_name FROM THE (SELECT dependents FROM
objects.employee WHERE employee_id = 2);
```

```
FIRST_NAME           LAST_NAME
-------------------- --------------------
Jared                Freeman
Elizabeth            Freeman

--Insert a new record into the employee table, adding a new
--child to the dependent record.
INSERT INTO THE (SELECT DEPENDENTS FROM employee WHERE
employee_number=20000)
VALUES(1,'FREEMAN','SARAH','F');

--Update the dependent record. In this case we are going to
--make the name all uppercase for Jared.
UPDATE
THE(SELECT DEPENDENTS FROM employee WHERE employee_number=20000)
SET LAST_NAME='FREEMAN', FIRST_NAME='JARED'
WHERE LAST_NAME='Freeman' and FIRST_NAME='Jared';
```

VARRAYs

As you've seen, a **VARRAY** is much like a nested table in some ways. The referential integrity between the master table and the **VARRAY** is automatically maintained by the database, just as with a nested table. The **VARRAY** differs from the nested table in that the maximum number of rows that can be stored is fixed when the **VARRAY** type is created. In addition, a **VARRAY** is stored inline with the rest of the table data as a **RAW** data type as long as it is not over 4,000 bytes. If it is greater than 4,000 bytes, the **VARRAY** is stored out of line with the rest of the row data, as a **BLOB** data type. Generally, Oracle suggests using a **VARRAY** for very short lists of data that will be of finite length. In any other case, using nested tables is preferred. Listing 5.8 shows an example of using a **VARRAY** to create the dependents table.

Listing 5.8   Creating a **VARRAY**.

```
--We are going to recreate our employee table again, this
--time as with a VARRAY for the dependents instead of a
--nested table.
--Create a custom data type object with attributes of the
--nested table you wish to create.
CREATE OR REPLACE TYPE objects.type_dependents AS OBJECT
(
     dependent_no      number,
     last_name         varchar2(20),
     first_name        varchar2(20),
     sex               varchar2(1)
);
--Create a table type for the custom object created above.
```

```
CREATE OR REPLACE TYPE objects.type_dependents_varray
IS VARRAY(10) OF objects.type_dependents;

--Now create the nested table.
CREATE TABLE objects.employee
(
    employee_number  NUMBER,

    address_info     objects.ADDRESS_TYPE,
    dependents       objects.type_dependents_varray
);
```

Using SQL On **VARRAY**s

Unfortunately, working with **VARRAY**s is more difficult than working with nested tables. You cannot directly refer to an individual record within a **VARRAY** like you can with a nested table. Within PL/SQL, however, a number of collection methods for accessing **VARRAY**s are provided. A collection method is a built-in procedure or function that works on collections. Table 5.1 provides the methods you can use on **VARRAY**s and nested tables in PL/SQL.

You should understand what a nested table is, and what a **VARRAY** is, for the Oracle8 exam. You should also understand how they store the data and what the differences between the two are.

Table 5.1	Collection methods used in PL/SQL to access VARRAY collection objects.
Method	**Function Of The Method**
COUNT()	Returns the number of elements in the collection
DELETE()	Removes one, all, or a range of elements from a collection
EXISTS()	Verifies the existence of an element
EXTEND()	Adds one element or several, or makes copies of elements
FIRST()	Returns the smallest index number of a collection
LAST()	Returns the largest index number of a collection
LIMIT()	Returns the maximum number of elements in a VARRAY type
NEXT()	Returns the next index number
PRIOR()	Returns the previous index number
TRIM()	Removes one or more elements from a collection

Object Tables

Oracle8 introduces the notion of an object table, again only available if the Objects option is installed. In this section we will look at what an object table is, how it is created, and how to use it.

Definition And Creation Of An Object Table

Object tables allow you to define a table within the database based on object types only. An object table is not a relational table; you do not define a table with relational columns in an object table. Instead, you first define object types that contain the attributes you wish to be stored in the object table. Then you create the object table itself. When you store a row in an object table, the row is called a *row object reference*, and each row is an object unto itself and is not relational data. When you create an object table, Oracle assigns it an object type attribute known as an *object identifier (OID)*. Oracle indexes this attribute, and it becomes the object table's primary key. An object table is said to be *persistent*, and only persistent objects are assigned OIDs. To create an object table, you must define the types to be contained in the table. Once the types are defined, you then create an object table that contains these types.

Object References

To allow the expression of a one-to-many relationship with object tables Oracle has provided the **REF** data type. A **REF** provides a means of expressing a relationship between two tables when at least one object in the relationship is row object. The **REF** data type stores the object's OID to provide a quick reference to the related row object. A **REF** data type can be used in an object table or a relational table. You can use the **REF** to either examine the row it references or even update that row.

To create a table REF data type, you create the object table you wish to reference. Next, create the second table that you wish to add the reference to, adding a **REF** data type that will allow you to store the row object OID. You can now use the **REF** function to create the **REF** to the row. The **REF** function is typically used in a SQL **SELECT** statement, specifying the row you wish the OID returned for via the **WHERE** clause. The function takes the object table name as a function, returning the OID of the row object referenced. An example of such a query is shown in Listing 5.9.

Listing 5.9   An example of using the **REF** function.

```
SELECT REF(so) INTO OrderRef
       FROM sales_orders so
       WHERE so.id=100122;
```

Oracle provides the corollary function **DREF** to the **REF** function. The **DREF** function returns data in a row object to which the OID of the child record (passed to the **DREF** function) points. Unfortunately, using **REF**s can cause the parent record to be removed and the children to remain. In this case, **NULL**s will be returned, thus indicating orphaned records.

Listing 5.10 shows an example of creating an employee and dependents object tables. This listing includes the creation of an object reference between the two tables. The reference used relates the **employee_number** attribute of the employee table to the **employee_number** attribute of the dependents table. To facilitate this example, a new type is created in this example. The new type contains the attribute of the **employee_id**, which was originally an attribute of the employee table itself.

Listing 5.10   Creating object tables with object references, and querying them.

```
--Create a custom datatype object with attributes of the nested
--table you wish to create.
--Now create the nested table!
CREATE TYPE objects.type_employee AS OBJECT
(
      employee_number   NUMBER,
      last_name         varchar2(20),
      first_name        varchar2(20),
      middle_initial    char,
      address_info      objects.ADDRESS_TYPE
)
/


--Create the object table.
CREATE TABLE objects.employee OF objects.type_employee.
(employee_number PRIMARY KEY);

CREATE OR REPLACE TYPE objects.type_dependents AS OBJECT
(
      dependent_no      number,
      last_name         varchar2(20),
      first_name        varchar2(20),
      sex               varchar2(1),
      employee_number   REF objects.type_employee
)
/


--Create an object table for the type_dependents type.
CREATE TABLE objects.dependents OF objects.type_dependents
(dependent_no PRIMARY KEY);
```

One of the benefits of object tables is that you can eliminate complicated join queries by including the object references in the table. You can also create more-customized table structures that accommodate structures developed in object-oriented databases. The benefits of object tables and using object **REF**s should not be downplayed. Object tables and **REF**s allow users of the database to navigate the object tables and related object tables with fewer joins. Another benefit is potentially simplified SQL syntax. It might take you a few tries to get used to the new syntax required when navigating object tables in SQL, so don't be discouraged if you have trouble at first.

Object Dependencies

You have probably noticed that there is a particular order involved when you create object tables. First, you define the types to be used and then you define the object tables. There is even an order when you create object tables; you must first create the object tables that other object tables with object references will reference.

As with other Oracle objects, dependencies exist within the object world. It is possible for one or more attributes of an object to become invalid. An object will become invalid if one of its attribues (e.g., user-defined object types) becomes invalid. In other words, dependencies exist between an object and its attributes and the object types hat those attributes were created from. Further dependencies exist with regards to object references; dependencies on the presence of other objects exist, and if they are not present, problems can occur. Oracle does not allow you to drop an object that other objects depend on. It can be a frustrating exercise to change a type if several objects depend on it. You can use the **DBA_DEPENDENCIES** view to determine which objects have dependencies on other objects. You must drop child objects before you can drop parent objects. As a result, changing such things as object type attributes can be complicated.

 Because the relationships can get complicated, and changing object tables after the fact can be difficult, carefully consider your database design before you commit to it.

Listing 5.11 shows some examples of SQL statements that access the object tables you just created. Note how the extended dot notation refers to the object references within the object table as well as how the syntax for accessing the **ref** columns is much easier than the syntax of a SQL statement that joins two tables of a relational database design.

Listing 5.11 Manipulating object tables.

```
--INSERT a record INTO the employee table.
INSERT INTO objects.employee
VALUES
(1,'FREEMAN','ROBERT',NULL,objects.address_type
('2147 Baker',NULL,'Somewhere','FL','12345','US') );

--INSERT a record INTO the dependents table.
INSERT INTO objects.dependents
SELECT 1,'FREEMAN','JACOB','M',ref(d)
FROM objects.employee d WHERE employee_number=1

--SELECT FROM the table. Note the use of dot decimal values.
SELECT dependent_no,a.employee_number.employee_number FROM
objects.dependents a;
```

Types Of Methods

As first mentioned in the "Object-Oriented Development" section earlier in this chapter, methods within the object are the second part of an object. In object-oriented speak, methods are ways programs associated with the object that provide a way of manipulating data within the object. Methods are code (PL/SQL code) that is associated with the data within the object. When you create a method within an object, you create bodies of PL/SQL code that are stored as a part of the object.

Generally, in the object-oriented world, data and methods that belong to an object are said to be encapsulated: The data inside the object can be manipulated only by the methods, not from outside the object. This is not the case with Oracle8.0.5. At this time, Oracle does not offer encapsulation of an object's data and methods.

As you've already seen in this chapter, methods come in four flavors. The first is the **CONSTRUCTOR** method, which has already been discussed. The constructor is automatically produced when the object is created, and it takes the name of the object for its own name. The parameters of the **CONSTRUCTOR** are the same as the attributes of the object.

MEMBER Methods

The next method types are the **MEMBER** methods. *MEMBER methods* are stored procedures or functions that are part of the object. As with any other PL/SQL procedure or function, a **MEMBER** method can have parameters associated with it. For each **MEMBER** method, the first parameter is called **SELF** and is created automatically as a part of the method.

Also required with a **MEMBER** method is a **PRAGMA RESTRICT REF-ERENCES** specification. This specification controls the operations that the method can perform. Four states can be defined in the pragma: **WNDS** (write no database state), **WNPS** (write no package state), **RNDS** (read no database state), and **RNPS** (read no package state). **PRAGMA RESTRICT REFER-ENCES** is required in a **MEMBER** method, but is not new for Oracle8.

To create a method, you first define the method when defining the object type. You can then use the new Oracle **CREATE MEMBER BODY** syntax to create the methods. There are a few restrictions to methods, the biggest being that you cannot use a method to change data within the database itself. Oracle allows you to create a method that changes the data, but the **PRAGMA** you define prevents it from actually working. Listing 5.12 shows how to create a member method using a modified version of our employee table.

Listing 5.12   Creating a **MEMBER** method.

```
CREATE OR REPLACE TYPE employee_type AS OBJECT
(
      employee_id          NUMBER,
      last_name            VARCHAR2(30),
      first_name           VARCHAR2(30),
      middle_initial       char,
      street_address       VARCHAR2(40),
      apartment_number     VARCHAR2(10),
      city_name            VARCHAR2(30),
      state                VARCHAR2(2),
      zip                  VARCHAR2(10),
      country              VARCHAR2(20),
      MEMBER FUNCTION in_state
      (
            state_name                  varchar2
      ) RETURN NUMBER,
      PRAGMA RESTRICT_REFERENCES(in_state,WNDS)
)
/

CREATE TABLE employees OF employee_type
(employee_id PRIMARY KEY);

CREATE OR REPLACE TYPE BODY employee_type AS
MEMBER FUNCTION in_state
(
      state_name                  varchar2
```

```
) RETURN NUMBER IS
    BEGIN
        IF SELF.STATE=state_name
        THEN
            return 1;
        else
            return 0;
        END IF;
    END;
END;
/

insert into employees values
(1,'FREEMAN','ROBERT',NULL,'1200 Jaguars
Dr.',NULL,'Jacksonville','FL','44331','US');

select decode(e.in_state('FL'),1,'TRUE',0,'FALSE','UNKNOWN')
"IN STATE"
from employees e where e.employee_id = 1;
```

MAP And ORDER Methods

In this section, we will address the **MAP** and **ORDER** methods and their use. One of the design issues you need to contend with when designing object tables is sorting or grouping attributes contained within the object. For example, you might issue the following query:

```
SELECT a.emp_no, a.emp_name.emp_last_name FROM emp a
ORDER BY a.emp_name;
```

which will return an ORA 22950 error (cannot **ORDER** objects without the **MAP** or **ORDER** method). The **MAP** and **ORDER** methods define how to compare data within an object. If you do not declare a **MAP** or **ORDER** method, Oracle can do only equality and inequality operations, and then only for objects of the same type.

The **MAP** method does not take any parameters as input, and it returns a scalar data type. The **ORDER** method takes two parameters: **SELF**, which is implicit, and the object type. Oracle uses the **MAP** and **ORDER** methods for several operations, including the following:

➤ Equality operations

➤ Inequality operations (less than and greater than)

➤ **BETWEEN** predicate

➤ **IN** predicate

➤ **ORDER BY** operations

➤ **GROUP BY** operations

➤ **DISTINCT** clauses

➤ **UNIQUE** constraints and **PRIMARY KEY** constraints

Creating an **ORDER** method is a bit more involved than creating a **MAP** method. With an **ORDER** method, you create a function that returns one of three values:

➤ -1 when **SELF** < the other input parameter

➤ 0 when **SELF** = the other input parameter

➤ 1 when **SELF** > the other input parameter

Listing 5.13 shows an example of creating **MAP** and **ORDER** methods.

Listing 5.13   Creating **MAP** and **ORDER** methods.

```
--Define the type, with the MAP function defined.
CREATE OR REPLACE TYPE employee_type AS OBJECT
(
     employee_id        NUMBER,
     last_name          VARCHAR2(30),
     first_name         VARCHAR2(30),
     middle_initial     char,
     street_address     VARCHAR2(40),
     apartment_number   VARCHAR2(10),
     city_name          VARCHAR2(30),
     state              VARCHAR2(2),
     zip                VARCHAR2(10),
     country            VARCHAR2(20),
     MAP MEMBER FUNCTION employee_map RETURN VARCHAR2
)
/
--Define the member now.
CREATE OR REPLACE TYPE BODY employee_type (
MAP MEMBER FUNCTION employee_map RETURN VARCHAR2 IS
BEGIN
     RETURN first_name||last_name||middle_initial;
END;
/

--Define the order now.
CREATE OR REPLACE TYPE employee_type AS OBJECT
(
     employee_id        NUMBER,
```

```
     last_name              VARCHAR2(30),
     first_name             VARCHAR2(30),
     street_address         VARCHAR2(40),
     apartment_number       VARCHAR2(10),
     city_name              VARCHAR2(30),
     state                  VARCHAR2(2),
     zip                    VARCHAR2(10),
     country                VARCHAR2(20),
     ORDER MEMBER FUNCTION employee_map (other employee_type)
RETURN NUMBER
)
/


--Define the map member now.
CREATE OR REPLACE TYPE BODY employee_type (
ORDER MEMBER FUNCTION employee_map (other employee_type)
RETURN NUMBER
IS
self_name     varchar2(200) := self.last_name||self.first_name
   ||middle_initial;
other_name    varchar2(200) :=
other.last_name||other.first_name||middle_initial;
BEGIN
     if self_name < other_name
     THEN
            return -1;
     elseif self_name > other_name
     THEN
            return 1;
     ELSE
            return 0;
     END IF;
END;
);
```

Make sure you are clear on the four different types of methods and what they are used for. Make sure you clearly understand the differences between the four method types.

Creating Object Views In Oracle8

Along with the new functionality of Oracle8 and the Objects option, Oracle has made changes to views to facilitate use of objects within the views. Oracle8 will even allow you to create a view that will display existing relational tables as object tables. The next section discusses views in Oracle as they relate to the Objects option.

Object Views

Just as you may wish to create views on relational tables, you can create *object views* on object tables. Creating an object view requires that you create an object type that defines the format of the view. In some cases, when it is not clear which column uniquely identifies the rows the view returns, you must use the **WITH OBJECT_OID** clause to specify which attribute of the objects uniquely identifies the correct OID of the view.

To create an object view, you first create an object type that defines the attributes of the view. Once you have done that, you can create the object view. Listing 5.14 shows how to create an object view of the employee object table. For security reasons, the view user will not be allowed to query the **employee_id** column in this view.

Listing 5.14   Creating object views.

```
--First we need to create a type that describes the shape of
--the view.
CREATE OR REPLACE TYPE objects.type_view_employee AS OBJECT
(
        last_name            VARCHAR2(30),
        first_name           VARCHAR2(30),
        middle_initial       char,
        street_address       VARCHAR2(40),
        apartment_number     VARCHAR2(10),
        city_name            VARCHAR2(30),
        state                VARCHAR2(2),
        zip                  VARCHAR2(10),
        country              VARCHAR2(20)
)
/

CREATE OR REPLACE VIEW objects.v_employee OF
objects.type_view_employee AS
SELECT e.last_name, e.first_name, e.middle_initial,
e.address_info.street_address, e.address_info.apartment_number,
e.address_info.city_name,e.address_info.state,e.address_info.zip,
e.address_info.country
from
objects.employee e;
```

Views That Represent Object Tables As Relational Tables

In an effort to make the migration to object tables easier, Oracle provides a method to create a view on an object table that makes it appear as a relational table. The same restrictions on views apply to object relational views. However, by using **INSTEAD OF** triggers, you can create PL/SQL code that allows you to manipulate the data within the view. See Chapter 7 for more information on **INSTEAD OF** triggers.

The creation syntax is fairly straightforward. First, choose the table you wish to access through the object view. Next, create the type for the user-defined data type(s) in which you wish the view to return the data. Finally, create the view, defining which columns in the relational table associate with the attributes of the type you have defined. Listing 5.15 shows an example of such a view.

Listing 5.15   Creating a view that represents an object table as a relational table.

```
--Create the type for item information.
CREATE OR REPLACE TYPE item_information AS OBJECT
(
     item_id            NUMBER,
     effective_date     DATE,
     expire_date        DATE
);
--Create the object table using the ITEM_INFORMATION structure
--we defined above.
CREATE OR REPLACE TYPE type_price
(
     price_id           NUMBER PRIMARY KEY,
     item_detail        ITEM_INFORMATION
);
--Create the object table.
CREATE TABLE price of type_price
(price_id PRIMARY KEY);
--Now we need to define a type with attributes that reflect
--how the view will appear.
CREATE OR REPLACE TYPE type_price_relational
(
     price_id           NUMBER PRIMARY KEY,
     item_id            NUMBER,
     effective_date     DATE,
     expire_date        DATE
);
--Now create the view.
CREATE OR REPLACE VIEW view_price_relational OF
type_price_relational WITH OBJECT_OID OID (price_id) AS
SELECT price_id, item_information(item_id, effective_date,
expire_date)
FROM price;

--Create the view that expresses this as a relational object.
CREATE OR REPLACE VIEW view_price
```

Views That Represent Relational Tables As Object Tables

Oracle also allows you to perform the reverse operation, creating an object view on a relational table. Note that Oracle added some new syntax when it created the view. In particular, the **WITH OBJECT_OID** clause indicates the attribute of the view to identify as the unique OID of the object view.

Listing 5.16 demonstrates the creation of an object view on a relational table called price. We then create the price table as an object table and demonstrate how to create a view expressing the price object table as a relational table.

Listing 5.16   Creating a view that represents a relational table as an object table.

```
--Create a relational table for employees.
CREATE OR REPLACE TABLE price
(
     price_id            NUMBER PRIMARY KEY,
     item_id             NUMBER,
     effective_date      DATE,
     expire_date         DATE
);

--Now create the object view. We will use the item_information
--type created earlier.
CREATE OR REPLACE VIEW view_price (price_id,
item_id,effective_date,expire_date)
AS
SELECT price_id,objects.item_information(item_id,effective_date,
expire_date)
FROM price;
```

Managing Objects In Oracle8

The views that you can use to manage objects in Oracle8 will be explained in this section. Many of these views are new, and DBAs who want to be ready for the exam should study them.

Data Dictionary Views For Managing Object Types

Several views are available to DBAs for managing defined object types and collections. These views include:

➤ *DBA_COLL_TYPES*—Displays all collection types in the database

➤ *DBA_DEPENDENCIES*—Provides dependency information on objects, including types

➤ *DBA_METHOD_PARAMS*—Describes method parameters of types in the database

➤ *DBA_METHOD_RESULTS*—Describes method parameters of types in the database

➤ *DBA_NESTED_TABLES*—Displays descriptions of nested tables in all tables that contain them

➤ *DBA_OBJECT_TABLES*—Displays descriptions of all object tables in the database

➤ *DBA_REFS*—Describes the **ref** columns and **ref** attributes in object type columns of all the tables in the database

➤ *DBA_TYPE_ATTRS*—Displays the attributes of types in the database

➤ *DBA_TYPE_METHODS*—Describes methods of all types in the database

➤ *DBA_TYPES*—Describes all abstract types in the database

A Final Word On Administering Objects

A few more administrative notes: Any user who wants to create an object type must have the **CREATE TYPE** system privilege. This privilege is also associated with the **RESOURCE** role. In addition, the data types that you can define for attributes of an object are limited. You cannot create an object of the following types:

➤ **LONG**

➤ **LONG RAW**

➤ **NCHAR**

➤ **NCLOB**

➤ **NVCHAR2**

➤ **ROWID**

Also, you cannot use PL/SQL data types such as **BINARY_INTEGER, BOOLEAN,** and the like.

Practice Questions

Question 1

Which items are collection types? [Choose two]

☐ a. **VARRAY**

☐ b. Relational table

☐ c. Method

☐ d. Nested table

☐ e. Penny

Answers a and d are correct. Answer b is incorrect because a relational table is not a collection type. Answer c is incorrect because a method is part of an object and is not a collection. Answer e is incorrect. Although you may have a penny collection, Oracle does not.

Question 2

If a nested table's row length is fewer than 4,001 bytes, how is it stored?

○ a. Inline with the row data as a **RAW** data type

○ b. Out of line with the row data in a separate object

○ c. Out of line with the row data as a **LONG**

○ d. Inline with the row data, as a **BFILE**

○ e. **INSERT** will generate an error because nested tables cannot be greater than 4,000 bytes in size.

Answer b is correct. When you create a nested table, a second segment in which to store the nested data is created. This is a trick question because you might get nested tables and **VARRAY**s confused and therefore choose answer a. Answer a would be correct for a **VARRAY**, which stores the data in two ways depending on its size. Answer c is incorrect for either a nested table or a **VARRAY**. Answer d is also incorrect because a **BFILE** type is a type for externally stored Oracle data and has no relationship to a collection's storage. Answer e is incorrect because a nested table can be larger than 4,000 bytes.

Question 3

What is true about a method created with an object table?

○ a. A method can manipulate data in tables related to the object table, relieving the developer from having to design more code.

○ b. A method is PL/SQL code that can be created with an object table.

○ c. There are two different kinds of methods: a **CONSTRUCTOR** method and a **DESTRUCTOR** method.

○ d. Methods are the only way to manipulate data within an object table.

○ e. None of the above.

Answer b is correct. Answer a is incorrect because methods cannot manipulate data in other tables in the database. Answer c is incorrect because there is no **DESTRUCTOR** method, and the other three types of valid methods (**ORDER, MAP, MEMBER**) are not listed. Answer d is incorrect because there is not encapsulation in Oracle and thus you can manipulate data within objects directly with SQL. Answer e is incorrect because a correct answer is given.

Question 4

When manipulating **VARRAY**s, what special SQL clause do you use?

○ a. The **THE** clause

○ b. The **FROM** clause

○ c. The **WHERE** clause

○ d. The **SANTA** clause

○ e. None of the above

Answer e is correct. You cannot directly manipulate **VARRAY** values through SQL. You must use PL/SQL to deal with the data contained in these types. This is a trick question because if you were thinking of nested tables, you might be tempted to choose answer a. Answers b, c, and d are incorrect for both **VARRAY**s and nested tables.

Question 5

Which statement is true regarding a method?

○ a. A method can add values and return the results.

○ b. A method can change data in the table with which the method is associated.

○ c. A method can modify any table in the database.

○ d. A method does not require **PRAGMA RESTRICT REFERENCES**.

○ e. All of the above are correct.

Answer a is correct. A method can add and subtract values and return the results. Answer b and c are incorrect because a method cannot manipulate any database object data. Answer d is incorrect because a method does require a restrict references pragma. Answer e is incorrect because only one answer is correct.

Question 6

A flattened subquery is used for what purpose?

○ a. To define the rows of a collection object to return for one master record

○ b. To take a multi-rowed result from a SQL query and display the result all on one line

○ c. To define the attributes of an object table

○ d. To define what database actions a method allows

○ e. To generate aggregate results from multiple rows in the parent object table

Answer a is correct. A flattened subquery returns one or more rows of a collection type in a table for one row in that table. Answer b is incorrect because the flattened subquery has nothing to do with displaying multi-row results on one row. Answer c is incorrect because the subquery is not responsible for defining the attributes of an object table. Answer d is incorrect because a pragma is what is used to restrict references on database actions. Answer e is incorrect. Because a flattened subquery can only reference a single row from the parent object, aggregate results on the parent are not possible.

Question 7

You need to redefine a user-defined object type, adding a new attribute to it. What view will you query to determine what objects are using the user-defined object type?

O a. **DBA_TABLES**

O b. **DBA_DEPENDENCIES**

O c. **DBA_COL_TYPES**

O d. **DBA_SEGMENTS**

O e. **DBA_TYPES**

Answer b is correct. The **DBA_DEPENDENCIES** table lists the dependencies of objects within the database. You must drop dependent objects before dropping the objects they depend on, so this view is critical. Answer a is incorrect because **DBA_TABLES** does not provide dependency information. Answer c is incorrect because **DBA_COL_TYPES** defines collection types in the database and, again, does not provide dependency information. Answers d and e are incorrect because they do not provide dependency information.

Question 8

MAP and **ORDER** methods are used for what function?

O a. To assist in locating row addresses and returning either the extended or restricted **ROWID** of those rows in an object table.

O b. The **MAP** and **ORDER** methods are created when the object is created. One allows you to extract the data directly from a **SELECT** statement, and the other allows you to access the attributes of objects when you are using **INSERT**, **UPDATE**, or **DELETE** statements.

O c. The **MAP** method allows you to define where you wish the data to be stored (inline or out of line), and the **ORDER** method defines the sort order of the object's stored data.

O d. To allow attributes of an object to be sorted and compared correctly.

O e. None of the above.

Answer d is correct. Both **MAP** and **ORDER** methods are created to allow sorting of data in object types. Answer a is incorrect because these methods have nothing to do with locating data or providing **ROWID**s. Answer b is incorrect because these are not the correct functions of the **MAP** and **ORDER** methods. Answer c is incorrect because the map method does not allow you to define where you want data to be stored in the database. Answer e is incorrect because a correct answer is given.

Question 9

What is the purpose of the **REF** keyword?

○ a. A **REF** returns the parent rows for a query against a child object table.

○ b. A **REF** is an object attribute that references another object via the OID.

○ c. A **REF** creates a unique index on the column that is being defined in the **REF**.

○ d. A **REF** creates a foreign key relationship between an object table and a collector.

○ e. When used, the **REF** keyword causes an index to be built on the foreign key relationship between the parent-child relationship created in a nested table.

Answer b is correct. A REF is used when creating an object table to create a relationship between a child table and a parent table. Answer a is incorrect because a REF is not used to return parent rows in a select statement, though it can be used to return the parent table OID. Answer c is incorrect because no index is created when you include a REF type in an object table definition. Answer d is incorrect because a REF does not create any relationship to collector types. Answer e is incorrect because the REF keyword has nothing to do with the creation of indexes.

Question 10

What kinds of comparison or sort operations can be done on an object that does not have an **ORDER** or **MAP** method? [Choose two]

❏ a. Equality

❏ b. Between

❏ c. Order

❏ d. Inequality

❏ e. Distinct

Answers a and d are correct. Answers b, c, and e are incorrect because they require that a map or an order method be created. If a sort method is not created for these three incorrect answers, an Oracle error results.

Need To Know More?

Ault, Michael R.: *Oracle8 Black Book*. The Coriolis Group, 1998. ISBN 1-57610-187-8. This book deals in great depth with several new Oracle8 features, including partitioning.

Bobrowski, Steve: *Oracle8 Architecture*. Oracle Press/Osborne McGraw Hill, 1998. ISBN 0-07-882274-2. This book covers basic topics, including objects in Oracle8 and how to use them.

Curtis, Mike: *Oracle8 and Windows NT Black Book*. The Coriolis Group, 1998. ISBN 1-57610-248-3. A superior text that discusses objects in a clear and concise way with many examples.

www.support.com is Oracle's Metalink Web site. It is a wonderful resource if you have Oracle Metals Support.

Oracle8 Parallel DML And DDL

Terms you'll need to understand:

√ Parallel Data Manipulation Language (DML) and Data Definition Language (DDL)

√ Parallel Query Coordinator

√ Degree of parallelism

√ Parallel server process

√ Parallel server pool

√ Inter-operation parallelism

√ Intra-operation parallelism

Techniques you'll need to master:

√ Understanding the concepts behind parallel processing in Oracle

√ Understanding the rules associated with the various parallel processing options in Oracle

√ Learning to use hints to control parallel processing of a statement

√ Learning to use the data dictionary views to manage parallel query processing

This chapter reviews the new parallel processing features available in Oracle8. The Oracle Certified Professional (OCP) Exam will expect you to know—and this chapter will cover—how to process *Data Manipulation Language (DML)* and *Data Definition Language (DDL)* in parallel. You need to understand which DML and DDL statements you can parallelize and what rules are associated with parallel processing of these statements. You must also know how to enable parallel DML within a session and how to use hints to request an operation be executed in parallel. You should understand how to execute a parallel **INSERT** in direct path mode as well as how to do parallel **UPDATE** and **DELETE** operations on partitioned tables and the restrictions Oracle puts on these operations. Finally, you should understand the data dictionary views and how to use them in Oracle8.

Why Use Parallel DML And DDL?

Until Oracle8, most DML and DDL operations on large tables had to be executed serially. To review, DML is Data Manipulation Language, which includes such operations as **INSERT**s, **UPDATE**s, and **DELETE**s. DDL is Data Definition Language which includes all other operations, most of which effect objects in the database.

In large database environments, DML or DDL can be a very time-consuming task, and time is critical in 24×7 operations. Oracle7 introduced the parallel query option, which allowed large **SELECT** operations to be divided into several smaller operations, each working a specific range of data. On large queries against tables, parallel queries could increase throughput on a query several-fold in many cases. Oracle7 also allowed you to parallelize the creation of indexes, speeding up that process as well. The parallel query option can reduce the execution time of operations that might otherwise would not be able to run in given time constraints.

Now, Oracle8 introduces several new operations DML operations—as well as many DDL operations, such as the creation of indexes—that can be parallelized. Large data warehouses can now do mass updates of tables in parallel, the effect being a reduction in the time required for the completion of these operations. Staged data can be inserted into other tables within the database much quicker. These new parallel options make managing large amounts of data much easier and more efficient than serial operations. However, with the introduction of these new features comes the introduction of many rules and restrictions. These will all be elaborated on as we progress through this chapter.

Not all occasions call for parallel processing. The overhead associated with parallel processing makes it inefficient for operations on smaller tables. The additional processes associated with parallel statements, the additional CPU, and disk and memory requirements all add up to resource requirements that your system may not be able to handle. Typically, DBAs use parallel processing operations to speed up large operations in large databases. Although parallelism is not a likely candidate for sub-second response oriented online transaction processing (OLTP) queries, you may in fact use it during nightly batch job runs on an OLTP database. Tables in a data warehouse often need periodic refreshes of large amounts of data, for which parallel DML is tailor-made. Parallelism may be the key to keeping your processing schedule on schedule.

One final note: If you use parallel processing, you may need to think a bit more about your database design. Much of the new parallel processing functionality depends on the use of partitioning (see Chapter 4 for more on partitioning). If you are not taking advantage of partitioning in your database, you cannot fully take advantage of many of Oracle8's new parallel processing abilities.

Oracle8 Parallel Architecture

In Oracle8, the features of Oracle7's parallel query option are now included with the base database product and are installed when you install the database server software. When enabled, parallel processing allows SQL queries to be split into different units of work so that a single parallel coordinator process can manage multiple parallel query processes. The multiple parallel query processes split the work into smaller chunks, and process these smaller chunks of work in parallel at the same time. By using this divide-and-conquer method to attack large volumes of data—on hardware sufficiently powerful to handle the additional workload—Oracle can significantly increase the performance of queries and DDL. This section examines the architecture that Oracle uses to execute parallel statements.

Preparing The Database For Parallel Processing

Before actually attempting to do parallel queries, you must set up the database to effectively manage the parallel query process. To do so, follow these steps:

1. Determine if the hardware will support the use of parallel query.

2. Determine if the database structures will support the type of parallel queries you intend to use.

3. Correctly set the init.ora parameters for your database so that the parallel query processes will be efficient.

Let's look at each of these items in more detail.

Hardware Support Of Parallel Queries

Trying to do parallel queries on a system that is already CPU-constrained might actually negatively impact the response time of the queries. Oracle recommends that you do not attempt parallel queries on a system that runs at less than 25 to 30 percent idle. Parallel query and the processes associated with it have additional memory requirements. In addition, if the query is processing larger data volumes, other memory requirements might increase as well (e.g., you may need to increase the **hash_area_size** parameter). Some parallel processes also require additional disk space; many create temporary segments in the database that are used to process the query. When you are planning to use parallel queries, consider these resource requirements.

Database Architectural Support For Parallel Queries

The "Parallel Processing Of DML" section later in this chapter lists the requirements associated with doing parallel DML or DDL in Oracle8. One of these requirements is that if you want to do parallel updates on tables, tables must be partitioned. If you have not taken advantage of partitioning in Oracle8, you often cannot use parallel query; performing updates is one such occurrence. In most situations with parallel DDL, Oracle does not return an error when you instruct it to do a parallel process and it chooses not to perform the action in parallel. You should review your current database design in light of these requirements to determine if you can actually perform the parallel actions you want to perform.

Correctly Setting The init.ora Parameters For Efficient Parallelism

Efficient use of parallelism includes setting the init.ora parameters for the instance you are working on. Incorrectly setting initialization parameters can cause serious performance degradation, again causing parallel queries to have an unexpected effect. Parameters that will affect parallel query include:

➤ *compatible*—Make sure it is set to the correct version of Oracle you are running.

➤ *cpu_count*—Should have been set properly during the install of the database. Check platform specific documentation to determine the number this parameter should be set to.

➤ *db_file_multiblock_read_count*—Determines how many blocks are read during a full table scan during one I/O pass.

➤ *db_file_simultaneous_writes*—Determine the number of writes that will be made to a specific datafile. When using parallel server, this should be set to the degree of parallelism or to the number of striped disks for the parallel operation.

➤ *dml_locks*—This parameter represents the maximum number of concurrent transactions times the number of DML locks.

➤ *enqueue_resources*—Should be set higher than **dml_locks**.

➤ *hash_area_size*—The default value is two times the size of **sort_ area_size**. This is the maximum amount of memory that can be used for hash joins.

➤ *optimizer_percent_parallel*—Determines the weight of index scan solutions over serial based plans. The greater the setting (0 to 100), the more that table scans will be favored.

➤ *parallel_min_servers*—Minimum number of parallel servers to start at system startup.

➤ *parallel_max_servers*—Maximum number of parallel server processes that will be allowed to be started at once.

➤ *shared_pool_size*—Will require additional memory allocations if using parallel DML/DDL.

➤ *always_anti_join*—Recommended setting is **hash**. This causes **not in** predicates to be evaluated in serial rather than parallel.

➤ *db_block_size*—Affects memory allocations, such as **hash_area_size** and how large it should be.

➤ *db_block_buffers*—Holds datafile blocks read in by parallel queries (and normal queries for that matter).

➤ *sort_direct_writes*—Allows for sorts to be written to the buffer cache or to avoid it. Avoiding the buffer cache can have significantly positive effects on performance.

➤ *sort_read_fac*—This parameter should be set based on the recommendation of the platform specific documentation.

Use caution when setting these parameters, and follow Oracle guidelines for the platform and version of Oracle you are using. We will cover several of these parameters in more detail in various sections of this chapter.

Parallel Query Processes

Before exploring the process of how parallel queries work, let's look at the architecture that surrounds it. This section reviews the individual database processes associated with parallel processing operations. These processes include the Parallel Query Coordinator and the parallel server processes. Finally, we will look at the server pool.

The Parallel Query Coordinator

The *Parallel Query Coordinator* is the foreground process for the SQL statement being executed in parallel. If you are using Multi-Threaded Server (MTS), it is the server process (see the "The Parallel Server Processes" section later in this chapter) that is executing the query plan. If you're not using MTS, the Parallel Query Coordinator is the user process that Oracle spawns off when you connected to the database. The Query Coordinator's first duty is to determine how many *parallel server processes* will be used during a query. The Coordinator process then obtains server processes from the parallel server pool (see the "The Server Pool" section later in this chapter) and assigns them to the query. These processes will be used for operations within the query, and once they are complete, they can be reused for other operations in the same query or released back to the parallel server pool. The number of parallel server processes used for one operation in the query is known as the *degree of parallelism*.

The degree of parallelism (defined in hints, object definitions, or the database default values) represents the number of parallel server processes that the query coordinator requests for one operation of the the query. The degree of parallelism can be defined at either the statement level (by using a SQL hint) or at the table or index level (as part of the **PARALLEL** definition of that object). Generally, hints take precedence over object-level settings, which take precedence over the default settings (I will deal more in specifics about these cases throughout the chapter). The default degree of parallelism is set according to several criteria, including the number of disks or CPUs present on the database server. The number of processes actually used in parallelizing a SQL statement may vary based on:

➤ How many processes are available in the parallel server pool

➤ The instance of init.ora settings that relate to parallelism

➤ If inter-operation parallelism is possible (for more information on this topic, see the "Parallel Query Operations" section later in this chapter)

Here's an example of what is meant by the degree of parallelism. When a SQL statement is executed, the parallel query coordinator determines the degree of parallelism for that statement. It does this based on the statement type and the rules associated with that statement type. Each statement has rules about how to determine the degree of parallelism for that type of statement. Assuming the coordinator process determines that the degree of parallelism is 6, the query coordinator process dispatches six parallel query server processes from the server pool for the first operation (assuming they are available).

These processes are used to process the first operation of the plan that the optimizer has produced for the query. If six processes are dispatched for that operation, the degree of parallelism for that statement (the whole statement, not just the operation in the statement) is six. It is possible (even probable) that Oracle will start additional processes for other parts of the query's execution plan (e.g., one set of processes for the full table scan and a wholly different set of processes for the subsequent sort) at the same time. In this case, the degree of parallelism is the largest number of processes assigned to one operation of the statement. Figure 6.1 shows an example of multiple parallel processes working on multiple operations of a SQL statement.

Finally, if in the processes of attempting to allocate server processes the coordinator cannot allocate any more parallel server processes, the coordinator processes the query in serial rather than in parallel, and it does so without error or notification. Once the parallel server processes have completed their work, the Parallel Query Coordinator is responsible for coordinating the result sets returned from the server processes.

The Parallel Server Processes

The parallel server processes are assigned at system startup to the *parallel server pool*. The initial number of parallel server processes started in the pool is determined by the init.ora setting **parallel_min_servers**. The default value for this parameter is 0, and the valid range of values is between 0 and the value of **parallel_max_servers**. Determine how to set **parallel_max_servers** based on how many parallel operations you would expect to occur on your system.

As system demand increases, Query Coordinators start other parallel server processes until the maximum number has been started, as defined by the init.ora setting **parallel_max_servers**. **parallel_max_servers** has a default value that varies by platform (its maximum value is generally 256). The recommended setting of this parameter is two times the number of CPUs plus one, although it can go higher if your system will handle the load.

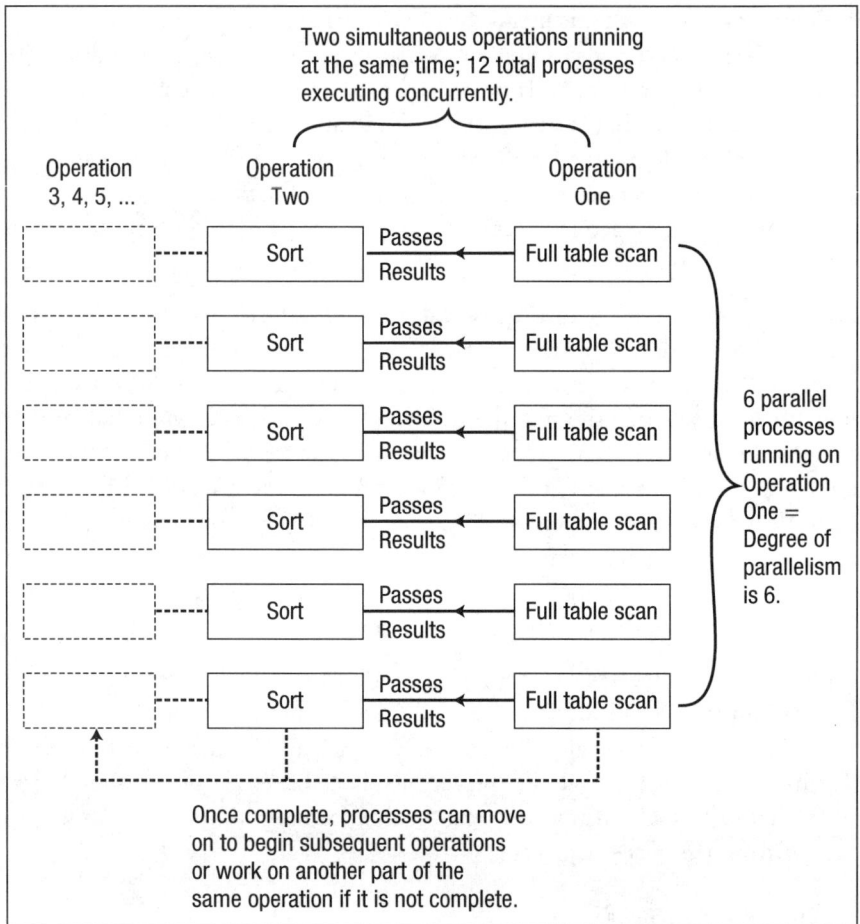

Figure 6.1   The degree of parallelism in multiple operations.

If a certain number of seconds passes, as defined by **parallel_server_idle_time,** Oracle reduces the number of unused server processes in the pool to the value **parallel_min_servers.**

It is the responsibility of the parallel server processes to take chunks of data that the parallel coordinator process has assigned to them and process them, returning the results to the coordinator. Once the server process has completed its task, it may be used for another parallel operation in the same transaction, or the query coordinator may return it to the server pool for reuse.

Note: In some cases, the parallel server processes (e.g., SELECT statements) are returned to the pool immediately. However, with other transactions, until the transaction is completed via a COMMIT, the parallel server processes used during the operation are not available for other operations outside that transaction.

One of the benefits of the multiple parallel server process design is that each parallel server process is assigned its own rollback segment. Although one parallel server process may share a rollback segment with another (for example, you have more parallel server processes running than available rollback segments), it is more likely that the server processes will be distributed among different rollback segments. Oracle uses a simplified two-phase commit process to manage the processes and the "undo" they generate. Oracle guarantees, through this process, that you will never see a partially committed parallel operation. This is one of the primary reasons that you can execute only one parallel DML operation per transaction.

Another final consideration has to do with recovery if a parallel process fails. When recovery of a failed transaction/user process occurs, SMON rolls back the operation serially. This means that it can take much longer to do the rollback; in fact, a rollback of a failed parallel transaction by the SMON process is calculated as the degree of parallelism of the process × the process run time up until the point of the failure. Figure 6.2 shows a diagram about how a parallel server and the query coordinator work together to execute a simple parallel query.

For the purposes of the OCP exam, you need a general working knowledge of what the Query Coordinator is and what the parallel server processes are, and how these two processes work together.

The Server Pool

When the Oracle instance is started, the server pool is established with a number of parallel query servers started and ready to be called to action by the query coordinators. The number of parallel query servers that are started is defined by the **parallel_min_servers** init.ora parameter. Unused servers are removed from this pool when the server has reached **parallel_server_idle_time**, up to a maximum of **parallel_min_servers**. Oracle never allows fewer than **parallel_min_servers** parallel servers to be available at any time. Keep in mind that these are actual Oracle processes being started; therefore, they have some impact on CPU and memory even when they are not in use.

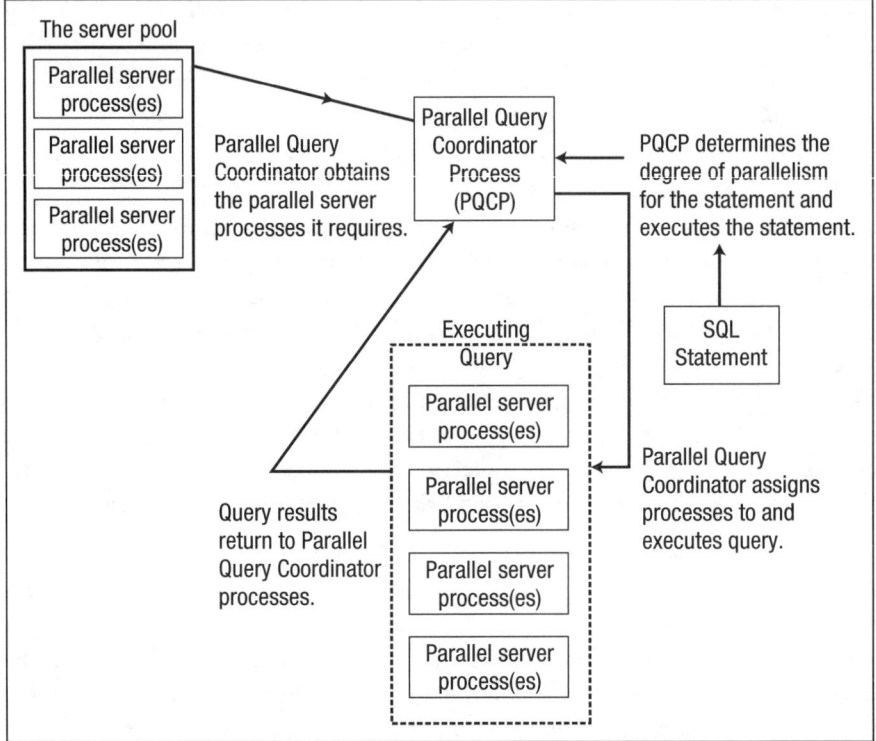

Figure 6.2 How a parallel server and the Query Coordinator work together.

Parallel Query Operations

To properly answer the questions on the Oracle OCP exam, it is important that you understand how Oracle parallelizes DML and DDL statements, and how the different processes are used in parallel processing. In this section, we will review the overall workings behind parallel query operations.

Preparing For The Query

When a user submits a SQL statement to the database to be processed, the statement is parsed, going through the normal syntax and shared pool checks. Then, the optimizer and the Parallel Query Coordinator work together to decide if the statement is a candidate for parallelization. First, the optimizer determines the execution plan of the statement (assuming it's not already in the shared pool, in which case the existing plan is used). Then, the Parallel Query Coordinator determines the parallelization method for each operation. The Coordinator decides whether the operation can even be done in parallel. If it can, the Coordinator determines the number of server processes—or the degree of parallelism—to be assigned to the operation. Oracle determines this by looking at the hint included in the statement.

If there is no hint, Oracle refers to the *reference table* to determine the degree of parallelism. The definition of a reference table is somewhat different depending on the kind of parallelism being done. For a parallel query (e.g., **SELECT**), Oracle looks at the tables and indexes in the part of the query that will be parallelized. The object with the highest degree of parallelism set is chosen. The highest degree of parallelism is also known as the *maximum query directive*. With parallel DML, the reference table is the object being modified. If the DML statement includes a subquery, that operation's degree of parallelism is the same as the degree of parallelism defined on the table being modified. Finally, for parallel DDL, the reference table is the object being created, rebuilt, split, or moved. Again, if the statement contains a subquery, that subquery uses the same level of parallelism as the main statement.

Once the number of parallel server processes is decided on, the Parallel Query Coordinator determines how the work is to be divided amongst the server processes, thus determining the *redistribution requirement* of the operation, or determining how each parallel operation should access the rows.

Once the Parallel Query Coordinator has completed its job, the optimizer determines the operations' order of execution, and then the final execution plan is crafted. It is critical to understand that in the execution plan, there are *parent operations* and *child operations*. A parent operation requires output from its child operation before it can begin its processing. A parent operation can begin its processing once a child starts to send output to it; there is no need for the parent operation to wait until the child operation has completed its operation before it begins processing rows. This is known as a *producer/consumer relationship*, with child processes (producers) sending results to parent operations (consumers).

Executing The Query

Both the parent and child operations can be done in parallel at the same time, each operation having its own set of parallel server processes. This is known as *inter-operation parallelism*. The process of a single operation being parallelized is known as *intra-operation parallelism*. Thus, in Oracle, not only can a single operation be done in parallel, but up to two operations can also be done in parallel at the same time. Note the primary restriction is that only two inter-operation parallelized operations may occur at the same time (and, actually given Oracle's design, this is all that need be run at any given time).

> *Note: When one server process has completed an operation for a step in the execution plan of the query, it will move onto another operation*

within the same step of the execution plan (for example, a full table scan of a table). If the step is complete, the server process will begin working on the subsequent operation (for example, a sort operation).

Finally, there are times when you will not have enough parallel server processes available to process an operation with the degree of parallelism that is requested. If there are not enough server processes available, the statement might actually process more slowly than if it were processed by single, nonparallelized operations. You may specify a minimum number of server processes by including the **parallel_min_percent** parameter in the init.ora. This parameter specifies the minimum number of parallel processes that must be available as a percentage of the total number of processes requested (either through a hint, the setting assigned to the table, or the default system setting). If the number of server processes cannot be used, an error is returned to the calling process.

Figure 6.3 shows an example of the inter-operation and intra-operation parallelism of the following SQL statement:

```
SELECT * FROM parts ORDER BY part_no;
```

In this example, assume that the **PARTS** table has no indexes and that it is a partitioned table.

In this diagram, there is a sort operation after the partitioned full table scan. The use of the **ORDER BY** clause forces the sort operation, but this operation can be done in parallel also. Although the degree of parallelism is 4, there are actually 8 parallel processes running at the same time in the figure, an example of inter-operation parallelism. Four are processing the rows from the table (the child processes), and the other four are operating on the sort (the parent processes). As rows are returned from the child processes, they are assigned to the correct parent process for the sorting process. Thus, a table scan returning an employee row with a name that begins with "C%" is assigned to the subsequent processes that are sorting the results. There will be multiple sort processes running. Oracle will pass a row returned to the process that will handle the "C" range, which would perhaps be a process processing the range of letters A through G.

Once the optimizer and the parallel coordinator have completed pre-processing the statement in the parse phase, the statement is executed and the data is fetched. In summary, when a parallel statement is executed, the following steps occur during the parallel operation:

1. The foreground process executing the SQL statement becomes the parallel coordinator.

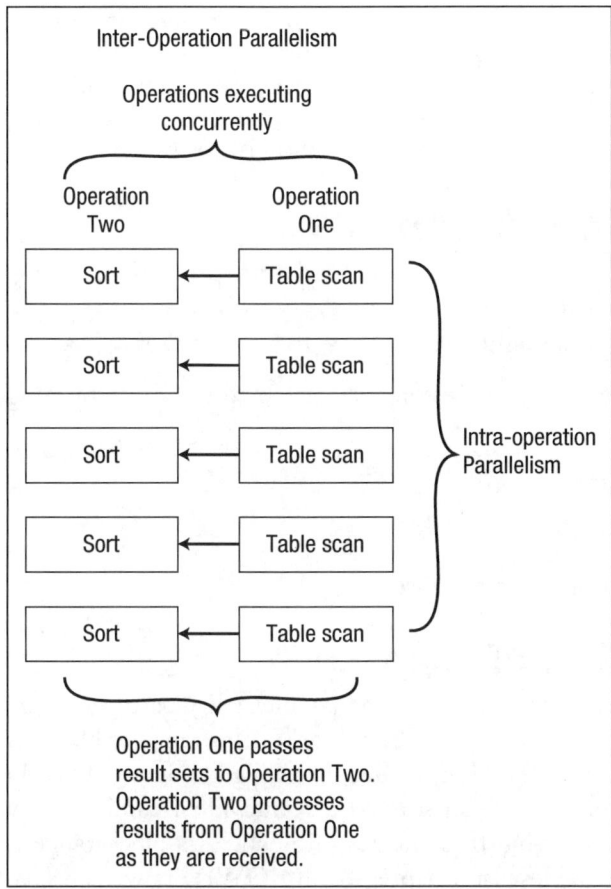

Figure 6.3   Inter-operation and intra-operation parallelism.

2. The execution plan is decided, the degree of parallelism is determined, and the execution of the statement begins.

3. The coordinator obtains the number of parallel server processes from the shared server pool. If more are needed, the coordinator starts these additional processes.

4. Oracle executes each operation of the statement in parallel, if possible. Up to two separate operations may be parallelized at a time.

5. When the statement has been processed, the coordinator returns any resulting sets of data to the user process that issues the statements and then returns the parallel server processes back to the server pool.

 Make sure you are clear on how Oracle determines how many parallel processes to use. Typically, hints take precedence over table settings and table settings take precedence over defaults. Also, make sure you understand the difference between inter-operation parallelism and intra-operation parallelism.

Parallelization Methods

Now that you understand the processes associated with parallel processing, let's review in a bit more detail the various parallel execution paths that can be taken as well as see what you might need to know to pass your OCP exam.

When using parallel query, Oracle uses one of these methods of performing parallel queries or DML:

1. Parallelize by block range

2. Parallelize by partition

3. Parallel processing using slave processes

Parallelize By Block Range

When executing a parallel query that uses the parallelize by partition range method, Oracle divides the table into ranges of blocks. This range of blocks is also known as a *ROWID range*, and it is divided into a high and low **ROWID** range for the purposes of the parallel scans. Each individual parallel query process then works on processing these ranges of blocks. If a block range is being used on partitioned tables (see Chapter 4), no **ROWID** range can span more than one partition; however, each partition may consist of one or more range partitions within the partition boundaries. Also, a parallel query on a partitioned table might be able to take advantage of partition pruning, thus making it faster than an equivalent nonpartitioned block range query on the same object.

For a block range lookup, Oracle starts as many parallel query processes as it determines are needed, up to the maximum number configured in init.ora. The number of processes that are chosen is defined in this hierarchical order:

1. The number of processes defined in the hint associated with the SQL being executed.

2. In the absence of a hint, the default degree of parallelism established for the table.

3. In the absence of the first two, the default values as established by the Oracle server based on the number of CPUs or disks.

When Oracle uses parallelize by block range to process parallel queries on **SELECT** statements, the scan of one table in the query must be a full table scan. In addition, a parallel query on a **SELECT** statement occurs only if the table queried on has been defined with a parallel clause, or if a parallel hint is included in the SQL query (see specific query type rules in the section entitled "Parallel Processing of DML").

The following operations on tables and indexes can be parallelized by using the block range method:

➤ Queries using table scans (including queries in DML and DDL statements)

➤ Partition operations: **MOVE, SPLIT,** and **REBUILD** index partitions

➤ **CREATE INDEX** on a nonpartitioned index

➤ **CREATE TABLE...AS SELECT** on nonpartitioned tables

Figure 6.4 shows an example of a parallel operation by block range.

Statements That Parallelize By Partition

When executing a query using the parallelize by partition method, Oracle requires that one object in the query be partitioned. The partition is the most granular unit that Oracle uses in a parallelized operation that involves

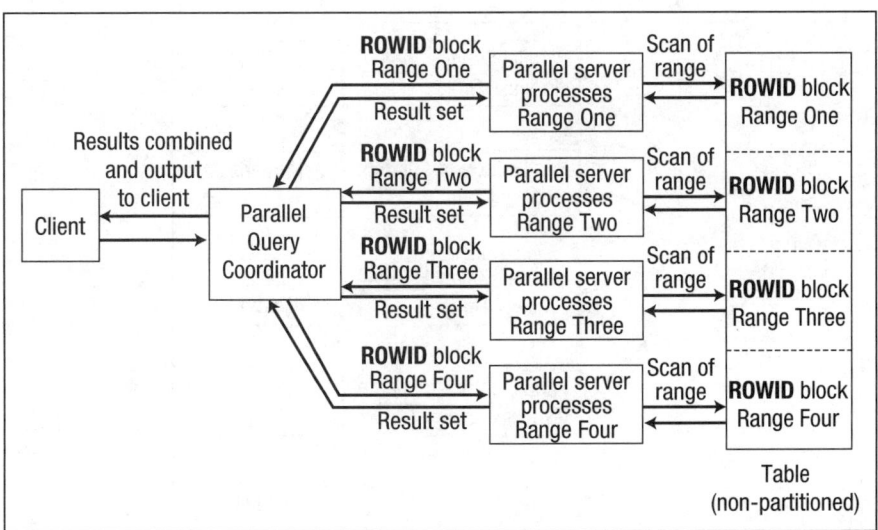

Figure 6.4 Diagram of a parallel operation by block range.

partitioned objects. No separate parallelization operations take place within the partition itself.

When a parallelize by partition operation is executed on a partitioned object, a parallel server process is assigned to each partition of the table or index, which is needed for the query. Again, partition pruning may well reduce the numbers of partitions that need to be processed during the query, further speeding the process and reducing the number of parallel server processes needed.

The number of partitions may exceed the number of parallel server processes used in the query, so only one parallel server process accesses a single partition. However, that single server process may, in fact, process multiple partitions.

Oracle uses parallelize by partition for several operations, including:

➤ **CREATE INDEX**

➤ **CREATE TABLE...AS SELECT**

➤ **UPDATE** and **DELETE** operations

➤ **INSERT...SELECT**

➤ **ALTER INDEX...REBUILD**

➤ Queries that use range scans on a partitioned index

Figure 6.5 shows an example of a parallel operation by partition.

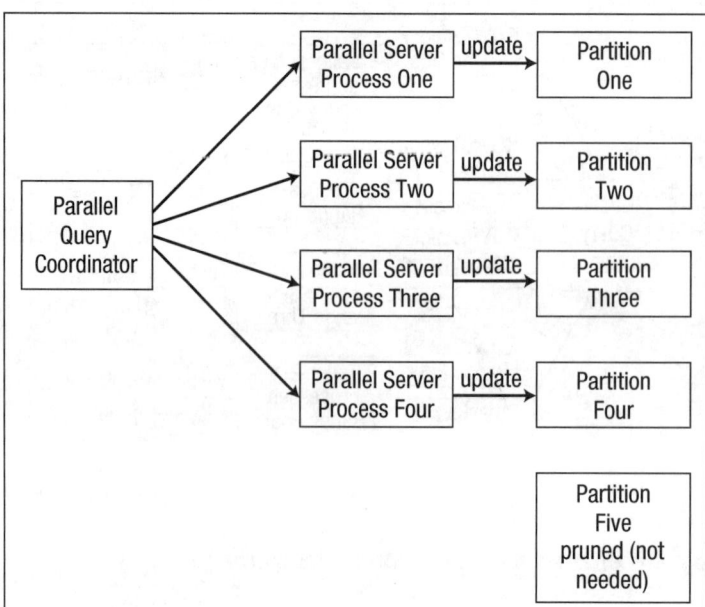

Figure 6.5   Diagram of a parallel operation by partition.

Parallelize By Parallel Server Processes

This option is available only for **INSERT...SELECT** on nonpartitioned tables. It allows the multiple parallel server processes to divide the work on an insert operation. The insert operation distributes part of the **INSERT** operation among the parallel server processes, which proceed to insert the information into the object.

Parallel Processing Need-To-Knows

This section contains some miscellaneous need-to-know items that relate to parallel processing. This includes the new Oracle8 **NOLOGGING** option, how to enable parallel DML, and using hints in your SQL code.

NOLOGGING In Oracle8

In Oracle8, a new option, **NOLOGGING**, is made available to further enhance the performance of many DML commands. This option, used in combination with parallel DML/DDL, can significantly speed up the processing of updates, new table creation, or data movement operations. The **NOLOGGING** feature disables redo logging on the database, generating less I/O and improving performance. Once the **NOLOGGING** operation is complete, the administrator should back up the database because you cannot recover the **NOLOGGING** operation (but forward recovery of all the other database objects is not compromised). You can define objects as **NOLOGGING** when they are created. In addition, you can change at any time the **NOLOGGING** attribute of the table, partition, or index that you create. You can set the **NOLOGGING** mode for a table, partition, index, or tablespace. **NOLOGGING** mode can also be applied to these statements:

➤ SQL*Loader direct loads

➤ Direct load **INSERT** statements

➤ CREATE TABLE...AS SELECT

➤ CREATE INDEX

➤ ALTER TABLE...MOVE PARTITION

➤ ALTER TABLE...SPLIT PARTITION

➤ ALTER INDEX...SPLIT PARTITION

➤ ALTER INDEX...REBUILD

➤ ALTER INDEX...REBUILD PARTITION

Enabling Parallel DML

You must enable parallel DML in a session in order to be able to issue commands that use parallel DML. You do this at the session level using the **ALTER SESSION** command in each session. There is no method of enabling DML database-wide. You must issue this statement at the beginning of a transaction, or an error will be returned. After you enable parallel DML, if a statement fails, parallel DML is not disabled. You can issue parallel DDL without enabling parallel DML. To enable parallel DML, issue the following command:

```
ALTER SESSION ENABLE PARALLEL DML;
```

Several types of queries can disable parallel DML from being executed. Issuing serial **UPDATE**, **INSERT**, or **DELETE** statements in a transaction prevents you from doing parallel operations in that transaction. Executing a **SELECT FOR UPDATE** or issuing a **LOCK TABLE** or **EXPLAIN PLAN** command also prevents you from executing parallel DML until you have committed the transaction. These restrictions do not apply to running multiple parallel **SELECT** queries.

Setting Object Definitions To Enable Parallelism

When you are creating tables, indexes, and partitions within tables and indexes, the **PARALLEL** clause is available for you to use. This clause indicates that a default degree of parallelism is preferred when issuing a query against the object. You can set the **PARALLEL** clause when you are creating the object, or you may set it by altering an object that already exists. You may unset the option by using the **ALTER TABLE** command and then using the **NOPARALLEL** option.

Hints

Several hints are available with Oracle8 to manipulate parallel processing of a statement. Hints are embedded in comment delimiters (/* and */) at the beginning of the SQL statement, appearing after the command keyword (e.g., **SELECT**). When using hints, you begin the hint with a /*. Following the opening of the hint, a + immediately follows the /* with no spaces. A hint is very particular about syntax, and the + must be immediately after the /*, and no spaces are allowed. A SQL statement with a hint might look something like this:

```
SELECT /*+ PARALLEL(EMP, 6) */ count(*) from EMP;
```

Note that the **PARALLEL** keyword is used in the hint. The table name and the requested degree of parallelism are then also included in parentheses.

If you have a multi-table join, you may use multiple **PARALLEL** statements within the same hint for each table for which you wish to request a parallel scan. Hints do not return errors if they are coded incorrectly, so be careful and always make sure the statement you execute is doing what you expect it to do. If the hint is incorrect, the statement executes serially. When you issue the **PARALLEL** directive (and in the parentheses define the table and request the degree of parallelism to be assigned to that table), your statement executes in parallel.

The hints available to request parallelism of an operation and their meaning are:

➤ *PARALLEL*—Indicates a request to parallelize the process.

➤ *NOPARALLEL*—Indicates a request to disable parallel processing for the statement.

➤ *APPEND*—Used for direct load inserts (see section titled "Direct Load Insert" later in this chapter for more information). This mode is used by default for a parallel insert. This hint can apply to both serial and parallel operations.

➤ *NOAPPEND*—Disables direct load inserts.

Parallel Processing Of DML

This section reviews specific rules that are associated with different query types. This includes in what conditions a query can be parallelized, what degree of parallelization is selected, restrictions, and other information. This is the meat of what's likely to be on the OCP exam.

DML Statements You Can Parallelize In Oracle8

Oracle8 now allows you to parallelize many database operations, including:

➤ Full table scan operations

➤ Nested loop joins

➤ Sort merge joins

➤ Hash joins

➤ Index accesses

➤ **NOT IN** clauses

➤ **GROUP BY** statements

➤ **SELECT DISTINCT** statements

➤ **UNION** and **UNION ALL** statements

➤ Group (aggregate) operations

➤ PL/SQL functions called from SQL

➤ **ORDER BY** operations

➤ **UPDATE** and **DELETE** operations

➤ **INSERT** operations using the **SELECT** clause

➤ Star query transformations

We will now look at the different DML statement types that can be parallelized in Oracle8. They include **SELECT, INSERT, UPDATE,** and **DELETE** statements. We will also talk about parallel inserts when using the **SELECT** clause and direct load inserts. Finally, we will discuss general restrictions on parallel DML.

SELECT Statements

A **SELECT** statement is parallelized only if a **PARALLEL** hint is included in the query, or if one of the objects associated with the query was created or altered to include a **PARALLEL** declaration. Additionally, **SELECT** statements must contain one of the following operations:

➤ Full table scan

➤ Multiple partition index range scan

The degree of parallelism for a **SELECT** statement is determined by the value in the hint in the query. Lacking a hint, the degree of parallelism is determined by the highest **PARALLEL** declaration value for one of the objects being accessed. The specification in the hint always takes precedence over the object settings.

One particular thing to note in Oracle8 regarding indexes is parallelism. Previous to Oracle8, only full table scans could be parallelized. Now with Oracle8, operations against partitioned indexes (e.g., Index Range Scans) can be parallelized as well.

Below is an example of a SQL **SELECT** query with a **PARALLEL** hint.

Here, you are requesting that the **emp** table be processed in parallel with a degree of parallelism of 6:

```
SELECT /*+ PARALLEL(EMP, 6) */ count(*) FROM emp;
```

UPDATE And DELETE Statements

UPDATE and DELETE operations can be parallelized only if the objects are partitioned (see Chapter 4 for more information on partitioning). In addition, Oracle does not parallelize operations within a partition. A result is that DELETEs on a single partition will not be parallelized (for example, if you are deleting all of the first quarter's data, which sits all in one partition, that DELETE operation will not be parallelized). (As you saw in Chapter 4, however, you will benefit from partition pruning.) Oracle parallelizes the UPDATE and DELETE operations only if a parallel hint is included in the operation, or if the table being modified has a parallel specification.

The degree of parallelism for UPDATE and DELETE statements is determined by the UPDATE/DELETE PARALLEL hint or by the PARALLEL declaration value of the objects being updated or deleted from. The specification in the hint always takes precedence over the object settings.

Subqueries of an UPDATE or DELETE statement may also be parallelized, though this requires that they have their own parallel hint or clause. Parallelism done in a subquery has no effect on the decision to parallelize the main UPDATE or DELETE operation. In addition, the level of parallelism of a subquery is independent of the main query's level of parallelism.

If the parallel hint is used, the degree of parallelism is determined first by the degree of parallelism specified in the hint. If no hint is given, then the degree of parallelism is that of the table the operation is being performed on. The maximum degree of parallelism is the total number of partitions that are assigned to the table. Only one parallel server process can update or delete from a single partition at any time. Once the parallel UPDATE or DELETE operation is complete, you must commit the transaction before you can issue another SQL command.

Below is an example of a SQL DELETE query with a PARALLEL hint. Here, you are requesting that the **emp** table be processed in parallel with a degree of parallelism of 3:

```
DELETE /*+ PARALLEL(EMP, 3) */ from EMP;
```

INSERT...SELECT Statements

You can parallelize inserts that take advantage of the **SELECT** subquery. Both the **INSERT** and **SELECT** operations are parallelized separately, except for the degree of parallelism.

> *Note: A table does not have to be partitioned to have an **INSERT**... SELECT operation parallelized. This is because Oracle8 can use multiple query servers to insert into rows simultaneously.*

You can use several ways to cause the **INSERT...SELECT** statement to be parallelized. First, you can use hints in the **INSERT** statement and/or the **SELECT** statements. Further, if you do not use hints but have defined **PARALLEL** clauses for the tables being inserted into or being queried as a part of the index, Oracle attempts to parallelize the statement. The **INSERT** operation may not be parallelized, whereas the **SELECT** operation can be, depending on the hints used and the way the tables are defined.

Oracle decides the degree of parallelism based on the whole statement once it has decided to parallelize it. The degree of parallelism is based on a selection in this order:

1. Oracle uses the degree of parallelism defined in the **INSERT** hint for the entire operation.

2. If there is no hint in the **INSERT** statement, the parallel declaration specification for the inserting table is used.

3. If a hint in the **INSERT** statement is not set, the maximum query directive is used, which means that among the tables and indexes in the query, the one object with the highest degree of parallelism determines the degree of parallelism for the entire statement.

Once the parallel **INSERT...SELECT** operation is complete, you must commit the transaction before you can issue any other DML commands (except **SELECT**) on that object.

Below is an example of a SQL **INSERT...SELECT** statement with a **PARALLEL** hint. Here, you are requesting that the **invoice_archive** (aliased as **iarc**) table be processed with a degree of parallelism of 3. The table alias, rather than the table name, is used in this hint:

```
INSERT /*+ PARALLEL(iarc,6) */ INTO invoice_archive iarc
SELECT * FROM sales WHERE invoice_no < 10000;
```

Direct Load **insert**

New for Oracle8 is the ability to do a direct load insert. Direct load insert can enhance the performance of inserts by directly formatting and writing the data to the object being inserted into without using the database buffer cache. The direct load insert appends the rows above the high-water mark of the table, much like using direct load in SQL*Loader. You can do direct load inserts into partitioned and nonpartitioned tables. Direct load insert is the default method used for **INSERT...SELECT** statements, regardless of whether the statement is executed in parallel or not.

Direct load inserts avoid both redo and undo logging, so they perform faster than normal **INSERT** statements or **CREATE TABLE...AS SELECT** statements. Another benefit that improves the performance of direct load insertS is that you can parallelize direct load inserts. A direct load insert may also be preferable for loading tables over SQL*Loader. The operation is an atomic operation and rolls back the operation if the index load fails, preventing an index from being left in **DIRECT LOAD** state, after a direct load in SQL*Loader.

To use direct load inserts, you must use the **INSERT...SELECT** form of the **INSERT** statement. The form of the statement with the **VALUES** clause does not perform a direct load insert. You use the **APPEND** hint to indicate that you wish the **INSERT** statement to do a direct load insert. You can also parallelize the direct load inserts; the degree of parallelism is first determined by the **PARALLEL** hint in the **INSERT** statement. If no **PARALLEL** hint is given, and if the table being inserted into has a **PARALLEL** definition, that definition will determine the degree of parallelism.

Three variations of direct load inserts are available:

➤ Serial or parallel

➤ Inserting into partitioned or nonpartitioned tables

➤ With or without the redo logging

Serial direct insert loads into tables (partitioned or nonpartitioned) at the high-water mark of the table or partition segment being inserted into. The high-water mark is actually moved once a commit is made, completing the transaction.

With parallel direct load inserts into a nonpartitioned table, the parallel server processes allocate new temporary segments and insert data into these temporary segments. Upon a commit, the coordinator process merges the temporary segments into the primary table segment (for more information on this mode of processing, see the "Managing Parallel Processes" section later in this chapter).

When you are doing parallel direct load inserts into a partitioned table, each parallel server process is assigned one (or more) partition(s). No more than one parallel process will work on any partition. Data is inserted beyond the high-water mark of the table. The high-water mark is then moved after the commit, to its new value. Only after the commit does the data become visible to others. Finally, to do direct load inserts, parallel DML must be enabled.

Here is an example of a SQL INSERT...SELECT statement that uses the direct load method (via a hint), along with a PARALLEL hint (a degree of parallelism of 6 is requested):

```
INSERT /*+ APPEND PARALLEL(iarc,6) */ INTO invoice_archive iarc
SELECT * FROM sales WHERE invoice_no < 10000;
```

General Restrictions On Parallel DML

There are several restrictions on parallel DML you should be aware of. These restictions are:

➤ Multiple tables can be modified by one transaction, but only one parallel statement in a transaction can access an individual table within that transaction.

➤ Queries to a table are allowed before the parallel DML statement, but not after. Any attempt to execute an operation after a parallel operation returns an error to the user.

➤ UPDATE and DELETE operations are not parallelized on nonpartitioned tables.

➤ Global unique indexes are not supported for parallel update operations.

➤ If the init.ora parameter row_locking=intent is set, no parallelism of INSERTs, UPDATEs, or DELETEs is performed.

➤ You cannot perform parallel actions on a table with enabled triggers associated with it.

➤ Replication does not support parallelism.

➤ Parallel DML cannot occur on tables with object columns, lob columns, or index-organized tables.

➤ Once you have executed a parallel operation, the transaction associated with that operation cannot become a distributed transaction. In other words, once parallel DML has occurred, until the commit, you cannot attempt DML on another table through a database link.

➤ Parallel DML does not support clustered tables.

➤ Parallel inserts are not supported for any global index.

➤ Only DML statements without functions or with functions that do not read or write to the database are parallelized.

 You should become familiar with these rules before you take your OCP exam.

Oracle does not warn you if you have violated any of these rules, and instead just runs the statement serially. The only exception to this is the first rule which will cause an Oracle error to be generated.

Additional rules relate to integrity restrictions and parallel DML. They are:

➤ Queries on tables with **NOT NULL** and **CHECK** constraints can be parallelized with no problem.

➤ Queries with **UNIQUE** and **PRIMARY KEY** constraints can be parallelized only if the index associated with that key is local.

➤ Tables with foreign key restrictions have parallel restrictions because of Oracle's requirement to check the relationship. The restrictions are:

 ➤ **INSERT** statements issued on the child table of a foreign key (FK) relationship are not parallelized.

 ➤ **UPDATE** and **DELETE** statements on the parent and the child may be parallelized.

 ➤ **DELETE CASCADE** operations are not parallelized.

➤ If a table has self-referential integrity established, parallelism can occur only if the primary keys of the table are not involved in the operation.

➤ If a table has deferred integrity constraints associated with it, parallel operations are not permitted.

Parallel Processing Of DDL

Oracle8 allows many different types of DDL to be parallelized as well. This allows for the creation of database objects in a potentially much shorter time frame that was previously possible. This section addresses parallel DDL and the rules associated with it.

DDL Statements You Can Parallelize In Oracle8

Oracle8 now allows you to parallelize many database operations, including:

➤ **CREATE** and **ALTER INDEX...REBUILD** commands

➤ **REBUILD INDEX PARTITION**

➤ **SPLIT** and **MOVE PARTITION** operations

➤ **CREATE TABLE AS SELECT**

➤ The **ENABLE CONSTRAINTS** command

Let's look at the different DDL statement types that can be parallelized, as listed in the bullets above.

CREATE INDEX Or ALTER INDEX...REBUILD

The only way to achieve parallel execution of an **ALTER INDEX** statement to create a new index is to use the **PARALLEL** clause in the **CREATE INDEX** or **ALTER INDEX** command. When rebuilding an existing index, use the **ALTER INDEX...REBUILD** operation. The **ALTER INDEX...REBUILD** operation can be parallelized only for a nonpartitioned index. To rebuild index partitions, use the **ALTER INDEX...REBUILD PARTITION** statement, which can be parallelized by a **PARALLEL** clause. The **PARALLEL** clause for the **REBUILD** and **CREATE** operations determine the degree of parallelism for the entire operation. If these operations are not specified, the degree of parallelism is the number of CPUs.

Here is an example of a **CREATE INDEX** statement that requests a degree of parallelism of 4:

```
CREATE INDEX ix_emp_01 ON EMP(emp_id)
PARALLEL (DEGREE 4);
```

MOVE Or SPLIT PARTITION

The **MOVE** or **SPLIT PARTITION** operations can also use the **PARALLEL** clause to speed up execution. These statements manipulate partitions in partitioned tables and indexes, and can thus take a great deal of time to execute. Partitioning will speed up the movement or split of a partition. The degree of parallelism is defined in the statement using the **PARALLEL** clause. If the degree of parallelism is not defined in these statement, it defaults to the number of CPUs.

CREATE TABLE AS SELECT

The **CREATE TABLE AS SELECT** statement contains both DDL and DML. Both operations can be parallelized, and the **CREATE** part of the command follows the same rules as other DDL operations do. Oracle cannot parallelize this command when creating and populating clustered tables.

The decision to parallelize the **SELECT** statement is fairly straightforward. First, the query must contain a **PARALLEL** hint; if it doesn't, the **SELECT** statement may be parallelized if the **CREATE TABLE** part of the SQL statement has a **PARALLEL** clause. Finally, if the objects being queried have a **PARALLEL** declaration associated with them, the **SELECT** is parallelized. The next requirement for the **SELECT** statement is that it must be either a full table scan or a multi-partition index range scan. If both of these requirements are met, the **SELECT** statement is parallelized.

To parallelize the **CREATE TABLE** statement, the **PARALLEL** clause must be included with the **CREATE TABLE** statement. Oracle will attempt to parallelize both the **CREATE** and **SELECT** portions of the statement in this case. Of course, the **SELECT** operation can be parallelized independent of the **CREATE TABLE** operation.

The degree of parallelism is first defined for the entire statement if the **PARALLEL** clause of the **CREATE** statement is used. If this is not the case, the number of CPUs becomes the default.

*Note: The degree specified in the hint of the **SELECT** clause will be ignored in a **CREATE TABLE AS…SELECT** statement.*

Here is an example of a **CREATE TABLE… AS SELECT** statement with a degree of parallelism of 4 requested on the operation:

```
CREATE TABLE temp_emp PARALLEL(DEGREE 4)
AS SELECT * FROM emp;
```

Summary Of Rules

Table 6.1 summarizes what can be a confusing set of rules associated with which operations can take advantage of parallel DML with nonpartitioned tables, and which ones cannot.

Table 6.1	DML statements and allowance of parallelized DML.			
SQL Statement To Be Executed	Parallel Allowed When Non-Partitioned	Parallel Allowed When Partitioned	Method To Determine If Statement Should Be Parallelized*	Method To Determine Degree Of Parallelism
SELECT	If a full table scan is used, *or* Index range scan spanning multiple partitions is used	Yes	Hint, Table	Maximum Query Directive, Hint, Table
UPDATE/ DELETE**	No	Yes	Hint, Table (Being modified)	Hint, Table (Being modified)
INSERT	Yes	Yes	Hint, Table (Being inserted)	Hint (Insert), Table, Maximum Query Directive (query table)

*Note that the order in the column *Method To Determine If The Statement Should Be Parallelized* does not matter. The order in the column *Method To Determine The Degree Of Parallelism* does matter, and the degree of parallelism is determined in the order listed.

Note that subqueries are parallelized separately. The decision to parallel subqueries is based on **SELECT *parallelism criteria, as listed above. They will not determine parallelization of the associated* **UPDATE/DELETE** *statement.*

In addition, Table 6.2 summarizes what can be a confusing set of rules associated with which operations can take advantage of parallel DDL with nonpartitioned tables, and which ones cannot.

It is critical that you understand what operations can be parallelized and which ones cannot. You should understand which operations can be parallelized on partitioned tables and which ones do not require partitioning.

Table 6.2	DDL statements and when parallelized DDL is allowed.			
SQL Statement To Be Executed	Parallel Allowed When Non-Partitioned	Parallel Allowed When Partitioned	Method To Determine If Statement Should Be Parallelized*	Method To Determine Degree Of Parallelism
CREATE INDEX	Y	Y	PARALLEL directive	PARALLEL directive
ALTER INDEX ...REBUILD	Y	N	PARALLEL directive	PARALLEL directive
ALTER INDEX ...REBUILD PARTITION	N/A	Y	PARALLEL directive	PARALLEL directive
CREATE TABLE ...AS SELECT (CREATE PART)	Y	Y	PARALLEL directive	PARALLEL directive
(Query)	Y (Follows SELECT query rules)	Y	Hint, PARALLEL clause in DDL statement, PARALLEL directive in definition of of table being created	PARALLEL clause in DDL statement, default degree of parallelism

Note that the order in the column Method To Determine If Statement Should Be Parallelized does not matter. The order in the column Method To Determine Degree Of Parallelism does in fact mater and the degree of parallelism will be determined in the order listed.

Managing Parallel Processes

This section covers issues revolving around management of parallel processing. In it we will cover space management issues that arise out of the use of parallelism, and what the DBA needs to be cautious about in terms of space availability. Also we will look at the various views Oracle provides to manage parallel DML/DDL operation.

Space Management Issues

When you issue parallel DDL CREATE requests, you must consider the additional space requirements associated with these operations. As the parallel processes create tables or indexes, they allocate an extent equivalent to the next extent size defined for the object that is being built. When you are creating a table, Oracle may trim some of the space from the table after the parallel operation. For example, if you parallelize a **CREATE TABLE...AS SELECT** operation with six parallel processes, and the table is defined with an **INITIAL** extent of 5M, you end up with a requirement for 30M of space (six parallel processes times 5M per process). The coordinator then combines the extents. At this time, it may decide to trim some of the extents, making the final size of the table less than the 30M used during processing. The same type of operation occurs when you create indexes in parallel. Oracle allocates extents for each query server process of size **INITIAL**.

During parallel creation of tables and indexes, you may create fragmentation problems within the database. In certain cases, Oracle decides to trim free space from the table, returning it to the database. This space is generally small enough to not be very usable by the database because it contains few contiguous free blocks. In other cases, the additional space is not returned to the system and instead is represented by empty blocks in the object that was created. In this situation, the space is available for **INSERT**s and **UPDATE**s into the object in the future.

The determination as to whether the space is returned to the system is based on the **minextents** parameter, set when a tablespace is created. If the unused space is greater than this amount, the unused space is returned to the database. If the free space amount is smaller than the **minextents** parameter, it is retained in the object.

Parallel Query Views For Database Administrators (DBAs)

Oracle has provided several views for DBAs to reference. They are useful when they are trying to determine:

➤ If a statement is running using parallel processing in a given session

➤ The status of the parallel slaves

➤ Other administrative issues

These views, their descriptions, and example queries from each are listed below.

View **V$PQ_SESSTAT** contains summary information on a session's use of parallel SQL statements. It is visible only from the session that is executing the statements. See Listing 6.1 for an example of the output from **V$PQ_SESSTAT**.

Listing 6.1   Using the **V$PQ_SESSTAT** view.

```
SQL> SELECT * FROM v$pq_sesstat;

STATISTIC                        LAST_QUERY SESSION_TOTAL
-------------------------------- ---------- -------------
Queries Parallelized                     0             1
DML Parallelized                         1             1
DFO Trees                                1             2
Server Threads                           4             0
Allocation Height                        4             0
Allocation Width                         0             0
Local Msgs Sent                          0            96
Distr Msgs Sent                          0             0
Local Msgs Recv'd                        0            96
Distr Msgs Recv'd                        0             0
```

View **V$PQ_SLAVE** contains information on the parallel query slaves, including current and total CPU time used by each slave, the number of messages sent back and forth, and if they are idle or active. You can use this view to verify that a particular transaction is doing parallel queries (if it is the only transaction running). You can also use it to see how many query slave processes the database has started. See Listing 6.2 for an example of the structure and output of the **V$PQ_SLAVE** table.

Listing 6.2   Using the **V$PQ_SLAVE** table.

```
SQL> DESC v$pq_slave
Name                              Null?    Type
-------------------------------- -------- ----
SLAVE_NAME                                VARCHAR2(4)
STATUS                                    VARCHAR2(4)
SESSIONS                                  NUMBER
IDLE_TIME_CUR                             NUMBER
BUSY_TIME_CUR                             NUMBER
CPU_SECS_CUR                              NUMBER
MSGS_SENT_CUR                             NUMBER
MSGS_RCVD_CUR                             NUMBER
IDLE_TIME_TOTAL                           NUMBER
BUSY_TIME_TOTAL                           NUMBER
CPU_SECS_TOTAL                            NUMBER
MSGS_SENT_TOTAL                           NUMBER
MSGS_RCVD_TOTAL                           NUMBER

SQL> SELECT slave_name,status,sessions FROM v$pq_slave;
```

```
SLAV STAT  SESSIONS
----  ----  --------
P000  IDLE        22
P001  IDLE        22
P002  IDLE        22
P003  IDLE         9
P004  IDLE         6
P005  IDLE         6
P006  IDLE         0
P007  IDLE         0

8 rows selected.
```

View **V$PQ_SYSSTAT** contains rollup totals for session statistics that relate to parallel query processing. It contains columns that tell you how many parallel servers are active and how many are busy. See Listing 6.3 for detailed output of the **V$PQ_SYSSTAT** table.

Listing 6.3   Using the **V$PQ_SYSSTAT** view.

```
SQL> SELECT * FROM v$pq_sysstat;

STATISTIC                         VALUE
-----------------------------   --------
Servers Busy                         0
Servers Idle                         8
Servers Highwater                    6
Server Sessions                     87
Servers Started                      0
Servers Shutdown                     0
Servers Cleaned Up                   0
Queries Initiated                    9
DML Initiated                       12
DFO Trees                           23
Sessions Active                      0
Local Msgs Sent                    961
Distr Msgs Sent                      0
Local Msgs Recv'd                 1006
Distr Msgs Recv'd                    0
```

View **V$PQ_TQSTAT** contains a session-specific detailed report of parallel server message traffic between the servers and the coordinator. It contains only information for the session that is querying the view. See Listing 6.4 for a description of the columns in the **V$PQ_TQSTAT** view and sample output from the view.

Listing 6.4 Using the **V$PQ_TQSTAT** view.

```
SQL> DESC v$pq_tqstat
Name                            Null?    Type
------------------------------- -------- ----
DFO_NUMBER                               NUMBER
TQ_ID                                    NUMBER
SERVER_TYPE                              VARCHAR2(10)
NUM_ROWS                                 NUMBER
BYTES                                    NUMBER
OPEN_TIME                                NUMBER
AVG_LATENCY                              NUMBER
WAITS                                    NUMBER
TIMEOUTS                                 NUMBER
PROCESS                                  VARCHAR2(10)
INSTANCE                                 NUMBER

SQL> SELECT dfo_number, tq_id, server_type,num_rows
  2  FROM v$pq_tqstat;

DFO_NUMBER     TQ_ID SERVER_TYPE  NUM_ROWS
---------- --------- -----------  --------
         2         0 Producer         1186
         2         0 Producer            0
         2         0 Producer          568
         2         0 Consumer         1754
```

Other views that existed in Oracle7 can assist in parallel query administration:

➤ The **V$PARAMETER** view can assist in finding out if and how the database is configured for parallel queries.

➤ The **V$SYSSTAT** and **V$SESSTAT** views can be used for gathering such statistics as the number of queries and the number of DML and DDL statements issued for a query.

➤ The **pdm** column of the **V$SESSION** view is particularly useful if you wish to find out if parallel DML has been enabled for your session.

Practice Questions

Question 1

> Which Oracle statement cannot be parallelized?
>
> ○ a. **INSERT...SELECT**
>
> ○ b. **SELECT**
>
> ○ c. **INSERT...VALUES**
>
> ○ d. **DELETE**
>
> ○ e. **UPDATE**

Answer c is correct. Oracle does not parallelize **INSERT** statements using the **VALUES** clause. There is really no reason to parallelize such a statement because it inserts only a single value into a table. Answers a and b are incorrect because you can parallelize these statements. Answer d is incorrect because you can parallelize **DELETE** statements (note, however, that this is restricted to partitioned tables). Answer e is incorrect because an **UPDATE** can be parallelized. Again this is restricted to partitioned tables.

Question 2

> Which line causes the query to return an error?
>
> ○ a. **INSERT /*+ PARALEL(3) */**
>
> ○ b. **INTO SALES_HISTORY**
>
> ○ c. **SELECT * FROM SALES**
>
> ○ d. **WHERE QUARTER = 1;**
>
> ○ e. This statement does not return an error.

Answer e is correct. The statement itself runs serially without an error, even though **PARALLEL** is clearly misspelled. Remember, a misspelling of a hint is ignored, and would not return any type of error notification. Because the rest of the statement is syntactically correct, the statement does not return an error.

Question 3

> Given this situation:
>
> ```
> CREATE TABLE new_emp PARALLEL 3
> AS SELECT * FROM emp WHERE ROWNUM=0;
>
> INSERT INTO new_emp SELECT * FROM old_emp;
> ```
>
> what will be the degree of parallelism that Oracle chooses to use on this **INSERT** statement: **INSERT INTO emp SELECT * FROM old_emp; ?**
>
> ○ a. 0
> ○ b. 3
> ○ c. 6
> ○ d. 7
> ○ e. None of the above

Answer b is correct. The degree of parallelism is first determined by any hints. No hints were given in the statement, so the default level of parallelism is based on the parallel directive associated with the table itself. The **NEW_EMP** table was created using the **PARALLEL 3** clause, so by default, three parallel server processes are requested for use on the query. Answers a, c, and d are therefore incorrect. Note that this statement would not run unless the **ALTER SESSION ENABLE PARALLEL DML** command had previously been issued in the session. Answer e is incorrect because a correct answer is given.

Question 4

> When doing a parallel **SELECT** statement, how does Oracle determine the degree of parallelism?
>
> ○ a. Based on the hint included in the statement and then on the **PARALLEL** attribute setting of the object being queried
>
> ○ b. First based on the **PARALLEL** attribute setting of the object being queried and then on the database default setting based on CPUs
>
> ○ c. Based on the default database **PARALLEL** attribute set in init.ora
>
> ○ d. First based on the hint in the statement, then on the **PARALLEL** attribute of the object being queried, and finally on the default **PARALLEL** setting established in init.ora
>
> ○ e. Based on the **PARALLEL_DEGREE** setting in the init.ora

Answer a is correct. With a **SELECT** query, the degree of parallelism is defined based on a **PARALLEL** hint in the statement. If one is not included, the **PARALLEL** attribute of the table is used. Answer b is incorrect because the first consideration to parallelism is a hint, and there is not a database default degree of parallelism for **SELECT** statements. Answer c is incorrect because there is no **PARALLEL** attribute to be set in init.ora. Answer d is incorrect because it mentions a nonexistent **PARALLEL** attribute to be set in init.ora. Answer e is incorrect because there is no **PARALLEL_DEGREE** setting in the init.ora.

Question 5

As a DBA, you wish to know how many of your parallel query slaves are currently active. Which view might you select to determine this information?

○ a. **V$PQ_SESSTAT**

○ b. **V$_PQ_STAT**

○ c. **V$PQ_SLAVE**

○ d. **V$PQ_SLAVE_STATS**

○ e. **DBA_PARALLEL_SLAVES**

Answer c is correct. The **V$PQ_SLAVE** view tells you how many parallel query slaves are currently active. You could also use the **V$PQ_SYSSTAT** view for summary information on idle and active query slaves. Answer a is incorrect because the **V$PQ_SESSTAT** view provides only session-level information for parallel processes for that session. Answers b and d are incorrect because these are invalid view names. Answer e is incorrect because a correct answer is given.

Question 6

One parent and one child operation are executed on a query being parallelized. The child is sending information to the parent. What kind of process is the parent?

○ a. Consumer

○ b. Organic

○ c. Producer

○ d. Dependent

○ e. Demonstrative

Answer a is correct. The parent process that receives the data from the child is the consumer process. Answer b is incorrect because the database itself is not alive and thus is not organic. Answer c is incorrect because the child is the producer process in this case. Answer d is incorrect because there is no dependent-type relationship with parallel processing in Oracle. Answer e is incorrect there is no demonstrative relationship with parallel processes in Oracle (well...I suppose one might say there was, but it's not officially called that!).

Question 7

You issue the command **ALTER INDEX REBUILD** on a nonpartitioned table. Can this statement be parallelized?

○ a. Yes.

○ b. No.

○ c. Insufficient information exists to answer the question.

Answer b is correct. You cannot parallelize an **ALTER INDEX REBUILD** operation if an index is partitioned. You may execute the command **ALTER INDEX REBUILD PARTITION,** which allows you to parallelize a partitioned index. Answers a and c are incorrect by default.

Question 8

What will be the degree of parallelism requested for the transaction demonstrated by this example?

```
ALTER TABLE emp   PARALLEL= 6;
SELECT /*+ PARALLEL */ count(*)   from emp;
```

○ a. Six.

○ b. The degree of parallelism will default to the number of CPUs on the system.

○ c. An incorrect hint is given so it will default to six, the table setting for parallelism on that table.

○ d. No parallel processing will be done because this is a full table scan.

○ e. None of the above.

Answer a is correct. A degree of parallelism of six is requested for the transaction. Answer b is incorrect because a **SELECT** statement does not default to the number of CPUs to determine parallelism. Answer c is incorrect because **PARALLEL**, by itself, is a valid hint, and the hint syntax was not in error. Answer d is incorrect because full table scans can be parallelized with **SELECT** queries. Answer e is incorrect because a correct answer is given.

Question 9

Assume the parameter **parallel_min_servers** is set to 16, the parameter **parallel_max_servers** is set to 30, and the parameter **parallel_min_servers** is set to 50. For which of these cases will a process that requests parallelism fail?

○ a. The process will fail if **parallel_max_servers** processes have already been started.

○ b. The process will fail if **parallel_min_servers** processes have already been started.

○ c. The process will fail if the number of parallel server processes available to be assigned to the statement falls below 50 percent of the requested degree of parallelism.

○ d. The process will fail if it attempts to parallelize using more than **parallel_max_servers**.

○ e. The request will not fail in any event.

Answer c is correct. If the percentage of parallel servers, as defined by **parallel_min_servers**, is not available to process a query, that query fails and returns an error. Answer a is incorrect because it is possible for **parallel_max_servers** to have already been started, but the parallel server processes may be in an idle state and ready for use. Answer b is incorrect because **parallel_min_servers** defines how many server processes start when an instance is started. It has no real relationship to a process failing due to lack of parallel server processes. Answer d is incorrect because a request for a degree of parallelism above **parallel_max_servers** is adjusted to fit within the number of parallel server processes available and does not cause statement failure. Answer e is incorrect because the process will fail if the percentage of parallel servers, as defined by **parallel_min_servers**, is not available to process a query.

Question 10

What is the primary purpose of parallel DML?

○ a. To speed up transactions that require quick response, such as OLAP transactions

○ b. To speed up various operations on large tables that frequently take a great deal of time

○ c. To reduce CPU and memory requirements for a system

○ d. To allow more users to access a table at one time

○ e. To provide redundancy for important transactions

Answer b is correct. Parallelism speeds up various operations on large tables. It is provided to assist DBAs in managing large data volumes present in environments such as data warehouses. Answer a is incorrect because the additional overhead of parallel processing is generally not conducive to increased performance in an OLAP-type environment. These environments generally require quick response to queries, as these queries are generally retrieved by index lookup. Answer c is incorrect because parallel query processing actually increases the overhead on the system. Answer d is incorrect because parallel processing does not aim to let the database handle more users. Answer e would only be answered by someone from NASA where redundancy is a favorite buzz word (especially when you are traveling in the shuttle at several times the speed of sound). Parallelism has nothing to do with redundancy.

Need To Know More?

 Ault, Michael R.: *Oracle8 Black Book*. The Coriolis Group, 1998. ISBN 1-57610-187-8. This book deals in great depth with several new Oracle8 features, including partitioning and parallel DML.

 Bobrowski, Steve: *Oracle8 Architecture*. Oracle Press, 1998. ISBN 0-07-882274-2. This book is a good basic introduction to Oracle8 changes and in particular parallel DML and partitioning.

 Curtis, Mike: *Oracle8 and Windows NT Black Book*. The Coriolis Group, 1998. ISBN 1-57610-248-3. This book is a great book on partitioning. It contains a lot of practical information on partitioning as well as examples.

 Niemiec, Richard K.: *Oracle Performance Tuning, Tips, & Techniques*. Oracle Press, 1999. ISBN 0-07-882434-6. This is a good book on performance tuning that contains some good information on using parallel DML and DDL to tune your database.

 www.support.com is Oracle's Metalink Web site. Metalink is a vast resource of Oracle knowledge. It contains forums, search engines to find problem and bug reports, and many other features to assist the DBA.

New Oracle8 Large Object Data Types

7

Terms you'll need to understand:

√ **LOB** (Large Object) data types

√ **BFILE**

√ **BLOB**

√ **CLOB**

√ **NCLOB**

√ Internal **LOB**

√ External **LOB**

√ **LOB** locator

√ **LOB** segment

√ **LOB** index

Techniques you'll need to master:

√ Understanding the differences between **LONG** data types and **LOB** data types

√ Understanding the use and purpose of **LOB**s

√ Creating tables using **LOB**s, including defining storage clauses properly

√ Understanding how to use the **DBMS_LOB** package to manipulate **LOB**s

New Oracle8 Data Types: An Introduction

Oracle8 has introduced new data types called *LOBs* to support storage of large amounts of data, both in text and binary form, and for storage of data outside the database itself. This chapter reviews the new Oracle8 data types, why they are superior to the data types they replace, and the new **DBMS_LOB** package that Oracle provides to manipulate them.

The Demise Of The **LONG** Data Type

The introduction of Oracle8 signals the demise of the **LONG** and **LONG RAW** data types in Oracle. They store large pieces of data (sound, images, text, and the like). Although Oracle still supports the use of these data types in Oracle8, their ongoing use is not recommended. It is likely that these data types will not be supported in the future. **LONG** and **LONG RAW** data types have several inherent failings. Problems revolving around these data types include:

➤ Only one **long** or **long raw** can exist in a table at a time.

➤ You cannot index a **long** or **long raw** column.

➤ A **long** or **long raw** column can be no more than 2GB.

➤ A **long** or **long raw** column is very difficult to manipulate. In Oracle7, you could effectively manipulate a **long** or **long raw** column only by calls using the Oracle Call Interface (OCI) or convoluted PL/SQL code using the dynamic SQL package **DBMS_SQL**.

➤ A **long** or **long raw** column is stored inline with the rest of the row it is associated with, possibly causing performance problems.

➤ A **long** or **long raw** column cannot be manipulated in a trigger.

Oracle8 has addressed the shortcomings of the **LONG** and **LONG RAW** data types by introducing new **LOB** data types: CLOB, NCLOB, BLOB, and BFILE.

Introducing The Oracle8 **LOBs**

Oracle8 has introduced four **LOB** data types to replace **LONG** and **LONG RAW**. **LOBs** are database data types that store large amounts of data, much like the **LONG** and **LONG RAW** data types. **LOBs** can be contained as columns of a relational table, or they can be attributes of an object (with the exception of **NCLOBs**, which cannot be attributes of an object). The following list gives basic information about the four new Oracle8 **LOB** types, the type of **LOB** they are (**LOB**s can be internal or external, discussed shortly), and the type of data that they contain:

➤ *CLOB* (*internal LOB*)—Used to store single-byte, fixed-width character data that corresponds to the character set defined for the database

➤ *NCLOB* (*internal LOB*)—Composed of fixed-width multibyte character data that corresponds to the national character set defined for the Oracle database

➤ *BLOB* (*internal LOB*)—Composed of unstructured binary data

➤ *BFILE* (*external LOB*)—An externally stored operating system file that contains binary data

 You should know what the four types of **LOB**s are and what they are generally used for (to store character or binary data).

Oracle8 Internal **LOBs**

This section looks at the **CLOB, NCLOB**, and **BLOB LOB** data types. These **LOB** data types are called *internal* **LOB**s because the data is stored internally within the database. With the *external* **LOB** (the **BFILE** data type, examined later in this chapter), data is stored outside the database in operating system files. This section discusses how internal **LOB**s store data in the database, how to create tables that contain internal **LOB**s, and the benefits of internal **LOB**s over **LONG** and **LONG RAW** data types. For more information on manipulating internal **LOB** data types, see the "Accessing **LOB**s With SQL" section later in this chapter.

Creating Tables Using Internal **LOB** Columns

Creating a table with an internal **LOB** data type is really no different than creating a table with any other data type. When you create a table with an internal **LOB**, the data in that **LOB** may be stored inline or out of line, depending on the size of the data and the storage parameters selected when the table was created.

For each **LOB** stored out of line, a *LOB locator*—which provides a pointer to the storage location of the **LOB** column data belonging to that row—is inserted into the row of the table. The **LOB** locator then points to the actual data being stored in a **LOB** (internal or external), which is known as the

LOB's *value*. The **LOB** locator acts as a pointer to the internal **LOB** value, which may be stored inline with the rest of the row or out of line in a separate *LOB segment*.

The **LOB** segment is a separate segment created when the table with the **LOB** data type is created. A separate **LOB** segment is created for each **LOB** column defined. Data that is stored out of line is stored in the **LOB** segment. The **LOB** segment is created automatically when the internal **LOB** is created. You can define specific storage parameters when the table is created. This allows you to establish a separate tablespace and separate space storage parameters for the inline **LOB** segment. This ability to separate the **LOB** segment into a separate tablespace can have a significant positive impact on performance by allowing the I/O to the data to be distributed among different devices.

Another object created when you add an internal **LOB** column to a table is the *LOB index*. The system automatically generates this index. One index is defined for each **LOB** column and is maintained internally by Oracle. You cannot rebuild or rename the index using the **ALTER INDEX** command, and the only limited changes that you can make are through the **ALTER TABLE** command, which allows changes to storage parameters and the like. When you create the table, you can name the index, or Oracle assigns it a system-generated name by default. You can also assign the index to a separate tablespace and define its own storage specifications.

 Make sure you understand that two other objects are created when you create an internal **LOB**: the **LOB** index and the **LOB** segment. Also, you should understand that a separate **LOB** index and **LOB** segment are created for each **LOB** created in a table. Finally, you should be clear on the fact that each **LOB** index and **LOB** segment can have separate tablespaces.

Listing 7.1 shows an example of creating tables that contain internal **LOB** data types.

Listing 7.1   Creating tables with internal **LOB** data types.

```
CREATE TABLE CLOB_TEST_TABLE
( row_key          NUMBER,
  clob_column      CLOB );

CREATE TABLE BLOB_TEST_TABLE
( row_key          NUMBER,
  blob_column      BLOB )
TABLESPACE DATA_TAB
STORAGE(INITIAL 10M NEXT 10M);
```

Storage Characteristics Of Oracle8 Internal **LOB**s

The method Oracle8 uses to store **LOB** data is rather different than how it has stored data in the past. This includes out-of-line storage of data and certain storage clauses that have been added for more granular control of where data is stored. This section will review the new storage clauses Oracle8 makes available to use with **LOB**s.

Specifying Storage Of Internal **LOB** Row Data And Internal **LOB** Indexes

Several new clauses have been added to the **CREATE TABLE** command for the management of **LOB** creation in a table. These include:

➤ DISABLE STORAGE IN ROW

➤ PCTVERSION

➤ CACHE and NOCACHE

➤ LOGGING and NOLOGGING

➤ CHUNK

DISABLE STORAGE IN ROW Clause

With the **DISABLE STORAGE IN ROW** clause, Oracle has made an effort to improve performance and allow for more flexibility with **LOB**s. In Oracle7, **LONG** and **LONG RAW** data types stored all of their data inline with the rest of the row, which could cause performance problems. Oracle8 has provided the **DISABLE STORAGE IN ROW** clause to force all rows of an internal **LOB** to be stored out of line as opposed to the default action. By default, the **LOB** is stored out of line if the **LOB**'s value is larger than the maximum size of a **CHAR** (which is 4,000 bytes, but there is some overhead associated with this number; the actual maximum size of an inline **LOB** is really 3,964 bytes). If the **LOB** size is smaller than this threshold size, the **LOB** is stored inline with the rest of the row. If a row subsequently grows so that it is greater than the maximum size that can be stored inline, it is moved out of line with the rest of the row.

PCTVERSION Clause

When the **LOB** value is stored out of line, read consistency and transaction management are performed differently than with regular database objects. Changes to a **LOB** value result in a completely new version of the **LOB** value being stored. The old version of the data is retained to maintain read consistency for other transactions and for transaction recovery, much like old versions of blocks are stored in rollback segments for read consistency. The only undo generated by an out-of-line **LOB** is the redo generated by changes to the **LOB** index and the **LOB** locator. If the **LOB** value is stored inline, the traditional method of using rollback segments to store undo and for read consistency is maintained.

You use the **PCTVERSION** clause of the **CREATE TABLE** or **ALTER TABLE** command to establish or change the percentage of space that old versions of **LOB** value pages should be allowed to use. Once this threshold is reached, Oracle attempts to start reclaiming space from the old **LOB** pages. If **PCTVERSION** is set incorrectly, it can cause **SNAPSHOT TO OLD** error messages during long-running transactions. Also, incorrectly setting **PCTVERSION** can cause the **LOB** storage to increase in size more than it needs to, which uses excessive space.

Internal **LOB** values have a one-to-one relationship with the **LOB** locator assigned to them. Thus, if a row that contains a 2GB **LOB** is duplicated, 4GB is required after the duplication has completed (2GB for the original **LOB** data and 2GB for the new copy of the **LOB** data). When multiple internal **LOB** locators exist, each points to a separately stored **LOB** value, even though the **LOB** values may be equivalent.

Listing 7.2 shows an example of creating an internal **LOB** that stores its data using different storage clauses and separate storage specification.

Listing 7.2   Creation of an internal **LOB** with different storage clauses.

```
CREATE TABLE BLOB_TEST_TABLE
( row_key          NUMBER,
  blob_column      BLOB )
LOB(blob_column)
STORE AS blob_column_name(
    TABLESPACE blob_segment
    STORAGE(INITIAL 10M NEXT 10M)
    INDEX idx_blob_segment (
        TABLESPACE blob_segment
        STORAGE(INITIAL 10M NEXT 10M)
    )
  )
TABLESPACE blob_data
STORAGE(initial 5M next 5M);
```

CACHE And NOCACHE Clauses

The **CACHE** and **NOCACHE** clauses determine the method that the database uses to read data from a **LOB**. They have no effect on data stored inline with a row. They affect only the out-of-line **LOB** segment data being read or written. If a **LOB**'s storage clause is set to **NOCACHE** (the default), all reads from **LOB** segments are done using direct reads and writes. This is much like a direct load in that the data does not pass through the buffer cache. When the **CACHE** option is set, the reads and writes go through the database buffer cache and are put at the most recently used (MRU) end of the cache.

LOGGING And NOLOGGING Clauses

The **LOGGING** (default) and **NOLOGGING** clauses allow redo logging to be disabled on a **BLOB**, which reduces I/O requirements. This, of course, could impact the recovery of the object; changes to the internal **BLOB** when it is set up in **NOLOGGING** mode are marked as corrupt during recovery. **BLOB** values stored inline are not affected by the **nologging** parameter and thus always generate redo. Finally, the **nologging** parameter can be used only if it is prefixed by the **NOCACHE** option. Using the **CACHE** option enables **LOGGING** by default.

CHUNK Clause

The **CHUNK** clause defines how many blocks of data are read in one I/O from an out-of-line **LOB** segment. This number is represented in bytes and is rounded up to the next highest multiple of the **DB_BLOCK_SIZE**.

> *Note: The storage clauses **INITIAL** and **NEXT** should be larger than the rounded **CHUNK** value for out-of-line **LOB** segments.*

Benefits Of New Oracle8 Internal LOBs

The new Oracle8 internal **LOB**s have several benefits that set them apart from the old **LONG** and **LONG RAW** data types. These benefits include:

➤ Oracle8 **LOB**s have a maximum size of 4GB as opposed to the 2GB limit imposed on **LONG** and **LONG RAW** data types.

➤ **LOB**s can be stored out of line with the rest of the row data, increasing the performance of queries against tables that contain **LOB**s, particularly if you are querying columns other than the **LOB** columns.

➤ You can manipulate Oracle8 **LOB**s through the Oracle8 OCI, as was possible for **LONG** and **LONG RAW** data types. You can now also manipulate the new Oracle8 **LOB**s through a new Oracle PL/SQL package, **DBMS_LOB**, and SQL DML statements. Full transactional consistency is provided as with any other Oracle data type.

➤ An unlimited number of Oracle8 **LOB** columns may exist in a table (up to the maximum number of columns allowed in a table of course!).

➤ You can manipulate **LOB**s with triggers.

➤ Oracle automatically indexes a **LOB** column. You cannot create a regular index on a **LOB** column, however.

➤ With the exception of **NCLOB** data types, objects can have **LOB** attributes assigned to them.

➤ Methods can take **LOB**s as arguments.

➤ An internal **LOB** can be used as a bind variable.

➤ An internal **LOB** can be accessed randomly, as opposed to serial access required for **LONG** and **LONG RAW** data types.

 Make sure you understand the benefits of **LOB**s and how those benefits contrast with those of the **LONG** and **LONG RAW** data types.

The Oracle8 External **LOB**: BFILE

This section looks at the **BFILE LOB** data type and discusses how it references external operating system data files. We will look at creating tables with external **LOB**s. It examines how **BFILE** stores references to this external data in the database, and how to create tables that contain the **BFILE** data type. Finally, it reviews the benefits of external **LOB**s over **LONG** and **LONG RAW** data types. For more information on manipulating **BFILE** data types, see the "Accessing **LOB**s With SQL" section later in this chapter.

Creating Tables Using External **LOB** Columns

BFILE **LOB**s represent external files (or external **LOB**s) on the operating system. These operating system data files can exist on disk drives, CD-ROMs, and like devices. No single **BFILE LOB** may span more than one device, however, and the operating system must support the stream I/O associated with reading **BFILE**s. With a **BFILE**, you can do only read-only stream I/O access to the external file. Using SQL commands to write data to the operating system file is not supported, nor is there transactional support for **BFILE**s.

*Note: Unlike with internal **LOB** types, a table created with a **BFILE** column does not have an index generated for it, nor is there any need for a **LOB** segment.*

Before creating a **BFILE** data type in a table, you must define a *directory object.* Doing so allows for access to **BFILE**s by defining the directory they are located in. This directory object is the alias name for a physical directory on the database server. These directories are where the **BFILE** operating system files can be accessed through Oracle.

To create the directory, use the new **CREATE DIRECTORY** command. You can query the **DBA_DIRECTORIES** table to see a list of accessible directories. You use the **DROP DIRECTORY** SQL command to remove directory aliases that are no longer needed. You can create directory entries with the **CREATE DIRECTORY** command that do not actually exist on the operating system. No error will be generated when you create a directory entry for a file system that does not exist.

There is a limit to how many **BFILE**s can be open at one time. This is defined by the init.ora setting **SESSION_MAX_OPEN_FILES**. The default for this per-session limit is 10, so consider if you may need to open more when setting up your database for **BFILE**s.

*Note: When you access a **BFILE**, the information read from the **BFILE** is in hexadecimal format. You may need to convert this information into another format (for example ASCII) in order to use it properly.*

Security is a concern when it comes to users accessing **BFILE** type **LOB**s. A user must have been granted the **CREATE ANY DIRECTORY** privilege to create directory entries. Of course, the **DROP ANY DIRECTORY** grant must also be given to allow a user to drop a directory. In addition, when creating directory entries, database administrators (DBAs) should ensure that the security of critical file systems is not compromised. It would not, for example, be a good idea to create a directory entry for ORACLE_HOME.

In addition, system privileges may be granted or revoked, allowing others to read directory entries. The **GRANT READ ON DIRECTORY** and **REVOKE READ ON DIRECTORY** commands control read privileges to directories and control who can access what files. If a user has read access to the table, but not read access to the directory, that user cannot access the **BFILE** he or she is trying to access.

Note: The file being accessed must be readable by Oracle in order to be accessed.

You can **AUDIT** dictionary access as well.

Listing 7.3 shows how to use the **CREATE DIRECTORY** command and the **GRANT READ ON DIRECTORY**. In this case, you are creating a directory alias main_dir that points to the /tmp directory.

Listing 7.3   Using the **CREATE DIRECTORY** command.

```
CREATE DIRECTORY main_dir as '/tmp';
GRANT READ ON DIRECTORY main_dir TO robert;
DROP DIRECTORY main_dir;
```

Creating a table with a **BFILE** data type is no different than creating a table with any other data type. Listing 7.4 shows an example of creating tables that contain **bfile** columns.

Listing 7.4   Creating tables with a **BFILE** data type.

```
CREATE TABLE BFILE_TEST_TABLE
( row_key           NUMBER,
  bfile_column      BFILE )
TABLESPACE bLOB_data
STORAGE(initial 5M next 5M);
```

Benefits Of New Oracle8 External **LOBs** (**BFILEs**)

The new Oracle8 **BFILE LOBs** have several benefits that set them apart from the old **LONG** and **LONG RAW** data types. These benefits include:

➤ They have a maximum size of 4GB as opposed to the 2GB limit imposed on **LONG** and **LONG RAW** data types. The maximum type is constrained by any operating system limits that might exist on external files.

➤ You can store data outside the database in separate operating system files. Data from these operating system files is never stored inline and is read-only.

➤ You can manipulate Oracle8 **BFILEs** through the OCI, as was possible for **LONG** and **LONG RAW** data types. You can now also manipulate the new Oracle8 **BFILEs** through a new Oracle PL/SQL package, **DBMS_LOB**, and SQL DML statements. **bfile** columns are read-only, so no transactional consistency is provided.

➤ An unlimited number of Oracle8 **bfile** columns may exist in a table (up to the maximum number of columns allowed in a table of course!).

➤ Objects can have **BFILE** attributes assigned to them.

➤ The **BFILE** can be accessed randomly, as opposed to serial access required for **LONG** and **LONG RAW** data types.

LOB Restrictions

LOBs are much more versatile than **LONG** or **LONG RAW** data types. Unfortunately, however, there are some restrictions associated with **LOB**s:

➤ You cannot convert or migrate a **LONG** data type to a **LOB** or vice versa. Oracle supports some workarounds to this problem, but these are beyond the scope of this book and are not covered on the Oracle Certified Professional (OCP) exam.

➤ Distributed **LOB**s are not supported.

➤ **LOB**s cannot be exported using direct load method. Only the table definition will be exported.

➤ The **compress=y** parameter of export has no effect when exporting **LOB**s.

In fact, no new Oracle8 data types can be exported using direct load. This includes nested tables, **VARRAY**s, **LOB**s, **REF**s, or object type columns.

➤ You cannot use a **LOB** locator in a **SELECT** or **WHERE** clause, nor can you use it in **DBMS_LOB** programs (see "Using The **DBMS_LOB** Package" later in the chapter).

➤ SQL*Loader does not support **LOB**s that use either the direct or conventional path.

➤ **LOB**s are not allowed in partitioned or clustered tables, or in index-only tables.

➤ **LOB**s cannot be used in **GROUP BY, ORDER BY, SELECT DISTINCT**, or aggregate SQL statements. They can be used in **UNION ALL. UNION, MINUS**, and **SELECT DISTINCT** are allowed on **LOB** attributes of objects if the object type has a **MAP** or **ORDER** function associated with it.

➤ LOB columns are not analyzed when you use the **ANALYZE** command.

➤ LOBs are not allowed in **VARRAY**s.

➤ Triggers are not supported in **LOBs**, but you can use a **LOB** in the body of a trigger with some restrictions. First, you cannot write to a **LOB** with a trigger. Second, you cannot read the **:new** value of the **LOB**. It is possible to read the **:old** value of the **LOB**. With **INSTEAD OF** triggers (see Chapter 8), you can read the **:old** and **:new** value for a **LOB**.

Views To Administer **LOBs**

Oracle provides some views to assist DBAs in administering **LOBs**. They include:

➤ *DBA_LOBS*—Is general **LOB** information, including **LOB** index names and **LOB** segment names

➤ *DBA_DIRECTORIES*—Includes directory information on **BFILE** directories that have been created

Each of these views listed has the usual **USER** and **ALL** views associated with them.

Accessing **LOBs** With SQL

This section looks at how to manipulate the various types of LOBs in SQL. It examines **INSERT**s, **DELETE**s, **UPDATE**s, and **SELECT**s from tables that contain internal and external **BLOB** data types.

Inserting, Updating, and Deleting Rows From **LOBs**

This section addresses inserting rows into internal and external **LOBs**. We will review the rules associated with these inserts and the use of the **EMPTY_BLOB()** and **EMPTY_CLOB()** functions. We will also review the process of updating existing rows and deleting existing rows that contain **LOB** types.

Inserting Rows Into Internal **LOBs**

Once the table with the internal **LOB** column has been created, you can populate the internal **LOB** column through SQL just as you would any other column. No special syntax is required. You can also initialize an internal **LOB** by using the **EMPTY_BLOB()** or **EMPTY_CLOB()** functions, or by initializing them with **NULL**. You must use the **EMPTY_BLOB()** or **EMPTY_CLOB()** functions when creating a row in a table that contains columns of these types if you expect to use the **DBMS_LOB** package on the rows. Listing 7.5 shows an example of inserting a value into a table with an internal **LOB** and then inserting a row using the **EMPTY_CLOB()** function.

Listing 7.5   Inserting rows into a table with an internal **LOB** data type.

```
INSERT INTO clob_test_table
(row_key,clob_column)
VALUES
(1,'THIS IS A TEST, INSERTING INTO A LOB!');

INSERT INTO clob_test_table
(row_key,clob_column)
VALUES
(2,EMPTY_CLOB());

INSERT INTO clob_test_table
(row_key,clob_column)
VALUES
(3,NULL);
```

Inserting A Row Into An External **LOB** To Initialize It

You have created a table with an external **LOB** earlier in Listing 7.4, and created a directory entry that defines the location of the **BFILE**. You now need to initialize a row in the table that contains the **BFILE** information needed to reference the operating system physical file. To do so, use an **INSERT** statement and the **BFILENAME()** function to insert the correct operating system file information into the **bfile** column that will be required to find the file in subsequent operations.

The **BFILENAME()** function takes two **VARCHAR2** data types as parameters (and thus they belong in single quotation marks). The first is the directory alias that was created with the **CREATE DIRECTORY** command. The second parameter is the actual name of the file that is associated with the row being inserted.

> *Note: You can populate a BFILE column with a file name that does not exist, and no error will be generated. An error is generated only upon an attempt to access the operating system file.*

Listing 7.6 shows an example of inserting a row into **BFILE_TEST_TABLE** that will point the **bfile** column (**BFILE_COLUMN**) to a file called **TEST**.

Note that I use the directory alias that you created earlier in Listing 7.3 called "**MAIN_DIR**". Oracle then looks for the file called "test" in the directory "/ tmp", which is the directory assigned to the alias **MAIN_DIR**.

Listing 7.6   Inserting a row into a table with an internal **LOB** data type.

```
INSERT INTO bfile_test_table(row_key,bfile_column)
VALUES
(1,bfilename('MAIN_DIR','test'))
```

Deleting Rows From Internal And External **LOB**s

The process of deleting records from internal **LOB**s is the same as deleting external **LOB**s. Simply use the **DELETE** statement as you would with any other SQL operation. Keep in mind that although you may remove the row with a **bfile** column associated with an external operating system file, the physical file itself is never removed by such an action. This operation must take place at the operating system level. The following is an example of a **DELETE** statement; it removes one of the rows you added earlier in Listing 7.5.

```
DELETE FROM clob_test_table WHERE row_key = 3;
```

Updating Rows From Internal **LOB**s

Updates to rows in internal **LOB**s are generally the same as with any normal **UPDATE** SQL command. Listing 7.7 shows an example of such an update.

Listing 7.7   Updating a row from the **CLOB_TEST_TABLE**.

```
UPDATE clob_test_table
SET clob_column = 'New update In this column'
WHERE row_key = 2;
```

Updating Rows From External **LOB**s

As with **INSERT**s, **UPDATE**s of **bfile** columns require the use of the **BFILE-NAME()** function. Beyond that requirement, they are the same as any other update. Listing 7.8 shows an example of an update to the **BFILE_TEST_TABLE**.

Listing 7.8   Updating a row from the **BFILE_TEST_TABLE**.

```
UPDATE bfile_test_table
SET bfile_column = bfilename('MAIN_DIR','test1')
WHERE row_key = 1;
```

Selecting Rows From **LOB**s

When you select from a **LOB,** you do not actually get the value, but rather the **LOB** locator value. If you try to select from a **LOB** in SQL, you may get an error if you are not using the **DBMS_LOB** package. To retrieve stored data in **LOB** data types, you need to use the **DBMS_LOB** package or OCI calls. OCI calls are outside the scope of this book and are not covered in the OCP exam. The **DBMS_LOB** package, on the other hand, is covered. It's up next.

Using The **DBMS_LOB** Package

The **DBMS_LOB** package provides extensive access to internal and external **LOB**s. It makes working with **LOB**s much more flexible than working with **LONG**s in Oracle7. This section reviews the various functions available in **DBMS_LOB** and then reviews some examples of how to use the package.

DBMS_LOB Functions And Procedures

The **DBMS_LOB** package contains several subprograms (procedures and functions) that assist you in managing **LOB** data. The two categories of subprograms in the **DBMS_LOB** package are *mutators* and *observers*. Mutators change data, whereas observers simply display data. Generally, the **DBMS_LOB** package programs do not allow **NULL**s to be in the **LOB** column and will return an error if NULLS are present. To avoid getting an error when creating a row with a **LOB** column that you wish to leave empty, use the **EMPTY_CLOB,** **EMPTY_BLOB,** and **EMPTY_BFILE** functions.

The next sections discuss each subprogram available in the **DBMS_LOB** package. They explain whether the subprogram is a mutator or an observer, as well as describe the parameters they require and what they do.

dbms_lob.append

The **dbms_lob.append** procedure is a mutator. The **append** procedure takes the contents of one **LOB** and appends those contents to another **LOB** of the same type. This procedure can be used on both **BLOB** and **CLOB LOB** data types. The source parameter is the **LOB** that is appended to be the destination parameter. The procedure takes two parameters, as shown below.

```
PROCEDURE DBMS_LOB.APPEND(DEST_LOB IN OUT BLOB, SCR_LOB IN BLOB);
```

This procedure is overloaded with this additional specification available:

```
PROCEDURE DBMS_LOB.APPEND
(DEST_LOB IN OUT CLOB CHARACTER SET ANY_CS,
 SCR_LOB  IN     CLOB CHARACTER SET DEST_LOB%CHARSET);
```

The descriptions of the parameters are:

➤ *dest_lob*—The **LOB** that will be appended to

➤ *scr_lob*—The **LOB** to append to the **DEST_LOB**

DBMS_LOB.COMPARE

The **DBMS_LOB.COMPARE** function is an observer. The function returns an **INTEGER** type. The return value is 0 if the compare is successful, and non-zero if it is not. The **COMPARE** function will compare entire **LOB**s or only compare specific parts of two **LOB**s. The **LOB**s compared must be of the same type. You may compare **CLOB**, **BLOB**, or **BFILE LOB**s of the same type. The **bytes_to_compare** parameter determines the maximum number of bytes to compare between the two objects and defaults to the maximum size of a **LOB**. You can use the **offset1** and **offset2** parameters to define the offset byte positions to begin the compare. The **COMPARE** function type description is found below:

```
FUNCTION DBMS_LOB.COMPARE
(LOB_1    IN  BLOB | CLOB CHARACTER SET ANY_CS,
 LOB_2    IN  BLOB | CLOB CHARACTER SET ANY_CS,
 AMOUNT   IN  INTEGER := 4294967295,
 OFFSET_1 IN  INTEGER := 1,
 OFFSET_2 IN  INTEGER := 1)
 RETURN INTEGER;
```

As stated, if the function is overloaded, the second definition is as shown below:

```
FUNCTION DBMS_LOB.COMPARE
(LOB_1    IN  BFILE,
 LOB_2    IN  BFILE,
 AMOUNT   IN  INTEGER,
 OFFSET_1 IN  INTEGER := 1,
 OFFSET_2 IN  INTEGER := 1)
 RETURN INTEGER;
```

The parameters of the **DBMS_LOB.COMPARE** function are shown next:

➤ *lob_1*—The first **LOB** of the comparison

➤ *lob_2*—The second **LOB** of the comparison

➤ *amount*—Number of bytes (**BFILE** or **BLOB**) or characters (**CLOB**, **NCLOB**) to compare

➤ *offset_1*—Location of the byte of character to begin the comparison

➤ *offset_2*—Location of the byte of character to begin the comparison

dbms_lob.copy

The **dbms_lob.copy** procedure is a mutator. The **copy** procedure is used to copy all or part of the source **LOB** to the destination **LOB**. The **copy** procedure can be used only on internal **LOB**s. You determine where you start the **copy** with the **source_offset** parameter and where the copy begins for the destination with the **dest_offset** parameter. As a result, it is possible to overwrite **LOB** value data in the destination. If the **source_offset** parameter defined is beyond the end of the source data, zero-byte fillers or spaces are inserted. The procedure specification appears as follows:

```
PROCEDURE DBMS_LOB.COPY
(DEST_LOB     IN  OUT    BLOB,
  SRC_LOB      IN  BLOB,
  AMOUNT       IN  INTEGER,
  DEST_OFFSET  IN  INTEGER := 1,
  SRC_OFFSET   IN  INTEGER := 1);
```

As with other procedures in the **DBMS_LOB** package, the **dbms_lob.copy** procedure is also overloaded. The alternate specification appears below:

```
PROCEDURE DBMS_LOB.COPY
(DEST_LOB     IN  OUT    CLOB  CHARACTER SET ANY_CS,
  SRC_LOB      IN         CLOB  CHARACTER SET DEST_LOB%CHARSET,
  AMOUNT       IN  INTEGER,
  DEST_OFFSET  IN   INTEGER := 1,
  SRC_OFFSET   IN   INTEGER := 1);
```

The parameters for this procedure are as follows:

➤ *dest_lob*—The **LOB** being copied to

➤ *src_lob*—The **LOB** being copied

➤ *amount*—The number of bytes to copy from the **SRC_LOB** to the **SRC_OFFSET** location

➤ *dest_offset*—Byte or character offset to begin copying to in the **DEST_LOB**

➤ *src_offset*—Byte or character offset to begin copying from in the **SRC_LOB**

dbms_lob.erase

The **dbms_lob.erase** procedure is a mutator. The **erase** procedure erases part or all of an internal **LOB**. The offset parameter determines, in bytes, where the erasure action begins, and the amount parameter defines how many bytes to erase from that location. The actual number of bytes erased is returned in the amount parameter because the number of bytes erased can differ from the number of bytes requested to be erased. The package specification follows:

```
PROCEDURE DBMS_LOB.ERASE
(LOB_LOC   IN   OUT   BLOB | CLOB   CHARACTER SET ANY_CS,
   AMOUNT   IN   OUT   INTEGER,
   OFFSET   IN         INTEGER := 1);
```

The parameters of the package are described below:

➤ *lob_loc*—The locator of the **LOB** to erase

➤ *amount*—The number of bytes/characters to erase

➤ *offset*—The position to begin the erasure; defaults to 1

dbms_lob.fileclose

The **dbms_lob.fileclose** procedure is a mutator. The **fileclose** procedure closes a **BFILE** that has been opened. The **file_loc** parameter is the **LOB** locator associated with the **BFILE**. The package specification is below:

```
FUNCTION DBMS_LOB.FILECLOSE
( FILE_LOC     IN    BFILE )
RETURN INTEGER;
```

The parameter for the function is:

➤ *file_loc*—The file locator of the file you wish to determine the existence of

dbms_lob.filecloseall

The **dbms_lob.filecloseall** procedure is a mutator with no parameters. The **filecloseall** procedure closes all **BFILE**s that have been opened in a session.

DBMS_LOB.FILEEXISTS

The **DBMS_LOB.FILEEXISTS** function is an observer. The **FILEEXISTS** function is used to determine if a **BFILE LOB** locator points to a file that exists on the operating system. The function returns a non-zero integer if the file exists and a 0 if the file does not exist. The function specification is found next:

```
FUNCTION DBMS_LOB.FILEEXISTS
( FILE_LOC     IN    BFILE )
RETURN INTEGER;
```

The parameter for the function is:

➤ *file_loc*—The file locator of the file you wish to determine the existence of

dbms_lob.filegetname

The dbms_lob.filegetname procedure is an observer. The **filegetname** procedure takes the **BFILE LOB** locator in the **file_loc** parameter. It returns the directory alias for the file in the **dir_alias** parameter and the name of the file associated with the **file_loc LOB** locator. The specification of the procedure is as follows:

```
PROCEDURE DBMS_LOB.FILEGETNAME
( FILE_LOC     IN    BFILE,
    DIR_ALIAS    OUT   VARCHAR2,
    FILENAME     OUT   VARCHAR2);
```

The parameters of the procedure are as follows:

➤ *file_loc*—The file locator of the file you wish to determine the existence of.

➤ *dir_alias*—The directory alias name associated with the **FILE_LOC** sent into the procedure. This is returned by the procedure.

➤ *filename*—The filename associated with the **FILE_LOC** sent into the procedure. This is returned by the procedure.

DBMS_LOB.FILEISOPEN

The DBMS_LOB.FILEISOPEN function is an observer. The FILEISOPEN function is used to discover if a **BFILE** was opened with the given **file_loc** locator. If **file_loc** was never opened using the **dbms_lob.fileopen** procedure, the file is not considered to have been opened by the locator passed into the function. It is possible for another **file_loc LOB** locator to open the same **BFILE**. This function returns an **INTEGER**.

```
FUNCTION DBMS_LOB.FILEISOPEN
( FILE_LOC     IN    BFILE )
RETURN INTEGER;
```

The parameter for the function is:

➤ *file_loc*—The file locator of the file you wish to determine the existence of

dbms_lob.fileopen

The **dbms_lob.fileopen** procedure is a mutator. The **fileopen** procedure is used to open a **BFILE**. Remember that a **BFILE** is read-only and may not be written to in Oracle. The header for the procedure follows:

```
PROCEDURE DBMS_LOB.FILEGETNAME
( FILE_LOC   IN   BFILE,
  OPEN_MODE  IN   BINARY_INTEGER:= FILE_READONLY);
```

The parameters of the procedure are as follows:

➤ *file_loc*—The file locator of the file you wish to determine the existence of

➤ *open_mode*—Used to indicate access type; currently the default of **FILE_READONLY** is valid

DBMS_LOB.GETLENGTH

The **DBMS_LOB.GETLENGTH** function is an observer that returns an **INTEGER**. The integer returned is the length of the **LOB** in bytes or characters, depending on the **LOB** type. The function will return a **NULL** if the **LOB** is NULL. The **GETLENGTH** function is used to get the length of the **LOB** specified in the locator parameter, which is the **LOB** locator. Other causes for the function to return a **NULL** are if the locator is a **BFILE** type and the directory or operating system (OS) file privileges are not sufficient, or if there is an OS read error on the file. The package specification of the function follows:

```
FUNCTION DBMS_LOB.GETLENGTH (LOB_LOC   IN   BLOB)
RETURN INTEGER;
```

The parameter of the function is:

➤ *lob_loc*—The locator of the **LOB**

DBMS_LOB.INSTR

The **DBMS_LOB.INSTR** function is an observer. The **INSTR** function is used to determine if a pattern set forth in the pattern parameter is present. Using the nth parameter, you can tell the function that you wish it to check for the pattern happening nth number of times, and only return a true if the pattern occurs on the **nth** time. The search starts at the offset location for the match. For a search on a **BFILE**, the file must have already been opened using **FILEOPEN**. The function returns an integer that represents the offset of the start of the matched pattern, or it returns a 0 if the pattern is not found. The function specification is listed next:

```
FUNCTION DBMS_LOB.INSTR
(  LOB_LOC   IN   BLOB | BFILE,
   PATTERN   IN   RAW,
   OFFSET    IN   INTEGER   :=  1,
   NTH       IN   INTEGER   := 1)
RETURN INTEGER;
```

The function is overloaded and also contains this specification:

```
FUNCTION DBMS_LOB.INSTR
(  LOB_LOC   IN   CLOB   CHARACTER SET ANY_CS,
   PATTERN   IN   VARCHAR2 CHARACTER SET LOB_LOC%CHARSET,
   OFFSET    IN   INTEGER   :=  1,
   NTH       IN   INTEGER   := 1)
RETURN INTEGER;
```

The parameters of the function have the following definitions:

➤ *lob_loc*—The locator of the **LOB**

➤ *pattern*—The pattern to search for in the **LOB**

➤ *offset*—Location of the byte of character in the **LOB** to begin the search

➤ *nth*—Search for the **NTH** occurrence of the **PATTERN** in the **LOB**

dbms_lob.loadfromfile

The **dbms_lob.loadfromfile** procedure is a mutator. The **LOADFROMFILE** function copies all or part of a **BFILE LOB** defined by the **src** parameter to an internal **LOB** as defined by the **dest** parameter. Again, the **dest_offset** parameter and the **src_offset** parameters represent the offsets to copy to and copy from. The number of bytes to copy is defined by using the **amount** parameter.

In order to use this function, the **BFILE** to be copied from must have already been opened, and the **BFILE** must be the same character set as the **LOB** it is being copied into. You can overwrite existing contents in the destination **LOB** by defining the **dest_offset** to a point before the current end-of-file (EOF) of the destination **LOB**. The offsets all default to 1 if not specified. The specification of the procedure is found below:

```
PROCEDURE DBMS_LOB.LOADFROMFILE
(DEST_LOB      IN  OUT   BLOB | CLOB  CHARACTER SET ANY_CS,
 SRC_LOB       IN        BFILE,
 AMOUNT_IN     IN        INTEGER,
 DEST_OFFSET   IN        INTEGER := 1,
 SRC_OFFSET    IN        INTEGER := 1);
```

The parameters for this procedure are as follows:

➤ *dest_lob*—The locator for the destination internal **LOB**

➤ *src_lob*—The file locator of the external **LOB**

➤ *amount_in*—The number of bytes to load into the **DEST_LOB**

➤ *dest_offset*—Byte or character offset to begin copying to in the **DEST_ LOB**

➤ *src_offset*—Byte offset of the **BFILE** to begin copying from in the **SRC_LOB**

dbms_lob.read

The **dbms_lob.read** procedure is an observer. The **read** procedure is used to read a piece of a **LOB** and returns the specified number of bytes or characters read to the **buffer** parameter. The number of bytes or characters read is returned in the **amount** parameter. The package specification is as follows:

```
PROCEDURE DBMS_LOB.READ(
      LOB_LOC   IN    BLOB  |  BFILE,
      AMOUNT    IN    OUT       BINARY_INTEGER,
      OFFSET    IN              INTEGER,
      BUFFER    OUT             RAW );
```

The package is overloaded with this alternate header:

```
PROCEDURE DBMS_LOB.READ(
      LOB_LOC   IN    CLOB      CHARACTER SET ANY_CS,
      AMOUNT    IN    OUT       BINARY_INTEGER,
      OFFSET    IN              INTEGER,
      BUFFER    OUT   VARCHAR2 CHARACTER SET LOB_LOC%CHARSET );
```

The parameters of the procedure are:

➤ *lob_loc*—The locator for the **LOB**

➤ *amount*—The number of bytes/characters to erase

➤ *offset*—The position to begin the erasure; defaults to 1

➤ *buffer*—Returns the bytes or characters read from the **LOB**

DBMS_LOB.SUBSTR

The **DBMS_LOB.SUBSTR** function is an observer. Much like the SQL SUBSTR function, the **DBMS_LOB.SUBSTR** function returns the value of the bytes or characters as defined in the **amount** parameter, starting at the offset. As a result, the **SUBSTR** function returns a portion of the characters or bytes of the **LOB**. When the function is called, the data is read from the **LOB** pointed to by the **locator** parameter, the first parameter of the function. The data will be read from the **LOB** starting at the location identified by the offset parameter. The number of bytes to be read is defined by the second parameter, **amount**. The header for this function is found below:

```
FUNCTION DBMS_LOB.SUBSTR
( LOB_LOC   IN  BLOB  |  BFILE,
  AMOUNT    IN  INTEGER  :=  32767,
  OFFSET    IN  INTEGER  :=  1)
  RETURN        RAW;
```

This function is overloaded as well and an alternate header is defined next:

```
FUNCTION DBMS_LOB.SUBSTR
( LOB_LOC   IN  CLOB  CHARACTER SET  ANY_CS,
  AMOUNT    IN  INTEGER  :=  32767,
  OFFSET    IN  INTEGER  :=  1)
  RETURN        VARCHAR2  CHARACTER SET LOB_LOC%CHARSET;
```

The function's parameters are defined below:

➤ *lob_loc*—The locator for the lob

➤ *amount*—The number of bytes/characters to erase

➤ *offset*—The position to begin the erasure; defaults to 1

dbms_lob.trim

The **dbms_lob.trim** procedure is a mutator. The **trim** procedure trims the internal **LOB** locator in the **locator** parameter to a length in bytes or characters as defined by the **newlen** parameter. The package specification is as follows:

```
PROCEDURE DBMS_LOB.TRIM
(LOB_LOC  IN  OUT  BLOB|CLOB  CHARACTER SET ANY_CS,
  NEWLEN  IN INTEGER);
```

The parameters for the procedure are:

➤ *lob_loc*—The locator for the lob

➤ *newlen*—The length to trim the **LOB** to, in bytes or characters depending on the type of **LOB**

dbms_lob.write

The **dbms_lob.write** procedure is a mutator. The **write** procedure writes a specific amount of data as defined in the amount parameter to the **LOB** locator defined in the locator parameter. The write starts at the location defined by the **offset** parameter, and the buffer written from is defined by the **buffer** parameter. The **write** procedure overwrites any data already stored in the **LOB**. The specification for the procedure is as follows:

```
PROCEDURE DBMS_LOB.WRITE
( LOB_LOC   IN   OUT BLOB
  AMOUNT    IN       BINARY_INTEGER,
  OFFSET    IN       INTEGER,
  BUFFER    IN       RAW );
```

The procedure is overloaded with this second specification:

```
( LOB_LOC   IN   OUT CLOB  CHARACTER SET   ANY_CS,
  AMOUNT    IN       BINARY_INTEGER,
  OFFSET    IN       INTEGER,
  BUFFER    IN       VARCHAR2  CHARACTER SET LOB_LOC%CHARSET );
```

The parameters for the function are:

➤ *lob_loc*—The locator for the lob

➤ *amount*—The number of bytes/characters to erase

➤ *offset*—The position to begin the erasure; defaults to 1

➤ *buffer*—The buffer holds the contents of the write operation

Examples Of **DBMS_LOB**

This section looks at a couple of examples of how to use the **DBMS_LOB** package. These examples are fairly simple and give you a general idea of how to interact with **LOB** data types. The first example, Listing 7.9, simply queries a row assigned to a **BFILE** and derives the name of the file and the directory alias it is assigned to.

Listing 7.9   Using PL/SQL to determine which directory and file are assigned to a **BFILE LOB**.

```
CREATE OR REPLACE PROCEDURE find_file AS
      bfile_lob          BFILE;
      dir                VARCHAR2(30);
      filename           VARCHAR2(30);
BEGIN
```

```
SELECT bfile_column INTO bfile_lob
      FROM bfile_test_table
      WHERE row_key = 1;
SELECT bfile_column INTO bfile_LOB
FROM bfile_test_table
WHERE row_key=1;
DBMS_LOB.FILEGETNAME(bfile_ lob,dir,filename);
DBMS_OUTPUT.PUT_LINE('The directory is '||dir||
                     ' The file is '||filename);
END;
```

The second example, Listing 7.10, creates some PL/SQL that opens, reads, and closes a **BFILE LOB**. For the purposes of this example, I have created a file called "test" in a directory called "/tmp". I will open the file and display its contents.

> *Note: The output generated when you read a **BFILE** is binary in nature. If you wanted to convert it to ASCII, you would have to write a function to convert the binary value to ASCII. Oracle does not provide such a function, and it is outside the scope of this book to do so. For sources that cover this topic, see the "Need To Know More?" section at the end of this chapter.*

Listing 7.10   Opening, reading, and closing a **BFILE LOB**.

```
CREATE OR REPLACE PROCEDURE test_one AS
      bfile_ lob           BFILE;
      buffer               VARCHAR2(200);
      amount               BINARY_INTEGER := 2;
      position             INTEGER := 1;
BEGIN
      SELECT bfile_column INTO bfile_lob
      FROM bfile_test_table
      WHERE row_key = 1;
      DBMS_LOB.FILEOPEN(bfile_lob,DBMS_LOB.FILE_READONLY);
      LOOP
           DBMS_LOB.READ(bfile_lob, amount, position, buffer);
           DBMS_OUTPUT.PUT_LINE('Data stream, read '||buffer);
           position := position + amount;
      END LOOP;
      EXCEPTION
           WHEN NO_DATA_FOUND THEN
           DBMS_OUTPUT.PUT_LINE('End of the data read '
                 ||position);
      END;
```

Practice Questions

Question 1

> Which of the following is not a **LOB** type?
>
> ○ a. **BLOB**
>
> ○ b. **CLOB**
>
> ○ c. **NCLOB**
>
> ○ d. **BFILE**
>
> ○ e. **DLOB**

Answer e is correct. **DLOB** is not a valid **LOB** type. Answer a is incorrect because a **BLOB** is a binary **LOB**. Answer b is incorrect because **CLOB** is a **LOB** that contains character information. Answer c is incorrect because an **NCLOB** is a **LOB** composed of fixed-width, multi-byte character data that corresponds to the national character set defined for the Oracle database. Answer d is incorrect because a **BFILE** is a **LOB** that allows you to access outside operating system files.

Question 2

> When creating a directory object, you specify an operating system directory that does not exist on the file system. When should the DBA expect to receive an error?
>
> ○ a.   When the **CREATE DIRECTORY** statement is executed
>
> ○ b.   When the **BFILE** physical file is created
>
> ○ c.   When the **BFILE** physical file is accessed
>
> ○ d.   When the physical directory is created
>
> ○ e.   When the **BFILE** physical file is copied into the physical directory

Answer c is correct. An error is generated when the physical file referenced in the **BFILE** column in the row is not present when you attempt to access it through the database. Answer a is incorrect because you can create the **DIRECTORY** entry without any error being generated. Answers b, d, and e are incorrect because there is no direct connection between Oracle and the operating system until you attempt to access the external file. Creating, copying, or removing the file (or the directory as in answer d) in the file system has no impact on the database or the row with the **BFILE** in it until it is actually accessed.

Question 3

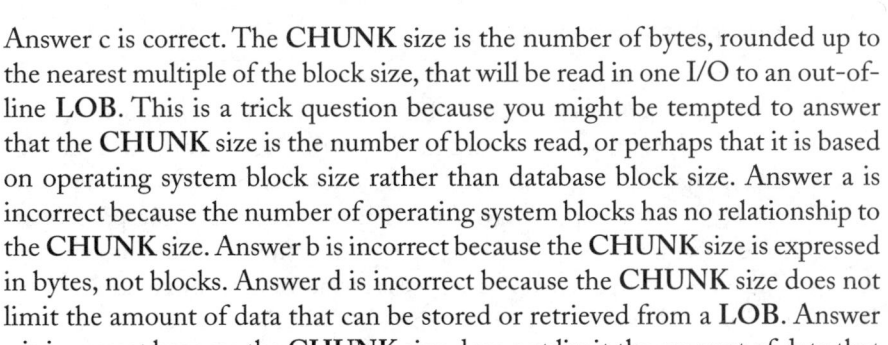

What is the **CHUNK** size of a **LOB**?

○ a. The number of operating system blocks read per I/O for a **LOB**

○ b. The number of database blocks read per I/O for a **LOB**

○ c. The number of bytes that will be read in one I/O from an out-of-line LOB. The number of bytes read will be rounded to the nearest block size multiple.

○ d. The maximum number of bytes that an inline **LOB** can be before it is stored out of line

○ e. The maximum size of an external **BFILE**

Answer c is correct. The **CHUNK** size is the number of bytes, rounded up to the nearest multiple of the block size, that will be read in one I/O to an out-of-line **LOB**. This is a trick question because you might be tempted to answer that the **CHUNK** size is the number of blocks read, or perhaps that it is based on operating system block size rather than database block size. Answer a is incorrect because the number of operating system blocks has no relationship to the **CHUNK** size. Answer b is incorrect because the **CHUNK** size is expressed in bytes, not blocks. Answer d is incorrect because the **CHUNK** size does not limit the amount of data that can be stored or retrieved from a **LOB**. Answer e is incorrect because the **CHUNK** size does not limit the amount of data that can be read from an external database data file.

Question 4

Which is a valid component of the **LOB**?

○ a. The location   ·

○ b. The locator

○ c. The pointer

○ d. The control

○ e. The type

Answer b is correct. The locator is one of two components of the **LOB**, the other being the value. The locator acts as a pointer to the out-of-line storage of the internal or external **LOB**. Answer a is incorrect because the location is not a component of the **LOB**. Answer c is incorrect because although the locator is much like a pointer, there is no pointer used by **LOB**s. Answers d and e are incorrect because there is no component of the **LOB** by either of these names.

Question 5

When you create a table with a **BLOB** data type, what other objects are created by default? [Choose two]

- ❑ a. A **LOB** index is created.
- ❑ b. An external operating system datafile is created for the out-of-line storage of the **BLOB**.
- ❑ c. A **LOB** segment is created for out-of-line storage of **LOB** data.
- ❑ d. A new tablespace is created by default to store the out-of-line **LOB**.
- ❑ e. No new objects are created by default.

Answers a and c are correct. When a table with a **BLOB** data type is created, two additional segments are created. The first is the **LOB** index, and the second is a **LOB** segment that is designated for out-of-line storage of the **LOB** data. These segments can be assigned to their own separate tablespaces. Answer b is incorrect because no external operating system datafiles are created. Answer d is incorrect because no tablespaces are automatically created when a **BLOB** is created. Answer e is incorrect because additional objects are created when the **BLOB** data type is created.

Question 6

Which is not a valid procedure or function of the **DBMS_LOB** package?

- ○ a. **APPEND**
- ○ b. **COMPARE**
- ○ c. **COPY**
- ○ d. **WRITETOBFILE**
- ○ e. **GETLENGTH**

Answer d is correct. There is no **WRITETOBFILE** function in the **DBMS_LOB** package. Because you cannot write out to a **BFILE**, there would be no purpose for such a function. Answer a is incorrect because the **APPEND** function appends data from one **LOB** to another **LOB**. Answer b is incorrect because the **COMPARE** function compares two **LOBs** and reports if they match or not. Answer c is incorrect because the **COPY** function copies data from one **LOB** to another. Answer e is incorrect because the **GETLENGTH** function determines the length of a **LOB**.

Question 7

In gigabytes, what is the maximum size of a **LOB**?

○ a. 2

○ b. 4

○ c. 6

○ d. 8

○ e. 10

Answer b is correct. Answers a, c, d, and e are incorrect because they do not represent the maximum size of a **LOB**.

Question 8

If you have created a table and have included the **DISABLE STORAGE IN ROW** clause in its creation, what is the result?

○ a. **LOBs** smaller than 4K will be stored inline.

○ b. No **LOBs** will be stored out of line.

○ c. All **LOBs** will be stored out of line.

○ d. No **LOBs** larger than 4K can be stored in the column.

○ e. You will not be able to store **LOBs** in the table until you issue an **ALTER TABLE** command using **ENABLE STORAGE IN ROW**.

Answer c is correct. The **DISABLE STORAGE IN ROW** clause forces all **LOBs** to be stored out of line. Answer a is incorrect because the **DISABLE STORAGE IN ROW** clause does not allow any inline storage to occur. Answer b is incorrect because all **LOBs** will be stored out of line if you use the

DISABLE STORAGE IN ROW clause. Answer d is incorrect because the DISABLE STORAGE IN ROW does not force all LOBs to be stored inline; therefore it will not cause errors if trying to store larger sized LOBs. Answer e is incorrect because the DISABLE STORAGE IN ROW clause does not prevent storage of LOBs in any way.

Question 9

What types of categories of subprograms are there in **DBMS_LOB**? [Choose two]

❑ a. Mutator

❑ b. **LOB** locator

❑ c. Originator

❑ d. Destructor

❑ e. Observer

Answers a and e are correct. The two types of subprograms are mutators, which manipulate data, and observers, which simply display data read from a LOB. Answer b is incorrect because a LOB locator is a pointer to data that is stored out of line in the row; it is not a type of subprogram in DBMS_LOB. Answers c and d are incorrect because neither has any relationship to the DBMS_LOB package.

Question 10

What is the purpose of the **BFILENAME()** function?

○ a. To insert a **LOB** into a **BFILE**

○ b. To create a file in the operating file system so that you can later insert data into the file in subsequent operations

○ c. To define the file name and directory alias for the file that the **BFILE** column in a row will point to

○ d. To create the **LOB** segment for out-of-line storage

○ e. None of the above

Answer c is correct. The **BFILENAME** function, when used with an **INSERT** statement, creates the pointer in the **bfile** column of a row in a table to an external operating system data file. Answer a is incorrect because **BFILE LOBs** are read-only, and you cannot insert data into them. Answer b is incorrect because the **BFILE LOBs** do not create data files and are read-only. Answer d is incorrect because the **BFILENAME** function has no relationship to out-of-line storage of **LOBs**. Answer e is incorrect because a correct answer is given.

Need To Know More?

Curtis, Mike: *Oracle8 and Windows NT Black Book.* The Coriolis Group, 1998. ISBN 1-57610-248-3. This is an excellent book on Oracle8. It covers Oracle8 **LOB**s in great detail and gives several very good examples of how to use this Oracle8 feature.

Feuerstein, Steven, et al.: *Oracle Built-in Packages.* O'Reilly & Associates, 1998. ISBN 1-56592-375-8. This is an excellent book that dives into Oracle-supplied packages like the **DBMS_LOB** package. I highly recommend this book for any DBA.

Koch, George and Kevin Loney: *Oracle8: The Complete Reference.* Oracle Press, 1997. ISBN 0-07-88-2396-X. This book is a good general Oracle reference for the DBA. It contains sections on the use of **LOB** data types, including how to setup and use the **BFILE** data types.

Oracle's documentation is good reference material. Oracle has numerous guides available on CD or in hardcover.

www.support.com is Oracle's Metalink Web site, a wonderful resource if you have Oracle Metals support.

Miscellaneous New Oracle8 Features

Terms you'll need to understand:

√ Index-organized table

√ Index fast full scan

√ Overflow tablespace

√ Reverse key index

√ Deferred constraint enforcement

Techniques you'll need to master:

√ Creating an index-organized table

√ Understanding and creating reverse key indexes

√ Understanding what deferred constraints are and how to create them

√ Understanding and using enforced constraints

Storage Types And Features In Oracle8

If you are still with me, then rejoice; you are past the worst of it. If you have made it here without deciding to retire early from the database world, good job! You are more than halfway done learning what you need to know for the Oracle Certified Professional (OCP) exam, and, in fact, this book has already covered about 80 percent of the exam's material. I call this chapter the milk and cookies chapter. It's short and sweet, so grab your milk and a couple of ginger snaps and let's move on.

Oracle8 introduces new storage types such as index-organized tables and reverse key indexes. New trigger functionality was added with **INSTEAD OF** triggers, and new constraint functionality was added with the introduction of *deferred triggers*. In this chapter, we will look at these new features and how they work.

New Oracle8 Storage Types

In this section, we will look at some new object types that are introduced in Oracle8. These include index-organized tables and reverse key indexes. We will also cover the **NOLOGGING** option that Oracle8 introduces, which replaces the **UNRECOVERABLE** option of some Oracle7 commands.

Index-Organized Tables

The introduction of index-organized tables in Oracle8 provides potential performance benefits for the database user, depending on the nature of the data in the table and how it will need to be accessed. This section reviews index-organized tables, what they are, and how to create them.

Introducing Index-Organized Tables

The traditional method of storing data in Oracle is to create tables and store the data within the tables. One of the rules of building relational database models is that data stored in tables is not stored in any particular order. Also a table that has been created without an index will have no guarantee that a row in it is unique. Therefore, performance can become very slow if you are looking for a specific row, and of course, you cannot guarantee uniqueness. Thus, to complete any query, Oracle would have to read through the entire table to retrieve the appropriate rows.

To solve these problems, there are indexes. Indexes are used, of course, to provide a quick reference to data stored in a table as well as to enforce uniqueness for primary keys and unique keys of a table. Indexes are wonderful things, but there are certain problems with them. For one thing, an index adds additional I/O requirements on the database. Whenever you change a table's row, you must also modify the related indexes. In certain cases, too, an index can be a detriment to performance because the database must read both the index and the table to retrieve rows through an index lookup. Often, depending on the cardinality of the data (or how distinct a row is in a table), index lookups can become much slower than if the database just read through the entire table. Sometimes, however, a seemingly inefficient index can be beneficial to use. This may be true in the case where the index will cause what was a sort-merge join operation to become a nested loop operation. What to index and what not to index can turn into a war of sorts and is really outside the scope of this book.

In later versions of Oracle7, an access method called *index fast full scan (FFS)* sped up certain types of index accesses. You do an FFS by creating an index that contains the rows that a query might need to return. For example, you might have a table called **EMPLOYEE** with many columns that represent each employee's address, phone number, employment status, and so on. Perhaps a particular application needs to retrieve only the **employee_id** and the address of specific employees. In such a case, FFS lookups might excel. If the correct index has been created on the **employee_id** column (which is the primary key) and the address information columns as well, Oracle could just scan the index to return the result set. Oracle would never need to access the table, significantly reducing the I/Os required. An FFS may not be appropriate in all cases, but it can improve performance in many situations.

Clustered tables have been available in Oracle for some time. Clustered tables are a group of tables that share the same data blocks. Generally they share common columns and are often used together in joins. A clustered table makes for very fast lookup performance but very poor **INSERT, UPDATE,** or **DE-LETE** performance. For more information on clustered tables or FFS of indexes, see the Oracle8 concepts guide. FFSs and clustered tables are not covered in the OCP exam. However, I mention them as an introduction to Oracle8's newest enhancement: index-organized tables, a topic that may appear on the exam.

An *index-organized table* is like the combination of a table and an index. It can be a potential alternative to a clustered table, where the cluster key maps to the primary key of the table. An index-organized table can also be an alternative to a table indexed only on its primary key. The index-organized table stores one or more columns. The rows in an index-organized table must be unique; this is enforced through a primary key established on the table. The index-organized table is stored in a B*tree structure, as with a regular index, with the B*tree index storing this data in the format: [primary key] [column1] [column2] and so on.

As you might guess, performance on index-organized tables can be significantly better than performance on regular table/index type architectures. When you are deciding to create an index-organized table over a regular table/index setup, consider the following:

➤ An index-organized table cannot have any indexes built on it.

➤ An index-organized table cannot be partitioned, as can a table and its indexes.

➤ A primary key for an index-organized table must be established because it identifies a row in an index-organized table (as opposed to a **ROWID**, which identifies a specific row in a table). A table does not require that a primary key index be created for it, whereas an index-organized table does.

➤ An index-organized table has no **ROWID** pseudo-column.

➤ Index-organized tables are not supported when you are doing distributed databases or replication.

➤ Index-organized tables cannot be made **NOLOGGING**.

For those who are familiar with indexes, you will know that the structure of a B*tree index can have problems with growth and block usage as you delete records from the index. As you do so, the records are removed from the leaf blocks of the index. Unlike with a table, the leaf blocks are not reused for other values until the entire leaf block has been cleared out. This is known as *index browning*. Thus, an index tends to grow, which can become a serious problem because you can end up with blocks that may contain only one or two records. Typically, DBAs rebuild indexes from time to time to solve this problem. Rebuilding an index-organized table is not a cheery option for the DBA because it will make the data unavailable for the time of the rebuild.

Index browning becomes a problem with index-organized tables, particularly with very large rows. Oracle has addressed this problem, in part, with an overflow area. To establish the overflow area, you use the **OVERFLOW TABLESPACE** clause (as shown in Listing 8.1 below). When you create an index-organized table, you define the tablespace to contain the overflow area, which Oracle creates and maintains. In addition, you can define a threshold, with the use of the **pctthreshold** parameter. If a row to be stored in a table is greater than the percentage of the block size defined by the **pctthreshold** parameter, the non-key columns of that row will be stored in the location defined by the **overflow tablespace** parameter.

Be careful! In Oracle8.0.5, there is a bug with the import utility and index-organized tables. Although you can export an index-organized table without error, attempting to import an index-organized table results in an error. This is corrected in Oracle8.0.6.

Creating Index-Organized Tables

To create an index-organized table, you use the **CREATE TABLE** command. Of course, the syntax you use is slightly different than what you use when creating a regular table. You use the new **ORGANIZATION INDEX** clause of the **CREATE TABLE** command, which indicates that the table is supposed to be an index-organized table. The default value for the **ORGANIZATION** clause is **ORGANIZATION HEAP**, which indicates that a regular table is to be created. You may then follow the **ORGANIZATION INDEX** clause with various statements to define storage parameters, the tablespace assignment of the index-organized table, and the overflow area.

Finally, the **INCLUDING** option of the command defines the split of which records are stored in the index and which are stored in the overflow area. The column listed in the **INCLUDING** clause is the last column stored in the index, and all subsequent columns are stored in the overflow area. The column in the **INCLUDING** clause must be either the last column of the primary key or any column after the primary key.

Listing 8.1 shows an example of creating an index-organized table. Note that you are creating a table for state codes that an application might use. You make the state_code the primary key, and you must define a primary key for an index-organized table. You assign the index-organized table to a tablespace called all_overflow.

Listing 8.1   Creating an index-organized table.

```
CREATE TABLE state_code
(STATE_CODE NUMBER PRIMARY KEY,
STATE_NAME VARCHAR2(30) NOT NULL)
ORGANIZATION INDEX TABLESPACE all_data
PCTTHRESHOLD 10
OVERFLOW TABLESPACE all_overflow;
```

Make sure you clearly understand what an index-organized table is and how to create one.

NOLOGGING Option

In Chapter 4 we mentioned the **NOLOGGING** option, which allows DBAs to ease some of the overhead associated with redo logging. This option is useful, for example, for a table that has significant activity but that does not need to be recovered if the database itself requires recovery. **NOLOGGING** is also helpful if the table is subject to some long-running DML statement. You can create a table in **NOLOGGING** mode when you issue the **CREATE TABLE** command, or you can use the **ALTER TABLE** command to set a table to **NOLOGGING** mode.

The following objects can be set to **NOLOGGING**:

➤ Tables

➤ Indexes

➤ Snapshots

➤ Snapshot logs

➤ Tablespace default settings (the tablespace default settings define the default for objects stored in the tablespace)

Reverse Key Indexes

Reverse key indexes, new in Oracle8, can help improve the performance of indexes in certain cases. Reverse key indexes can be helpful in keeping indexes balanced, thus reducing index brown out. If you insert into the index key values that represent some ascending value, and you then delete rows with a lower value, reverse key indexes may help keep the indexed balanced, thus assisting in performance. For example, assume you created a reverse key index on a table column called **code**. Assume one of the codes is 'LIGHT100C10', perhaps for a 100-watt lightbulb. In a regular index, Oracle stores the value as 'LIGHT100C10' and then stores the **ROWID** associated with that value. In a reverse key index, the value is instead stored as '01C001THGIL' followed by the **ROWID**.

Note that with the reverse key index, if codes 'LIGHT100C0' through 'LIGHT100C5' were deleted, the index entries would remain balanced because the range of codes would not be stored—clustered together—in the index. Instead, they would be balanced based on the reverse values because '0C001THGIL' and '5C001THGIL' are much more different than the reverse.

Reverse key indexes have some drawbacks. For example, you cannot use them to do a range scan or an FFS on an index, and, of course, they take up space.

 There may be at least one question about reverse key indexes in the exam. Make sure you understand what they are and how they are created.

Creating Reverse Key Indexes

To create a reverse key index, you use the **CREATE INDEX** clause, including the **REVERSE** keyword. Listing 8.2 is an example of creating a reverse key index.

Listing 8.2   Creating a reverse key index.

```
CREATE UNIQUE INDEX ix_emp_01_rev ON emp (emp_no)
REVERSE
STORAGE (INITIAL 5M NEXT 5M PCTINCREASE 0)
TABLESPACE emp_data;
```

New Oracle8 Features

As we have seen in this and previous chapters, Oracle8 introduces several new features that make it much more versatile than Oracle7. Two additional new features include the introduction of **INSTEAD OF** triggers, and deferred constraints. In this section, we will review each of these new features and how they are used.

INSTEAD OF Triggers In Oracle8

In Oracle8, views have become much more versatile than in Oracle7: You may now construct triggers around views. Oracle8's new trigger that you can use on views is the **INSTEAD OF** trigger. It is a row-level trigger only, and it gives you much more flexibility to manipulate views than was previously possible. You can create the trigger only on relational views or object views.

Previously, Oracle had some restrictive rules regarding how you could manipulate a view with DML. For example, updates on primary key values of join views were not allowed, nor were changes to views that included aggregate values. The **INSTEAD OF** trigger corrects these problems by allowing the trigger to "intercept" an action on a view, such as an **INSERT**, and execute PL/SQL code to perform a set of actions "instead of" that action.

Listing 8.3 uses the **EMPLOYEE** and **DEPENDENTS** tables in preparation for using an **INSTEAD OF** trigger. The listing creates the tables, as well as generates primary keys on each, a foreign key between the two, and a view.

Listing 8.3 Creating the **EMPLOYEE** and **DEPENDENTS** tables.

```
CREATE TABLE employee
(emp_no    NUMBER PRIMARY KEY,
 name      VARCHAR2(30) );

CREATE TABLE dependents
(dep_no    NUMBER ,
 emp_no    NUMBER ,
 name      VARCHAR2(30) )

ALTER TABLE dependents ADD PRIMARY KEY (dep_no, emp_no);

ALTER TABLE dependents
ADD CONSTRAINT fk_emp_dep
FOREIGN KEY (emp_no)
REFERENCES employee(emp_no);

CREATE VIEW ed_VIEW AS SELECT a.emp_no,a.name,b.dep_no,b.name
AS dep_name FROM employee a, dependents b
WHERE a.emp_no = b.emp_no;
```

You are now prepared to create an **INSTEAD OF** trigger on this view. First, as shown in Listing 8.4, try to update the view without the **INSTEAD OF** trigger. This fails because updates to views must be key preserved, which means that you cannot change the join key columns.

Listing 8.4 Trying to update **ed_view**.

```
INSERT INTO ed_view
(emp_no, name, dep_no, dep_name)
VALUES
(1,'RF',1,'JF');

ERROR at line 2:
ORA-01779: cannot modify a column that maps to a
non key-preserved table
```

Whoops, a minor problem here. It appears that you cannot update the **ed_view**. There is a solution, however. The cavalry has arrived in the form of an **INSTEAD OF** trigger. So, get out your PL/SQL coder hats and create the bit of code in Listing 8.5 to solve your problem!

Listing 8.5 Creating an **INSTEAD OF** trigger to solve the problem.

```
CREATE OR REPLACE TRIGGER ed_instead_trigger_01
INSTEAD OF INSERT ON ed_view
```

```
FOR EACH ROW
BEGIN
     INSERT INTO employee (emp_no, name)
     VALUES (:new.emp_no, :new.name);
     INSERT INTO dependents (dep_no, emp_no, name)
     VALUES (:new.dep_no, :new.emp_no, :new.dep_name);
END ed_instead_trigger_01;
```

Bravo! You are a PL/SQL coder deluxe. Now, let's see if this puppy works! Listing 8.6 reveals that it does indeed work, and our manager will take all the glory and all we will have is a story to tell.

Listing 8.6   A working insert.

```
INSERT INTO ed_view
(emp_no, name, dep_no, dep_name)
VALUES
(1,'RF',1,'JF');
```

One thing to be careful about when you are dealing with **INSTEAD OF** triggers is *subversion*. This is a case in which you execute one action, but the trigger takes a completely different action. With subversion, you can take a view that intercepts an **INSERT** statement and have it actually delete data, update data, or take a host of other unexpected actions. Be careful when using triggers, and as a DBA, be more careful about the developers who use them. Subversion can be a big security issue, so make sure that developers do what you expect them to do with **INSTEAD OF** triggers. **INSTEAD OF** triggers make views much more useful, much more powerful, and much more effective.

Constraints In Oracle8

Oracle8 has added new constraint functionality—including the introduction of deferred constraints and enforced constraints—to assist DBAs in doing their jobs. These new constraint types address problems revolving around constraint enforcement that DBAs and database designers have had for some time. The Oracle OCP exam will likely have at least one question about each on it.

Deferred Constraint Enforcement

Until Oracle8, constraints were enforced after each statement finished processing. For example, take the case of an insert into a child table that has a foreign key (FK) relationship established with a parent table. That FK constraint is checked immediately after any DML action is performed on the child table to ensure that the related record existed in the parent table. Having constraints being checked immediately does not always mesh with certain business rules, such as relationships that are mandatory going in each direction. For example, assume that in your database with an **EMPLOYEE** table there is also a table called **INSURED**. This table defines whom the company insured as a part of its internally funded health program. For the sake of example, assume that one of the business rules is that if an employee is in the **EMPLOYEE** table, a record for the employee must also exist in the **INSURED** table and that this relationship is mandatory. Before Oracle8 and delayed constraint enforcement, the concurrent update of parent and child tables was a serious and difficult-to-solve problem.

Deferred constraint enforcement allows the delay of the constraints' enforcement until the end of the transaction. If the constraint checks fail at the end of the transaction, the entire transaction fails and is rolled back. You enable delayed constraint enforcement when you establish a constraint on a table. Listing 8.7 shows an example of setting up a deferred constraint by using the **DEPENDENTS** table again. In the example, we establish the foreign key between the **DEPENDENTS** and **EMPLOYEE** tables, making it a deferred constraint. You might then choose to set it deferrable or nondeferred, depending on your needs. Note that if it is left deferrable, the constraint will not be checked until a commit, whereas if it is changed to be nondeferred, the constraint will be checked at the time the statement is executed.

Listing 8.7   Creating a deferred constraint.

```
alter table dependents
add constraint fk_emp_dep
FOREIGN KEY (emp_no)
REFERENCES employee(emp_no)
DEFERRABLE INITIALLY DEFERRED;
```

Note the new clause **DEFERRABLE INITIALLY DEFERRED**. It establishes the nature of the constraint. The clause begins with **DEFERRABLE INITIALLY** and then has two options: **DEFERRED** or **IMMEDIATE**. If the **DEFERRED** option is used, the constraint is a deferred constraint. If the **IMMEDIATE** option is used, the constraint is an immediate constraint (the default setting).

You can define all deferrable constraints in a session as deferred. To do so, issue the **ALTER SESSION** statement, using the **SET CONSTRAINTS=DEFERRED** syntax and the **SET CONSTRAINTS=IMMEDIATE** syntax to re-enable constraints. The above command (**ALTER SESSION SET CONSTRAINTS = DEFERRED**) does not work on constraints that are defined as **NOT DEFERRABLE** because defining a constraint as **NOT DEFER-RABLE** forces constraints to be immediate and will not allow them to become deferrable. **NOT DEFERRABLE** is the default value for a constraint.

Constraint Enforcement

Oracle8 allows you to re-enable constraints using a new syntax option called **ENFORCE** in place of **ENABLE**. When you use this syntax, it causes Oracle to not check existing data in the relationship when the constraint is enabled. Instead, the **ENFORCE** option simply enables the constraint and enforces it for all future changes. Therefore, large bulk loads can run, and constraints after the run are enabled without you having to wait for the database to check each related column. The ability to tell the database not to validate constraints when re-enabling them can also save you time when you are reorganizing tables and tablespaces.

In Oracle8, there are a couple new statuses to constraints to support enforced constraints. The **ENABLED VALIDATE** status indicates an enabled constraint that has validated the data in the tables when it was enabled. The **ENABLED NOVALIDATE** status indicates a constraint enabled with the **ENFORCE** clause, which did not validate the data before enabling.

Using Enforced Constraints

Building on the **EMPLOYEE** and **DEPENDENTS** tables introduced earlier in this chapter, let's see how to use the enforced constraint option. Listing 8.8 shows an example in which the foreign key is disabled between the two tables. You then add a row to the **DEPENDENTS** table that does not have a related row in the **EMPLOYEE** table. Next, you try to re-enable the constraint with the **ENABLE** clause and get an error message in return. After the error, you enable the constraint using the **ENFORCED** clause instead, which enables the constraint without any checking of the relationship, thus generating no errors. You see in the final SQL insert that you have indeed re-enabled the constraint because it fails a subsequent attempt to insert an invalid row into the **DEPENDENTS** table.

Listing 8.8   Using the **ENFORCED** option when enabling a foreign key.

```
ALTER TABLE dependents DISABLE CONSTRAINT fk_emp_dep;
Table altered.

INSERT INTO dependents (dep_no, emp_no, name)
VALUES (1,55,'TED');
1 row created.
```

```
ALTER TABLE dependents ENABLE CONSTRAINT fk_emp_dep;
ERROR at line 1:
ORA-02298: cannot enable (SYSTEM.FK_EMP_DEP) -
parent keys not found

ALTER TABLE dependents ENFORCE CONSTRAINT fk_emp_dep;

INSERT INTO dependents (dep_no, emp_no, name)
VALUES (1,57,'FRED');

ERROR at line 1:
ORA-02291: integrity constraint (SYSTEM.FK_EMP_DEP)
violated - parent key not found
```

Practice Questions

Question 1

What is one of the new statuses available for integrity constraints?

○ a. **DEFERRED**

○ b. **CONSTANT**

○ c. **ENABLED NOVALIDATE**

○ d. **PENDING**

○ e. **DEFINED**

Answer c is correct. Only **DEFERRED** is a new status available for integrity constraints. Answers a, b, d, and e are incorrect because they are not valid constraint settings.

Question 2

What type of action is not possible against an index-organized table?

○ a. **CREATE TABLE...TABLESPACE**

○ b. **ALTER INDEX**

○ c. **ALTER TABLE...ADD CONSTRAINT**

○ d. **DROP TABLE**

○ e. **RENAME**

Answer b is correct. An index-organized table cannot have other indexes created against it. Therefore, you cannot issue an **ALTER INDEX** command against the index-organized table. Answer a is incorrect because you can define the tablespace in which to store an index-organized table. Answer c is incorrect because you can create foreign keys between index-organized tables and regular tables. Answer d is incorrect because you can drop an index-organized table with the **DROP TABLE** command. Answer e is incorrect because you can rename an index-organized table as you can with any kind of table.

Question 3

Each option is a portion of a whole SQL statement. Given the following SQL statement that is executed against an index-organized table, which line causes an error?

○ a. SELECT a.emp_no, a.emp_name, ROWID

○ b. FROM emp a

○ c. WHERE emp_no < 1

○ d. AND emp_no > 1000

○ e. AND hire_date < SYSDATE - 365;

Answer a is correct. It causes an error because the **ROWID** pseudocolumn is not available when you are **SELECT**ing against an index-organized table. All the other choices are incorrect because they do not cause an error in the statement.

Question 4

Given the following,

```
CREATE TABLE parts
  (part_no         NUMBER PRIMARY KEY,
   description     VARCHAR2(30) );


CREATE TABLE orders
  (order_no    NUMBER ,
   line_no     NUMBER ,
   part_no     NUMBER );


ALTER TABLE orders ADD PRIMARY KEY (order_no,
       line_no);


ALTER TABLE orders
ADDC CONSTRAINT fk_order_part
FOREIGN KEY (part_no)
REFERENCES employee(part_no)
DEFERRABLE INITIALLY DEFERRED;
```

(continued)

Question 4 *(continued)*

what is the result, given the following statements entered in SQL*Plus:

```
INSERT INTO ORDERS (order_no, line_no, part_no)
VALUES (100,1,1234567);
INSERT INTO parts
(part_no, description)
VALUES (1234567,'Wiget');
COMMIT;
```

○ a. Because of the foreign key restriction, the first SQL **INSERT** will fail.

○ b. The **ALTER SYSTEM SET CONSTRAINTS = DEFERRED** command wasn't entered first, so the first **INSERT** will fail because it attempts to validate the foreign key during the insert.

○ c. The transaction will succeed without failure.

○ d. The transaction will fail at the **COMMIT** because a correct parent record was never created in the "parts" table.

○ e. The transaction will fail because the **INSERT** syntax is incorrect for a deferred constraint.

Answer c is correct. The foreign key constraint was established with the clause **DEFERRABLE INITIALLY DEFERRED,** so all validations of the constraint will take place at the end of the transaction. Answer a is incorrect because the deferred constraint that was created does not attempt to validate the first SQL statement until after the transaction is completed. Answer b is incorrect because the constraint was set up with **INITIALLY DEFERRED,** which means that the relationship is established as a deferred relationship to begin with. If the statement had been **DEFERRABLE INITIALLY IMMEDI-ATE,** the statement would fail unless the **ALTER SYSTEM SET CONSTRAINTS = DEFERRED** command was entered. Answer d is not correct since the foreign key restriction would be satisfied at the time of the commit. Answer e is not correct because the **INSERT** syntax is indeed correct.

Question 5

> If I insert a name SMITH into an index-organized table primary key column, how will that name be stored?
>
> ○ a. The name is stored normally as SMITH.
>
> ○ b. The name is stored in reverse order as HTIMS.
>
> ○ c. The name is stored in overflow storage.
>
> ○ d. The name is stored in overflow storage and in reverse order.
>
> ○ e. You cannot store a character value in an index-organized table.

Answer a is correct. An index-organized table stores data in the normal format, just as a regular index. This is a trick question because you might have gotten an index-organized table and a reverse key index confused. Answer b is incorrect because this is the format in which a reverse key index would store it, leading to the trick nature of the question. Answers c and d are incorrect because they allude to storing the name in offline storage, and the primary key of an index-organized table is never stored offline. Answer e is incorrect because you can store character values in an index-organized table.

Question 6

> What is the purpose of an **INSTEAD OF** trigger?
>
> ○ a. To make any changes to a table that are required after a mass **INSERT...SELECT** statement
>
> ○ b. To intercept DML statements on views and to execute PL/SQL code based on what the action being intercepted is
>
> ○ c. To provide various trigger options on a table based on the type of DML being generated
>
> ○ d. To provide a method of doing **DELETE CASCADE**s on tables
>
> ○ e. To provide audit actions for **SELECT** statements on views or tables

Answer b is correct. **INSTEAD OF** triggers intercept DML commands executed against view and perform specific actions as defined in PL/SQL code associated with the trigger. Answer a is incorrect because an **INSTEAD OF** trigger cannot be created on a table and does not intercept **SELECT** statements (because the **SELECT** of the **INSERT...SELECT** could be from a view). Answers c, d, and e are incorrect because **INSTEAD OF** triggers do not apply to tables.

Question 7

What new constraint option will allow you to enable a constraint without checking the parent and child rows already in place in the tables?

- ○ a. **DEFERRED**
- ○ b. **ENABLED VALIDATE**
- ○ c. **IMMEDIATE**
- ○ d. **ENFORCED**
- ○ e. **ENABLE**

Answer e is correct. You issue an **ALTER TRIGGER ENABLE** command to enable a constraint without checking the data that already exists in the tables constrained by the constraint. Answer a is not correct; deferred constraints allow you to defer constraint checking until the transaction is complete. Answer b is incorrect. **ENABLED VALIDATE** is actually a status for a constraint, indicating that it has been enabled and that it validated the relationships when it was re-enabled. Answers c and d are incorrect because they are not valid commands.

Question 8

An overflow tablespace can be defined when you create what kind of object?

- ○ a. A bitmap index
- ○ b. An object that has deferred constraints
- ○ c. An index-organized table
- ○ d. A reverse keyed index
- ○ e. Any object created with the **NOLOGGING** command to ensure object recovery

Answer c is correct. When you create an index-organized table you define the overflow tablespace for the data in the rows that exceeds the **pcthreshold** parameter's percentage of the block size. Answers a, b, d and e are incorrect because they have no relationships to overflow tablespaces.

Need To Know More?

 Ault, Michael R.: *Oracle8 Black Book*. The Coriolis Group, 1998. ISBN 1-57610-187-8. This is a great reference guide to Oracle8. The book covers, in depth, the topics covered in this chapter.

 Curtis, Mike: *Oracle8 and Windows NT Black Book*. The Coriolis Group, 1998. ISBN 1-57610-248-3. This is a wonderful Oracle8 reference. Covers topics such as reverse key indexes and deferred constraints.

 **www.support.com** is Oracle's Metalink Web site. It is a useful resource if you have Oracle Metals Support.

9

Oracle8 Security, Advanced Queuing, And External Procedures

Terms you'll need to understand:

√ Profile

√ utlpwdmg.sql

√ **FAILED_LOGIN_ATTEMPTS**

√ **PASSWORD_GRACE_TIME**

√ **PASSWORD_LIFE_TIME**

√ **PASSWORD_LOCK_TIME**

√ **PASSWORD_REUSE_MAX**

√ **PASSWORD_REUSE_TIME**

√ **PASSWORD_VERIFY_FUNCTION**

√ Advanced Queuing (AQ)

√ Consumer

√ Producer

√ Queue processes

√ Enqueue

√ Dequeue

Techniques you'll need to master:

√ Enabling and using Oracle8 security features

√ Understanding AQ and how it works in Oracle8

√ Understanding the concepts of external procedures in Oracle8

New Oracle8 Security Features

With version 8, Oracle introduces several new security features. These features make Oracle8 much more secure, and introduce features that database administrators (DBAs) have wanted to have at their disposal for years. Right up front in the security arena is password management. With password management, you can configure user accounts to force password changes and to disable passwords after a certain number of failed login attempts. In addition, you can control how passwords are used by not allowing reuse of passwords and requiring that a certain number of characters and numbers be used in the password. Oracle8 adds a great amount of flexibility to the new password security architecture by allowing DBAs to create PL/SQL scripts to enforce password security standards.

Profile Management And Security

Oracle8 uses profiles to manage password security. In the profiles, you establish the criteria for various password functions. Once created, the profile is then assigned to the user and the user is subject to the password criteria established for that profile. This section reviews what profiles are and then looks at the new profile settings available in Oracle8.

Using Profiles

As an Oracle7 DBA, you should already be familiar with profiles. *Profiles* are used to enforce certain restrictions (such as maximum idle time or CPU time) on users. Once you create the profile, you assign the profile to the user, enforcing the profile's constraints upon the user.

To create a profile, use the **CREATE PROFILE** command, as shown in Listing 9.1. Here, this command creates a profile called "developer," which might be used to constrain developer sessions. In Listing 9.1, you allow a developer's session to be idle for only one day, preventing the developer from just signing onto the database and leaving the session logged on all weekend. The **CREATE PROFILE** command has changed to adapt to the needs of Oracle8. Listing 9.1 also shows an example of the **ALTER PROFILE** command (which alters existing profiles) as well as the **DROP PROFILE** command (which drops an existing profile).

Listing 9.1   Using commands to administer profiles.

```
CREATE PROFILE developer
LIMIT
IDLE_TIME 1
```

```
FAILED_LOGIN_ATTEMPTS 3
PASSWORD_LOCK_TIME 1/24
PASSWORD_LIFE_TIME 90
PASSWORD_GRACE_TIME 3;

ALTER PROFILE developer
LIMIT
IDLE_TIME 2;

DROP PROFILE developer;
```

You can look at profiles and how they are defined in the system by examining the **DBA_PROFILES** table. Listing 9.2 shows the **DBA_PROFILES** table and what entries are there. Note that the **DEFAULT** profile appears in this listing. This is the profile assigned to users if they are not explicitly assigned a profile when their username is created.

Listing 9.2   Displaying settings using the **DBA_PROFILES** view.

```
SQL> select * from dba_profiles
  2  order by profile;
```

PROFILE	RESOURCE_NAME	RESOURCE	LIMIT
DEFAULT	COMPOSITE_LIMIT	KERNEL	UNLIMITED
DEFAULT	FAILED_LOGIN_ATTEMPTS	PASSWORD	UNLIMITED
DEFAULT	SESSIONS_PER_USER	KERNEL	UNLIMITED
DEFAULT	PASSWORD_LIFE_TIME	PASSWORD	UNLIMITED
DEFAULT	PASSWORD_REUSE_TIME	PASSWORD	UNLIMITED
DEFAULT	PASSWORD_REUSE_MAX	PASSWORD	UNLIMITED
DEFAULT	PASSWORD_VERIFY_FUNCTION	PASSWORD	UNLIMITED
DEFAULT	PASSWORD_LOCK_TIME	PASSWORD	UNLIMITED
DEFAULT	PASSWORD_GRACE_TIME	PASSWORD	UNLIMITED
DEFAULT	IDLE_TIME	KERNEL	UNLIMITED
DEFAULT	PRIVATE_SGA	KERNEL	UNLIMITED
DEFAULT	CONNECT_TIME	KERNEL	UNLIMITED
DEFAULT	LOGICAL_READS_PER_CALL	KERNEL	UNLIMITED
DEFAULT	LOGICAL_READS_PER_SESSION	KERNEL	UNLIMITED
DEFAULT	CPU_PER_CALL	KERNEL	UNLIMITED
DEFAULT	CPU_PER_SESSION	KERNEL	UNLIMITED
DEVELOPER	COMPOSITE_LIMIT	KERNEL	DEFAULT
DEVELOPER	SESSIONS_PER_USER	KERNEL	DEFAULT
DEVELOPER	CPU_PER_SESSION	KERNEL	DEFAULT
DEVELOPER	PRIVATE_SGA	KERNEL	DEFAULT
DEVELOPER	CONNECT_TIME	KERNEL	DEFAULT
DEVELOPER	PASSWORD_GRACE_TIME	PASSWORD	3

```
DEVELOPER   IDLE_TIME                        KERNEL   1
DEVELOPER   PASSWORD_LOCK_TIME               PASSWORD 1
DEVELOPER   LOGICAL_READS_PER_CALL           KERNEL   DEFAULT
DEVELOPER   PASSWORD_VERIFY_FUNCTION         PASSWORD DEFAULT
DEVELOPER   LOGICAL_READS_PER_SESSION        KERNEL   DEFAULT
DEVELOPER   PASSWORD_REUSE_MAX               PASSWORD DEFAULT
DEVELOPER   CPU_PER_CALL                     KERNEL   DEFAULT
DEVELOPER   PASSWORD_REUSE_TIME              PASSWORD DEFAULT
DEVELOPER   PASSWORD_LIFE_TIME               PASSWORD 90
DEVELOPER   FAILED_LOGIN_ATTEMPTS            PASSWORD 3
```

New Security Profile Settings

Oracle8 introduces security concepts new to Oracle, but they're not new to the rest of the computing world. In an answer to critics who claim that Oracle password security was nonexistent, Oracle8 introduced the following options:

➤ *Account locking*—Allows DBAs to lock and unlock an account at will.

➤ *Password aging*—Allows DBAs to set passwords to expire after a certain amount of time, forcing the user to change them with some regularity.

➤ *Password expiration*—Allows DBAs to set passwords to expire in the event of unsuccessful login attempts as well as to have the account unlock after some predetermined time.

➤ *Password history*—Keeps track of previous passwords used over a specified time and prevents their reuse during that time interval. Generally used to help make passwords more secure.

➤ *Custom password authentication routines*—Force the user to select passwords that are more secure. As an administrator, you can introduce controls that will force the user to create passwords of a specific length, a certain number of characters and numbers, and so on. This can make Oracle8 passwords much more secure than the old Oracle7 passwords.

 Make sure you understand all the new security features in Oracle8. The test may have specific questions that involve the new security features and how to implement them.

You establish each of these new password options by using profiles. Refer back to Listing 9.2, noting the two profiles listed (**DEFAULT** and **DEVELOPER**). The first profile is the *default*, the profile a user is assigned to when the user is created if the user is not explicitly assigned to another profile. The second profile is the developer profile, which you just created in Listing 9.2.

Note: Each row in Listing 9.2 lists the value for the profile or the value ***DEFAULT***. *If a value for a parameter is not assigned specifically when you create a profile, then that new profile will take on the default setting for that parameter.*

When created, the password profile settings do not have defaults assigned to the default profile; they are all unlimited. You can enable default profiles by doing one of the following:

➤ Altering the default profile and changing the password profile settings to the default settings at which you wish them to be set.

➤ Running the Oracle-supplied script utlpwdmg.sql (included in the ORACLE_HOME/rdbms/admin directory on Unix). When you run this script, it sets up default password settings for the new password parameters (documented with each parameter later in this chapter). The script also loads a sample user-defined password authentication PL/SQL script. Review this file and run it if it suits your purpose.

 Some books and documentation are unclear about the require-ment of running the utlpwdmg.sql script. You do not have to run this script to be able to use password management. All the utlpwdmg.sql script does is set up the default settings (which are set to unlimited when you create a database) and install a user-defined password authentication program. The bottom line is this: Once you install Oracle8, you can use password man-agement immediately. The only bug I could find affects the pass-word function when it is set to **NULL** on more than one profile. This bug is supposed to be corrected in 8.0.6.

Password-Related Profile Settings

Oracle has introduced several new profile settings associated with the new security features present in Oracle8. These profile settings revolve around the users and their passwords. The new profile settings for Oracle are:

➤ *failed_login_attempts*—This setting represents the number of failed login attempts that can be tried before Oracle locks out an account. Note that the user receives an error message: "ERROR: ORA-28000: the account is locked" upon the locking out of the account due to excessive failed connect attempts. The default profile setting of this parameter is **unlimited** upon install and is set to 3 after the DBA runs the utlpwdmg.sql script.

➤ *password_grace_time*—This setting is the amount of time a user has to change his or her password once the password expires (for more information on expiring passwords, see the **password_life_time** description, next). This parameter is set by using either a number that represents days or a number that represents a fraction of a day. The default profile setting for this parameter is **unlimited** upon install, and the default is reset to 10 days after the DBA runs the utlpwdmg.sql script.

To express a fraction of a day for the setting, use the notation y/z. In this format, z is the total of the fractional part of the day you are representing. Therefore, if you use hours, z is 24 (because there are, of course, 24 hours in a day). If you use minutes, z is 1440 (because there are 1,440 minutes in a day). If you use seconds, use the value 86400 for z. (There are a lot of seconds in the day, but it never seems there are enough hours! Go figure!)

The y part of the fraction, then, is the fractional part of the z quantity you wish to represent. For example, if you didn't want to immediately shut a user off when his or her password expired—but wanted to give the user six hours to change the password—you would use the setting of 1/4 (which is really 6/24, because 1/4 of a day is six hours, which is when we would want the password to expire). Let's try another example because this can be confusing. Assume you wished to give the user 90 minutes of grace time before you expired the password. The proper setting would then be 1/16 (90/1,440 mathematically reduced), which comes out as, you guessed it, 90 minutes! If you wish to immediately expire the accounts, you could set this to 0 in the profile.

*Note: The format above for expressing time is used on several of the password profile settings. This includes **password_grace_time**, **password_life_time**, **password_lock_time**, and **password_reuse_time**.*

➤ *password_life_time*—This setting determines how long a user's password is good for if a user is assigned to this profile. Once the time has passed, the password expires and the user cannot sign onto the system. To delay the password expiration, use the **password_grace_time** parameter (discussed above). The default setting for the parameter when the database is created is **UNLIMITED**, and the default is reset to 90 days when the utlpwdmg.sql script is executed.

➤ *password_lock_time*—This setting determines how long an account will remain locked out if the number of failed attempts, as defined by **FAILED_LOGIN_ATTEMPTS**, is exceeded. The default setting for the parameter when the database is created is **UNLIMITED**, and the default is reset to 1 minute when the utlpwdmg.sql script is executed.

➤ *password_reuse_max*—This setting defines the number of times a password has to be changed before it can be reused. If this parameter is set, the **password_reuse_time** parameter must be set to unlimited. The default setting for the parameter when the database is created is **UNLIMITED**, and the default remains at **UNLIMITED** after the utlpwdmg.sql script is executed.

➤ *password_reuse_time*—This setting defines the number of days before a password can be reused. The default setting for the parameter when the database is created is **UNLIMITED**, and the default is reset to 1800 days when the utlpwdmg.sql script is executed.

➤ *password_verify_function*—This setting defines the user-defined PL/SQL function that is called to control the complexity of the password. The default setting for the parameter when the database is created is **UNLIMITED**, and the default is reset to use the **PASSWORD_VERIFY_FUNCTION** when the utlpwdmg.sql script is executed. **verify_function** is loaded into the database when the utlpwdmg.sql script is run. For more details about this setting, see the "PASSWORD VERIFY Function" section later in this chapter.

Make sure you clearly understand how to enable password management in profiles and how to make sure users are assigned to those profiles. Be sure to understand the new profile settings and what each does.

Locking Users Out And Letting Them Back In

Once users are locked out by password management, the only way they can be let back in is to call the DBA and beg for forgiveness, or in some cases, wait for the amount of time set in **password_lock_time** to pass, or…you know the score. Because we DBAs are such a great lot, and because Oracle decided that maybe we should be able to unlock locked accounts, we have the **ALTER**

USER UNLOCK command at our disposal. Also, DBAs can now use the ALTER USER LOCK command to lock out user accounts; Oracle got tired of DBAs complaining that they could not lock out userids easily (in Oracle7, in order to lock out a user without just removing their account, you would have to change the password or remove rights to connect to the database, all very messy stuff). Make sure you tell your most annoying users about this command in a threatening tone.

Oracle8 also allows DBAs to expire passwords, forcing users to change their password before they can get back in the system. This is good if you want to force a whole group of users to change their passwords. (Of course, make sure you provide some way for them to change their passwords, or the pointy-haired boss will come a-knocking.) Finally, you can create a user with an expired password. When you expire passwords using the CREATE USER or ALTER USER command, **password_grace_time** does not have any effect; you must reset users when they want to use the account, or provide a method for them to reset their own password (if that is desirable). Listing 9.3 shows some examples of these commands.

Listing 9.3   Using the **CREATE USER** and **ALTER USER** command.

```
CREATE USER quamquat IDENTIFIED BY oooogracie
TEMPORARY TABLESPACE temp
DEFAULT TABLESPACE users
PASSWORD EXPIRE;

ALTER USER bad_guy ACCOUNT LOCK;
ALTER USER good_guy UNLOCK;
ALTER USER criminal PASSWORD EXPIRE;
```

Dictionary Changes For Security

Of course, the additional security added in Oracle8 has required some changes to the views that DBAs use to determine the status of accounts. The DBA_USERS view has a new column called **account_status** along with several new status codes associated with the new column. These codes are:

➤ *OPEN*—Indicates the user can access the account

➤ *EXPIRED*—Indicates the account password has expired

➤ *EXPIRED(GRACE)*—Indicates an account that has expired but is still accessible because of the **password_grace_time** setting

➤ *LOCKED*—Indicates the account is locked out

➤ *LOCKED(GRACE)*—Indicates the account is locked out after **password_grace_time** has expired

➤ *LOCKED(TIMED)*—Indicates the account is locked out after **password_lock_time** has been activated (for example, after multiple sign-on failures)

The **ACCOUNT_STATUS** code may even display multiple status codes, such as **EXPIRED(GRACE)** and **LOCKED(TIMED)**. Other new columns include **lock_date**, which indicates when the account was locked out, and **expiry_date**, which indicates when the password will expire.

Another table that has changed is **DBA_PROFILES**. This table was obviously changed to display the new profiles available with Oracle8. The **resource_type** column has been added to distinguish between password and kernel resource settings.

Finally, there is a new view, **USER_PASSWORD_LIMITS**, which shows the password limits applied to a specific user. This view allows you to see what password limits the DBA has established for your userid. Note that there is no related **DBA_** or **ALL_** views for this view.

PASSWORD VERIFY Function

As already noted, Oracle allows you to define a custom **PASSWORD VERIFY** function. The function can be any name, so you can actually have multiple verify functions if you desire. **SYS** must own this function in order for it to be used to validate passwords. Listing 9.4 defines this function.

Listing 9.4   Defining the **PASSWORD VERIFY** function.

```
CREATE OR REPLACE FUNCTION sys.name_your_verify_function_here
( user_id            IN          VARCHAR2(30),
  new_password       IN          VARCHAR2(30),
  old_password       IN          VARCHAR2(30)
)
RETURN BOOLEAN;
```

Listing 9.5 shows an example of a **PASSWORD VERIFY** function and how it is used. This is a simplified function, an example just to show you how it is done.

> *Note: The Oracle Certified Professional (OCP) exam will not ask you to write a function, but it is good to know how it all works when you take the exam.*

In this example, you will ensure that the password is not the same as the old password, and that the new password is longer than five characters.

Listing 9.5   Creating a **PASSWORD VERIFY** function.

```
CREATE OR REPLACE FUNCTION sys.f_pwd_verify_01
( user_id            IN            VARCHAR2,
  new_password       IN            VARCHAR2,
  old_password       IN            VARCHAR2
)
RETURN BOOLEAN
IS
BEGIN
     -- check the length of the password > 5 characters.
     IF LENGTH(new_password) < 6
     THEN
          RETURN (FALSE);
     END IF;
     IF new_password = old_password
     THEN
          RETURN(FALSE);
     END IF;
     RETURN(TRUE);
EXCEPTION
WHEN OTHERS
THEN
     RETURN(FALSE);
END f_pwd_verify_01;
```

Now that you have created the profile, you need to test it. You first add the function to an existing profile. Next, try to create a user with a password that does not fit the required length. Then, create a user that does and see what happens. Listing 9.6 shows the results.

Listing 9.6   Testing the **PASSWORD VERIFY** function.

```
--First, we alter the profile and assign it the password
--verify function!
SQL>  alter profile developer
  2     limit
  3     password_verify_function SYSTEM.F_PWD_VERIFY_01;

  Profile altered.

--Now try to create the user.
SQL>  create user max identified by max
  2     temporary tablespace temp
```

```
   3   default tablespace payroll_data
   4   profile developer;
 create user max identified by max
 *
 ERROR at line 1:
 ORA-28003: password verification for the specified password failed
 ORA-28003: password verification for the specified password failed

 --Now let's create the user with a valid profile!
 SQL>  create user max identified by thisisalongpassword
   2   temporary tablespace temp
   3   default tablespace payroll_data
   4   profile developer;

 User created.
```

Changes To The Security Of The **SYS** Schema

Oracle has made a change to the security of the **SYS** schema. In previous versions of Oracle, if a **GRANT** that included the **ANY** syntax (for example, **GRANT SELECT ANY TABLE**) was issued, this grant was effective for the entire database. This caused potential problems with securing the **SYS** schema. Now, the **GRANT ANY** commands do not allow you to manipulate the **SYS** schema. **GRANTS** to **SYS** objects must be given specifically to a user or through a role.

New Oracle8 Advanced Queuing (AQ)

Advanced Queuing (AQ) is a new feature introduced in Oracle8. I briefly touched on it in Chapter 3 when I discussed the new processes associated with AQ. This section digs a bit deeper into AQ, ensuring you know everything you ever needed to know about it for the exam but were afraid to ask.

AQ Concepts

If there was ever a fun topic that DBAs huddle around the coffee machine to discuss, it's got to be the concepts around Oracle8's AQ. The concept behind AQ is that you can queue a message up by one process, and then one or more processes can read this message. AQ allows for a finite control of message queuing (including being able to return error messages) and for control of the order of job step execution.

Message Queues And Queue Processes

To facilitate AQ, Oracle establishes *message queues* in the database to store queued messages. There can be one or more message queues in a database. The message queue is created with the **DBMS_AQADM** package (discussed in the "Using The **DBMS_AQADM** Package" section later in this chapter). A message queue is like a middleman, a repository where Oracle supplied packages (discussed in the "Using The **DBMS_AQ** Package" and "Using The **DBMS_AQADM** Package" sections later in this chapter) place messages and retrieve them. The message queue also aids in the processing of failure messages. Oracle provides two types of queues: normal queues and exception queues.

There are several terms you should be aware of in respect to advanced queuing. They are:

➤ *Normal queues*, the main queues in AQ, used to store and pass messages on to other processes.

➤ *Exception queues* store messages that have generated exceptions. The messages stored were originally in normal queues.

➤ *Consumers* of queue information, those who extract messages from queues, are also known as *subscribers* to a queue.

➤ *Producers* are those that create the messages in the queues for the consumers to use and that can restrict a consumer's ability to dequeue a message. Consumers and producers can place and retrieve messages from queues.

➤ The term *agents* is a collective term used to describe consumers and producers.

➤ *Messages* are the smallest units used in queue processes and are stored in normal queues.

Setting Up AQ In Oracle

Before you can use AQ, you must first set up the processes and users that it requires. This includes setting up database processes, and in many cases, installing the Objects option for Oracle8 and enabling user accounts to use AQ through the granting of roles. In this section, we will addresses these issues in more detail.

Setting Up The Required Database Processes

Oracle8 *queue processes* must be started in order to facilitate the execution of time-based management of the queue processes in Oracle. There are several options that depend on the use of the queue processes (also known as the *time manager*), including expiration, delay, and retention operations. To start the queue processes, set the init.ora setting **AQ_TM_PROCESSES = 1**. As discussed in Chapter 3, there can currently be only one **AQ_TM_PROCESS** started on an Oracle8 database.

Message propagation is another feature of AQ. A single message can be distributed to multiple databases and multiple queues. Message propagation is facilitated through the Oracle8 job scheduler. In order to enable message propagation, you must set the init.ora parameter **job_queue_processes** to a value greater than 0.

Finally, to take full advantage of AQ, you should have purchased and installed the Objects option. AQ works without objects being installed; however, without being able to create objects, you will not enjoy the full flavor of AQ.

Roles Associated With AQ

To enable an account to use AQ, you must assign it to one of two roles. These roles are:

➤ *AQ_ADMINISTRATOR_ROLE*—Grants **EXECUTE** privileges to all programs in the **DBMS_AQ** and **DBMS_AQADM** packages (see below for more on these packages). The user **SYS** must grant this role.

➤ *AQ_USER_ROLE*—Grants **EXECUTE** privileges to the **DBMS_AQ** package, allowing the message queue facilities to be used, but not allowing any administration of the queuing facilities. A user with the **AQ_ADMINISTRATOR_ROLE** must grant this role to other users.

Setting Up The Database For AQ

To use AQ, you must first set up the database as described earlier. Once the AQ processes are running, you generally create a queue administrator account from the **SYS** account, assigning it the role **AQ_ADMINISTRATOR_ROLE**. In addition, you execute the **DBMS_AQADM** procedure **grant_type_access** to allow the administrator to support multiple consumers. Once you have done so, you sign into the administrator account.

The administrator then creates objects that define the *payload* (the format of the message) that the queues store. The payload can take on a logical structure (defined by using the **CREATE TYPE** command) to create a user-defined object type, or you can use a scalar type (e.g., **VARCHAR2**). The Objects option is a good companion with use of AQ functions because it can use defined object types in queues.

Once the payload type is defined, you create the queue table. You do this using the **DBMS_AQADM.CREATE_QUEUE_TABLE** command (the **DBMS_ AQADM** package is documented in "Using The **DBMS_AQADM** Package" in this chapter). Once the queue table is created, you create a queue to be associated with it. To create the queue, use the **DBMS_AQADM.CREATE_ QUEUE** command. Once you have created the queue, you must start it using the—you guessed it—**DBMS_AQADM.START_QUEUE** command.

The processes for removing a queue and a queue table are much the same. You stop the queue (**DBMS_AQADM.STOP_QUEUE**), drop the queue (**DBMS_AQADM.DROP_QUEUE**), and then drop the queue table (**DBMS_AQADM.DROP_QUEUE_TABLE**), all using the **dbms_aqadm** procedure.

Enqueueing A Message

Once the queues are created and ready for use, you place messages in the main queues with an *enqueue*. To do an enqueue, use the **dbms_aq.enqueue** procedure. When you enqueue a message, it is placed in the normal queue (there can be many queues) specified in the message ready to be processed. Once you are ready for the message to be queued up, commit the transaction.

Several features are associated with enqueuing, which means that:

➤ Users can assign specific identifiers to queued messages for later retrieval.

➤ Multiple queues can be established for different subscribers. Multiple consumers can consume a single message.

➤ Queue administrators can specify a list of subscribers with a subscription list for a particular queue and thus, different queues can have many different subscribers. To further cloud the issue, though, specific messages in a queue can be directed to specific recipients who may not be subscribers to the queue, overriding the subscription list.

➤ You can assign messages priority and an order.

➤ One application can use AQ to communicate with another application while connected to different databases and different queues.

➤ Messages can be grouped in a queue so that only one consumer at a time can use them.

➤ Messages placed in a queue can be marked with delay intervals and expiration intervals. A message can be marked as available only within a certain window of time.

Dequeuing A Message

Messages are removed from queues through *dequeuing*. To dequeue messages, use the **dbms_aq.dequeue** procedure. The message is delivered to the application for processing.

Several features are associated with dequeuing. They include:

➤ You need to store a message in a queue only once, even if it is destined for multiple subscribers.

➤ Users have multiple options for selecting messages from the queue. They can select the first message, and subsequently select following messages, or retrieve specific messages using a message identifier.

➤ You can choose to only browse messages, leaving them in the queue for future reference if required, or to remove messages from the queue as they are dequeued.

➤ You can dequeue against an empty queue, defining the time to wait for new messages to be queued.

➤ You can make the dequeue action part of the transaction you are executing, making the results of the dequeue visible to the world only after a **COMMIT**. Alternatively, you can make the dequeue operation a transaction unto itself, making the results of the request visible to the world as soon as the dequeue statement is issued.

➤ Exception queues are made available for messages that are not consumed within the given constraints (e.g., expire time) of the message.

Using The **DBMS_AQ** Package

The **DBMS_AQ** package contains the procedures for the **ENQUEUE** and **DEQUEUE** functions. This package also contains several record specifications related to these functions. Later in this chapter, the "Putting It All Together" section shows how to use and set up **ENQUEUE** and **DEQUEUE**.

dbms_aq.enqueue Procedure

The **dbms_aq.enqueue** procedure adds a message to a specified queue:

```
PROCEDURE DBMS_AQ.ENQUEUE(queue_name   IN VARCHAR2,
enqueue_options      IN   DBMS_AQ.ENQUEUE_OPTIONS_T,
message_properties   IN   DBMS_AQ.MESSAGE_PROPERTIES_T,
payload              IN   <type_name>,
msgid                OUT  RAW);
```

Here is a description of the parameters:

➤ *queue_name*—The name of the message queue into which the message is to be enqueued.

➤ *enqueue_options*—A record that contains enqueuing options using the **ENQUEUE OPTIONS** record type. See the "Record Types Associated With Enqueue And Dequeue Operations" section later in this chapter for the definition of the **ENQUEUE_OPTIONS_T** record type.

➤ *message_properties*—A record that contains the message properties using the message properties record type. See the "Record Types Associated With Enqueue And Dequeue Operations" section for the definition of the **MESSAGE_PROPERTIES_T** record type.

➤ *payload*—The data to be placed in the queue: an object, a **RAW**, or a **NULL**.

➤ *msgid*—The message ID that Oracle returns. It is a unique identifier for that enqueue request. Using this identifier, you can dequeue the specific message.

dequeue Procedure

The dequeue procedure removes a message from a specified queue. The procedure header looks like Listing 9.7.

Listing 9.7 Using the **dequeue** procedure.

```
DBMS_AQ.ENQUEUE(queue_name      IN VARCHAR2,
dequeue_options       IN    DBMS_AQ.ENQUEUE_OPTIONS_T,
message_properties    IN    DBMS_AQ.MESSAGE_PROPERTIES_T,
payload               IN    <type_name>,
msgid                 OUT   RAW);
```

Here is a description of the parameters:

➤ *queue_name*—The name of the queue into which the message is to be dequeued.

➤ *dequeue_options*—A record that contains dequeuing options using the dequeue options record type. See the "Record Types Associated With Enqueue And Dequeue Operations" section for the definition of the **DEQUEUE_OPTIONS_T** record type.

➤ *message properties*—A record that contains the message properties using the message properties record type. See the "Record Types Associated

With Enqueue And Dequeue Operations"section for the definition of the **MESSAGE_PROPERTIES_T** record type.

➤ *payload*—The data to be placed in the queue: an object, a **RAW,** or a **NULL.**

➤ *msgid*—The message ID that Oracle returns.

Record Types Associated With **enqueue** And **dequeue** Operations

The **ENQUEUE_OPTIONS_T** record type is used by the **enqueue** procedure. It contains the option settings selected for an enqueued message. The type's structure is shown below.

```
TYPE DBMS_AQ.ENQUEUE_OPTIONS_T IS RECORD
(visibility          BINARY_INTEGER DEFAULT  DBMS_AQ.ON_COMMIT,
relative_msgid       RAW(16)     DEFAULT   NULL,
sequence_deviation  BINARY_INTEGER DEFAULT NULL);
```

Here is a description of the attributes:

➤ *VISIBILITY*—Determines the transactional behavior of the enqueue request. There are two possible settings: **DBMS_AQ.ON_COMMIT** and **DBM_AQ.IMMEDIATE.**

➤ *RELATIVE_MSGID*—Specifies the message identifier of the message referenced in the **SEQUENCE_DEVIATION** operation. Valid only if **BEFORE** is specified in the **SEQUENCE_DEVIATION** field.

➤ *SEQUENCE_DEVIATION*—Determines if the message being enqueued should be dequeued before other messages already in the queue. There are three valid settings:

　➤ *DBMS_AQ.BEFORE*—Enqueue the message ahead of the message specified by the **RELATIVE_MSGID** field.

　➤ *DBMS_AQ.TOP*—Enqueue this message ahead of any others.

　➤ *NULL*—Specifies that no deviation from normal sequencing should be done. This is the default.

The **DEQUEUE_OPTIONS_T** record type is used by the **dequeue** procedure. It contains the option settings selected for a dequeued message. The type's structure is shown below.

```
TYPE DBMS_AQ.DEQUEUE_OPTIONS_T IS RECORD
(consumer_name      VARCHAR2(30)     DEFAULT   NULL,
```

```
dequeue_mode       BINARY_INTEGER    DEFAULT   DBMS_AQ.REMOVE,
navigation         BINARY_INTEGER    DEFAULT   DBMS_AQ.NEXT_MESSAGE,
visibility         BINARY_INTEGER    DEFAULT   DBMS_AQ.ON_COMMIT,
wait               BINARY_INTEGER    DEFAULT   DBMS_AQ.FOREVER,
msgid              RAW(16)           DEFAULT   NULL,
correlation        VARCHAR2(128)     DEFAULT   NULL);
```

Here is a description of the attributes:

➤ *CONSUMER_NAME*—The name of the consumer of the message. **NULL** is the default. If a consumer is specified, only that consumer can access the message.

➤ *DEQUEUE_MODE*—Specifies locking behavior associated with the **dequeue** operation. Valid options are:

  ➤ *DBMS_AQ.BROWSE*—Read the message without acquiring any locks.

  ➤ *DBMS_AQ.LOCKED*—Read and obtain a write lock on the message.

  ➤ *DBMS_AQ.REMOVE*—Read and delete the message from the queue. This is the default.

➤ *NAVIGATION*—Specifies the position of the message to be retrieved next. Valid options are:

  ➤ *DBMS_AQ.NEXT_MESSAGE*—Retrieve the next message that is available.

  ➤ *DBMS_AQ.NEXT_TRANSACTION*—Skip the remainder of the current transaction group. Instead, retrieve the first message of the next transaction group.

  ➤ *DBMS_AQ.FIRST_MESSAGE*—Get the first message that is available. Resets the current position of the message pointer to the beginning of the queue.

➤ *VISIBILITY*—Determines the transactional behavior of the enqueue request. There are two possible settings: **DBMS_AQ.ON_COMMIT** and **DBM_AQ.IMMEDIATE.**

➤ *WAIT*—The number of seconds to wait if no message is in the queue. Two values are valid: **DBMS_AQ.FOREVER** (which causes the wait to last forever) and **DBMS_AQ.NO_WAIT** (which causes the program not to wait at all).

➤ *MSGID*—Allows specification of a message identifier for the message to be dequeued.

➤ *CORRELATION*—Allows you to use a correlation string passed when the message was enqueued to assist in doing pattern matching of messages. See the section on **MESSAGE_PROPERTIES_T** later in this chapter for more information on sending a correlation string.

The **MESSAGE_PROPERTIES_T** record type is used by the **enqueue** procedure. It allows you to associate a set of properties to a message. You can also receive most of the properties when you dequeue a message. The type's structure is shown below.

```
TYPE DBMS_SQ.MESSAGE_PROPERTIES_T IS RECORD
(priority                BINARY_INTEGER      DEFAULT 1,
 delay                   BINARY_INTEGER      DEFAULT
DBMS_AQ.NO_DELAY,
 expiration              BINARY_INTEGER      DEFAULT DBMS_AQ.NEVER,
 correlation             VARCHAR2(128)       DEFAULT NULL,
 attempts                BINARY_INTEGER,
 recipient_list          DBMS_AQ.AQ$_RECIPIENT_LIST_T,
 exception_queue         VARCHAR2(51)        DEFAULT NONE,
 enqueue_time            DATE,
 state                   BINARY_INTEGER );
```

Here is a description of the attributes:

➤ *PRIORITY*—Specifies the priority of the message you are sending. A smaller number is a higher priority. It can be any number, including negatives, and the default is 1.

➤ *DELAY*—Specifies the delay of the message once enqueued, before it becomes available for dequeuing. The default is no delay.

➤ *EXPIRATION*—The time in seconds after which the message expires. The default behavior is to never expire. If the message expires while still in the queue, it is moved into the exception queue in an **EXPIRED** state.

➤ *CORRELATION*—Allows you to send producer-specified identification for the message to be enqueued. You can use this value to later identify the message.

➤ *ATTEMPTS*—The number of attempts that have been made to dequeue the message. It is available only when the message is dequeued.

➤ *RECIPIENT_LIST*—A table that contains a list of agents. It defaults to subscribers of the queue. The parameter is valid only for queues that allow multiple consumers.

➤ *EXCEPTION_QUEUE*—The name of the exception queue for the message if it cannot be processed successfully.

➤ *ENQUEUE_TIME*—The time the message was enqueued. It is available only when the message is dequeued.

➤ *STATE*—The state of the message at the time of the dequeue. It can have several values:

   ➤ *DBMS_AQ.WAITING*—The message delay has not been reached yet.

   ➤ *DBMS_AQ.READY*—The message is ready to be processed.

   ➤ *DBMS_AQ.PROCESSED*—The message has been processed and is retained.

   ➤ *DBMS_AQ.EXPIRED*—The message has been moved to the exception queue.

Using The **DBMS_AQADM** Package

As you might surmise, you use the **DBMS_AQADM** package to administer the AQ features of Oracle8. The package contains several subprograms that break down into three categories:

➤ Queue table management functions

➤ Queue management functions

➤ Time manager management functions

The following are queue table management functions:

➤ CREATE_QUEUE_TABLE

➤ DROP_QUEUE_TABLE

The following are queue management functions:

➤ CREATE_QUEUE

➤ ALTER_QUEUE

➤ START_QUEUE

➤ STOP_QUEUE

➤ DROP_QUEUE

➤ VERIFY_QUEUE_TYPES

➤ UNSCHEDULE_PROPAGATION

➤ SCHEDULE_PROPAGATION

➤ GRANT_TYPE_ACCESS

The following are time manager management functions:

➤ START_TIME_MANAGER

➤ STOP_TIME_MANAGER

➤ ADD_SUBSCRIBER

➤ REMOVE_SUBSCRIBER

➤ QUEUE_SUBSCRIBERS

Queue Table Management Functions

The **CREATE_QUEUE_TABLE** function creates queue tables. The function accepts up to eight parameters.

```
DBMS_AQADM.CREATE_QUEUE_TABLE (queue_table   IN VARCHAR2,
queue_payload_type   IN VARCHAR2,
storage_clause       IN VARCHAR2,
sort_list            IN VARCHAR2 DEFAULT NULL,
multiple_consumers   IN VARCHAR2 DEFAULT NULL,
message_grouping     IN BINARY_INTEGER DEFAULT NULL,
comment              IN VARCHAR2 DEFAULT NULL,
auto_commit          IN BOOLEAN  DEFAULT NULL);
```

When the **CREATE_QUEUE_TABLE** function is invoked, the queue table is created. Also created is an exception queue table with the naming convention AQ$*QUEUE_TABLE*_E, where *QUEUE_TABLE* is the name of the main queue table being created. A read-only view of the queue table called AQ$*QUEUE_TABLE* and a table or an index organized table called AQ$*QUEUE_TABLE*_T are also created.

The parameters of this function are as follows:

➤ *queue_table*—The name of the queue table to be created.

➤ *queued_payload_type*—The name of the type of user data to be stored. This is the name of a type already created by the user (an object type created with the **CREATE TYPE** command), or it is the string "RAW", which indicated the payload is a single **Large Object (LOB)** column.

➤ *storage_clause*—The storage parameter for the queue table. It can include the following specific parameters: **pctfree, pctused, initrans, maxtrans, tablespace, lob,** and a table storage clause (**INITIAL, NEXT,** and so on).

➤ *sort_list*—Columns to be used as the sort key.

➤ *multiple_consumers*—If **TRUE,** the queue can have more than one consumer per message. The default is **FALSE.** The user who is creating the queue must have been granted the ability to create multiple consumer queues by the DBA having used the **dbms_aqadm. grant_type_access** procedure to allow the user access to create queues that can handle multiple consumers.

➤ *message_grouping*—Message grouping behavior for queues created in the table. It has two valid arguments: **DBMS_AQADM.NONE** (which is the default and indicates that messages are treated individually) and **DBMS_AQADM.TRANSACTIONAL** (which causes one set of messages enqueued during a transaction to be treated as a group and dequeued as a group).

➤ *comment*—The user description of the queue table. It is added to the queue catalog.

➤ *auto_commit*—Defines the setting of queues created in the table in relation to transactions. If it is set to **TRUE,** the current transaction commits before the drop action is executed. If it is set to **FALSE,** the drop action occurs as a part of the current action and takes place only when the session issues a **COMMIT.**

The **DROP_QUEUE_TABLE** function drops existing queue tables. The function takes up to three parameters.

```
DBMS_AQADM.CREATE_QUEUE_TABLE(queue_table  IN VARCHAR2,
force              IN     BOOLEAN default FALSE,
auto_commit        IN     BOOLEAN default TRUE);
```

Here is an explanation of the parameters:

➤ *queue_table*—The name of the queue table to be dropped.

➤ *force*—If set to **FALSE,** it causes the drop action to fail if all queues have not been dropped. **TRUE** forces the drop of the table regardless of whether queues are assigned to the table. Queues are dropped as a result of the action.

➤ *auto_commit*—If set to **TRUE**, it causes the current transaction to commit before the drop action is executed. If it is set to **FALSE**, the drop action occurs as a part of the current action and takes place only when the session issues a commit.

When the **drop_queue_table** procedure is executed, it drops the queue table defined in the parameters of the procedure.

Queue Management Functions

The **CREATE_QUEUE** function creates a queue in a previously created queue table. Oracle requires queue names to be distinct within a schema.

```
DBMS_AQADM.CREATE_QUEUE(queue_name      IN      VARCHAR2,
queue_table            IN        VARCHAR2,
queue_type             IN        BINARY_INTEGER
                       default DBMS_AQADM.NORMAL_QUEUE,
max_retries            IN        NUMBER,
retry_delay            IN        NUMBER,
retention_time         IN        NUMBER    DEFAULT 0,
dependency_tracking    IN        BOOLEAN   DEFAULT FALSE,
comment                IN        VARCHAR2  DEFAULT NULL,
auto_commit            IN        BOOLEAN   DEFAULT TRUE);
```

Here is a description of the parameters:

➤ *queue_name*—The name of the queue you are creating.

➤ *queue_table*—The name of the queue table you created that this queue is associated with.

➤ *queue_type*—The type of queue. It can take two values: **DBMS_AQADM.NORMAL_QUEUE** (for regular queues) or **DBMS_AQADM.EXCEPTION_QUEUE** (for exception queues).

➤ *max_retries*—Defines the maximum number of times that a dequeue with the **REMOVE** command can be attempted on a queue message. The number of retries is counted, and once this number is reached, the message is moved to the exception queue. The default is 0.

➤ *retry_delay*—Defines the number of seconds to delay after an application rollback before the message is scheduled for processing again. The default is 0, and this parameter is ignored if **max_retries** is set to 0.

➤ *retention_time*—The number of seconds a message will remain in the queue table after being dequeued from the queue. The default is 0. The **DBMS_AQADM.INFINITE** constant causes messages to be retained forever.

➤ *dependency_tracking*—Reserved for future use. The default is **FALSE**.

➤ *comment*—User comments associated with the message queue in the queue catalog.

➤ *auto_commit*—It is **FALSE** if you wish to make the **CREATE_QUEUE** operation part of the current transaction. If it is **TRUE** (the default), the current transaction commits before the **CREATE_QUEUE** transaction executes.

The **ALTER_QUEUE** function alters existing queues.

```
DBMS_AQADM.ALTER_QUEUE(queue_name    IN    VARCHAR2,
max_retries            IN      NUMBER   DEFAULT NULL,
retry_delay            IN      NUMBER   DEFAULT NULL,
retention_time         IN      NUMBER   DEFAULT NULL,
auto_commit            IN      BOOLEAN  DEFAULT TRUE);
```

Here is a description of the parameters:

➤ *queue_name*—The name of the queue you are creating.

➤ *max_retries*—Defines the maximum number of times that a dequeue with the **REMOVE** command can be attempted on a queue message. The number of retries is counted, and once this number is reached, the message is moved to the exception queue. The default is 0.

➤ *retry_delay*—Defines the number of seconds to delay after an application rollback before the message is scheduled for processing again. The default is 0, and this parameter is ignored if **max_retries** is set to 0.

➤ *retention_time*—The number of seconds a message will remain in the queue table after being dequeued from the queue. The default is 0. The **DBMS_AQADM.INFINITE** constant causes messages to be retained forever.

➤ *auto_commit*—It is **FALSE** if you wish to make the **CREATE_QUEUE** operation part of the current transaction. If it is **TRUE** (the default), the current transaction commits before the **CREATE_QUEUE** transaction executes.

The **START_QUEUE** function starts existing queues. You must execute this once the queue has been created in order to use the queue.

```
DBMS_AQADM.START_QUEUE(queue_name      IN    VARCHAR2,
enqueue      IN    BOOLEAN   DEFAULT   TRUE,
dequeue      IN    BOOLEAN   DEFAULT   TRUE );
```

Here is a description of the parameters:

➤ *queue_name*—The name of the queue you are creating.

➤ *enqueue*—The flag that indicates if the queue is available for enqueuing.

➤ *dequeue*—The flag that indicates if the queue is available for dequeuing.

> *Note: The ENQUEUE and DEQUEUE flags have no real function. You cannot create an ENQUEUE or DEQUEUE only type queue. The only way to disable a queue is to use the STOP_QUEUE command.*

The **STOP_QUEUE** function stops existing queues.

```
DBMS_AQADM.START_QUEUE(queue_name      IN    VARCHAR2,
enqueue      IN    BOOLEAN   DEFAULT   TRUE,
dequeue      IN    BOOLEAN   DEFAULT   TRUE
wait         IN    BOOLEAN   DEFAULT   TRUE);
```

Here is a description of the parameters:

➤ *queue_name*—The name of the queue you are creating.

➤ *enqueue*—The flag that indicates if the queue is available for enqueuing.

➤ *dequeue*—The flag that indicates if the queue is available for dequeuing.

➤ *wait*—If it is **TRUE** (the default value), the program waits for any outstanding queue transactions to be completed. No new enqueue or dequeue transactions are allowed while the program is waiting. If you specify **FALSE**, the program does not wait on the queue to stop; it returns an ORA_24023.

The **DROP_QUEUE** function drops queues, once the queue itself has been stopped. An error is returned if you do not stop the queue first.

```
DBMS_AQADM.START_QUEUE(queue_name      IN    VARCHAR2,
auto_commit        IN    BOOLEAN   DEFAULT    TRUE);
```

Here is a description of the parameters:

➤ *queue_name*—The name of the queue you are creating.

➤ *auto_commit*—It is **FALSE** if you wish to make the **CREATE_ QUEUE** operation part of the current transaction. If it is **TRUE** (the default), the current transaction commits before the **CREATE_ QUEUE** transaction executes.

The **VERIFY_QUEUE_TYPES** function allows you to determine if two queues have the same payload type. This function is used before propagation between two queues is established to ensure that the queue payloads are compatible. The definition of the procedure is shown below.

```
DBMS_AWADM.VERIFY_QUEUE_TYPES(src_queue_name    IN    VARCHAR2,
dest_queue_name      IN    VARCHAR2,
destination          IN    VARCHAR2,
rc                   OUT   BINARY_INTEGER);
```

Here is a description of the parameters:

➤ *src_queue_name*—The name of the first queue of the verify. Typically, this is the queue from which messages propagate.

➤ *dest_queue_name*—The name of the second queue of the verify. Typically, this is the queue to which messages propagate.

➤ *destination*—The database link for the destination queue. If it is **NULL**, the destination queue is assumed to be on the same database as the source queue.

➤ *rc*—The return code. Returns a 0 if the verify is successful. Any non-zero code is an error.

The **UNSCHEDULE_PROPAGATION** function stops propagation of a queue.

```
DBMS_AWADM.UNSCHEDULE_PROPAGATION(src_queue_name    IN    VARCHAR2,
destination             IN    VARCHAR2);
```

Here is a description of the parameters:

➤ *src_queue_name*—The name of the source queue from which messages are no longer to be propagated.

➤ *destination*—The database link for the destination queue. If it is **NULL**, the destination queue is assumed to be on the same database as the source queue.

The **SCHEDULE_PROPAGATION** function schedules propagation of messages from one queue to another.

```
DBMS_AWADM.SCHEDULE_PROPAGATION(src_queue_name    IN     VARCHAR2,
destination          IN     VARCHAR2
start_time           IN     DATE  DEFAULT SYSDATE,
duration             IN     NUMBER,
next_time            IN     VARCHAR2  DEFAULT NULL,
latency              IN     NUMBER    DEFAULT 60
);
```

Here is a description of the parameters:

➤ *src_queue_name*—The name of the source queue from which messages are to be propagated.

➤ *destination*—The database link for the destination queue. If it is **NULL**, the destination queue is assumed to be on the same database as the source queue.

➤ *start_time*—The initial start date-time when the propagation should begin.

➤ *duration*—The length of time (in seconds) for the propagation to be allowed to run. A **NULL** value allows constant propagation until the propagation is unscheduled.

➤ *next_time*—An expression of a date value that defines the next time the propagation from the queue should begin. A **NULL** value causes the propagation to stop when the current propagation process has completed.

➤ *latency*—The maximum wait time (in seconds) that a message may sit in a queue after propagation has begun before it is propagated. The default is 60 seconds. This setting controls how long the queue monitor waits before checking for messages in the queue after the queue manager has finished propagating all messages currently in the queue.

The **GRANT_TYPE_ACCESS** function grants the user specified in the argument to the procedure the ability to create message queues that will support multiple consumers. The procedure is:

```
DBMS_AQADM.GRANT_TYPE_ACCESS(user_name    IN     VARCHAR2);
```

The **user_name** parameter is the name of the user who is creating queues that need to be allowed to support multiple consumers.

Time Manager Management Functions

DBMS_AQADM includes several time manager management functions as well. We will address these parts of the package in this section.

The **START_TIME_MANAGER** function allows you to start the queue monitor process. You can use this procedure to start the queue monitor process if you had previously stopped it or if you did not start the database with a monitor process. There are no parameters for this call.

The **STOP_TIME_MANAGER** function allows you to stop the queue monitor process. You can use this procedure to stop the queue monitor process. The actual queue monitor process on the system does not stop when this call is issued. There are no parameters for this call.

The **ADD_SUBSCRIBER** procedure adds a subscriber to the queue.

```
DBMS_AQADM.ADD_SUBSCRIBER(queue_name    IN    VARCHAR2,
subscriber              IN    VARCHAR2   SYS.AQ$_AGENT);
```

Here is a description of the parameters:

➤ *queue_name*—The name of the queue to which the subscriber is being added.

➤ *subscriber*—The subscriber to be added. Note that this is not an actual name but an object of type **SYS.AQ$_AGENT**.

The **REMOVE_SUBSCRIBER** function allows you to remove a subscriber from a queue.

```
DBMS_AQADM.REMOVE_SUBSCRIBER(queue_name    IN    VARCHAR2,
subscriber              IN    VARCHAR2   SYS.AQ$_AGENT);
```

Here is a description of the parameters:

➤ *queue_name*—The name of the queue from which the subscriber is being removed.

➤ *subscriber*—The subscriber to be removed. Note that this is not an actual name but an object of type **SYS.AQ$_AGENT**.

The **QUEUE_SUBSCRIBERS** function returns a current list of subscribers associated with a specific queue.

```
DBMS_AQADM.QUEUE_SUBSCRIBERS(queue_name    IN      VARCHAR2)
RETURN  DBMS_AQADM.AQ$_SUBSCRIBER_LIST_T;
```

The **queue_name** parameter is the name of the queue from which the subscriber is being removed.

Data Dictionary Views Associated With Queues

You can query several data dictionary views that are associated with Advanced Queuing. They are:

➤ *DBA_QUEUE_TABLES*—Used to obtain information about all queue tables created. The related **USER_QUEUE_TABLES** view shows information on all queue tables defined in your schema.

➤ *DBA_QUEUES*—Used to obtain information about all queues created in the database. The related **USER_QUEUES** shows you information about all queues created in your schema.

➤ *DBA_JOBS*—Used to view schedules for message propagation.

Two dynamic statistic views are also available for you to use:

➤ *GV$AQ*—Provides information about the numbers of messages and their various states.

➤ *V$AQ*—Contains information about the messages in a specific database instance.

Putting It All Together

Well, this chapter has covered a lot of ground about AQ. The discussion finishes with an example of how to take advantage of AQ. The example in Figure 9.1 creates an AQ administrator, creates a type to be used for the payload of a message, sets up the queues, and finally enqueues the message and dequeues it, displaying it after dequeuing it. Thanks to Mike Ault for allowing me to use this figure.

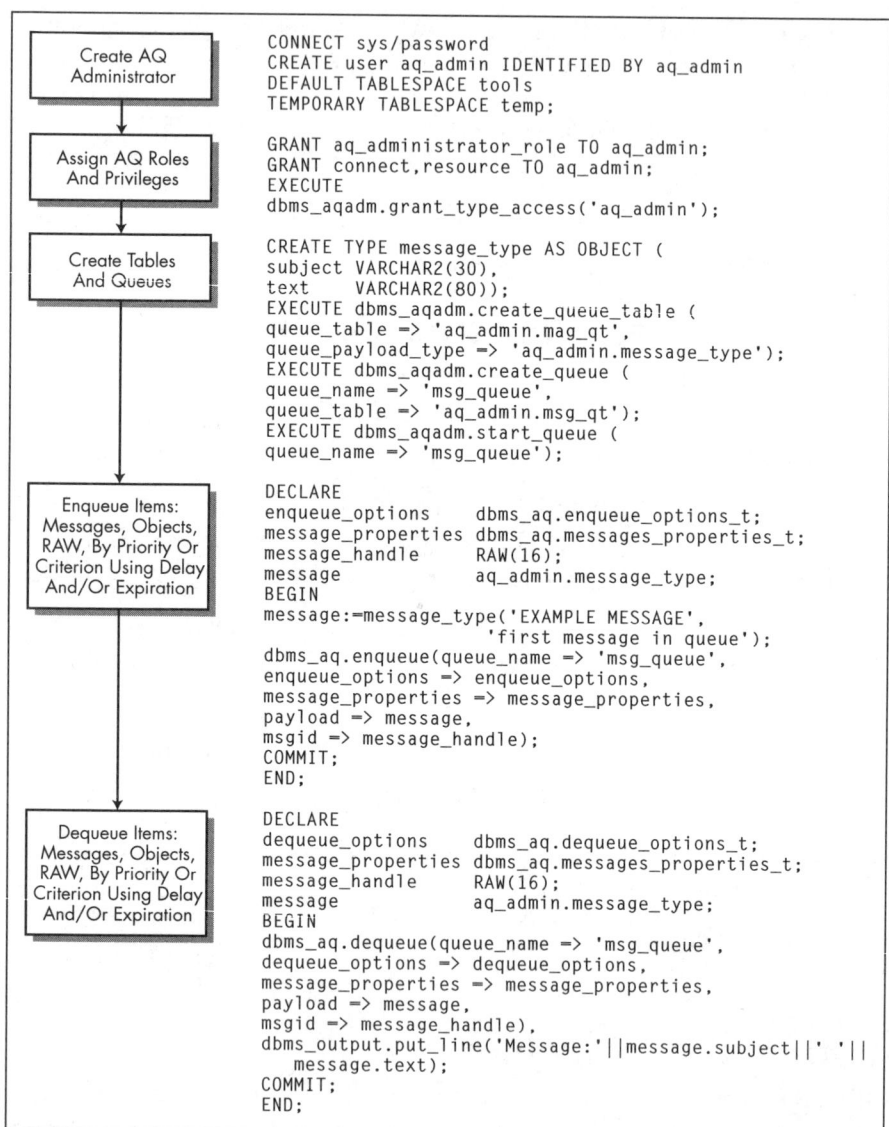

```
                              CONNECT sys/password
  ┌──────────────┐            CREATE user aq_admin IDENTIFIED BY aq_admin
  │  Create AQ   │            DEFAULT TABLESPACE tools
  │ Administrator│            TEMPORARY TABLESPACE temp;
  └──────────────┘
         │                    GRANT aq_administrator_role TO aq_admin;
  ┌──────────────┐            GRANT connect,resource TO aq_admin;
  │Assign AQ Roles│           EXECUTE
  │And Privileges │           dbms_aqadm.grant_type_access('aq_admin');
  └──────────────┘
         │                    CREATE TYPE message_type AS OBJECT (
  ┌──────────────┐            subject VARCHAR2(30),
  │ Create Tables│            text    VARCHAR2(80));
  │  And Queues  │            EXECUTE dbms_aqadm.create_queue_table (
  └──────────────┘            queue_table => 'aq_admin.mag_qt',
         │                    queue_payload_type => 'aq_admin.message_type');
                              EXECUTE dbms_aqadm.create_queue (
                              queue_name => 'msg_queue',
                              queue_table => 'aq_admin.msg_qt');
                              EXECUTE dbms_aqadm.start_queue (
                              queue_name => 'msg_queue');

  ┌──────────────┐            DECLARE
  │Enqueue Items:│            enqueue_options     dbms_aq.enqueue_options_t;
  │Messages, Objects,│        message_properties dbms_aq.messages_properties_t;
  │RAW, By Priority Or│       message_handle      RAW(16);
  │Criterion Using Delay│     message             aq_admin.message_type;
  │And/Or Expiration │        BEGIN
  └──────────────┘            message:=message_type('EXAMPLE MESSAGE',
                                              'first message in queue');
                              dbms_aq.enqueue(queue_name => 'msg_queue',
                              enqueue_options => enqueue_options,
                              message_properties => message_properties,
                              payload => message,
                              msgid => message_handle);
                              COMMIT;
                              END;

  ┌──────────────┐            DECLARE
  │Dequeue Items:│            dequeue_options     dbms_aq.dequeue_options_t;
  │Messages,     │            message_properties dbms_aq.messages_properties_t;
  │RAW, By Priority Or│       message_handle      RAW(16);
  │Criterion Using Delay│     message             aq_admin.message_type;
  │And/Or Expiration │        BEGIN
  └──────────────┘            dbms_aq.dequeue(queue_name => 'msg_queue',
                              dequeue_options => dequeue_options,
                              message_properties => message_properties,
                              payload => message,
                              msgid => message_handle),
                              dbms_output.put_line('Message:'||message.subject||' '||
                                  message.text);
                              COMMIT;
                              END;
```

Figure 9.1   Using AQ in Oracle8.

Oracle8 External Procedure Calls

Oracle8 allows you to call externally created procedures. These procedures are dynamically linked libraries (DLLs) created in C. In order to access these external procedures, you create **LIBRARY**s. Much like **BFILE**s are pointers to files outside the database, **LIBRARY**s contain pointers to the external DLLs that are called from within the database.

For the purposes of the OCP exam, you should understand the fundamentals of external procedure calls.

You create **LIBRARY**s with the **CREATE LIBRARY** command. The command takes this form:

```
CREATE LIBRARY lib_alias AS lib_path;
```

where **lib_alias** is the alias name of the library you wish to create and **lib_path** is the path and name of the DLL that the user references in executing an external procedure call.

Developers can create PL/SQL procedures to then call the external procedures. When the request is made, the listener process **extproc** starts a separate Net8 process. Calls are sent through **extproc**, which starts a second separate process for the user call. This second process protects the user process from problems like memory corruption. In addition, **extproc** passes variables between the two processes.

A few restrictions to note about external procedure calls are as follows:

➤ Oracle currently supports calls to DLLs created in C only.

➤ You cannot pass as variables into external calls cursor variables, records, collections, or instances of an object type.

➤ You cannot use a database link to specify a remote library in the **LIBRARY** clause.

➤ You must start the Net8 listener agent **extproc** on the host that runs the Oracle server.

➤ The maximum number of parameters that can be passed to an external procedure is 127.

Practice Questions

Question 1

> Given the following code, how long will it be until a user is forced to change his or her password?
>
>
>
> ```
> CREATE PROFILE user_profile
> LIMIT
> IDLE_TIME 1
> FAILED_LOGIN_ATTEMPTS 3
> PASSWORD_LOCK_TIME 30
> PASSWORD_LIFE_TIME 90
> PASSWORD_GRACE_TIME 30;
> ```
>
> ○ a. 30 days
>
> ○ b. 30 weeks
>
> ○ c. 1 year
>
> ○ d. 30 months
>
> ○ e. 90 days

Answer e is correct. This value is set by the **password_life_time** parameter. Answer a is incorrect, although you might choose this answer based on **password_lock_time** being set to 30. **password_lock_time**, however, has nothing to do with when the password expires. **password_lock_time** is how long an account is locked out if a user attempts to sign into an account with a wrong password. Answer b is incorrect because times are not represented in weeks in these settings, but rather in days. Answer c is incorrect, and I'll be darned if I know how you would guess it. Answer d is incorrect, although you might have chosen this answer if you didn't know that the time was measured in days, and if you thought that **password_lock_time** or **password_grace_time** were the parameters. **password_grace_time** is the amount of time you are given to change your password after **password_lock_time** has expired.

Question 2

Which of the following is not one of the new security features introduced in Oracle8?

○ a. Account locking

○ b. Password aging

○ c. Password expiration

○ d. Password history

○ e. Auditing of **SELECT** statements on tables

Answer e is correct. Although it might be a nice enhancement request for Oracle9 (or even 8.1.x), auditing of **SELECT** tables is not yet with us in Oracle8. Answer a is incorrect because account locking is a feature of Oracle8. It allows the DBA to lock out a user's account without needing to mess with old methods like changing passwords or revoking grants. Answer b is incorrect because it is also introduced in Oracle8. It allows the DBA to force users to change their passwords or be forced to ask the DBA for account reinstatement. Answer c is incorrect because it is a feature of Oracle8. Password expiration allows you to expire passwords with the flick of a command, or expire passwords based on potentially illicit multiple login attempts. Answer d is incorrect because it is a feature of Oracle8. It allows you to ensure that users select different passwords every time.

Question 3

While trying to log into the database, the user receives the error message, "ORA-2800 The account is locked". The user calls you and you need to correct the problem. What do you do?

○ a. Call Oracle support for assistance.

○ b. Issue an **ALTER USER PROFILE <profile_name>;** to assign the user to an Oracle8 security profile.

○ c. Issue an **ALTER USER UNLOCK ACCOUNT;** command.

○ d. Issue an **ALTER USER UNLOCK;** command.

○ e. Drop and recreate the user.

Answer d is correct. The **ALTER USER UNLOCK** command unlocks a user account that has been locked. Answer a is incorrect because although you could contact Oracle support, this is not the best answer to the problem. Answer b is incorrect because changing a user's profile does not unlock the account. Answer c is incorrect because it is not a valid command. Answer e is incorrect because although dropping and recreating the user may well solve the problem, it is nowhere close to the best solution.

Question 4

Which roles are associated with advanced queuing? [Choose two]

- ❑ a. **AQ_ADMINISTRATOR_ROLE**
- ❑ b. **AQ_USER**
- ❑ c. **AQ_ADMIN_ROLE**
- ❑ d. **AQ_USER_ROLE**
- ❑ e. **AQ_DEVELOP_ROLE**

Answers a and d are correct. The roles **AQ_ADMINISTRATOR_ROLE** and **AQ_USER_ROLE** are both associated with AQ. The **AQ_USER_ROLE** allows the user to execute the **DBMS_AQ** package allowing the user the enqueue and dequeue messages to and from queue tables. The **AQ_AD-MINISTRATOR_ROLE** allows the user to execute the **DBMS_AQ** package as well and in addition the **DBMS_AQADM** packages which allow administration of AQ. Answers b, c, and e are incorrect because they are not valid roles.

Question 5

What is the correct order of operations when you are passing messages back and forth to an existing queue?

- ○ a. Create the queue, create the queue table, start the queue, enqueue, and dequeue.
- ○ b. Start the queue, dequeue, and enqueue.
- ○ c. Dequeue, create the queue table, start the queue, and enqueue.
- ○ d. Enqueue and dequeue the message.
- ○ e. Create the queue table, create the queue, start the queue, and enqueue.

Answer d is correct. You enqueue the message and then dequeue it from an existing queue. Answer a would be correct if the queue had not already existed. However, the question indicates that it already exists, which is why this is a trick question. Therefore, answer a is incorrect. Answers b and c are incorrect because the order of operations is incorrect. Answer e is incorrect because it calls for creating the queue (which already exists) and it does not include a dequeue operation.

Question 6

Which command creates a **LIBRARY** for external calls from Oracle?

○ a. **CREATE PROCEDURE**

○ b. **CREATE LIBRARY**

○ c. **CREATE STORAGE AREA**

○ d. **CREATE TABLESPACE**

○ e. **CREATE EXTERNAL LOCATION**

Answer b is correct. The **CREATE LIBRARY** command creates library entries for external procedures. Answer a is incorrect because it is for creating stored procedures. Answer c is incorrect because it is not even a SQL statement. Answer d is incorrect because it creates tablespaces. Answer e is incorrect because there is no such command.

Question 7

What init.ora parameter must be set in order for time management processes to work when you are using advanced queuing?

○ a. **AQ_TM_SERIES = YES**

○ b. **AQ_TIMER = YES**

○ c. **AQ_TM_PROCESSES = 1**

○ d. **AQ_TM_ACTIVATE = 1**

○ e. **AQ_TM_ACTIVE = YES**

Answer c is correct. **AQ_TM_PROCESSES = 1** establishes one AQ timer process, which is currently the maximum number of processes that you can run in Oracle8. Answers a, b, d, and e are incorrect because they are all invalid Oracle options.

Need To Know More?

 Ault, Michael R.: *Oracle8 Black Book.* The Coriolis Group, 1998. ISBN 1-57610-187-8. This book deals in great depth with several new Oracle8 features, including partitioning.

 Feuerstein, Steven, et al.: *Oracle Built-in Packages.* O'Reilly & Associates, 1998. ISBN 1-56592-375-8. I consider this book to be the definitive work on Oracle-supplied packages; it contains a whole chapter on Oracle8 AQ.

 Theriault, Marlene, et al.: *Oracle Security.* O'Reilly & Associates, 1998. ISBN 1-56592-450-9. This book contains several chapters that relate to security issues and implementing security in Oracle8.

 Oracle's online documentation, including *Oracle8 Concepts*, *Oracle8 Administrators Guide*, and *Oracle8 Tuning*, is on CDs supplied with the Oracle database server product. This documentation is a principle source of information for any Oracle feature you wish to use.

 **www.support.com** is Oracle's Metalink Web site. It is a wonderful resource if you have Oracle Metals support.

Oracle8 Backup And Recovery

Terms you'll need to understand:

√ Recovery Manager (RMAN)

√ Backup sets

√ Backup pieces

√ Multiplexing

√ Full backup

√ Incremental backup

√ Image copies

√ Recovery catalog

Techniques you'll need to master:

√ Setting up a backup repository

√ Registering a database in a repository using RMAN

√ Backing up an Oracle8 database with RMAN

√ Recovering a database backed up using RMAN

√ Making image copies of datafiles with RMAN

√ Generating reports and lists with RMAN

Oracle8 And RMAN

This chapter addresses issues relating to RMAN that you will be expected to know for the Oracle Certified Professional (OCP) exam. The chapter looks at the architecture and features of RMAN, and then details how to set up RMAN properly. It then addresses how to back up databases with the product, including how to create backup scripts. The chapter then examines how to do recoveries with RMAN. Finally, it covers the reporting features available in RMAN and looks at management issues with RMAN and the views Oracle provides to manage RMAN. First, a word from the author.

The Author On His Soapbox

If you have already read Chapter 2, you might have found yourself thinking, "Boy, this guy is backup-happy." Backups are among the first priorities of database administrators (DBAs). Databases must be backed up, and they must be recoverable.

Oracle7 offered a product called Enterprise Backup Utility (EBU) to back up Oracle7 databases in concert with other vendor-supplied interfaces into tape backup systems. I was never really all that crazy about the product myself and have had more than one client pull it out because of its shortcomings. Oracle8 introduces a replacement product to EBU called *Recovery Manager* (*RMAN*), which figures prominently in the Oracle8 OCP exam. To be sure, RMAN is much more flexible and boasts that it offers some great features. Time will tell if it will overcome EBU's shortcomings and (with some) bad reputation.

What's the bottom line? Backups, backups, backups. And test your backup strategy. Now, back to the text!

RMAN Features And Architecture

RMAN has many features of which DBAs should be aware, and that are covered on the OCP exam. This section introduces you to RMAN and its features, and then looks at the basic architecture of RMAN.

RMAN Features

RMAN is an Oracle-supplied backup and recovery utility that comes with the base database product. It manages backup and recovery of Oracle databases (once you have set up the databases) with a minimum of ongoing administrative work required. RMAN does the following kinds of operations:

➤ It configures frequently performed database backups. This includes hot and cold backups. These operations can be automated as well.

➤ It generates a log of all backup and recovery actions.

➤ It parallelizes backup and recovery operations.

➤ It performs incremental backups (only for hot backups). This new feature allows you to back up only those data blocks that have changed, which potentially saves you backup time. Of course, your recovery window increases, and you must use more advanced backup management strategies.

➤ It allows you to do hot backups RMAN without requiring that a tablespace be put into hot backup mode. This reduces overhead during the backup process that is caused because of the additional redo generated while the tablespace is in hot backup mode.

➤ It can back up the entire database, specific tablespaces, or datafiles.

➤ It provides automated datafile integrity checking.

➤ It allows you to execute backup and recovery operations interactively, through command files and through stored scripts.

You can run RMAN in two ways: interactively or in batch mode. Additionally, Oracle offers a graphical interface in Oracle Enterprise Manager (OEM). Also, an application programming interface (API) allows programmers to interface with RMAN and create programs that can manage backup and recovery. RMAN returns one of three return codes when it exits:

➤ *ex_succ*—Means that all RMAN statements succeeded

➤ *ex_warn*—Means that some RMAN statements were successful but the most recent was not

➤ *ex_fail*—Means that no command was successful

RMAN Backup Sets

When you use RMAN to back up a database, *backup sets* are created. These backup sets contain one or more datafiles or archive logs, but cannot contain both. Control file backups can also be contained in datafile backup sets. A backup set constitutes a complete full or incremental backup (see more on full and incremental backups later in this secton). Backup sets typically can go to disk or to tape, and there may be one or more sets for any given backup command, depending on how many backup devices you have available. As a result, you can parallelize writing to the backup sets and hopefully speed up the operation.

A backup set that contains datafiles and/or control files is a *datafile backup set*. A backup set that contains archived redo logs is an *archivelog backup set*. A backup set contains one or more *backup pieces*, each piece being a single output file. You can restrict the size of the backup pieces so that it does not exceed a particular maximum file size. This is handy if you are writing out to a filesystem with limited space or if your operating system has limitations on maximum file sizes. Oracle also provides block compression, which skips data blocks that have never been used, reducing the size and run time of the backup being executed.

Datafile backups can be *multiplexed*. Therefore, a single datafile can be stored noncontiguously in different backup pieces. Multiplexing also allows Oracle to selectively determine which tablespace or datafile is backed up. RMAN switches between backing up data in various tablespaces and datafiles, depending on the activity of the datafiles or tablespaces. If activity increases in one datafile, or within the tablespace, RMAN may choose to work on another tablespace or datafile of the backup, returning to the remaining tablespace or datafile when its activity has decreased or it is the only remaining piece of the backup.

RMAN allows you to do both full and incremental backup sets. A *full backup* set backs up the entire database, tablespace, or datafile. It is incorrect to associate a full backup with a backup of just the entire database because it can back up only a specific part of a database (e.g., a full backup backs up just a data file). Rather, you should contrast a full backup to what is known as an incremental backup. An *incremental backup* backs up only those blocks in the database that have changed since the last full backup, speeding up backup execution significantly.

Incremental backups are multilevel, allowing you to do incremental backups at different time periods that might replace incremental backups at lower levels. Therefore, you could implement a three-level backup strategy. You would use the level 0 backup, a full backup, once a month to back up the database. You would then use a level 1 backup once a week to back up that week's changes. You would also use a level 2 backup to back up daily changes. You would keep the level 2 backups until the next level 1 was done for recovery purposes, and you would keep all level 1 backups until the next full backup was performed on the entire database.

RMAN Image Copies

In addition to backup sets, RMAN allows you to do *image copies* of datafiles. These are exact copies of datafiles that you can use as-is to perform recovery; no compression is performed. An image copy is not unlike an operating system copy of the file, except that it has these benefits:

➤ An image copy has the data validated by the RMAN tool.

➤ The image copy is registered in the catalog and the control file.

➤ You can use RMAN to perform automated recovery with the image copy.

Image copies can be made only to disk and can be restored to another disk, if need be, to prevent overwriting the original datafile with the same name. You can also use operating system-created image copies and record them in the recovery catalog.

 Make sure you understand the differences between image copies and backup sets.

Block Corruption Detection

One central benefit of RMAN is that control and checksum information is contained in the backup pieces, providing a way to validate the data and protecting from a possible corrupted backup set. During the backup process, if RMAN detects corruption, it logs the corruption to the **V$BACKUP_COR-RUPTION** and **V$COPY_CORRUPTION** views for later reporting. The corrupted block is also reported to the control file and the alert log of the database being backed up.

You can limit the number of bad blocks that RMAN backs up without failing the backup job by using the **SET MAX CORRUPT** clause in RMAN, as shown here:

```
set maxcorrupt for datafile 1 to 0;
```

This causes the backup to fail if any corrupt blocks are found. You can disable block corruption by using the **NOCHECKSUM** option. Note that by default, any error will cause RMAN to exit with an error code.

RMAN Channels

Before you can execute a backup or recovery using RMAN, you must allocate a *channel* between the backup processes and the operating system. The following operations in RMAN must have at least one channel allocated to operate correctly:

➤ **BACKUP**

➤ **COPY**

➤ RESTORE

➤ RECOVER

To allocate a channel, you use the RMAN command **ALLOCATE CHAN-NEL**. When you allocate the channel, you also specify the type of device that will be used for the operation that will occur through that channel. Multiple channels can be allocated, allowing for multiple backup sets or file copies to run in parallel by the execution of just a single RMAN command. Each time you issue an **ALLOCATE CHANNEL** command, a separate connection between the backup processes and the operating system is created.

RMAN Recovery Catalog

The RMAN architecture revolves primarily around the *recovery catalog*. The recovery catalog is an Oracle database and associated objects in a schema that are created to manage RMAN backups. Although the recovery catalog is not required to use RMAN, some of the backup/recovery functions are not available without it being set up correctly. Generally, to set up a catalog, you identify the database in which the catalog will exist. Then, you create a user in that database and grant that user the **RECOVERY_CATALOG_OWNER** role.

What are the benefits of using the recovery catalog? With the recovery catalog in place, you can use these RMAN features, which are not available otherwise:

➤ Tablespace point-in-time recovery

➤ Stored scripts

➤ Recovery when the control file is lost or damaged

The bottom line is that Oracle strongly recommends that you use the recovery catalog.

Once you have set up the recovery catalog, you use the RMAN executable in concert with RMAN manual commands or stored scripts to back up, recover, and report on backups. The next few sections of this chapter look at the setup, backup, recovery, and reporting functions of RMAN. Finally, the chapter returns (in much more detail) to the recovery catalog and addresses maintenance issues and reporting from the views Oracle supplies for the DBAs. First, let's look at how to set up the catalog and use it to register, back up, and recover databases.

 The recovery catalog should always be a separate database from the one you are going to back up. Also, you need to back up the database that the recovery catalog is a part of!

Setting Up The RMAN Recovery Catalog

Setting up the recovery catalog RMAN is an important first task in using RMAN. This section looks at the basic steps required to set up the recovery catalog, in order of execution.

Creating The Recovery Catalog

Setting up the recovery catalog is not a terribly complicated process. It only requires setting up a user in the database you will use, granting certain user rights, and running a script. To begin the creation of the recovery catalog, you choose the database to be used to store the recovery catalog and then create the userid/schema in which to create the recovery catalog. Listing 10.1 shows the creation of a user/schema in a database that will store the recovery catalog.

Listing 10.1   Creation of recovery catalog user/schema.

```
CREATE USER RMAN IDENTIFIED BY RMAN
DEFAULT TABLESPACE RMAN_catalog_tbs
TEMPORARY TABLESPACE temp
QUOTA UNLIMITED ON RMAN_catalog_tbs;
```

Here are the steps you take once you have created the user/schema that contains the recovery catalog:

1. **GRANT** the userid the role **RECOVERY_CATALOG_OWNER** with the following:

   ```
   GRANT RECOVERY_CATALOG_OWNER TO eman;
   ```

   Doing so gives the user account the privileges that it needs to manage the recovery catalog. Note that this grant does not give connect access to the user account. You should assign this separately.

2. Once you have created the schema for the recovery catalog, sign into that user account. You must execute the SQL script catrman.sql from the account you just created to install the recovery catalog:

   ```
   @?/rdbms/admin/catman.sql
   ```

   This script is generally in the ORACLE_HOME/rdbms/admin directory on Unix or in the ORACLE_HOME\rdbms80\admin directory on NT. See "Registering A Database In The Recovery Catalog" later in this chapter for details on registering a database in the recovery catalog.

Using RMAN

The RMAN program allows you to manage the recovery catalog, start backups and recoveries, and generate reports on backups. You start RMAN from the command line, passing it parameters as required. An example call to RMAN might look like this:

```
RMAN target=system/manager@test1
rcvcat=RMAN_admin/RMAN_admin@backupdb
```

RMAN has several options that you can provide on the command line.

> *Note: You can use single or double quotation marks in the arguments to the strings—although some may require you to use escape characters (e.g., the \ character).*

The command-line options include:

➤ *APPEND*—This causes RMAN to append to the output file specified by **MSGLOG**.

➤ *CMDFILE*—This causes RMAN to get input from the filename given as the argument to this parameter. If it is not specified, the default is **STDIN**.

➤ *DEBUG*—This turns on the debug mode for RMAN.

➤ *MSGLOG*—This specifies the name of a file to which RMAN will send all messages. The default is **STDOUT**.

➤ *NOCATALOG*—This option is required if you do not have a recovery catalog.

➤ *RCVCAT*—This is the connect string to the recovery catalog username and database.

➤ *TARGET*—This is the target database connect string. If you wish to do the equivalent of connect internal, just type "target /" (without the quotation marks, of course).

> *Note: You can connect with RMAN to a target database by using the **nocatalog** parameter of the RMAN command. Doing so allows you to do backups and recoveries without the recovery catalog, within the constraints mentioned in the "RMAN Recovery Catalog" section earlier in this chapter.*

Recovery Manager Commands

When you use RMAN, you can execute RMAN commands, create and run scripts to execute a series of commands and operations such as backups and allocation of channels, and use RMAN to do reporting on a database's backup and recovery needs. Each RMAN command is terminated by a semicolon at the end of the command. Here are the commands (with examples) that you use to manage the recovery catalog as well as backups.

ALLOCATE CHANNEL

This command is used with backup and restore operations. It allows for communications between the recovery processes and the operating system (OS). When you allocate a channel, you assign it a name or a handle to which it will be referred. You can allocate the channel for such operations as saving backup sets to disk, to some other resource (e.g., tape), or to delete backup sets with the **FOR DELETE** clause. Listing 10.2 shows how to use the **ALLOCATE CHANNEL** command.

Listing 10.2   Example of the ALLOCATE CHANNEL command.

```
RMAN> ALLOCATE CHANNEL chan1 TYPE DISK;
RMAN> ALLOCATE CHANNEL chan2 FOR DELETE TYPE DISK;
RMAN> ALLOCATE CHANNEL chan3 FOR '/dev/rmt0';
```

BACKUP

This command creates backup sets of databases, archived redo logs, or control files. You can back up the target database when it is open (if it is in archivelog mode) or just mounted. The format of the **BACKUP** command is **BACKUP**(*options*)(*scope*). The **BACKUP** command has the following options available:

➤ *CHANNEL*—This names the channel that should be used for the backup set.

➤ *CUMULATIVE*—This flag, associated with an **INCREMENTAL LEVEL** backup, indicates that the backup is to be of all changes since the last level 0 backup.

➤ *DELETE INPUT*—This is used to delete archive logs after they have been backed up.

➤ *FILESPERSET num*—This defines the number of datafiles that can be multiplexed into individual backup sets.

➤ *FULL*—This is a level 0 backup, causing the full datafile to be backed up.

➤ *INCREMENTAL LEVEL*—This is a level 1 through 8 backup. Only blocks changed since the last full backup, or the last higher level incremental level backup, are backed up. There must be an associated level 0 backup in order to do an **INCREMENTAL LEVEL** backup.

➤ *MAXCORRUPT num*—This defines the maximum number of corrupted datafiles that can be backed up until the entire backup process fails.

➤ *NOCHECKSUM*—This flag indicates that no block checksums should be calculated during the backup.

➤ *SKIP*—This option defines datafile classes that are skipped. Three options are available: **INACCESSIBLE, OFFLINE**, and **READ-ONLY**.

➤ *TAG*—This name gives a name to the backup that can be used for identification later, and it should be meaningful.

Here are the scope options available to the **BACKUP** command:

➤ *ARCHIVELOG*—Backs up all archived redo logs. This scope option can further specify a filename pattern, sequence range, or date and time range.

➤ *BACKUP CONTROL FILE*—Backs up a backup control file.

➤ *BACKUPSET*—Backs up the primary key of a backup set on disk.

➤ *CURRENT CONTROLFILE*—Backs up the current control file.

➤ *DATABASE*—Backs up all datafiles and control files.

➤ *DATAFILE*—Backs up all datafiles by name or number. If named, the datafile must be a current datafile named in the control file.

➤ *DATAFILE COPY*—Backs up all datafiles by name or datafile number.

➤ *TABLESPACE tbs_name*—Backs up all datafiles for the specifically named tablespace.

Listings 10.3 and 10.4 are examples of the **BACKUP** command.

Listing 10.3   Running a full backup using RMAN and the **BACKUP** command.

```
RMAN> RUN
{ALLOCATE CHANNEL chan1 TYPE DISK;
BACKUP FULL TAG 'MY BACKUP' format '/backupdir/todays_backup/
```

```
db_t%t_s%s_p%p' (DATABASE);
RELEASE CHANNEL chan1;
}
```

Listing 10.4   Another example of running a full backup using
RMAN and the **BACKUP** command.

```
RMAN> RUN
{ALLOCATE CHANNEL chan1 NAME '/dev/rmt0';
BACKUP FULL FILESPERSET 5 SKIP OFFLINE
( database format '/backupdir/todays_backup/db_t%t_s%s_p%p');
RELEASE CHANNEL chan1;
}
```

CATALOG

This command is used to manually add items to the recovery catalog. Valid
arguments to the **CATALOG** command include **ARCHIVELOG**, **BACKUP**,
CONTROLFILECOPY, and **DATAFILECOPY**. Here is an example of
manually adding a datafile using the **CATALOG** command:

```
RMAN> CATALOG DATAFILECOPY '/backups/01011999/bigdb_system_01.dbf';
```

CHANGE

This command modifies the availability status of a backup item. When used
by itself, the **CHANGE** command refers to backups, the backup piece is referred to and, for archivelogs, the **ARCHIVELOG** keyword is used. When
the **CHANGE** command is used for image copies, you use the **DATAFILE-
COPY** keyword. For a backup of a control file, you use the **BACKUP
CONTROLFILE** keywords. The availability status keywords that you can
use are **AVAILABLE, DELETE, UNAVAILABLE**, and **UNCATALOG**.

> *Note: To delete a backup, you must first allocate a channel so that the OS
> can delete the file associated with that backup.*

The **UNAVAILABLE** option marks file(s) that are unavailable or offsite but
that you may wish to use again for recovery. Listing 10.5 shows an example of
using the **CHANGE** command to change the status of a backup control file in
the recovery catalog.

Listing 10.5   Using the **CHANGE** command in RMAN.

```
RMAN> ALLOCATE CHANNEL ch1 FOR DELETE TYPE DISK;
RMAN> CHANGE BACKUP CONTROLFILE '/backups/controlfiles/01011999/
backup.ctl' DELETE;
RMAN> RELEASE CHANNEL ch1;
```

COPY

This command allows you to create backup copies of the database datafiles. You use the **COPY** command to create image copies of datafiles, archived redo logs, and control files. You can use image copies to immediately recover a database without a **RECOVER** command. Several clauses are available with the **COPY** command. They include **ARCHIVELOG, DATAFILE,** and **DATAFILE-COPY**. Listing 10.6 shows an example of using the **COPY** command.

Listing 10.6   Using the RMAN **COPY** command.

```
RUN
{ALLOCATE CHANNEL chan1 NAME '/dev/rmt0';
COPY DATAFILE '/ora05/oracle/data/data01.dbf'
TO '/ora02/backup/database/data01.dbf';
RELEASE CHANNEL chan1;
}
```

DEALLOCATE CHANNEL

This command is used when there is no longer a need for the channel to be allocated. It closes the channel and the interface to the OS. This code snippet shows how to use the **DEALLOCATE CHANNEL**.

```
RMAN> DEALLOCATE CHANNEL chan1;
```

RECOVER

This command causes the database to begin recovery after a **RESTORE** operation. The **RECOVER** command restores archived redo logs as required to finish the database recovery. The following **RECOVER** options are available:

➤ *DATABASE*—Recovers the database in full unless the **UNTIL** clause is used for incomplete recovery.

➤ *DATAFILE datafile_name*—Recovers the datafile defined.

➤ *TABLESPACE tablespace_name*—Recovers the tablespace defined.

➤ *UNTIL*—Used for point-in-time recovery. You can use either the time that you wish to recover to, the system change number (SCN), or the redo log sequence number with this clause. If you wish to recover to a specific time, you must set the National Language Standard (NLS) system environment variables **NLS_DATE_FORMAT** and **NLS_LANG**. Doing so sets the format that you will use in the **UNTIL TIME** command. Listing 10.7 shows an example of using the **RECOVER DATABASE** command.

Listing 10.7   Using the **RECOVER DATABASE** command.
```
RMAN>RECOVER DATABASE;
RMAN>RECOVER TABLESPACE temp_tbs;
RMAN>RECOVER DATABASE UNTIL TIME 'JAN-01-1999 22:00:00';
```

REGISTER DATABASE

This command causes the target database to be registered in the recovery cata-
log. For more information, see the "Registering A Database In The Recovery
Catalog" section in this chapter. This code snippet shows the use of the **REG-
ISTER DATABASE** command:

```
RMAN>register database;
```

RELEASE CHANNEL

This command releases a channel created by the **ALLOCATE CHANNEL**
command. Here is an example:

```
RMAN> RELEASE CHANNEL chan1;
```

RESET DATABASE

This command is used if the target database has been opened with the
RESETLOGS command. If the **RESETLOGS** command is used in a target
database, a new incarnation of the database must be created in the recovery
catalog or no further access to the catalog for the target database is allowed
until the **RESET DATABASE** command is used. In certain cases (such as
incomplete media recovery), the DBA may need to actually revert to a previous incarnation of the database in the recovery catalog. To do so, first determine
the incarnation to which you wish to recover by using the **LIST INCARNA-
TION OF DATABASE** command to determine the incarnation number you
wish to return to. You then use the **RESET DATABASE TO INCARNA-
TION <#>** command to return to a previous incarnation of the database. Listing
10.8 shows an example of using the **RESET DATABASE** command.

Listing 10.8   Using the **RESET DATABASE** command in RMAN.
```
RMAN>RESET DATABASE;
RMAN>LIST INCARNATION OF DATABASE;
RMAN>RESET DATABASE TO INCARNATION 1;
```

RESTORE

This command recovers a database, tablespace, or datafile using backup sets
created with either the **BACKUP** or **COPY** command. The **RESTORE** command takes the form **RESTORE** *from_clause until_clause file_clause*. The

RESTORE command recovers the backup sets and then applies them to the database. The **RESTORE** command, by default, selects the most current backup to use to recover the database. When using the **RESTORE** command, you can choose to overwrite the existing datafiles (the default), or write the datafiles, control files, and archived redo logs to alternate locations. Doing so can be useful when you are trying to clone a database. The valid keywords in the from_clause are:

➤ *FROM BACKUPSET*—Restores files from the named backup set.

➤ *FROM DATAFILECOPY*—Restores files from the datafiles copies named on disk.

The valid options of the until_clause include time-based recovery, redo log sequence number recovery, and recovery to a specific SCN. The clause specifies the point in time to which the **RESTORE** should be done.

Finally, the file_clause has the following keywords:

➤ *ARCHIVELOG*—Restores named archive log files.

➤ *CONTROLFILE*—Restores control file to the location that is listed.

➤ *DATABASE*—Restores the file for the entire database, optionally skipping named tablespaces using the **SKIP** clause.

➤ *DATAFILE*—Restores a named datafile.

➤ *TABLESPACE*—Restores a named tablespace.

These three code snippets show how to use the **RESTORE** command:

```
RESTORE DATABASE UNTIL 605504033 SKIP TABLESPACE 'TEMP';

RESTORE CONTROLFILE TO '/ora054/oracle/db01/controlfile';

RESTORE DATABASE;
```

RESYNC CATALOG

This command resynchyronizes the recovery catalog with the target database. By default, it resyncs based on the current control file, though you may use a backup control file for the operation using the additional keywords **FROM BACKUP CONTROLFILE**. This code snippet shows an example of using the **RESYNC CATALOG** command:

```
RMAN>resync catalog;
RMAN>resync catalog from backup controlfile;
```

RUN

This command generally precedes the following commands: **BACKUP, COPY, RESTORE,** and **RECOVER.** The **RUN** command is followed by an open bracket, which is then preceded by commands. Then, the **RUN** command is closed by brackets after the commands have been completed. Typically, **ALLOCATE CHANNEL** commands and **DEALLOCATE CHANNEL** commands are associated with the **RUN** command. **RUN** commands are used in both interactive RMAN operations as well as scripts. Listing 10.9 shows an example of using the **RUN** command.

Listing 10.9   Using the **RUN** command in RMAN.

```
RMAN> RUN
{ALLOCATE CHANNEL chan1 TYPE DISK;
BACKUP FULL TAG 'MY BACKUP' format '/backupdir/todays_backup/
db_t%t_s%s_p%p' (DATABASE);
RELEASE CHANNEL chan1;
}
```

You can, within the confines of the **RUN** command, set certain variables or attributes by using the **SET** command. You can set the **maxcorrupt** parameter, which defines the maximum number of corrupted blocks that can be backed up. Another parameter is **newname,** which you can use to change the name of the datafile being restored. Finally, the **ARCHIVELOG DESTINATION** option can change the location where RMAN looks for archive logs files.

SETLIMIT CHANNEL

This command allows the DBA to set limits on certain facets of the activity channel. The DBA can limit such things as the maximum size of a backup piece, the number of files that can be opened at one time, or even the number of blocks that the **BACKUP** command can read per second. This code snippet shows an example of using the **SETLIMIT CHANNEL** command:

```
RMAN>RUN { SETLIMIT CHANNEL chan1 MAXOPENFILES 50 KBYTES 1024
READRATE 200 };
```

SWITCH DATAFILE TO DATAFILECOPY

This command can be used to take a datafile copy (image copies) into a current datafile. The **SWITCH** command changes the name of the datafile in the control file, emulating the **ALTER DATABASE README DATAFILE** command. This code snippet shows an example of using this command:

```
RMAN> RUN {SWITCH DATAFILE 'data01.dbf'
TO DATAFILECOPY 'data01bkp.dbf'};
```

SQL

This command causes SQL statements to be executed on the target database.

 When preparing for your exam, make sure you understand these commands and how to use them. In particular, you should pay special attention to the commands that revolve directly around database backup and recovery and catalog registration.

Using Format Strings

As you've probably noticed, when defining a backup set, you use format strings much like those used when defining the names of archive logs in a database. Here is an example of this format:

```
BACKUP FULL TAG 'MY BACKUP' format '/backupdir/todays_backup/
db_t%t_s%s_p%p' (DATABASE);
```

The format strings in this example are the **%t**, **%s**, and **%p**. The main purpose of the format strings is to ensure that the names of the backup datafile sets are unique for each backup, preventing accidental erasure of those files. These format strings are also known as substitution variables and the following are available:

➤ *%p*—This specifies the backup piece number within the backup set. The value begins at 1 and goes up by one for each backup set piece created.

➤ *%s*—This specifies the backup set number. This number comes from a counter in the control file of the target database and is incremented for each backup set. The counter begins at 1 and does not cycle unless a new control file is created.

➤ *%d*—This represents the name of the database.

➤ *%n*—This represents the database name of eight characters. The variable right-fills with "x" characters until it reaches eight characters. Thus, a database called "TEST" is represented as "TESTxxxx".

➤ *%t*—This is the timestamp of the backup set. You can use a combination of **%s** and **%t** to form a unique name for the database backup set.

➤ *%u*—This is an eight-character name that is created by combining a portion of the backup set number and the time of the backup.

Creating RMAN Scripts

You can create command scripts for RMAN. They can be stored in OS files or in the recovery catalog itself. To create a stored script in RMAN, you use the **CREATE SCRIPT** command. Listing 10.10 shows an example of using the **CREATE SCRIPT** command.

Listing 10.10   Using the CREATE SCRIPT command.

```
CREATE SCRIPT test_backup
{
     ALLOCATE CHANNEL chan1  TYPE DISK;
     BACKUP FULL format '/backupdir/todays_backup/db_t%t_s%s_p%p'
(DATABASE);
     RELEASE CHANNEL chan1;
}
```

Once you have created a script, you may need to replace it. To do so, use the **REPLACE SCRIPT** command. Listing 10.11 shows an example of this command.

Listing 10.11   Using the REPLACE SCRIPT command.

```
REPLACE SCRIPT test_backup
{
     ALLOCATE CHANNEL chan1  TYPE DISK;
     # Changed backup directory name
     BACKUP FULL format '/backupdirectory/todays_backup/
db_t%t_s%s_p%p' (DATABASE);
     RELEASE CHANNEL chan1;
}
```

Also available are the **DELETE SCRIPT** and **PRINT SCRIPT** commands. The **DELETE SCRIPT** command removes a script from the backup catalog, and the **PRINT SCRIPT** causes the script to print out. To execute a script once it has been created, use the **EXECUTE SCRIPT** command, prefixed by the **RUN** command, as shown here:

```
run {EXECUTE SCRIPT test_backup;}
```

So, once you have stored a script, how do you find out what is contained in it? First, you can use the **PRINT SCRIPT** command, mentioned above. What if you do not remember the name of the script though? You can query two views on the recovery catalog database. The **RC_STORED_SCRIPTS** view provides you with the names of all scripts stored in the recovery catalog. The **RC_STORED_SCRIPT_LINE** view provides you with the contents of the script.

Registering A Database In The Recovery Catalog

Once you have created the recovery catalog, use RMAN to register databases in the catalog. To register a database in the RMAN recovery catalog, start RMAN and use the **REGISTER DATABASE** command to register the database. You are then ready to back up the database.

To register a database is very simple operation. First you need to use the following RMAN command to start RMAN:

```
RMAN target=sys/password@database_to_backup rcvcat=sys/
password@recovery_catalog_database
```

Another variation on the command, if the recovery catalog and the database were on the same server, might be as shown:

```
oraenv
ORACLE_SID = [testo82] ? testo82

RMAN rcvcat=sys/password@recovery_catalog_database
RMAN> connect target

Recovery Manager: Release 8.0.5.1.0 - Production

RMAN-06005: connected to target database: TEST082
RMAN-06008: connected to recovery catalog database

RMAN>
```

Note that you can use the target database and the recovery catalog database on the command line, or you can use the recovery catalog on the command line and connect to the target in RMAN itself. Using the password on the command line is optional (and probably not a good idea). The RMAN product prompts you for the password. Once you have started the RMAN program, you see the RMAN prompt. This is the interactive prompt for RMAN. To register the database, simply issue this command:

```
RMAN>register database;
```

At this point, RMAN registers the database you have selected in the recovery catalog, and you are prepared to back up the database. You might, at some point, wish to verify if a database is registered in the recovery catalog. To do this, connect to RMAN and issue the command shown in Listing 10.12, **LIST INCARNATION OF DATABASE**, which will produce the output shown in the same listing.

Listing 10.12   Using the LIST INCARNATION OF DATABASE command.

```
RMAN> list incarnation of database;

RMAN-03022: compiling command: list
RMAN-06240: List of Database Incarnations
RMAN-06241: DB Key Inc Key DB Name DB ID        CUR Reset SCN    Reset Time
RMAN-06242: ------ ------  -------  -------      --- ---------    ---------
RMAN-06243: 298     299    TEST082 2518791340    YES 1                     10-OCT-99
RMAN-06243: 1       2      TMSD    3875339696    YES 554530139074 24-JUL-99
```

Note the **db id** column. Now, to verify if the database is already registered, issue the following query. Using the query shown in Listing 10.13, you can then validate the **DB ID** associated with the database and ensure that the database registered in the catalog is the incarnation of the database you are currently using.

Listing 10.13   Checking the BID of a database.

```
SQL> select to_char(dbid) from v$database;
TO_CHAR(DBID)
--------------------------------------
2518791340
```

Resyncing And Resetting The Recovery Catalog

Often, the recovery catalog requires *resyncing*. Many operations resync the recovery catalog implicitly. Other times, you may need to resync the recovery catalog by issuing the following command from RMAN:

```
RMAN>resync catalog;
```

You should resync the recovery catalog with the target database often, particularly if there are many archive log switches or if changes are made to the structure of the database. The catalog resync process is done mostly to allow for a proper control file recovery to occur, if needed. Although recovery is still possible even if the catalog was not resynced, it just becomes more labor intensive because you must manually add the new structures by using the RMAN **CATALOG** command.

RMAN performs two types of resyncing: *full resyncs* and *partial resyncs*. Full resyncs are done whenever you manually resync the catalog through RMAN and at the end of any backup through RMAN. Full resyncs update the recovery catalog with all control file information that has changed since the last resync. This includes changes to the physical architecture of the database.

Partial resyncs update the catalog with the following information only:

➤ Redo log

➤ Backup set

➤ Datafile copy information

Oracle recommends that you resync the catalog at intervals of no less than the **control_file_record_keep_time** parameter in the init.ora of the target database. This ensures that the recovery catalog is resynced before Oracle clears out the control files of the target database of information older than the time in days specified by the parameter.

Resetting the recovery catalog is necessary in the cases of database recovery that end in the use of the **ALTER DATABASE OPEN RESETLOGS** command. The **RESET** command creates a new incarnation of the database, which is required if the online redo logs are reset. You must create a new incarnation because the archive log sequence numbers are reset and because the database ID is changed. You can also use the **RESET** command to reset to a prior incarnation if required during a recovery operation. You do this using the **TO INCARNATION <NUM>** clause of the **RESET DATABASE** command.

Backing Up Databases With RMAN

So far, this chapter has covered a lot of territory. This section contains some practical examples of using RMAN to back up an Oracle8 database. This section assumes that you have already registered the Oracle database with the RMAN product as described in the "Creating The Recovery Catalog" section earlier in this chapter.

A Hot Or Cold Backup Of A Database

If you are going to back up a database in **NOARCHIVELOG** mode, some manual DBA intervention is required. RMAN does not shut down and then mount the database for you, so you must do these first. Because backups for databases in **NOARCHIVELOG** mode must be cold backups, the database must be mounted and not open. If the database is open, or if it is shut down, RMAN generates an error. Once you have mounted the database, you can back up the database as you normally would.

Once you deal with the issue of the database being mounted rather than open, the overall RMAN process for performing cold and hot backups is generally the same. Listing 10.14 shows an example of a hot or cold backup using RMAN.

Listing 10.14   A hot or cold backup using RMAN.

```
RMAN>  run {
2> allocate channel dev1 type disk;
3> backup full
4> format '/tmp/backup_dir/db_t%t_s%s_p%p' (database);
5> release channel dev1;
6> }


RMAN-03022: compiling command: allocate
RMAN-03023: executing command: allocate
RMAN-08030: allocated channel: dev1
RMAN-08500: channel dev1: sid=11 devtype=DISK

RMAN-03022: compiling command: backup
RMAN-03023: executing command: backup
RMAN-08008: channel dev1: starting datafile backupset
RMAN-08502: set_count=5 set_stamp=378771271
RMAN-08010: channel dev1: including datafile 1 in backupset
RMAN-08011: channel dev1: including current controlfile in
backupset
RMAN-08010: channel dev1: including datafile 2 in backupset
RMAN-08013: channel dev1: piece 1 created
RMAN-08503: piece handle=/tmp/backup_dir/test_001.fil comment=NONE
RMAN-03023: executing command: partial resync
RMAN-08003: starting partial resync of recovery catalog
RMAN-08005: partial resync complete

RMAN-03022: compiling command: release
RMAN-03023: executing command: release
RMAN-08031: released channel: dev1
```

A Backup Of A Tablespace And A Datafile

RMAN allows you to do backups of tablespaces and datafiles. Listing 10.15 executes a backup of a tablespace and a datafile all in the same backup command. This demonstrates how to merge two backups into one **RUN** command.

Listing 10.15   A tablespace backup using RMAN.

```
RMAN>  run {
2> allocate channel dev1 type disk;
3> backup
4> format '/tmp/backup_dir/db_t%t_s%s_p%p' (tablespace system);
5> backup
6> format '/tmp/backup_dir/db_t%t_s%s_p%p' (datafile 2);
5> release channel dev1;
6> }
```

```
RMAN-03022: compiling command: allocate
RMAN-03023: executing command: allocate
RMAN-08030: allocated channel: dev1
RMAN-08500: channel dev1: sid=18 devtype=DISK

RMAN-03022: compiling command: backup
RMAN-03023: executing command: backup
RMAN-08008: channel dev1: starting datafile backupset
RMAN-08502: set_count=11 set_stamp=378772507
RMAN-08010: channel dev1: including datafile 1 in backupset
RMAN-08011: channel dev1: including current controlfile in
backupset
RMAN-08013: channel dev1: piece 1 created
RMAN-08503: piece handle=/tmp/backup_dir/db_t378772507_s11_p1
comment=NONE
RMAN-03023: executing command: partial resync
RMAN-08003: starting partial resync of recovery catalog
RMAN-08005: partial resync complete

RMAN-03022: compiling command: backup
RMAN-03023: executing command: backup
RMAN-08008: channel dev1: starting datafile backupset
RMAN-08502: set_count=12 set_stamp=378772539
RMAN-08010: channel dev1: including datafile 2 in backupset
RMAN-08013: channel dev1: piece 1 created
RMAN-08503: piece handle=/tmp/backup_dir/db_t378772539_s12_p1
comment=NONE
RMAN-03023: executing command: partial resync
RMAN-08003: starting partial resync of recovery catalog
RMAN-08005: partial resync complete

RMAN-03022: compiling command: release
RMAN-03023: executing command: release
RMAN-08031: released channel: dev1
```

Creating And Using A Stored Script To Copy A Datafile To A Backup Location

This example combines the creation of an RMAN script with the use of the **COPY** command in RMAN. First, you need to load the script into RMAN and then execute it. Listing 10.16 demonstrates these actions.

Listing 10.16   Creating a stored copy datafile script and running it.

```
CREATE SCRIPT copy_script_001
{
     allocate channel dev1 type disk;
     copy datafile '/ora01/oracle/admin/testo82/link/new_tbs.dbf'
```

```
to
    '/tmp/backup_dir/new_tbs.dbf';
    release channel dev1;
}
RMAN> run {EXECUTE SCRIPT copy_script_001;}
RMAN-03021: executing script: copy_script_001
RMAN-03022: compiling command: allocate
RMAN-03023: executing command: allocate
RMAN-08030: allocated channel: dev1
RMAN-08500: channel dev1: sid=17 devtype=DISK

RMAN-03022: compiling command: copy
RMAN-03023: executing command: copy
RMAN-08000: channel dev1: copied datafile 2
RMAN-08501: output filename=/tmp/backup_dir/new_tbs.dbf recid=2
stamp=378773569
RMAN-03023: executing command: partial resync
RMAN-08003: starting partial resync of recovery catalog
RMAN-08005: partial resync complete

RMAN-03022: compiling command: release
RMAN-03023: executing command: release
RMAN-08031: released channel: dev1
```

Recovering Databases With RMAN

This section reviews some examples of recovering a database with RMAN. It looks at a recovery of an entire database from a cold backup, and then at an example of a recovery of a tablespace from a hot backup.

Example One: Recovery From A Cold Backup

Assume a database backed up in **NOARCHIVELOG** is lost due to total media failure. This, of course, requires full database recovery. Listing 10.17 shows an example of this type of recovery. First, the control files are recovered, and then the database data files are restored. Finally, the database is opened with an **ALTER DATABASE OPEN RESETLOGS** command. This recovery example assumes the database is in the **NOMOUNT** state, ensuring the instance is up and running. I have, for brevity, removed some of the output from RMAN, leaving the important details only.

Listing 10.17   Recovering a database from a cold backup.

```
RMAN> run {
allocate channel t1 type disk;
restore controlfile to '/ora05/oracle/data/testo82/control01.ctl';
restore controlfile to '/ora05/oracle/data/testo82/control02.ctl';
```

```
restore controlfile to '/ora05/oracle/data/testo82/control03.ctl';
sql "alter database mount";
restore database;
sql "alter database open resetlogs";
 }
2> 3> 4> 5> 6> 7> 8> 9>
RMAN-03022: compiling command: allocate
RMAN-03023: executing command: allocate
RMAN-08030: allocated channel: t1
RMAN-03022: compiling command: restore
RMAN-03023: executing command: IRESTORE
RMAN-08016: channel t1: starting datafile backupset restore
RMAN-08021: channel t1: restoring controlfile
RMAN-08505: output filename=/ora05/oracle/data/testo82/
control01.ctl
RMAN-08024: channel t1: restore complete
RMAN-03022: compiling command: restore
RMAN-03023: executing command: IRESTORE
RMAN-08021: channel t1: restoring controlfile
RMAN-08505: output filename=/ora05/oracle/data/testo82/
control02.ctl
RMAN-08023: channel t1: restored backup piece 1
RMAN-03022: compiling command: restore
RMAN-03023: executing command: IRESTORE
RMAN-08021: channel t1: restoring controlfile
RMAN-08505: output filename=/ora05/oracle/data/testo82/
control03.ctl
RMAN-08024: channel t1: restore complete
RMAN-03022: compiling command: sql
RMAN-06162: sql statement: alter database mount
RMAN-03023: executing command: sql
RMAN-03022: compiling command: restore
RMAN-03025: performing implicit partial resync of recovery catalog
RMAN-03023: executing command: IRESTORE
RMAN-08016: channel t1: starting datafile backupset restore
RMAN-08509: destination for restore of datafile 1:
/ora01/oracle/admin/testo82/link/testo82_system_01.dbf
RMAN-08019: channel t1: restoring datafile 2
RMAN-08509: destination for restore of datafile 2:
/ora01/oracle/admin/testo82/link/new_tbs.dbf
RMAN-08023: channel t1: restored backup piece 1
RMAN-08511: piece handle=
/tmp/backup_dir/db_t378856462_s16_p1 params=NULL
RMAN-08024: channel t1: restore complete
RMAN-03022: compiling command: sql
RMAN-06162: sql statement: alter database open resetlogs
RMAN-03023: executing command: sql
RMAN-08031: released channel: t1
```

You should clearly understand the purpose of the **ALLOCATE CHANNEL**, **RESTORE CONTROLFILE**, **SQL**, and **RESTORE DATABASE** commands. The OCP exam may present examples of a command (for example, **ALLOCATE CHANNEL**) and ask you what it does.

Example Two: A Backup Of A Tablespace And A Datafile

RMAN allows you to do recovery of backups of tablespaces and datafiles. Assume, for example, that you try to create a table in a tablespace called **NEW_TBS** and get the error shown in Listing 10.18.

Listing 10.18   Attempting to create a table in a tablespace that has errors.

```
SQL> create table robert
  2  (test number)
  3  tablespace new_tbs;
create table robert
*
ERROR at line 1:
ORA-00376: file 2 cannot be read at this time
ORA-01110: data file 2: '/ora01/oracle/admin/testo82/link/
new_tbs.dbf'
```

It would appear that the **NEW_TBS** tablespace has lost a datafile (in fact, this datafile is the only one assigned to this tablespace). In Listing 10.19, you recover the entire tablespace rather than the single datafile (though you could recover the datafile just as easily). Note again, for brevity's sake, some of the output of RMAN has been eliminated.

Listing 10.19   Recovering a tablespace.

```
run {
allocate channel t1 type disk;
restore tablespace new_tbs;
recover tablespace new_tbs;
sql "alter tablespace new_tbs online";
}
RMAN-03023: executing command: allocate
RMAN-08030: allocated channel: t1
RMAN-03022: compiling command: restore
RMAN-03023: executing command: IRESTORE
RMAN-08509: destination for restore of datafile 2:
/ora01/oracle/admin/testo82/link/new_tbs.dbf
RMAN-03023: executing command: partial resync
RMAN-08003: starting partial resync of recovery catalog
RMAN-08005: partial resync complete
```

```
RMAN-03022: compiling command: recover
RMAN-08054: starting media recovery
RMAN-08055: media recovery complete
RMAN-03022: compiling command: sql
RMAN-06162: sql statement: alter tablespace new_tbs online
RMAN-03023: executing command: sql
RMAN-08031: released channel: t1
```

Now, let's try to create the table again, and let's see what happens! Listing 10.20 shows the creation of a table after the tablespace was recovered.

Listing 10.20   Attempting to create an object after tablespace recovery.

```
SQL> CREATE TABLE robert
  2  (test NUMBER)
  3  TABLESPACE new_tbs;
Table created.
```

RMAN actually provides us with several options to recover from the problem in this example. In Listing 10.19, you restored and recovered the entire tablespace. Alternatively, you could have restored just the damaged datafile. Listing 10.21 shows an example of how to do this type of recovery.

Listing 10.21   Restoring a datafile in RMAN and recovering the tablespace.

```
run {
allocate channel t1 type disk;
restore datafile 2;
recover tablespace new_tbs;
sql "alter tablespace new_tbs online";
}
```

Finally, if more than one datafile had been corrupted, you might have chosen the form of recovery shown in Listing 10.22.

Listing 10.22   Restoring and recovering a single datafile.

```
run {
allocate channel t1 type disk;
restore datafile 2;
recover datafile 2;
sql "alter tablespace new_tbs online";
}
```

All **RECOVER** commands shown in Listings 10.19, 10.20, 10.21, and 10.22 would have resulted in the same action: the recovery of the datafile. Note that you can do this recovery action while the database is up and running, so your users may never even know that a problem occurred!

RMAN Management And Associated DBA Views

RMAN provides two commands to enable you to generate different kinds of reports and lists. The **REPORT** command reports on such items as datafiles that require backups and files that have not been backed up over a period of time. The **LIST** command provides reports of information about backup sets or copies in the recovery catalog.

The **REPORT** Command

The **REPORT** command includes reports on files that are not recoverable due to operations executed with the **UNRECOVERABLE** command. This can also produce a report that shows which backup files can be deleted and reports on what the physical schema of the database was at some previous point in time. The **REPORT** command has the following formats (with clauses delimited by curly brackets).

REPORT NEED BACKUP {NEED_BACKUP_OPERATOR} {REPORT_OBJECT_LIST} {DEVICE_TYPE_LIST};

This report lists all datafiles that need to be backed up based on criteria passed to the report on the command line. It assumes that the most recent report would be used if there was a restore.

REPORT OBSOLETE {REPORT_OBSOLETE_OPERATOR_ LIST} {DEVICE_TYPE_LIST};

You can use this report to list the backups sets and datafile copies that are redundant and no longer needed.

REPORT SCHEMA {AT_CLAUSE};

This report lists datafiles and tablespaces at a specific point in time. Also the report can be based on the SCN, or a redo log number.

REPORT UNRECOVERABLE {REPORT_OBJECT_LIST} {DEVICE_TYPE_LIST};

This report, when passed the correct parameters, lists all datafiles that are unrecoverable. An object is considered unrecoverable if an operation with the **UNRECOVERABLE** is executed on the object.

The clauses are defined as follows:

➤ *REPORT_OBJECT_LIST*—This specifies the datafiles that are to be reported on. You can specify the entire database by using the keyword **DATABASE,** or you can enter a list of datafiles or tablespaces.

➤ *DEVICE_TYPE_LIST*—This limits the devices that are reported on. For example, if you wished to report on only backup sets on disk, you would specify **DISK** in this clause.

NEED_BACKUP_OPERATOR

This is part of the **REPORT NEED BACKUP** command. This operator has the following valid options:

➤ *days {number}*—This parameter specifies the threshold of the number of days of archive logs that need to be applied to datafiles to make a complete recovery.

➤ *incremental {number}*—This parameter specifies the threshold to report on. When this report is executed, files that need more than {number} of incrementals applied for recovery are reported.

> *Note: If a file is offline and the most recent backup contains the un-changed contents of the file, it is not reported. Also, files that were offline and that are now online are reported only if they have been online for the specified number of days, if the most recent backup contains all changes up to the time the file was taken offline.*

➤ *redundancy {number}*—This specifies the minimum number of backups that are considered not needing backup. For example, a 2 would mean that there must be at least two backups of each datafile in order for it to not be considered in need of backup.

report_obsolete_operator_list

This parameter is part of the **REPORT OBSOLETE** command. It has the following valid options:

➤ *orphan*—This parameter specifies that backups and copies cannot be used because they are not predecessors of the current incarnation and are considered obsolete.

➤ *redundancy {number}*—This specifies the minimum number of backups that are considered not needing backup. For example, 2 would mean that there must be at least two backups of each datafile in order for it to not be considered in need of backup.

➤ *until clause*—If this is specified, no backup is considered obsolete or redundant if it contains changes beyond the time specified.

AT_CLAUSE
The clause begins with the keyword **AT** and then follows with one of these valid keywords:

➤ *LOGSEQ {log sequence number} thread {thread number}*—A number representing the log sequence number.

➤ *SCN*—An integer that represents the **SCN**.

➤ *TIME*—A quoted string that specifies the time.

Examples Of The **REPORT** Command
This section shows some examples of the report command and its output. The report shown in Listing 10.23 reports on datafiles that have not been backed up in more than a day.

Listing 10.23 Using the **REPORT** command.

```
RMAN> report need backup days 2 database;

RMAN-03022: compiling command: report
RMAN-06270: Report of files whose recovery needs more than 2 days
of archived lo
gs
RMAN-06271: File Days  Name
RMAN-06272: ----------------------------------------------------
RMAN-06273: 1    3     /ora01/oracle/admin/testo82/link/
testo82_system_01.dbf
RMAN-06273: 2    3     /ora01/oracle/admin/testo82/link/new_tbs.dbf
```

The report shown in Listing 10.24 reports on a specific tablespace and if it requires recovery beyond the specific number of days.

Listing 10.24   Reporting on databases that should be backed up.

```
RMAN> report need backup days 2 tablespace system;

RMAN-03022: compiling command: report
RMAN-06270: Report of files whose recovery needs more than 2
  days of archived logs
```

```
RMAN-06271: File Days   Name
RMAN-06272: ---- ----   ----------------------------------------------
RMAN-06273: 1    3      /ora01/oracle/admin/testo82/link/
testo82_system_01.dbf
```

The report shown in Listing 10.25 reports on the target database, providing a list of datafiles, their size, and the tablespace they belong to.

Listing 10.25   Using the **REPORT** command to report on a schema.

```
RMAN> report schema;

RMAN-03022: compiling command: report
RMAN-06290: Report of database schema
RMAN-06291: File K-bytes      Tablespace           RB segs Name
RMAN-06292: ---- ----------   --------------------  ------ ----------
RMAN-06293: 1        51200 SYSTEM                   YES    /ora01/
oracle/admin/testo82/link/testo82_system_01.dbf
RMAN-06293: 2         5120 NEW_TBS                  NO     /ora01/
oracle/admin/testo82/link/new_tbs.dbf
```

The **LIST** Command

The **LIST** command produces reports about specific backup sets or copies that are in the recovery catalog. The following **LIST** commands are available.

LIST BACKUPSET OF {LIST_OBJECT_LIST} {LIST_QUALIFIER_LIST};

This list command produces information about backup sets.

LIST COPY OF {LIST_OBJECT_LIST} {LIST_QUALIFIER_LIST};

This lists information about datafile copies and archive logs.

LIST INCARNATION OF {IDENTIFIER} {LIST_QUALIFIER_LIST};

This lists information about incarnations of a database. This includes the primary keys of all database incarnation records for the specific database.

The parameters of the **LIST** command are as follows:

list_object_list

This parameter specifies the tablespaces, datafiles, or archivelogs whose backup sets are to be listed. It is followed by the following parameters:

➤ *archivelog_record_specifier*—This is the archivelog record number to report on.

➤ *database {skip_clause}*—This lists all backup sets or datafiles copies of the current database. You may include tablespaces to be skipped in the **skip_clause**.

➤ *datafile {datafile_names_or_numbers}*—This lists datafile names or numbers to report on.

➤ *tablespace {tablespace_names}*—This lists tablespace names. This option also causes backup sets or datafile copies from the specified tablespaces.

LIST_QUALIFIER_LIST

This specification limits the objects whose backup sets or copies are to be listed. The parameters of this clause are:

➤ *from {time} or until {time}*—This specified time range qualifies all files.

➤ *list {file_name_pattern}*—You can restrict datafile copies and archived logs by using a file name pattern as defined in the **file_name_pattern**. You can use Oracle pattern matching characters such as **%** and **_**.

➤ *tag {tag}*—You can restrict the datafile copies or backup sets to the tags specified with this parameter.

device_type_list

This limits the devices that are reported on. For example, if you wished to report only on backup sets on disk, you would specify **DISK** in this clause.

Examples Of The **LIST** Command

In the first example, Listing 10.26, we use the **LIST** command to product a list of all backup sets of the target database. This includes the completion data of the backup and the type of backup.

Listing 10.26 Using the **LIST** command in RMAN to list backup sets.

```
RMAN> list backup set of database;

RMAN-03022: compiling command: list
RMAN-06230: List of Datafile Backups
RMAN-06231: Key   File Type  LV Completion_time Ckp SCN   Ckp Time
RMAN-06232: ----  ---- ----  -- -------------- ---------  --------
RMAN-06233: 714   1    Full     14-OCT-99       78315     14-OCT-99
RMAN-06233: 723   1    Full     14-OCT-99       78332     14-OCT-99
```

```
RMAN-06233: 714  2    Full    14-OCT-99        78315        14-OCT-99
RMAN-06233: 723  2    Full    14-OCT-99        78332        14-OCT-99
```

The next example, Listing 10.27, lists the backup sets of a specific datafile.

Listing 10.27   Using the **LIST** command to list a backup set of
                    a datafile.

```
RMAN> list backup set of datafile 1;

RMAN-03022: compiling command: list
RMAN-06230: List of Datafile Backups
RMAN-06231: Key   File Type  LV Completion_time Ckp SCN   Ckp Time
RMAN-06232: ----  ---- ----  -- -------------- ---------- --------
RMAN-06233: 714   1    Full     14-OCT-99        78315      14-OCT-99
RMAN-06233: 723   1    Full     14-OCT-99        78332      14-OCT-99
```

RMAN Data Dictionary Views

Several views exist to assist the DBA in interacting with RMAN. Some of these are new for Oracle8, whereas some of them existed in Oracle7 but have new columns. The views from the target database include:

➤ *V$ARCHIVED_LOG*—Displays information about archived redo logs from the control file.

➤ *V$BACKUP_CORRPUTION*—Displays information about corrupted blocks discovered during database backups with RMAN.

➤ *V$BACKUP_DATAFILE*—Provides information from the control file about backup datafiles and control files.

➤ *V$BACKUP_DEVICE*—Provides information about various devices available from various third-party manufacturers.

➤ *V$BACKUP_PIECE*—Displays information about all backup sets from the control file.

➤ *V$BACKUP_REDOLOG*—Displays information about backed up redo logs in backup sets.

➤ *V$BACKUP_SET*—Displays information about all backup sets from the control file.

➤ *V$DATAFILE*—Lists datafile information from the database.

➤ *V$DATAFILE_HEADER*—Lists information about database datafile headers.

Selected views that are available from the recovery catalog that may be of interest include:

➤ *RC_COPY_CORRUPTION*—Contains reports of corruption detected during backups using the recovery catalog.

➤ *RC_STORED_SCRIPT*—Contains the database names and script names for scripts that are stored in RMAN.

➤ *RC_STORED_SCRIPT_LINE*—Contains the text of scripts stored in the recovery catalog.

There are other recovery catalog views that you may wish to explore, but they will not appear on the exam.

Duplexing Archive Logs

Finally, a short note on a new Oracle8 parameter: **log_archive_duplex_dest**. This new parameter allows you to define not one but two archived redo log storage locations. You can define it as a can or must succeed operation by setting the **log_archive_min_succeed_dest** parameter. This second parameter, if set to 1, does not require that the archived redo log copy to the duplex destination be complete; otherwise, if the parameter is set to a 2, both copies must be successful. If the parameter is set to 2, the database halts until the reason that the archive log cannot be copied is corrected.

Practice Questions

Question 1

> If you wish to use RMAN to back up a database, what operation must you first perform to set up the database in the recovery catalog?
>
> ○ a. **REGISTER DATABASE;**
>
> ○ b. **RECOVER DATABASE;**
>
> ○ c. **INSTALL DATABASE IN CATALOG;**
>
> ○ d. **INSTALL DATABASE;**
>
> ○ e. Using an **INSERT** statement, insert the correct parameters for the database into the **RC_BACKUP_DATABASE** table

Answer a is correct. You use the **REGISTER DATABASE** command to register a database to set it up in the recovery catalog in preparation for backup with RMAN. Answer b is incorrect because the **RECOVER DATABASE** command recovers a database from an RMAN backup. Answers c and d are incorrect because they are not valid RMAN commands. Answer e is incorrect because you should never manually add or change data in the recovery catalog.

Question 2

> Which command opens communication between RMAN and the OS to allow movement of data to a backup device?
>
> ○ a. **ALLOCATE DISK DEVICE;**
>
> ○ b. **OPEN DEVICE DISK;**
>
> ○ c. **CONNECT RAW DEVICE;**
>
> ○ d. **CONNECT OPERATING SYSTEM;**
>
> ○ e. **ALLOCATE CHANNEL;**

Answer e is correct. You use the **ALLOCATE CHANNEL** command to initiate the connection between RMAN and the OS. Answers a, b, c, and d are incorrect because they are not valid RMAN commands.

Question 3

> Which command is NOT a valid command-line parameter of RMAN?
>
> ○ a. **cmdfile**
>
> ○ b. **rcvcat**
>
> ○ c. **target**
>
> ○ d. **msglog**
>
> ○ e. **backupfile**

Answer e is correct because **backupfile** is not a valid RMAN command-line parameter. Answer a is incorrect because the **cmdfile** parameter allows you to use an external script to execute RMAN commands. Answer b is incorrect because the **rcvcat** parameter specifies the recovery catalog and username to use. Answer c is incorrect because the **target** parameter defines the target database for backup operations. Answer d is incorrect because **msglog** specifies an output file for messages to be sent to from RMAN.

Question 4

> Which script creates the recovery catalog?
>
> ○ a. adminrecv.sql
>
> ○ b. catproc.sql
>
> ○ c. catalog.sql
>
> ○ d. catrman.sql
>
> ○ e. utlxplan.sql

Answer d is correct. The catrman.sql script is used to create the recovery catalog. Answer a is incorrect because there is no adminrecv.sql script associated with RMAN. Answer b is incorrect because you use the catproc.sql script when creating a database; it does not create the recovery catalog. Answer c is incorrect because you use the catalog.sql script when creating a database; it does not create the recovery catalog. Answer e is incorrect because the utlxplan.sql script creates the **EXPLAIN_PLAN** table, which is used for query tuning, not for the recovery manager.

Question 5

What types of backups are possible with RMAN? [Choose two]

- ❑ a. **COMPLETE**
- ❑ b. **FULL**
- ❑ c. **INTERMEDIATE**
- ❑ d. **INCREMENTAL**
- ❑ e. **ACCUMULATING**

Answers b and d are correct. Full and incremental backups are the types of backups that RMAN can do (along with image copies, which are not mentioned in the question). This is a trick question because you might be tempted to choose answer a. Although a **FULL** backup might be termed a complete backup, in RMAN, there is no such thing as a **COMPLETE** backup. Answers c and e are incorrect because these types of backups do not exist.

Question 6

What is the purpose of the **RECOVER** command?

- ○ a. The command causes the datafiles and archive logs to be recovered from a backup.
- ○ b. The command prompts the database to execute media recovery.
- ○ c. The command causes datafile and archive logs to be recovered from a backup, forces a media recovery of the database, and then opens the database.
- ○ d. The command causes the recovery catalog to be restored from a backup created by RMAN.
- ○ e. The command creates a new incarnation of the database in the recovery catalog.

Answer b is correct. You use the **RECOVER** command after a **RESTORE** command to execute media recovery in the database. Answer a is incorrect because the **RECOVER** command does not recover datafiles or archive logs from backups; the **RESTORE** command does this. Answer c is incorrect again because the **RECOVER** command does not cause the datafiles or archive logs to be recovered, nor does it open the database. Answer d is incorrect because the recovery catalog is not created by the **RECOVER** command. Answer e is incorrect because the **RECOVER** command does not create a new incarnation of the database in the recovery catalog; this is the job of the **RESET** command.

Question 7

Which parameter defines the maximum number of corrupted blocks that can be backed up?

○ a. **corrupt**

○ b. **numcorrupt**

○ c. **maxcorrupt**

○ d. **total_corrupt**

○ e. **nocorrupt**

Answer c is correct. You can set the **maxcorrupt** attribute within a **RUN** command to limit the number of corrupt blocks that can be read before the **BACKUP** command aborts. Answers a, b, d, and e are incorrect because none of these answers is a valid command in RMAN.

Question 8

Which statement is true when you are contrasting backups to image copies?

○ a. Backups and image copies are both compressed.

○ b. Backups and image copies are both stored in backup pieces.

○ c. Backups and image copies are both ways that you can back up a database.

○ d. Backups are stored in the recovery catalog, whereas image copies are not.

○ e. Backups and image copies can both be stored on tape or disk.

Answer c is correct. You can use both backups and image copies to back up a database with RMAN. Answer a is incorrect because image copies are not compressed. Answer b is incorrect because image copies are exact copies of datafiles; they are not stored in backup pieces. Answer d is incorrect because image copies are stored in the recovery catalog. Answer e is incorrect because image copies can be stored to disk only by RMAN.

Question 9

> Upon opening a database with the **ALTER DATABASE OPEN RESETLOGS** com-
> mand, what command should you execute through RMAN to ensure that the
> recovery catalog is kept up to date?
>
> ○ a. **REGISTER DATABASE**
>
> ○ b. **RESET DATABASE**
>
> ○ c. **RESYNC CATALOG**
>
> ○ d. **REBUILD CATALOG**
>
> ○ e. **ALLOCATE CHANNEL**

Answer b is correct. The **RESET DATABASE** command creates a new incarnation of the database in the recovery catalog. Answer a is incorrect because
the **REGISTER DATABASE** command is used when you are registering a
database for the first time. Answer c is incorrect because the **RESYNC CATA-
LOG** command resynchronizes an existing incarnation of a database, and it is
generally done implicitly during backup operations. Answer d is incorrect because this is not a valid **RMAN** command. Answer e is incorrect because the
ALLOCATE CHANNEL does not maintain the recovery catalog.

Question 10

> If RMAN returns the **ex_succ** code, what does that indicate?
>
> ○ a. All operations were successful.
>
> ○ b. Some operations were successful, but the last one failed.
>
> ○ c. The last operation was successful.
>
> ○ d. No operation was successful.
>
> ○ e. The script file requested was found.

Answer a is correct. The **ex_succ** code indicates that all operations executed by
RMAN were successful. Answer b is incorrect because the **ex_warn** code indicates the condition where some operations succeeded but the last one failed.
Answer c is incorrect because there is no return code that indicates the success
of any specific operation in RMAN. Answer d is incorrect because the return
code **ex_fail** is returned when all the RMAN commands fail. Answer e is incorrect because there is no specific return code returned if a script fails to execute.

Need To Know More?

 Velpuri, Rama and Anand Adkoli: *Oracle8 Backup & Recovery Handbook*. Osborne/McGraw-Hill/Oracle Press, Berkeley, CA, 1998. ISBN 0-07-882389-7. Simply the best book ever on Oracle backup and recovery concepts. No DBA should be without it.

 Oracle's online documentation, including *Oracle8 Concepts*, *Oracle8 Administrators Guide*, and *Oracle8 Tuning*, is on CDs supplied with the Oracle database server product. This is a principal source of information for any Oracle feature you wish to use.

 **www.support.com** is Oracle's Metalink Web site. It is a wonderful resource if you have Oracle Metals Support.

Net8

Terms you'll need to understand:

√ Net8

√ Multiplexing

√ Connection pooling

√ Oracle Names Server (ONS)

√ Oracle Connection Manager (OCM)

√ Oracle Advanced Networking Option (ANO)

√ Oracle Security Server (OSS)

√ Net8 Easy Config

√ Net8 Assistant

Techniques you'll need to master:

√ Understanding the new features and benefits of Net8

√ Knowing and understanding the purpose of the new Net8 products

Net8: The Oracle8 Replacement For SQL*Net

For some time, Oracle7 database administrators (DBAs) have been using SQL*Net to manage the network connectivity between their databases and the clients/applications that need to access the database. Similar to SQL*Net is Oracle8's network-connectivity solution: Net8. This chapter looks at Net8 and some of its new features.

Net8 Internals

Net8 is the interface that Oracle provides between Oracle databases and the network communications layer. It replaces SQL*Net version 2, which was responsible for network connectivity in Oracle7. Net8 acts as the "middle man," allowing Oracle client and application processes to communicate with the database server. The database, therefore, never needs to directly interface with the network, and the client application never needs to directly talk with the network; rather, both layers talk to Net8, which takes care of the lower networking layers. In performing its networking interface job, Net8's various protocol adapters allow it to work over a variety of networks. In addition, Net8 has new enhancements and add-on products that further strengthen its robustness in the database world. Some of its enhancements are:

➤ Scalability

➤ Additional connectivity

➤ Security

➤ Performance

➤ Configuration

Net8 runs on both the client and the server on the Oracle network and consists of three layers:

➤ *Net layer*—This layer sits between the client or the server and the rest of the Net8 layers and the network. It makes client connections to the server appear transparent to the user, and permits the client and server to transmit data without the client or the server having to make any special networking calls.

➤ *Transparent Network Substrate (TNS) layer*—TNS is software that provides clients and servers with a common application programming interface (API) to standard network protocols. *TNS connections* are made between a client and a server, allowing for a persistent pathway to transmit data between the two nodes. One node is considered the *initiator*, which typically is the client, and the other is the *destination*, which is typically the server. Of course, two servers can communicate with each other as well (for example, distributed databases doing replication).

➤ *Protocol adapters*—Attached to the TNS stack, these adapters allow the clients and servers to translate TNS functionality into various network protocols such as TCP/IP, IPX/SPX, DecNet, and others.

Net8 New Features

Net8 introduces several new features and options, some of which are provided by add-on Net8 products. The new Net8 features and options that increase performance of the network connectivity between the database and the clients or applications are:

➤ Network protocol independence

➤ *Multiplexing*

➤ *Connection pooling*

➤ Multi-protocol support

➤ Listener load balancing

➤ Client server cache

➤ Enhanced security

➤ Backward compatibility with SQL*Net (if you already have a SQL*Net version 2 network in place, Net8 is completely compatible with your existing SQL*Net configuration files; you should literally be able to "plug and play" Net8 into your system with zero hassle)

➤ ODBC level 2 drivers (Net8 now supports them to allow direct access to stored procedures)

➤ Faster connections through TNS raw transport features (Net8 streamlines the network connection, removing the Net8 header, and uses low-level API calls, allowing it to bypass unnecessary network layers and reduce network traffic)

You should clearly understand the new features of Net8. In particular, make sure you understand multiplexing, connection pooling, and what services the other options provide.

Net8 Products

Several of Net8's features are associated with using one of the new Net8 products. Some old SQL*Net features and options have been integrated into these products as well. These new Net8 products are:

➤ Oracle Names Server (ONS)

➤ Oracle Connection Manager (OCM)

➤ Oracle Advanced Networking Option (ANO)

➤ Oracle Security Server (OSS)

➤ Net8 configuration tools

Oracle Names Server

Oracle Names Server (*ONS*) is a directory service that provides name-to-address resolution for Net8 services. With ONS, multiple name servers are available to store service name and network information. A client application then requests a connection, resolving the service name requested through the Names Server. Thus, Names Server provides for centralized administration of the name lookup process.

The Names Server eliminates the tnsnames.ora file on the client PC, relieving the administrator from having to maintain and distribute this file. Rather, Names Server uses the sqlnet.ora file, which provides an address to one or more Names Server services. ONS version 8 comes with three features that improve performance and help make administration easier.

Dynamic Service Registration

With dynamic service registration, Net8 services can register themselves with the ONS servers, relieving the administrator of this burden. ONS also provides facilities to allow the administrator to manually add names to the Names Server. Registration happens either when the service starts or when it is installed. When the service is shut down, the name is deregistered with the Names Server database.

Client Discovery Of Names Servers

This process allows the client to get a list of all Names Server addresses. It also allows the client to discover new Names Servers as they are added to the network. This reduces the administrative burden because the user/DBA is not required to perform any action for this discovery to occur. Clients have a cache established where names that have been looked up previously are stored for subsequent lookup. This reduces the interaction required with the Names Server, which decreases network traffic and speeds up the connect process.

If Names Server performs a lookup and the network name is not in the cache, the client attempts to resolve the network name through the preferred server that is defined in the sqlnet.ora file by using the **names.preferred_server** parameter. If this parameter is not set, the client looks for a well-known Names Server, a server on a TCP/IP network that is aliased to a name or a nameservr#, where # is some number distinguishing the various Names Servers that listen on port 1575.

Name Resolution Optimization

Two features of ONS version 8 optimize the speed of the service. These are:

➤ *Names Server performance optimization*—With this optimization, the client-side processes discover the fastest-responding Names Server and use it to enhance the performance of Names Server lookups. This process retrieves a list of all Names Servers and contacts each server in turn, timing the responses and ordering the response time list from the Names Servers from the fastest to the slowest. The resulting response times are stored, and the client queries the Names Server that responded the quickest during this test. The name of the file where this information is stored is sdns.ora.

➤ *Client-side cache*—This maintains a local list of services that have been retrieved from Names Servers. A client attempts to use this cache to resolve a service name first before proceeding to the Names Servers to resolve the lookup. This client-side cache is also useful if the Names Server becomes unavailable. All cached information lives only for a particular period of time before it becomes stale and is flushed from the cache. This period of time is called the *time to live (TTL)*. The TTL is 24 hours, and there is no way to change this value. The sdns.ora client file is used to maintain this cache as well.

As stated previously, each client's sqlnet.ora file is used to find the Names Server services. On the server side, you must configure the names.ora configuration file so that the control parameters for the Names Server are set correctly.

Oracle Connection Manager

Oracle Connection Manager (OCM) contains several features that you can use to enhance Oracle8 and SQL*Net. OCM acts as a gateway between Net8 and the network, providing additional services for Net8. It generally revolves around a principle of *concentrating* multiple user connections into a single connection to the database. OCM provides these features in Oracle:

➤ *Connection pooling*—Connection pooling allows a larger number of user sessions to share a single shared physical connection to the database server. This is very helpful when you have a large number of users who connect and remain connected to the database but who issue infrequent SQL statements; therefore, their sessions are generally inactive.

Note: Do not use connection pooling in an environment where users are issuing many queries very rapidly.

Connection pooling takes advantage of this inactivity trend of a group of users and manages them through one connection to the database. This reduces the memory and CPU overheads that would otherwise be associated with multiple server processes.

With connection pooling, when users connect to the database and issue a statement, their session is considered active. Once the statement is complete and the results have been received, a timer is started on the session. The session becomes idle after the timer expires if another SQL statement is not issued. Once the user session is idled, another user session takes the physical connection to the database, and thus the process is repeated.

➤ *Multiplexing*—Multiplexing allows the database to support a large number of users who are constantly active at the same time. Much like connection pooling, multiplexing allows a large number of users to share a single physical network connection to the database. Unlike connection pooling, however, multiplexing can handle multiple users that are all simultaneously issuing queries. If multiple users issue SQL all at the same time, OCM combines all the SQL statements and sends them over the network to the database server. The database processes the queries, and the result sets are bundled up and sent at the same time. OCM then sends the data to the correct users.

Multiplexing is best used in environments where there is a high transactional volume of short, quick transactions (such as data entry), or if threads need to maintain the physical connection to the database at all times (unlike connection pooling, which disconnects a session from the database until more activity occurs).

 Net8 and OCM make multiplexing and connection pooling mutually exclusive processes. In other words, you cannot run both at the same time. Also note that multiplexing requires the use of TCP/IP.

➤ *Multiprotocol support*—Multiprotocol support replaces the Multiprotocol Interchange product that was available in SQL*Net version 2. Multiprotocol support allows you to send Net8 information to a database on another network. A client can therefore use one protocol (e.g., TCP/IP), and a database server can use another (e.g., SPX/IPX). OCM translates the TCP/IP packets into SPX/IPX packets for data that goes to the server and performs the reverse operation for data that is being returned from the server to the client. Only your hardware restricts the number of network protocols that OCM can support because it has no inherent limits to the number of protocols that it supports.

➤ *Access control*—Access control is a function of OCM that controls which clients are allowed to connect to the server. You can define an exclusive list of users or an inclusive list, allowing only specific clients to connect or allowing all clients (except specific ones) to connect.

Oracle Advanced Networking Option

Oracle Advanced Networking Option (*ANO*) for Net8 is designed to provide high security for environments that require it. ANO provides encryption for Net8, a feature that Net8 does not provide by default. Encryption protects data that is being transmitted over the network from those who might attempt to intercept it and read it.

ANO also provides additional authentication and user-authorization options, not provided in the standard Oracle server and networking products, using several methods, including CyberSafe and SecurID.

Oracle Security Server

Oracle Security Server (*OSS*) contains various components that use various established protocols to provide several security features. User authentication allows centralized user authentication in the Oracle environment as well as distributed authentication. *Authentication* guarantees that the user who wishes to access one or more Oracle database servers is valid. *Authorization* assures that a given user can perform operations based only on privileges defined by an administrator. In addition, OSS provides enhanced network security when providing these authentication and authorization services. OSS consists of three components:

➤ *Oracle Security Server Manager*—Used to manage the OSS Repository. The Oracle Security Server Manager is a GUI available in the Oracle Enterprise Manager (OEM). The administrator uses OEM to define users and their authorizations.

➤ *Oracle Security Server Repository*—An Oracle database server that stores data that an administrator enters using the Oracle Security Server Manager. It is used to store user authentication and authorization data.

➤ *Oracle Security Server Authentication Adapter*—An interface from a client or a database server to the Oracle Security Server Repository. This adapter allows Oracle products to request, obtain, and use security information from the security repository.

With OSS, a *public key* and a *digital signature* authenticate a user. When the user logs in, that user receives a set of attributes. These attributes represent a list of privileges and roles to a *component* or *principle* (database, Web server, users, and so on) on the network. OSS allows the DBA to centrally manage authentication data. This is based on various security protocols such as X.509 version 1 certificates and key cryptography. By using these security protocols, the security server authenticates the user securely.

Net8 Configuration Tools

Oracle provides the *Net8 Easy Config* and the *Net8 Assistant* to assist the DBA in administering the network. These tools automate administrative tasks, placing them in the framework of a Windows 95/NT GUI program that prompts the administrator for the information that he or she needs to make the correct entries for the network files.

Net8 Easy Config (previously known as SQL*Net Easy Config) is the tool to use if you have a rather uncomplicated network setup. It guides you through all the steps required to set up the tnsnames.ora files for your client programs to use.

You should use Net8 Assistant for more complicated network setups. If you are going to use Oracle8 Names Server, for example, you use the Net8 Assistant to set up the sqlnet.ora and tnsnames.

Practice Questions

Question 1

Which product enhances security on the Oracle network?

○ a. Names Server

○ b. Oracle Security Server

○ c. Oracle Listener

○ d. Oracle RDBMS

○ e. Oracle Connection Manager

Answer b is correct. OSS enhances Oracle network security by encrypting network traffic. Answer a is incorrect because Names Server does not enhance security as much as it simplifies administration of the network authentication process by removing the need to have and maintain tnsnames.ora files on each client. Answer c is incorrect because the Oracle Listener process provides only network connectivity between the Oracle database and the external network and clients. The database itself, although secure, does not directly interact with the network. Rather, it interacts with Net8, which is responsible for communicating with the network layer. Answer e is incorrect because the Oracle Connection Manager provides several nonsecurity-related features to enhance network performance, but no new network security features.

Question 2

What are benefits of using ONS? [Choose two]

❏ a. ONS enhances the security of the network.

❏ b. ONS provides a central point of service name registration, decreasing the DBA's workload.

❏ c. ONS reduces network traffic.

❏ d. ONS provides for cached storage of server information on the client.

❏ e. ONS provides for fail-safe network access to a database server.

Answers b and d are correct. ONS provides a central point of control for the registration of service names. The DBA no longer must manage a rollout of the tnsnames.ora file to all clients every time a new database is created. Also, ONS provides for a client-side cache to store database names and access information, reducing network overhead and providing for some redundancy should the names server be unavailable. Answer a is incorrect because ONS adds no additional security layers onto the network. This is a trick question because you might be tempted to choose answer c or e. Answer c is incorrect because ONS does not reduce network traffic in any way. In fact, for queries to servers not already cached on the client side, network traffic is increased because of the query to the Names Server database. Answer e is incorrect because ONS should never be considered fail-safe. Several Names Servers should be established, and ONS in no way has anything to do with database redundancy.

Question 3

Connection pooling should be considered in what kind of environments?

- ○ a. High-transaction environments
- ○ b. OLAP environments
- ○ c. Environments with many users who remain connected but where infrequent transactional activity occurs
- ○ d. Environments with many users who remain connected but where frequent transactional activity occurs
- ○ e. Environments with many CPUs and additional memory

Answer c is correct. You should consider connection pooling when you have an environment with many users who remain connected, but who execute transactions infrequently. Answers a and d are incorrect because connection pooling is not designed for high-transaction environments; in fact, it would probably make performance in these environments worse if you implemented connection pooling. Answer e is incorrect because connection pooling actually reduces the CPU and memory requirements of a database because many users are sharing resources.

Question 4

Connection pooling and multiplexing require what Oracle option to be enabled?

○ a. CKPT

○ b. ARCH

○ c. MTC

○ d. ONS

○ e. MTS

Answer e is correct. In order to be used, connection pooling and multiplexing both require that the Oracle8 Multi-Threaded Server (MTS) be enabled on the database. Answer a is incorrect because CKPT is the checkpoint process in Oracle. This process is now required in Oracle8, but has no relationship with connection pooling or multiplexing. Answer b is incorrect because ARCH is the archive process, an optional process. Answer c is incorrect because there is no MTC process in Oracle. Answer d is incorrect because you don't have to enable ONS for connection pooling or multiplexing.

Question 5

Which of the following is a configuration tool for Net8?

○ a. Net8 Names Administrator

○ b. Net8 Easy Config

○ c. Net8 Network Configuration Manager

○ d. Net8—network in a bottle

○ e. Net8—networking administrator

Answer b is correct. Net8 Easy Config is a Windows 95/NT GUI program that allows you to configure a basic Net8 network. Answers a, c, d, and e are all incorrect because they do not configure the Net8 network.

Question 6

Which client configuration file is eliminated when you implement Oracle Names Server?

○ a. sqlnet.ora

○ b. tnsnames.ora

○ c. listener.ora

○ d. names.ora

○ e. init.ora

Answer b is correct. The tnsnames.ora file is not required if you implement ONS. Answer a is incorrect because sqlnet.ora is still required if you are using a Names Server. Answer c is incorrect because listener.ora is not a client file. Answer d is incorrect because names.ora is not a client file and because it is required on the server for ONS. Answer e is incorrect because the init.ora file is a server file, and it is needed whether or not ONS is implemented.

Question 7

What is the name of the file on the client in which ONS stores cached named server addresses?

○ a. sqlnet.ora

○ b. ons.ora

○ c. oras.ora

○ d. cache.ora

○ e. sdns.ora

Answer e is correct. The sdns.ora file stores cached server addresses as well as the location of names servers and which name server has responded the quickest. Answer a is incorrect because the sqlnet.ora file is not used to store named server addresses. Answers b, c, and d are incorrect because they are not valid file names.

Need To Know More?

 Bobrowski, Steve: *Oracle8 Architecture*. Osborne-McGraw-Hill, 1998. ISBN 0-07-882274-2. This book contains a short, but interesting, chapter on Net8.

 Curtis, Mike and Jacqueline King: *Oracle8 & Windows NT Black Book*. The Coriolis Group, 1998. ISBN 1-57610-248-3. This book contains a rather good chapter on Oracle Names Server and reviews other Net8 optional services.

 Theriault, Marlene, et al.: *Oracle Security*. O'Reilly & Associates, 1998. ISBN 1-56592-450-9. This book contains a good chapter on OSS as well as information on ANO.

 Oracle's documentation is good reference material. Oracle has numerous guides available on CD or in hardcover.

 www.support.com is Oracle's Metalink Web site. It is a wonderful resource if you have Oracle Metals support.

Sample Test

In this chapter, I provide pointers to help you develop a successful test-taking strategy, including how to choose proper answers, decode ambiguity, work within the Oracle testing framework, decide what you need to memorize beforehand, and prepare in general for the test. At the end of this chapter, I include a set of 60 questions on subject matter that is pertinent to **Exam 1Z0-010**, **"Oracle8: New Features for Administrators."** In Chapter 13, you'll find the answer key to this test. Good luck!

Questions, Questions, Questions

There should be no doubt in your mind that you are facing a test full of specific and pointed questions. The Oracle8: New Features For Administrators test consists of 60 questions that you must complete in 90 minutes.

Questions belong to one of two basic types: multiple choice with a single answer, and multiple choice with one or more answers.

Always take the time to read a question at least twice before selecting an answer, and always look for an Exhibit button as you examine each question. Exhibits include graphics information that pertains to the question. (An exhibit is usually a screen capture of program output or GUI information that you must examine to analyze the question's scenario and formulate an answer.)

Not every question has only one answer; many questions require multiple answers. Therefore, it's important to read each question carefully—not only to determine how many answers are necessary or possible, but to look for additional hints or instructions when selecting answers. Such instructions often occur in brackets immediately following the question itself (as they do for all multiple-choice questions in which one or more answers are possible).

Picking Proper Answers

Obviously, the only way to pass any exam is to select enough of the right answers to obtain a passing score. However, Oracle's exams are not standardized like the SAT and GRE exams; Oracle exams are far more diabolical and convoluted. In some cases, questions are strangely worded and deciphering them can be a real challenge. In those cases, you might need to rely on answer-elimination skills. Almost always, at least one answer out of the possible choices for a question can be eliminated immediately because it matches one of these conditions:

➤ It does not apply to the situation.

➤ It describes a nonexistent issue, an invalid option, or an imaginary state.

➤ It can be eliminated because of the question itself.

After you eliminate all answers that are obviously wrong, you can apply your retained knowledge to eliminate further answers. Look for items that sound correct but refer to actions, commands, or features that are not present or available in the situation the question describes.

If you're still faced with a blind guess among two or more potentially correct answers, reread the question. Try to picture how each of the possible remaining answers would alter the situation. Be especially sensitive to terminology, because sometimes the choice of words (*remove* instead of *disable*) can make the difference between a right answer and a wrong one.

Only when you've exhausted your ability to eliminate answers should you guess at an answer. An unanswered question offers you no points, but guessing gives you at least some chance of getting a question right. Just don't be too hasty when making a blind guess.

> You can wait until the last round of reviewing marked questions (just as you're about to run out of time or out of unanswered questions) before you start making guesses.

Decoding Ambiguity

Exams are meant to test knowledge on a given topic, and the scores from a properly designed test will have the classic bell-shaped distribution for the target audience, meaning a certain number will fail. A problem with this exam is that is has been tailored to Oracle's training materials even though some of the material in the training is hearsay, some is old DBA tales, and some is just incorrect. Where obvious errors in the exam questions exist, the previous chapters have attempted to point them out to you.

The only sure way to overcome some of the exam's limitations is to be prepared. You will discover that many of the questions test your knowledge of something that is not directly related to the issue that the questions raise. This means that the answers offered to you, even the incorrect ones, are as much a part of the skill assessment as the questions themselves. If you do not have a thorough grasp of all the aspects of an exam topic (in this case, Oracle8's new features), you will not be able to eliminate answers that are obviously wrong because they relate to a different aspect of the topic than the one the question addresses.

Questions can reveal answers, especially when dealing with commands. So, read a question and then evaluate the answers in light of common terms, names, and structure.

Another problem is that Oracle uses some terminology in its training materials that isn't found anywhere else in its documentation sets. Whether this is a deliberate attempt to force you to take its classes to pass the exam or simply a case of sloppy documentation is unknown.

Working Within The Framework

The test questions appear in random order, and many elements or issues that receive mention in one question also crop up in other questions. It's not uncommon to find that an incorrect answer to one question is the correct answer to another question, or vice versa. Take the time to read every answer to each question, even if you recognize the correct answer to a question immediately. This extra reading might spark your memory or remind you about a feature or function that helps you on another question elsewhere in the exam.

You can revisit any question as many times as you like. If you're uncertain of the answer to a question, check the box that's provided to mark it for easy return later on. You should also mark questions that you think may offer information that you can use to answer other questions. I usually mark somewhere between 25 and 50 percent of the questions. The testing software is designed to let you mark every question if you choose, so use this feature to your advantage. Everything you will want to see again should be marked; the testing software can then help you return to marked questions quickly and easily.

Deciding What To Memorize

The amount you must memorize for an exam depends on how well you remember what you've read, and how well you intuitively know the software. If you are a visual thinker and you can see the drop-down menus and dialog boxes in your head, you won't need to memorize as much as someone who's less visually oriented. Because the tests will stretch your recollection of commands, tools, utilities, and functions related to Oracle8's new features, you'll want to memorize—at a minimum—the following kinds of information:

➤ Various new Oracle8 features (for example, be clear you understand partitioning)

➤ Oracle8's new limitations

➤ How to perform a migration from Oracle7 to Oracle8

➤ Oracle8's new backup and recovery features, and how they work

If you work your way through this book while sitting at a machine with Oracle8 installed, and you try to manipulate the features and functions of the various commands, tools, and utilities as they're discussed, you should have little or no difficulty mastering this material. You might also wish, if possible, to perform a migration from Oracle7 to Oracle8 before you take the exam. Also, don't forget that The Cram Sheet at the front of the book captures the material that is most important to memorize, so don't forget to use it to guide your studies as well.

Preparing For The Test

The best way to prepare for the test—after you've studied—is to take at least one practice exam. I've included one in this chapter for that reason; the test questions are located in the pages that follow. (Unlike the preceding chapters in this book, the answers don't follow the questions immediately; you'll have to flip to Chapter 13 to review the answers.)

Give yourself 90 minutes to take the exam. Keep yourself on the honor system, and don't look at earlier text in the book or jump ahead to the answer key. When your time is up or you've finished the questions, you can check your work in Chapter 13. Pay special attention to the explanations for the incorrect answers; these can also help to reinforce your knowledge of the material. Knowing how to recognize correct answers is good, but understanding why incorrect answers are wrong can be equally valuable.

Taking The Test

Relax. Once you're sitting in front of the testing computer, there's nothing more you can do to increase your knowledge or preparation. Take a deep breath, stretch, and start reading that first question.

There's no need to rush; you have plenty of time to complete each question and to return to those questions that you skip or mark for return. If you read a question twice and remain clueless, you can mark it. Both easy and difficult questions are intermixed throughout the test in random order. Don't cheat yourself by spending too much time on a hard question early in the test, which deprives you of the time you need to answer the questions at the end of the test.

You can read through the entire test and, before returning to marked questions for a second visit, figure out how much time you've got per question. As you answer each question, remove its mark. Continue to review the remaining marked questions until you run out of time or you complete the test.

That's it for pointers. Here are some questions for you to practice on.

Sample Test

Question 1

How many columns can be contained in a partitioned key?

○ a. 16

○ b. 32

○ c. 8

○ d. 31

○ e. 255

Question 2

A user attempts to insert a record into the **SALES_DETAIL** table, shown in the following code, with a **date-of-sale** of **01-JAN-2000**. What will be the result of the **INSERT** command?

```
CREATE TABLE sales_detail_data
(date_of_sale      DATE      NOT NULL,
invoice_number     NUMBER    NOT NULL,
item_line_no       NUMBER    NOT NULL,
item_sku           NUMBER    NOT NULL,
qty_sold           NUMBER    NOT NULL
)
PCTFREE 10
PCTUSED 60
STORAGE (INITIAL 10K NEXT 10K)
PARTITION BY RANGE (date_of_sale)
(
PARTITION sales_q1_99 VALUES LESS THAN
        (to_date('1999-02-01','YYYY-MM-DD') )
  PCTFREE 10
  PCTUSED 60
  TABLESPACE quarter_one
  STORAGE (INITIAL 10K NEXT 10K ),
  PARTITION sales_q2_99 VALUES LESS THAN
        (to_date('1999-07-01','YYYY-MM-DD') )
  PCTFREE 10
  PCTUSED 60
```

(continued)

Question 2 *(continued)*

```
TABLESPACE quarter_two
  STORAGE ( INITIAL 10K NEXT 10K ),
PARTITION sales_q3_99 VALUES LESS THAN
        (to_date('1999-10-01','YYYY-MM-DD') )
  PCTFREE 10
  PCTUSED 60
  TABLESPACE quarter_three
  STORAGE ( INITIAL 20K NEXT 20K ),
  PARTITION sales_q4_99 VALUES LESS THAN
        (to_date('2000-01-01','YYYY-MM-DD') )
  PCTFREE 10
  PCTUSED 60
  TABLESPACE quarter_four
  STORAGE ( INITIAL 40K NEXT 40K ) );
```

- ○ a. The insert will succeed with the row being inserted into partition
  sales_q4_99.
- ○ b. The insert will fail because the partition is not defined for the date
  being inserted.
- ○ c. The insert will succeed with the row being inserted into the partition
  sales_q1_2000.
- ○ d. The insert will succeed, but the row will be in the incorrect partition,
  sales_q1_1999, because a **sales_q1_2000** partition did not exist.
- ○ e. The insert will fail due to the use of the **TO_CHAR** function in the
  partition clause.

Question 3

As a DBA, you discover an index partition has an **UNUSABLE** status. How
would you correct this status?

- ○ a. Issue a **DROP INDEX PARTITION** command followed by a **CREATE
  INDEX PARTITION** command.
- ○ b. Issue an **ALTER INDEX REBUILD** command to rebuild the entire index.
- ○ c. Issue an **ALTER INDEX REBUILD PARTITION** command to rebuild
  the index partition.
- ○ d. Issue an **ALTER INDEX PARTITION** command to rebuild the index
  partition.
- ○ e. Issue an **ALTER INDEX RECREATE PARTITION** command to rebuild
  the index partition.

Question 4

An automated process has truncated a partition in the **SALES_ROLLUP_
HISTORY** table that actually has no data in it. What action will be required on
the local prefixed index associated with that table?

○ a. The associated index partition will be invalidated and have an
INDEX UNUSABLE status. The partition of that index will need to be
rebuilt.

○ b. The entire index will be invalidated and need to be rebuilt.

○ c. The associated index partition will continue to be valid.

○ d. The entire index will have an **INVALID** status.

○ e. The index partition will be invalidated only if other partitions that
contained data were truncated at the same time.

Question 5

Which of the following is not part of the format of the new extended **ROWID**?

○ a. Database object number

○ b. Absolute datafile number

○ c. Relative datafile number

○ d. Data block number

○ e. Row number

Question 6

If your design calls for a table that will only need to be accessed by its primary key and the primary key has a high degree of cardinality, how should
you create the table for the best performance?

○ a. Create the table and create a primary key on that table.

○ b. Create the table without a primary key.

○ c. Create the table as an index-organized table.

○ d. Create the table with a **freelists** set at 5 or larger.

○ e. Correctly set **pctfree** and **pctused** on the table.

Question 7

A table is created with a constraint initially set up as **NONDEFFERRABLE**. A user, before making a change to the table, uses the SQL command **ALTER SESSION SET CONSTRAINTS=DEFERRED**. What will be the result of the user's attempt to insert a row into the table that violates the established constraint?

○ a. The insert will succeed and the constraint will not be checked.

○ b. The insert will fail, but only at the time that the user issues a commit.

○ c. The insert will fail upon execution of the insert statement, but the transaction will continue.

○ d. The insert will succeed at the time of execution and no rollback will occur later.

○ e. The entire transaction will fail at the time the user attempts to insert the row.

Question 8

By what method of parallel operation can an **INSERT...SELECT** statement on a nonpartitioned table be parallelized?

○ a. A **ROWID** range operation

○ b. Multiple **INSERT** statements

○ c. The **/*+ PARALLEL */** hint

○ d. Parallel server processes

○ e. Partition scan operation

Question 9

What package do you use to write to a **BFILE**?

○ a. **DBMS_LOB**

○ b. **DBMS_UTILITY**

○ c. **DBMS_ROWID**

○ d. **DBMS_WRITE**

○ e. None; **BFILE** objects are read-only

Question 10

What is the purpose of the **ALLOCATE CHANNEL** command in an RMAN script?

- ○ a. To establish communication between the RMAN processes and the operating system
- ○ b. To allow the script to execute external procedures
- ○ c. To begin the backup process
- ○ d. To allow scripts to execute SQL commands
- ○ e. To allocate memory for the backup

Question 11

What are the two kinds of backup sets that can be made in RMAN? [Choose two]

- ❑ a. Full
- ❑ b. Complete
- ❑ c. Online
- ❑ d. Offline
- ❑ e. Incremental

Question 12

Which of the following statements cannot be parallelized if the table is not partitioned?

- ○ a. **SELECT**
- ○ b. **INSERT...SELECT**
- ○ c. **UPDATE**
- ○ d. **CREATE TABLE...AS SELECT**
- ○ e. **CREATE INDEX**

Question 13

What type of method is used to insert data into an object that has been created?

○ a. Insert

○ b. Constructor

○ c. **MEMBER**

○ d. **MAP**

○ e. **ORDER**

Question 14

If a DBA defines attributes in an RMAN **RUN** command, how long will they remain defined?

○ a. For the duration of the session

○ b. Until the DBA brings the instance down

○ c. For the length of time the **RUN** command is active

○ d. The attributes are nonvolatile and will remain until changed

○ e. Attributes cannot be set in RMAN

Question 15

Which of the following is a valid command-line parameter for the Oracle8 migration utility?

○ a. **pfile**

○ b. **bfile**

○ c. **dbcopy**

○ d. **command_file**

○ e. **offline**

Question 16

Which schema owns the password verification function?

○ a. **SYSTEM**

○ b. **SEC_AUTH**

○ c. **SECURITY**

○ d. The schema of the user who created it

○ e. **SYS**

Question 17

What is the correct form for a hint that would be used to request a parallel scan on a table?

○ a. **/* PARALLEL (table_name, degree_of_parallelism) */**

○ b. **/*+ PARALLEL (table_name, degree_of_parallelism) */**

○ c. **/*+ PARALLEL (degree_of_parallelism, table_name) */**

○ d. **/*+ PARALLEL_SCAN(table_name) */**

○ e. **/*+ PARALLEL_DML(table_name,degree_of_parallelism) */**

Question 18

In Oracle AQ, where are message queues stored?

○ a. The SGA

○ b. An Oracle table

○ c. An outside memory structure

○ d. The AQ.ora file

○ e. An external file

Question 19

Which report command will cause RMAN to produce a report of all datafiles in need of backup?

- ○ a. **OBSOLETE**
- ○ b. **UNRECOVERABLE**
- ○ c. **NEED BACKUP**
- ○ d. **REQUIRE BACKUP**
- ○ e. **BACKED UP SINCE MM/DD/YYYY**

Question 20

Which Oracle product can help reduce the administrative burden associated with updating the tnsnames.ora file on clients?

- ○ a. Oracle Parallel Server
- ○ b. Oracle Parallel Query
- ○ c. Oracle Web Server
- ○ d. Oracle Lite
- ○ e. Oracle Names

Question 21

Which SQL script establishes default password settings in the **DEFAULT** profile?

- ○ a. utlpwdmg.sql
- ○ b. password.sql
- ○ c. setpass.sql
- ○ d. passdeflt.sql
- ○ e. setdfltpas.sql

Question 22

You discover after converting a database to Oracle8 that an application table has restricted **ROWID**s stored in it. The application group asks you to convert these **ROWID**s to the new extended Oracle8 format. Which package should you use to perform this conversion?

○ a. **DBMS_ROWID_CONVERT**

○ b. **DBMS_CONVERT**

○ c. **DBMS_ROWID**

○ d. **DBMS_UTILITY**

○ e. **DBMS_DDL**

Question 23

Using the following information, how would a user query the employee table to get the **street_name** of a specific employee?

```
CREATE TYPE address_t AS OBJECT
(  street_name            VARCHAR2(30),
   city_name              VARCHAR2(20),
   state_initial          VARCHAR2(4),
   zip_code               VARCHAR2(10) );

CREATE TABLE employee
( emp_id          NUMBER      NOT NULL,
  emp_address     address_t   NOT NULL,
  constraint emp_pk PRIMARY KEY (emp_id) );
```

○ a. **SELECT emp_address:street_name FROM employee;**

○ b. **SELECT emp_address.street_name FROM employee;**

○ c. **SELECT e.street_name FROM employee e WHERE emp_id=12345;**

○ d. **SELECT emp_address.street_name FROM employee WHERE emp_id=12345;**

○ e. **SELECT street_name FROM employee WHERE emp_id=12345;**

Question 24

The database design group has decided to split a partition containing data. This table has a local index on it, as well as a global index. What will be the result of the split operation on the global index?

- ○ a. The affected partition of the local index will be marked **UNUSABLE**, and any partition in the global index with **ROWID**s associated with the split partition will also be marked unusable.
- ○ b. The local index partition will be unaffected, and the global index will be marked as **UNUSABLE**.
- ○ c. The affected partition of the local index will be marked **UNUSABLE**, and the global index will be marked as **UNUSABLE**.
- ○ d. The operation will not affect the local index or the global index.
- ○ e. The global index will be updated and remain available, while the local index will become invalid and will require a rebuild.

Question 25

What two types of partitioning are available between two related objects in Oracle? [Choose two]

- ❏ a. Parallel partitioning
- ❏ b. Equipartitioned
- ❏ c. Equijoined
- ❏ d. Nonparallel partitioned
- ❏ e. Nonequipartitioned

Question 26

Which of the following is not a new Oracle **LOB**?

- ○ a. **BFILE**
- ○ b. **BLOB**
- ○ c. **CLOB**
- ○ d. **NCLOB**
- ○ e. **PLOB**

Question 27

A **REF** is a:

○ a. New type of check constraint

○ b. Built-in data type that allows an OID to be referenced in another table

○ c. New **LOB** data type that stores raw or character data

○ d. Unique identifier for an object

○ e. Collection of object attributes that make up an object table

Question 28

Which operation is not allowed on a partitioned index?

○ a. Dropping an index partition

○ b. Renaming an index partition

○ c. Adding an index partition

○ d. Modifying an index partition

○ e. Splitting an index partition

Question 29

What is one of the purposes of the large pool?

○ a. Provides a memory area for MTS sessions

○ b. Allows separation for commonly used SQL statements from transitory ones

○ c. Provides an area for large PL/SQL packages to be pinned into memory without affecting the rest of the shared pool

○ d. Provides an area for rarely used database data blocks to reside

○ e. Provides a separated dictionary cache, reducing contention in the shared pool

Question 30

You wish to query a partition table called **EMPLOYEE_RECORDS** for a specific record with a **record_id** of 12345. You know that the record exists on the partition called **new_employee** and that there is a like record on a partition called **OLD_EMPLOYEE**. What SQL statement would you use to **SELECT** only the record from the **new_employee** partition of the **EMPLOYEE_RECORDS** table?

○ a. **SELECT /*+ PARTITION(new_employee) */ * FROM employee_records WHERE record_id=12345;**

○ b. **SELECT * FROM employee_records where PARTITION (new_employee).record_id=12345;**

○ c. **SELECT * FROM employee_records PARTITION (new_employee) WHERE record_id=12345;**

○ d. **SELECT * FROM employee_records WHERE record_id=12345 USING PARTITON (new_employee);**

○ e. **SELECT * FROM employee_records WHERE record_id=12345 PARTITION (new_employee);**

Question 31

In Oracle8, how large can a **VARCHAR2** data type be?

○ a. 2,000 characters

○ b. 4,000 characters

○ c. 2 million characters

○ d. 4 million characters

○ e. 12 million characters

Question 32

In an extended **ROWID**, the relative file number is relative to:

○ a. A tablespace

○ b. The entire database

○ c. All other datafiles

○ d. The restricted **ROWID**

○ e. The OID of that tablespace

Question 33

What are the benefits of using Recovery Manager? [Choose two]

- ❑ a. Tablespaces, during hot backups, are not put in hot backup mode. Therefore, less redo is generated during the backup process.

- ❑ b. RMAN can make archive log backups directly to tape.

- ❑ c. RMAN will only combine backups into backup sets. You must use RMAN to recover all backups made. This has positive performance impacts.

- ❑ d. Backups can be full or incremental, thus allowing for the reduction in overall backup time.

- ❑ e. RMAN requires no DBA administration or setup.

Question 34

Which of the following is not a valid command-line parameter for RMAN?

- ○ a. **append**
- ○ b. **debug**
- ○ c. **msglog**
- ○ d. **nocatalog**
- ○ e. **catalog**

Question 35

What will happen when you attempt to run the script shown in the following example (which contains an RMAN backup script)?

```
RMAN> RUN
{ BACKUP FULL TAG 'MY BACKUP' format
  '/backupdir/todays_backup/db_t%t_s%s_p%p'
  (DATABASE);
RELEASE CHANNEL chan1;
}
```

(continued)

Question 35 *(continued)*

○ a. The backup will complete successfully.

○ b. The backup will fail, because there is no **END;** statement in the script.

○ c. The backup will fail, because a channel is not allocated.

○ d. The backup will complete with a warning, because the default operating system I/O device will have been used since an **ALLO-CATE CHANNEL** statement was not used.

○ e. The backup will fail, because braces are used instead of brackets after the **RUN** command and at the end of the script.

Question 36

What will happen when you attempt to run the script shown in the following code (which contains an RMAN backup script)?

```
RMAN> RUN
{ ALLOCATE CHANNEL chan1 TYPE DISK;
  BACKUP FULL TAG 'MY BACKUP' format
  '/backupdir/todays_backup/db_t%t_s%s_p%p'
  (DATABASE);
  RELEASE CHANNEL chan1;
}
```

○ a. The backup will complete successfully.

○ b. The backup will fail, because there is no **END;** statement in the script.

○ c. The backup will fail, because the **ALLOCATE CHANNEL** statement is incorrect.

○ d. The backup will complete with a warning, because the default operating system I/O device will have been used since an **ALLO-CATE CHANNEL** statement is incorrect.

○ e. The backup will fail, because braces are used instead of brackets after the **RUN** command and at the end of the script.

Question 37

The **RESET DATABASE** command in RMAN is used to:

○ a. Add a new database to the recovery catalog.

○ b. Force RMAN to perform an **ALTER DATABASE OPEN RESETLOGS** command on the database after it has completed recovering it.

○ c. Create a new incarnation of a database after a **RESETLOGS** command has been issued on that database.

○ d. Reset a database in the recovery catalog after the DBA has added or removed a datafile.

○ e. Wipe out the recovery catalog entry for a database that no longer exists.

Question 38

How would you verify whether a database is registered in the RMAN recovery catalog?

○ a. Issue the command **LIST INCARNATION OF DATABASE;** in RMAN.

○ b. Issue the command **LIST ALL INCARNATIONS;** in RMAN.

○ c. Sign onto the database that contains the recovery catalog and issue the **SELECT * FROM db_incarnations;** SQL command to get a listing of database incarnations.

○ d. It is not possible to determine the current incarnation. If you are concerned that the database incarnation is not correct, reissue the **REGISTER DATABASE** command.

○ e. Enter the command **SHOW INCARNATION** from RMAN.

Question 39

Multiplexing is best used when:

○ a. There are a large number of users on the database, and they are generating a large volume of SQL statements.

○ b. There are few users on the database, but those that are on it often issue long-running queries.

○ c. There are two databases that often need to communicate with each other through distributed links.

○ d. There is a need for high network security and the use of various security protocols.

Question 40

What packages are available to use and administer Advanced Queuing?
[Choose two]

- ❏ a. **DBMS_AQ**
- ❏ b. **DBMS_AQADM**
- ❏ c. **DBMS_AQWORK**
- ❏ d. **DBMS_AQENQUEUE**
- ❏ e. **DBMS_QUEUE**

Question 41

Which command must you run in order to create external pointers to external procedures in order to run those procedures in Oracle8?

- ○ a. **CREATE DIRECTORY**
- ○ b. **CREATE LIBRARY**
- ○ c. **CREATE PROCEDURE EXTERNAL**
- ○ d. **CREATE EXTERNAL FUNCTION**
- ○ e. **CREATE EXTERNAL PROCEDURE**

Question 42

When you define a **LOB** data type in a table, what other objects are created?
[Choose two]

- ❏ a. **LOB** segment
- ❏ b. **LOB** sort table
- ❏ c. **LOB** index
- ❏ d. **LOB** locator
- ❏ e. **LOB** accumulator

Question 43

A table with 15 partitions and an associated prefixed global index with 10 partitions is an example of:

○ a. Equipartitioning

○ b. Nonequipartitioning

○ c. Equijoining

○ d. Nonequijoining

○ e. Partition reliance

Question 44

If a user inserts

```
INSERT INTO sales_data (acct, name,
                amount, week)
VALUES (10000,'Joe's Place',100.00,51);
```

into the partitioned table created in the following code, into which partition will the insert go?

```
CREATE TABLE sales_data
( acct                NUMBER(5),
  name                CHAR(30),
  amount              NUMBER(6),
  week                INTEGER )
PARTITION BY RANGE ( week )
(PARTITION sales1 VALUES LESS THAN ( 4 )
 TABLESPACE ts0,
 PARTITION sales2 VALUES LESS THAN ( 8 )
 TABLESPACE ts1,
 PARTITION sales3 VALUES LESS THAN ( 12 )
 TABLESPACE ts1,
 PARTITION sales4 VALUES LESS THAN ( 16 )
 TABLESPACE ts1,
 PARTITION sales5 VALUES LESS THAN ( 20 )
 TABLESPACE ts1,
 PARTITION sales6 VALUES LESS THAN ( 24 )
 TABLESPACE ts1,
```

(continued)

Question 44 *(continued)*

```
PARTITION sales7 VALUES LESS THAN ( 28 )
TABLESPACE ts1,
PARTITION sales8 VALUES LESS THAN ( 32 )
TABLESPACE ts1,
PARTITION sales9 VALUES LESS THAN ( 36 )
TABLESPACE ts1,
PARTITION sales10 VALUES LESS THAN ( 40 )
TABLESPACE ts1,
PARTITION sales11 VALUES LESS THAN ( 44 )
TABLESPACE ts1,
PARTITION sales12 VALUES LESS THAN ( 48 )
TABLESPACE ts1,
PARTITION sales13 VALUES LESS THAN ( 52 )
TABLESPACE ts12 );
```

- ○ a. Partition **sales13**
- ○ b. Partition **sales12**
- ○ c. Partition **sales11**
- ○ d. Partition **sales1**
- ○ e. The insert will fail

Question 45

What will be the effect of the following statement on the local indexes associated with the table?

```
ALTER TABLE my_table MOVE PARTITION TABLESPACE new_tbs;
```

- ○ a. Global indexes will become **UNUSABLE**, and local indexes will remain valid.
- ○ b. Non-prefixed Global indexes will become **UNUSABLE**, but prefixed global and local indexes will remain available.
- ○ c. Affected partitions of the indexes will become invalid.
- ○ d. No indexes will be invalidated.
- ○ e. You cannot execute a **MOVE PARTITION** command on a table.

Question 46

Before issuing a DML statement to be executed in parallel, what action must you take?

○ a. You must be signed into the database as **SYSTEM** or **SYS**.

○ b. You must issue the SQL command **ALTER SESSION ENABLE PARALLEL DML;**.

○ c. You must issue the SQL command **ALTER DATABASE ENABLE PARALLEL DML;**.

○ d. You must set the init.ora setting **ENABLE_PARALLEL_DML=TRUE**.

○ e. You only need to issue the parallel DML statement. No other action is required.

Question 47

What is the effect of setting **parallel_max_servers=100** in the init.ora?

○ a. The parameter defines the number of parallel query servers to be started at instance startup.

○ b. The parameter defines the maximum number of parallel server processes that can be assigned to a single parallel query.

○ c. The parameter defines the absolute maximum number of parallel query processes that can be started for the database associated with the init.ora file.

○ d. The parameter defines the maximum number of user sessions that can be running parallel DML at one time.

○ e. The parameter defines the maximum degree of parallelism that any DML statement can have.

Question 48

What function do you use to grant a user the ability to support multiple consumer queues in Advanced Queuing?

○ a. **DBMS_AQ.ENABLE**

○ b. **DBMS_AQADM.SET_PERMISSIONS**

○ c. **DBMS_AQADM.GRANT_TYPE_ACCESS**

○ d. **DBMS_AQ.ENQUEUE**

○ e. **DBMS_AQ.DEQUEUE**

Question 49

What is the purpose of the Parallel Query Coordinator process?

- ○ a. Several Parallel Query Coordinator processes are started by the query server, which manages the parallel operation.
- ○ b. The Parallel Query Coordinator process is responsible for determining how many total parallel server processes can be started on the entire database. It manages all parallel query operations.
- ○ c. The Parallel Query Coordinator process is responsible for managing the parallel operation of a single statement. It begins one or more parallel server processes that divide the workload, processes the SQL statement, and returns the results to the Parallel Query Coordinator for processing.
- ○ d. The Parallel Query Coordinator allows multiple queries to be processed by one database server process.
- ○ e. The Parallel Query Coordinator is a new Net8 option that allows multiple connections to be pooled into one database connection.

Question 50

Which of the following is true regarding index-only tables? [Choose two]

- ❑ a. Index-only tables have no **ROWID**s.
- ❑ b. Index-only tables cannot contain **LOB** data types.
- ❑ c. Index-only tables cannot contain nested tables.
- ❑ d. Index-only tables can have multiple indexes built on them.
- ❑ e. An index-only table can be an object table.

Question 51

What is a primary difference between a nested table and a **VARRAY**?

- ○ a. A nested table can contain multiple records associated with one row, whereas a **VARRAY** can only contain one record per row.
- ○ b. Nested tables and **VARRAY**s are both independent of the master table, each having out-of-line storage.
- ○ c. Both nested tables and **VARRAY** data types can be indexed.
- ○ d. Both nested tables and **VARRAY**s allow for multiple related column values to be stored in a single row.
- ○ e. Neither **VARRAY**s nor nested tables have a limit to how many records you can insert into any particular row after they are defined.

Question 52

When creating a profile that includes password management, if you want a user's password to expire after 30 days but you do not want it to be locked out for 10 days after the expiration of the password, what parameters would you set?

○ a. **password_life_time=30** and **password_grace_time=10**

○ b. **password_life_time=30** and **password_lock_time=10**

○ c. **password_grace_time=30** and **password_reuse_max=10**

○ d. **password_grace_time=30** and **failed_login_attempts=10**

○ e. **password_reuse_max=30** and **failed_login_attempts=10**

Question 53

The Oracle8 Names Server _____.

○ a. dynamically assigns names to newly created databases

○ b. provides database name resolution to client applications

○ c. provides additional levels of security to Net8

○ d. provides a Web server for the Oracle8 database

○ e. provides extended protocol support to Net8

Question 54

Which of the following is not a feature of RMAN?

○ a. Backup and recovery of Oracle databases

○ b. Reporting of database backup status

○ c. Creation of copies of database datafiles

○ d. Incremental backups of databases

○ e. Recovery of control files without a recovery catalog

Question 55

You are concerned that another DBA in your company executed some operations within a tablespace that were executed as unrecoverable options. You need to check to make sure, and, if these operations have been done, you need to back up the database with RMAN. Using RMAN, how can you determine if unrecoverable operations have been done and require backup?

- ○ a. Check the **V$UNRECOVERABLE** view
- ○ b. Run the RMAN report **REPORT UNRECOVERABLE <DATABASE> DISK;**
- ○ c. Execute the report **REPORT NEED BACKUP 3 DAYS;**
- ○ d. Check the **ALERT.LOG** for Oracle messages related to the unrecoverable actions
- ○ e. Generate a report of all files needing to be backed up and sort by those with an unrecoverable status

Question 56

Issuing the **LIST BACKUP SET OF DATABASE** command in RMAN will:

- ○ a. List the last backup set of the target database
- ○ b. List the location that the files were copied to in the last backup set of the target database
- ○ c. Provide a list of all backup sets of the target database
- ○ d. Create a list of all backup sets of all databases in the recovery catalog
- ○ e. List and remove specific backup sets of the target database

Question 57

What procedures are available in the Oracle Advanced Queuing package **DBMS_AQ**? [Choose two]

- ❑ a. **dbms_aq.start_q**
- ❑ b. **dbms_aq.stop_q**
- ❑ c. **dbms_aq.enqueue**
- ❑ d. **ddms_aq.create_q**
- ❑ e. **dbms_aq.dequeue**

Question 58

What is the name for a complete RMAN backup that contains datafiles and/or control files?

○ a. Backup piece

○ b. Archivelog backup set

○ c. Datafile backup set

○ d. Image copy

○ e. Consistent backup copy

Question 59

What will be the result of the following operation, which might appear in a PL/SQL program if a valid **ROWID** is passed into **rowid_value**?

```
My_Rowid := DBMS_ROWID.ROWID_TO_EXTENDED
(rowid_value,'MYSCHEMA','MYTABLE',
ROWID_CONVERT_EXTERNAL);
```

○ a. **My_Rowid** will contain the extended **ROWID** of the given **ROWID** value of the **MYSCHEMA.MYTABLE** object.

○ b. **My_Rowid** will contain the restricted **ROWID** of the given **ROWID** value of the **MYSCHEMA.MYTABLE** object.

○ c. **My_Rowid** will contain a **NULL** value.

○ d. The operation is not a valid **DBMS_ROWID** function.

○ e. The function will cause all **ROWID**s to be stored in the database as extended **ROWID**s.

Question 60

In Oracle8, what is the maximum number of columns you can have in a table?

○ a. 255

○ b. 510

○ c. 1,000

○ d. 2,000

○ e. Unlimited

Answer Key

1. a
2. b
3. c
4. c
5. b
6. c
7. c
8. d
9. e
10. a
11. a, e
12. c
13. b
14. c
15. a
16. e
17. b
18. b
19. c
20. e

21. a
22. c
23. d
24. c
25. b, e
26. e
27. b
28. c
29. a
30. c
31. b
32. a
33. a, d
34. e
35. c
36. a
37. c
38. a
39. a
40. a, b

41. b
42. a, c
43. b
44. a
45. c
46. b
47. c
48. c
49. c
50. a, c
51. d
52. a
53. b
54. e
55. b
56. c
57. c, e
58. c
59. a
60. c

Question 1

The correct answer is a. You can create a partition key on as many as 16 columns. Answer b is incorrect and might almost be considered a trick answer because you might confuse a partition key with an index, which can be created with up to 32 columns. Answers c, d, and e are all incorrect values.

Question 2

The correct answer is b. The insert will fail, because a partition was not created for the date range being inserted and the **MAXVALUE** clause was not used. Answer a is incorrect. The insert will not succeed, because the value in the partition key must be lower than the value listed in the **VALUES LESS THAN** clause. The last **VALUES LESS THAN** clause was established for all dates before January 1, 2000, so any attempt to insert a date later than December 31, 1999, will fail. Answer c is incorrect, because there is no partition **sales_q1_2000** in the partitioned table. Answer d is incorrect. The insert will fail. The row will not find itself inserted in an incorrect partition, which **sales_q1_1999** would have been. Finally, answer e is incorrect, because the use of the **TO_CHAR** function is perfectly valid.

Question 3

The correct answer is c, because you must issue the **ALTER INDEX RE-BUILD PARTITION** command to rebuild the index partition. Answer a is incorrect. You do not need to drop the index partition and re-create it to correct the situation. Answer b is incorrect, because you need to specify the **PARTITION** keyword in the command. Answers d and e are incorrect, because the SQL commands are incorrectly formatted.

Question 4

Answer c is correct. When you truncate or split a partition that contains no data, the index will not be invalidated. Answers a and b are incorrect, because the partition is not invalidated and will not need to be rebuilt. Answer d is incorrect, because the entire index will not be invalidated. Finally, answer e is incorrect, because the partition is not invalidated at all, regardless of the status of any other truncates.

Question 5

The correct answer is b. There is no absolute datafile number in an extended ROWID. Answers a, c, d, and e are incorrect, because they are all part of the extended ROWID in Oracle8.

Question 6

The correct answer is c. You should create the table as an index-organized table. An index-organized table will perform better in the case of a table that will always be accessed using its primary key and the primary key has a high degree of cardinality. Answer a is incorrect, because, in this specific case, an index-organized table will perform better. Answer b is incorrect, because the lack of the primary key index will cause a query to perform quite slowly. Answer d is incorrect, because setting **freelists** will not help improve queries' response times. Finally, answer e is incorrect. Though setting **pctfree** and **pctused** can help space utilization, which can have some potential impact on performance, the more correct answer is to use an index-organized table, as described in answer c.

Question 7

The correct answer is c. Because the table was created with nodeferrable constraints, the use of ALTER SESSION SET CONSTRAINTS=DEFERRED will have no impact on the table or operations on it. Answer a is incorrect; the constraint will be checked, because it is not deferrable. Answer b is incorrect. The insert will fail at the time the user attempts to do it. Answer d is incorrect, because the insert will fail and the statement will be rolled back. Answer e is incorrect; only the insert will fail, not the entire transaction.

Question 8

The correct answer is d. An INSERT...SELECT statement on a non-partitioned table will use parallel server processes to execute the statement. Answer a is incorrect, because ROWID range operations are used for parallelizing SELECT operations. Answer b is incorrect. Using multiple insert statements is not a parallel process used by Oracle (though certainly a DBA could try). Answer c is incorrect. While there is a PARALLEL hint, it is not a process and does not guarantee that the statement will be processed in parallel. Answer e is incorrect, because parallel by partition operations are not used on INSERT...SELECT statements. Instead, they are used on such statements as UPDATE, DELETE, and other operations on partitioned tables.

Question 9

The correct answer is e. BFILE objects cannot be written to and are read-only. Answer a is incorrect. You cannot use the DBMS_LOB package to write to BFILE objects, but you can use the package to read from BFILE objects and manipulate other types of LOBs. Answers b, c, and d are incorrect, because none of the functions have any uses in regards to LOBs of any kind.

Question 10

The correct answer is a. The ALLOCATE CHANNEL command in RMAN is used to establish communications between the recovery processes and the operating system. You define which type of I/O device will be used to write the backup to with this command, as well. Answer b is incorrect, because the ALLOCATE CHANNEL command is not used to execute external procedures. Answer c is incorrect; you use the BACKUP command to start the backup processes. Answer d is incorrect; the SQL command is used to execute SQL scripts, not the ALLOCATE CHANNEL command. Finally, answer e is incorrect, because there is no command in RMAN to allocate memory.

Question 11

The correct answers are a and e. The two backup sets are full and incremental. Answer b is incorrect, because, while you can do complete backups with RMAN, complete is not a type of backup set. Answers c and d are incorrect, because neither answer provides a type of backup set associated with RMAN.

Question 12

The correct answer is c. A regular UPDATE statement cannot be partitioned on a nonpartitioned table. A table must be parallelized in order to perform a parallel UPDATE operation. Answer a is incorrect, because a parallel SELECT is done by using a ROWID range and multiple parallel query server processes. There is no requirement for a parallel SELECT to occur on a partitioned table. The same is true for answer b; INSERT...SELECT statements can be performed in parallel on a non-partitioned table. Answers d and e are incorrect for the same reasons. In both instances, CREATE TABLE...AS SELECT and CREATE INDEX, the statement can be parallelized on non-partitioned tables.

Question 13

The correct answer is b. The constructor method is implicitly created at the time the object type is created. This method is used to insert data into the attributes of the object. Answer a is incorrect, because there is no insert method in Oracle8. Answer c is incorrect. A **MEMBER** method is used to manipulate data that already exists in the object type instance. Answers d and e are incorrect, because the **MAP** and **ORDER** methods are used to provide the ability to order data within the objects.

Question 14

The correct answer is c. Attributes that are set will be valid for the duration of the **RUN** command they are associated with. Answer a is incorrect, because attributes' values are only valid until the end of a **RUN** command. Answer b is incorrect, because shutting down the instance has no effect on the attributes set. Answer d is incorrect, because attributes are not nonvolatile and will reset after the **RUN** command. Answer e is incorrect, because you can set attributes in RMAN.

Question 15

The correct answer is a. **pfile** is a valid command-line parameter for migration. It identifies the database parameter file to the migration utility. Answer b, **bfile**, is incorrect, because a bfile is an object type and has no relation to the migration utility. Answers c, d, and e are incorrect, because they do not represent valid parameters.

Question 16

The correct answer is e. The verification function must be compiled under the **SYS** account and is thus a member of the **SYS** schema. Answers a, b, c, and d are incorrect, because you cannot create a password verification function in any other schema other than **SYS**.

Question 17

The correct answer is b. To properly request a parallel scan, you use the hint syntax of /*+ followed by the **PARALLEL** keyword. This is followed by the **table_name** and the **degree_of_parallelisim** in parentheses. Answer a is incorrect, because the hint is missing the + symbol, which is part of the hint syntax.

Answer c is incorrect, because the order of the attributes of the **PARALLEL** clause is backwards. Answer d is incorrect, because the correct command is **PARALLEL**, not **PARALLEL_SCAN**, and the degree of parallelism is missing from the hint syntax. Finally, answer e is incorrect, because **PARALLEL_DML** is not a valid hint.

Question 18

The correct answer is b. A message queue is stored in an Oracle table. Answer a is incorrect, because the SGA is not used to store message queues (though blocks from the queue table can reside in the SGA). Answer c is incorrect, because no outside memory structure is used. Answers d and e are incorrect, because no external file of any type is used to store message queues.

Question 19

The correct answer is c. You use the **REPORT NEED BACKUP** command to generate a report of all datafiles that need to be backed up. Answer a is incorrect, because the **REPORT OBSOLETE** command generates a list of backups that are no longer needed. Answers d and e are incorrect, because the **REQUIRE BACKUP** and **BACKED UP SINCE** commands do not exist.

Question 20

The correct answer is e. Oracle Names can help alleviate the administrative burden of having to maintain tnsnames.ora files on a network consisting of a large number of clients. Using centralized name resolution, the client resolves the database alias from a Names Server or a local cache at the client that has been previously populated by a Names Server lookup. Answer a is incorrect, as the Parallel Server product is designed to allow multiple instances to work together on a single database, and has nothing to do with eliminating the tnsnames.ora file. Answer b is incorrect, because the Oracle Parallel Query has nothing to do with Oracle networking. Answers c and d are incorrect, because the Oracle Web Server and Oracle Lite products have nothing to do with the centralized resolution of alias names.

Question 21

The correct answer is a. utlpwdmg.sql is run to create default password security settings on the **DEFAULT** profile. Answers b, c, d, and e are incorrect, because the scripts are not used for the described purpose and are not Oracle-supplied scripts.

Question 22

The correct answer is c. You use the **DBMS_ROWID** package to convert the Oracle7 restricted **ROWID**s into Oracle8 extended **ROWID**s. Answers a and b are incorrect, because they are invalid Oracle8 packages. Answers d and e are incorrect, because, while they are valid packages in Oracle8, they have nothing to do with the conversion of Oracle8 **ROWID**s.

Question 23

The correct answer is d. Answer d will return just one record for the employee whose **emp_id** is 12345. Answer a is incorrect, because the colon is not a correct way to delimit the attribute of the type you wish displayed. Answer b is incorrect. While answer b might appear to be correct, if you read the question carefully, it states that you want the employee_id of a specific employee. Answer b will get addresses of all employees (and it would not be a very helpful query, because you won't know whose address goes with whom). Answer c is incorrect, because the attribute is improperly referred to. Answer e is incorrect, because there is no alias on the table, which is required when referring to objects.

Question 24

The correct answer is c. The **SPLIT PARTITION** operation will render the local index partitions unusable, unless one of the new partitions is empty. The global index will be marked **UNUSABLE**, and both will require maintenance to make them available. Answer a is incorrect, because the local index partitions are affected by the operation. Answer d is incorrect, because both local and global indexes are affected by the operation. Answer e is incorrect, because the global index will not be maintained during the split operation and will require a rebuild.

Question 25

The correct answers are b and e. The two types of partitioning between two related objects in Oracle are equipartitioned and nonequipartitioned. Answer a is incorrect; parallel partitioning is not a partition type between two objects. Answer c is incorrect; the term *equijoined* is not correct when referring to the partition relationship between two objects. Answer d, nonparallel partitioned, is not a partitioning option.

Question 26

The correct answer is e, **PLOB**. There is no **PLOB LOB** type in Oracle8. Answer a is incorrect, because a **BFILE** is a **LOB** that refers to an external file and is used in Oracle to allow the user to read from that external file. Answer b is incorrect, because a **BLOB** is a binary **LOB** in Oracle that holds raw, binary data. Answer c is incorrect, because a **CLOB** is a **LOB** used in Oracle to hold character data. Finally, answer d is incorrect, because an **NCLOB** is the **NLS** variant of the **CLOB LOB** data type, also holding character data.

Question 27

The correct answer is b. A **REF** is a built in data type that allows an object identifier (OID) to be referenced in another table. This can be used to provide one-to-many relationships between two Oracle objects when one side of the relationship is a row object. Answer a is incorrect. A **REF** is not a new type of check constraint. Answer c is incorrect. A **REF** is not a **LOB** and does not store raw or character data. Answer d is incorrect. A **REF** is a storage type that stores an **OID**, which is a unique identifier for an object type. Answer e is incorrect. A **REF** is not a collection of object attributes of an object table.

Question 28

The correct answer is c. You cannot add a partition to an index. Answer a is incorrect, because you can drop an index partition. Answer b is incorrect, because you can rename an index partition. Answer e is incorrect, because you can also split an index partition.

Question 29

The correct answer is a. The large pool stores session memory for sessions using MTS. Also, the large pool provides a memory area for server I/O processes and backup and restore operations using RMAN. Answer b is incorrect, because SQL statements are not stored in the large pool. Answer c is incorrect, because PL/SQL packages are not pinned into the large pool. Answer d is incorrect, because data blocks are not stored in the large pool, but are stored in the database buffer cache, and can be stored in one of three structures (the **KEEP**, **DEFAULT**, and **RECYCLE**). Finally, answer e is incorrect, because the large pool does not provide a separate dictionary cache area.

Question 30

The correct answer is c. You use the **PARTITION** clause after listing the table name in the **FROM** clause. Answer a is incorrect, because there is no **PARTITION** hint available to perform the desired action. Answer b is incorrect, because the **PARTITION** clause is in the wrong place. Answer d is incorrect, because there is no **USING PARTITION** clause in Oracle. Finally, answer e is incorrect, because the **PARTITION** clause is in the incorrect location.

Question 31

The correct answer is b. The **VARCHAR2** data type can now hold up to 4,000 characters of data. Answer a is incorrect for Oracle8, although it was true of Oracle7. Answers c, d, and e are incorrect, because the values they offer are much too large.

Question 32

The correct answer is a. The relative file number, the seventh through ninth characters of an extended **ROWID**, is a number relative to the tablespace. Answer b is incorrect, because it actually describes the old Oracle7 restricted format where the file number was relative to the entire database. Answers c, d, and e are all incorrect answers, because they do not describe the relative file number.

Question 33

The correct answers are a and d. Answer a is correct, because RMAN does not put tablespaces into hot backup mode. This reduces the I/O overhead caused by block images being saved in the online redo log files. Answer d is correct, because you can do full or incremental backups with RMAN. Because incremental backups only back up changed blocks since the last full backup (or previous, higher-level backup), you reduce the overall backup time. Answer b is incorrect, because RMAN cannot perform archive log backups directly to tape, but only to disk. Answer c is incorrect, because RMAN also provides the ability to produce image copies of datafiles that are not manipulated in any way. These copies can be used through RMAN to restore a database, create a new database, and even manually move these image copies to perform recovery functions manually. Answer e is incorrect, because, unfortunately, RMAN requires DBA administration and, especially, setup.

Question 34

The correct answer is e. There is no **catalog** command-line parameter in RMAN. Answer a is incorrect, because the **append** command-line parameter will cause the output from RMAN to be appended to the log file specified in the command-line parameter listed in answer c, **msglog**. Answer b is incorrect. The **debug** command-line parameter will turn debug mode on for RMAN. Answer d, **nocatalog**, is incorrect, because it is used if you need to use RMAN in a situation where there is no recovery catalog.

Question 35

The correct answer is c. The backup will fail, because a channel is not allocated to the backup. Allocation of a channel, which facilitates communication between the operating system and RMAN and which defines the I/O device to be used during the backup, is required before a backup command can be used. Answer a is incorrect, because the backup will fail. Answer b is incorrect, because no **END;** statement is required. Answer d is incorrect, because RMAN will not use a default I/O device if the **ALLOCATE CHANNEL** command is not used. Answer e is incorrect, because you do indeed use braces after the **RUN** command is issued and after all the statements of the **RUN** command have been entered.

Question 36

The correct answer is a. The backup will run successfully. Answer b is incorrect, because the backup does not require an **END;** statement. Answer c is incorrect, because the **ALLOCATE CHANNEL** statement is correct. Answer d is incorrect, because the backup will be successful and no warning message should be generated. Answer e is incorrect, because braces are expected, not brackets.

Question 37

The correct answer is c. The **RESET DATABASE** command in RMAN is used to create a new incarnation of the database after an **ALTER DATABASE OPEN RESETLOGS** command is issued, most likely after an incomplete recovery of that database. Answer a is incorrect, because you use the **REGISTER DATABASE** command to add a new database to the recovery catalog. Answer b is incorrect, because the **RESET DATABASE** does not force the target database to do an **ALTER DATABASE OPEN RESET-**

LOGS command. Answer d is incorrect, because you do not use the **RESET DATABASE** command to reset the recovery catalog after adding or removing a datafile. This will be done automatically or can be done manually with the **RESYNC CATALOG** command. Answer e is incorrect, because the **RESET DATABASE** command is not used to remove a recovery catalog entry for a database that no longer exists.

Question 38

The correct answer is a. You would use the **LIST INCARNATION OF DATABASE** command that is available in RMAN. This will provide a list of the current database incarnations stored in the RMAN recovery catalog. From this listing, you can determine whether the incarnation of the database you are concerned about is current. Answer b is incorrect, because the command shown will not work. Answer c is incorrect. While you can look at the underlying tables of the recovery catalog (a procedure not covered on the OCP exam and thus outside the scope of this book), it is not the preferred method. The SQL statement shown in answer c will also not show you the current incarnations. Answer d is incorrect, because it is possible to find the current incarnations. Even if the incarnations are incorrect, you would not issue the **REGISTER DATABASE** command again, but rather the **RESET DATABASE** command. Finally, answer e is incorrect, because there is no **SHOW INCARNATION** command in RMAN.

Question 39

The correct answer is a. Multiplexing is a part of Net8 and the new connection manager component. Multiplexing is useful in situations where there are lots of users who are issuing lots of SQL. It combines the SQL into one packet and then delivers the packet to the server. The server processes the packet and combines the results, returning them to communications manager, which distributes the results to the correct clients. Answer b is incorrect, because multiplexing is not as useful as connection pooling in the situation where there are lots of users but slow transactional volume. Answer c is incorrect, because multiplexing is not useful in situations where there are few users and long-running queries. Answer d is incorrect, because multiplexing is not designed to assist with databases communicating with each other, although if there was a lot of interdatabase SQL being generated, multiplexing might be of assistance. Answer e is incorrect, because multiplexing has no additional security features associated with its use.

Question 40

The correct answers are a and b. The **DBMS_AQ** package provides the **ENQUEUE** and **DEQUEUE** functions to allow users to use the queue tables to send queue messages. **DBMS_AQADM** is used by a DBA to administer advanced queuing functionality. Answers c, d, and e are incorrect, because they are not packages in Advanced Queuing.

Question 41

The correct answer is b. You issue the **CREATE LIBRARY** command to create the external pointer to the location of the external DLL that you wish to be able to access. Answer a is incorrect, because you use the **CREATE DIRECTORY** command to set up directories that point to the storage locations for **BFILES**. Answers c, d, and e are incorrect, because they are invalid Oracle commands.

Question 42

The correct answers are a and c. The **LOB** segment and the **LOB** index are created automatically when an object with the **LOB** storage data type is defined. The **LOB** segment is used for out-of-line storage of data for the **LOB**, and both the **LOB** segment and the **LOB** index can have separate storage specifications and reside on separate tablespaces. Answers b, d, and e are incorrect, because there is no **LOB** sort table, **LOB** locator, or **LOB** accumulator created when a **LOB** data type is created.

Question 43

The correct answer is b. Because the table and the prefixed global index have different partitions, answer b would be an example of nonequipartitioning. Answer a is incorrect, because the index and the table would have to have the same number of partitions; in this question, they would be equipartitioned. Answers c, d, and e are incorrect, because they are not related to partitioning.

Question 44

The correct answer is a. Because the week is 51, which is later than the partition range of partition **sales12(48)** and less than the partition range of partition **sales13(52)**, the row will fall into partition **sales13**. Answer b is incorrect for the same reason answer a is incorrect. Answers c and d are incorrect. The row will not be inserted in these partitions due to the value of the partition key. Finally, answer e is incorrect, because the insert will succeed.

Question 45

The correct answer is c; all affected partitions of all indexes will become invalid and require rebuilding. Answer a is incorrect, because the local index partitions will be invalidated, as well. Answer b is incorrect, because affected partitions in all indexes will be **UNUSABLE** and non-prefixed global indexes are no exception. Answer d is incorrect, because index partitions are affected. Finally, answer e is incorrect, because you can move an index partition.

Question 46

The correct answer is b. You must issue the **ALTER SESSION ENABLE PARALLEL DML** command to allow a DML statement (**UPDATE, INSERT**, or **DELETE**) to be executed in parallel. Answer a is incorrect, because any user can issue a parallel DML statement. Answer c is incorrect, because you enable parallel DML at the session level and not the database level. Answer d is incorrect, because there is no init.ora setting by the specified name. Finally, answer e is incorrect. If you do not issue the **ALTER SYSTEM ENABLE PARALLEL DML** command, the statement will not be run in parallel if so requested.

Question 47

The correct answer is c. The **parallel_max_servers** parameter defines the maximum number of parallel query processes that can be started by the database server for use with parallel queries. Answer a incorrect, because the parameter does not control the number of query server processes that will be started at instance startup. The **parallel_min_servers** parameter controls that number. Answers b, d, and e are incorrect. Answer b is not correct because **parallel_max_servers** does not control the maximum number of parallel server processes. There is no direct way to control the maximum number of processes used per query in Oracle. Answer d is not correct because the parameter has nothing to do with user sessions at all. Answer e is not correct because the setting does not have any effect on the degree of parallelism.

Question 48

The correct answer is c. You use the **DBMS_AQADM.GRANT_TYPE_ACCESS** function to grant a user the ability to support multiple consumers in a queue. Answers a and b are incorrect, because they are invalid functions in the **DBMS_AQ** and **DBMS_AQADM** packages. Answers d and e are incorrect. The specified functions are used to send messages to message queues and to receive messages from message queues.

Question 49

The correct answer is c. The parallel query coordinator manages parallel query operations of a single statement. It will start the required number of parallel server processes and manage the returning result sets from each of those processes. Answer a is incorrect, because it provides more of a description of the query server processes rather than the parallel query coordinator processes. Answer b is incorrect, because the parallel query coordinator is only responsible for the session that it is being used on. One parallel server process does not manage all parallel operations. Answer d is incorrect, because the parallel server coordinator does not affect serial query performance. Finally, answer e is incorrect, because the parallel query coordinator is not part of Net8, and it does not interact with the network directly in any way.

Question 50

The correct answers are a and c. Index-only tables have no **ROWID**s associated with the rows in the table. Also, an index-organized table cannot contain nested tables, object type tables, or **VARRAY**s. Answer b is incorrect, because you can create a nested table with a **LOB** data type. Answer d is incorrect, because you cannot create indexes on index-only tables. Answer e is incorrect, because index-only tables cannot be object tables.

Question 51

The correct answer is d; both nested-tables and **VARRAY**s allow you to store multiple values related to a column in a single row. This allows a one-to-many relationship between a column and a row. Answer a is incorrect. A **VARRAY** can contain more than one record per row. Answer b is incorrect, because **VARRAY**s are not stored out of line. Answer c is incorrect, because you cannot index **VARRAY** data type columns. Answer e is incorrect, because **VARRAY**s are created with a defined limit regarding the number of records they can hold.

Question 52

The correct answer is a. You use the **password_life_time** parameter to set how long a user, who is assigned to the profile associated with the setting, will have between forced password changes. You set the **password_grace_time** parameter to the number of days that you wish to give the user to change their password after the password has expired. Answer b is in correct, because the **password_lock_time** parameter is used to determine how long an account will be locked out if the number of failed login attempts exceeds the **failed_login_attempts** parameter. Answer c is incorrect, because the **password_reuse_max** setting is used to control how frequently a password can be repeated and has no association with forcing password changes. Answers d and e are incorrect, because they use password-setting parameters that do not apply to the question.

Question 53

The correct answer is b. Oracle8 Names Server is a directory service providing name-to-address resolution for Net8 services. It eliminates the need for localized tnsnames.ora files and, instead, does service alias name resolution at a central names server. Answer a is incorrect, because Oracle8 Names Server does not dynamically assign names to new databases. Answer c is incorrect, because the answer describes the Oracle8 security server. Answer d is incorrect, because Oracle8 Names Server is not a Web server. Answer e is incorrect, because Oracle8 Names Server does not provide new network protocol support for Oracle.

Question 54

The correct answer is e. RMAN will not recover a control file for a database unless the recovery catalog was used during the backup. Answers a, b, c, and d are incorrect, because they are all features of RMAN.

Question 55

The correct answer is b. The **REPORT UNRECOVERABLE** report will display datafiles that require backup due to unrecoverable actions performed on them since the last backup. Answer a is incorrect, because it is an invalid view for RMAN. Answer c is incorrect, because the wrong report is being executed, and its contents do not provide the needed information. Answer d is incorrect, because the alert.log does not contain messages relating to unrecoverable actions. Answer e is incorrect, because you cannot generate a report of the type described in RMAN.

Question 56

The correct answer is c. The **LIST BACKUP SET OF DATABASE** command will generate a list of all backup sets for the target database. Answer a is incorrect, because all backup sets are reported. Answer b is incorrect, because the location of the files is not reported with this command. Answer d is incorrect, because it only produces a listing of backup sets for the target database. Answer e is incorrect, because the command is only a reporting command and does not remove any backup sets.

Question 57

The correct answers are c and e. The **dbms_aq.enqueue** and **dbms_aq.dequeue** procedures are available in the **DBMS_AQ** package. Answers a, b, and d are incorrect, because the listed procedures are in the **DBMS_AQADM** package.

Question 58

The correct answer is c. A complete RMAN backup is contained in what is called a *backup set*. Answer a is incorrect, because a backup piece is comprised of the individual files that together create an entire backup set. Answer b is incorrect, because an archivelog backup set is a backup that contains archived redo logs. Answer d is incorrect, because an image copy is simply a direct copy of the datafile and is not part of an RMAN backup. Answer e is incorrect, because there is no such thing as a consistent backup copy.

Question 59

The correct answer is a. The **my_rowid** parameter will contain the extended **ROWID** of the object. Answer b is incorrect, because the specified functionality is provided by the **DBMS_ROWID.ROWID_TO_RESTRICTED** function. Answer c is incorrect, because a **NULL** will be returned in the case that the **ROWID** sent to the function is **NULL**. Answer d is incorrect, because **DBMS_ROWID.ROWID_TO_RESTRICTED** is a valid function. Answer e is incorrect, because the function has no effect on the database's limited internal use of **ROWID**s.

Question 60

The correct answer is c. You can have up to 1,000 columns in an Oracle8 table. Answers a, b, d, and e are incorrect answers.

Glossary

. . . .

Absolute datafile number—Used as a part of the **ROWID** in Oracle7, also known as a restricted **ROWID**. This is the file number where the row is located. This number is relative to the entire database.

Advanced Networking Option—A new Net8 networking option that allows for encryption of network traffic.

Advanced Queuing—Allows for advanced messaging functions, including the ability to send deferred messages, ordered messages, and messages to one or many recipients.

Agents—In advanced queuing, either producers or consumers of messages in queues.

Analyze—The process of gathering statistics on a table and/or indexes in Oracle. This is required in order to use the cost based optimizer.

Architecture—The logical design of a system.

Archive log—Mode in which an Oracle database must be set in order to facilitate hot backups. Causes the archival of online redo logs to offline redo log storage locations.

Archive log backup set—In RMAN, a backup set comprised of archived redo logs.

ASCII (American Standard Code for Information Interchange)—An eight-bit character system that's standard for transferring data between systems.

Attribute—Part of an object in Oracle, it defines either a scalar data type or another object type. It is one of two parts of an object, the other being methods.

Backup piece—In RMAN, a backup set may consist of one or more backup pieces.

Backup set—In RMAN, a backup set is the set of backup pieces that comprises a single complete backup. The backup may be a full, incremental, or archive log backup.

BFILE—An Oracle8 external **LOB**. It is a scalar data type used in Oracle to represent and facilitate read-only access to an external file from within the database.

BLOB—An Oracle8 internal **LOB**. A **BLOB** is a binary large object that is used to store binary data.

Block—The most granular unit of measurement of storage within Oracle. All oracle segments consist of multiple blocks. Once defined for an Oracle database the block size cannot be changed without recreating the database.

Block number—Used in both the Oracle7 restricted **ROWID** and the Oracle8 extended **ROWID**. This number identifies each block within a given datafile.

C—A programming language. In Oracle8, C is the only language that can be used to create external procedures.

Channel—Used in RMAN to facilitate communications between the operating system and the backup process.

Child operations—Operations that are spawned off by parent operations.

Chunk—Used in relation to Oracle8 **LOB**s. The **CHUNK** clause defines how many blocks of data will be read in a single I/O from an out-of-line **LOB** segment.

Client-side cache—Cache established on the client in association with the use of Oracle Names Server. Allows the client to quickly resolve name lookup requests in a local cache, thus reducing network traffic to the names server that might be required for this activity.

CLOB—An Oracle8 internal **LOB**. A **CLOB** is a large object that stores character data.

Cold backup—The process of backing up an entire Oracle database which requires shutting the database down, hence the database is cold (not running) during the backup.

Collection—One of two different types of new Oracle8 objects. A collection is either an object of a type of **VARRAY** or a nested table. These object types allow you to embed lists of values associated with a single row.

Connection manager—A new Net8 networking option that provides such functionality as multiplexing, connection pooling and provides multiprotocol support.

Connection pooling—Methodology provided in Oracle's connection manager product that allows multiple connections to share the same physical transport.

Constructor—Method created automatically when an object is created. A constructor method is used to create a new occurrence of an object type.

Consumer—In Oracle Advanced Queuing, the user of a message.

Data Object Number—Part of the Oracle8 extended **ROWID**. This number is used to keep track of the version number of every segment in the database.

Database buffer cache—Area of shared memory that is part of the SGA of an instance and is created at database startup. Used to store blocks of database data in memory to reduce disk I/O requirements for frequently used database blocks. Renamed **DEFAULT** buffer pool in Oracle8.

Database recovery—The process of recovering a database. This may include instance recovery, which requires no administrative action or media recovery that requires administrative action.

DBMS_AQ—Package used in Oracle's Advanced Queuing option to allow for queuing and dequeueing of messages by agents.

DBMS_AQADM—Package used in Oracle's Advanced Queuing option to allow for administration of advanced queuing features.

DBMS_LOB—Package provided by Oracle to allow manipulation of new Oracle8 **LOB** data types.

DDL (Data Definition Language)—Statements in Oracle used to create, drop and alter objects.

Default buffer pool—Replacement in Oracle8 for the database buffer cache. Has the same functionality as the database buffer cache in Oracle7.

Deferred constraint—A constraint that can optionally be checked at the end of a transaction rather than after the completion of a statement executed against the object the constraint is associated with.

Degree of parallelism—The requested number of parallel processes to be used in the execution of a SQL statement. Can be defined using several methods, including default settings on objects, hints, and directives in SQL statements.

Dequeue—The process of removing a message from a queue table in Oracle8 Advanced Queuing.

Direct load—The process of inserting data into a table that circumvents the standard Oracle insert processes (i.e. Use of the database buffer cache) and instead inserts data directly into the Oracle table.

DLL (Dynamically Linked Libraries)—Used when creating external procedures to be called from Oracle.

DML (Data Manipulation Language)—SQL statements used to manipulate data within Oracle objects. This includes **INSERT, UPDATE,** and **DELETE** statements.

Dot decimal notation—Process of using dots to separate various identifying characteristics of an object. For example, a dot is used between the schema owner name of an object and the object name.

Enforced constraint—An option, new in Oracle8, that allows a constraint to be enabled without checking the existing records in the relationship.

Enqueue—Process of placing a message in the message queue.

Equipartitioned—State of two Oracle partitioned objects where the partition of the one object corresponds to the partition of the other.

Exception queue—Used in Oracle Advanced Queuing to store messages that are removed from the queue tables for various reasons. Reasons for removal can include message expiration, errors attempting to deliver the message, and other problems.

EXPLAIN_PLAN—Oracle command used to determine access path that will be used by a SQL query. Results can be used for query performance tuning.

Export (EXP)—Oracle utility used to export part or all of an Oracle database. There exist several restrictions on the Oracle objects that can be successfully exported.

Extended ROWID—ROWID format used in Oracle8. The format of the extended **ROWID** contains four elements including the data object number, the relative file number, the block number, and the row number.

External LOB—An external large data type used to associate files external of the database with rows inside of the database.

Flattened subquery—A special SQL syntax introduced in Oracle8 to accommodate Oracle8 collection types. Using the Oracle8 keyword **THE**, the subquery returns one or more rows back for a query from an object that includes a collection type.

Full backup—A complete backup of a database created through RMAN.

Function—Stored PL/SQL code that returns a value.

Global index—An index that can be partitioned, that is not related directly to the table the index is created on. A global index allows an index to be nonequipartitioned with the table it is created against. Oracle is not aware of the relationship of the index and the table partitions.

Hint—Method in a SQL statement of tailoring the way the optimizer will create the execution path for that statement. Hints can include suggested indexes to use, parallelism requests, and other custom access paths to the data.

Hot backup—Process of backing up a database while the database is still running.

Image copy—In RMAN, an image copy is an exact copy of a data file copied somewhere else. This copy can be used to create another database or recover an existing database manually.

Import (IMP)—Oracle utility that allows the DBA to take a file created by the export utility and import that file into another database.

Incremental backup—RMAN feature that allows the DBA to backup only the data blocks that have changed.

Index fast full scan—Method of creating an index with columns that allows a query to scan only the index and return the data set requested.

Init.ora—Oracle parameter file that controls many different characteristics of the database. This file must be present to start the instance (nomount mode).

Instance recovery—An automatic Oracle process that is executed upon startup of the Oracle instance after an instance failure.

Instead of triggers—Triggers created to intercept DML commands on a view and perform specific database actions. These triggers run instead of the expected DML operation.

Internal LOB—An Oracle8 Large Object (**LOB**) that is stored inside the database. These include **BLOB, CLOB,** and **NCLOB** data types.

Inter-operation parallelism—The operation of one or more processes on more than one operation in the execution plan of a SQL statement at the same time.

Intra-operation parallelism—The operation of more than one process on a single operation of an execution plan of a SQL statement at the same time.

IO_SLAVES—An alternative to multiple DB writer processes, introduced in Oracle8. These can be used to mimic asynchronous I/O.

KEEP buffer pool—New memory pool in Oracle8 designed to store data blocks that should not be aged out of memory.

Large pool—New memory pool in Oracle8 designed for use with MTS sessions, I/O slaves, and RMAN.

LOB (Large Object)—These are new data types introduced in Oracle8 designed to store large objects. These data types are **BLOB, CLOB, NCLOB,** and **BFILE.**

LOB index—Index created at the same time a **LOB** column is defined.

LOB locator—Pointer to out-of-line stored **LOB** data, stored in a **LOB** segment.

LOB segments—Segment allocated at the time an object with a **LOB** data type is created.

Local index—Index created that is equipartitioned with the related partitioned table. The index's partition equivalency is known to the database.

Message—The unit of communication in Oracle Advanced Queuing between the producer and the consumer. The message contains the data the producer wishes to send plus other information such as the time the message was sent.

Message queue—Storage areas for Oracle8 Advanced Queuing messages. A message queue must be created before messages can be enqueued and dequeued.

Method—Part of an Oracle object, a method is a unit of code that is associated with the object. Oracle has four different kinds of methods: constructors, **MEMBER** methods, **MAP** and **ORDER** methods.

Migration—The process of moving a database from Oracle7 to Oracle8.

Migration utility—An Oracle provided utility to ease the migration of the Oracle7 database to an Oracle8 database.

Multiplexing—A feature of the Oracle Connection Manager that allows many user connections to use a single transport to access a database.

Names Server—A feature of Net8 that allows for remote resolution of a database alias for clients.

NCLOB—An Oracle8 **LOB** type that can store multibyte character data.

Nested table—An Oracle collection type that allows the storage of more than one value in a column in a single row.

Net8—Oracle networking software that provides networking facilities between the Oracle database and clients.

Network interface—An interface for Oracle8 servers and clients that handles the networking between the two. This layer, in part, makes the database and the client applications protocol independent.

NOLOGGING—Option for various objects in Oracle that prevents the creation of redo when DML is executed against those objects.

Nonequipartitioned—State of two Oracle partitioned objects where the partition of one object does not correspond to the partition of the other.

Nonprefixed index—An index in which the leading edge does not match the partition key of the partitioned table associated with that index.

Normal queue—In Oracle Advanced Queuing, the Normal Queue is the table that stores messages to be dequeued by consumers.

Object—A structure comprised of attributes and methods.

Object references—A reference in an object table or relational table to a row in an object table.

Object table—A nonrelational table that is a collection of objects and stored row object instances. Every row stored in an object table is an object itself.

OCP (Oracle Certified Professional)—One who has passed a battery of tests and has received official certification from Oracle of this status.

OID (Object Identifier)—16-byte number which is assigned to each object to make it unique throughout the entire database. Not used with relational tables.

Oracle installer—Program provided by Oracle, used to install the database, the migration utility and even execute the migration utility.

Out-of-line storage—Segment that is created when an object or table is created with a LOB datatype. This segment stores data greater than about 4000 bytes out of line with the rest of the row.

Overflow tablespace—Tablespace associated with an index-only table for rows of a length that exceeds a percentage of available space.

Package—Oracle programmatic construct that contains a collection of procedures and functions.

Parallel DDL/DML—DDL and DML operations that can be split concurrently into many different processes which can be executed at the same time.

Parallel query—A query that can have multiple processes working together to return the result set for the purpose of reducing the run time of the query.

Parallel Query Coordinator—Main process in parallel processing that is responsible for the management of parallel server processes and management of the data sets returned from those processes.

Parallel server processes—Processes that perform parallel operations and returns the results to the parallel query coordinator.

Parent operation—Operation that has started one or more operations and waits on the completion of those operations.

Partition key—The column or columns that a partitioned table is partitioned on.

Partition pruning—The process of removing a partition from consideration in a query based on it's partition key's relation to the where clause of the query.

Partitioning—The ability to split Oracle tables and indexes into different objects based on one or more partitioning criteria.

Password verify function—Function that is used to verify passwords that are changed by users.

Prefixed index—An index that is keyed on the same key as the partition key.

Procedure—Oracle programmatic construct that is stored in the database and does not return a value.

Producer—In Oracle Advanced Queuing, the creator of a message to be enqueued.

Recovery catalog—Schema in a database that stores RMAN backup data.

RECYCLE buffer pool—New Oracle8 memory structure in the SGA that is designed for buffers that are to be read into memory, but should not require retention in memory.

Redo—Records generated in the online redo logs that record all changes to the database. Once filled, online redo logs are copied to the archive log directory and become archived redo logs. These archived redo logs are used in recovery of Oracle databases.

Relative datafile number—Used in the new Oracle8 extended **ROWID** format, the relative datafile number is relative to the tablespace the datafile is associated with.

Restricted ROWID—The **ROWID** format used in Oracle7. Contains three elements, the block number, row number and absolute file number.

Reverse key index—An index in which key values are reversed in an effort to balance the index.

RMAN—New Oracle8 utility that facilitates backup and recovery of Oracle databases.

RMAN script—Collection of RMAN commands that can be stored in an operating system file or can be stored in the recovery catalog.

Row number—Used in both the Oracle7 restricted **ROWID** and the Oracle8 extended ROWID, the row number defines a unique row within a data block.

ROWID—Used in an Oracle database to uniquely identify a individual row in a database. Every row has a **ROWID** that is unique.

Scalar data type—Data types that are predefined in Oracle such as **NUMBER** and **VARCHAR2**.

Schema—Collection of Oracle objects (tables, indexes, and so on).

Security server—New Oracle8 Net8 option that allows for the encryption of network traffic and centralized database user authentication.

Server manager—Management interface into Oracle that allows the Database Administrator to manage the database.

Server pool—Pool of parallel server processes to be called upon when parallel processing servers are needed.

SGA (System Global Area)—Consists of the shared pool, the default buffer cache and the redo log buffer. It can also consist of optional structures including the large pool, the keep buffer pool and the recycle buffer pool.

Shared pool—Part of the Oracle SGA, used to store the data dictionary cache, the library cache and other memory structures.

Source database—In an Oracle migration from Oracle7 to Oracle8, the source database is the Oracle7 database.

SQL (Structured Query Language)—Used to access data within an Oracle database.

SQL*Loader—Oracle utility used to load raw data into an Oracle database. This data can be in various formats such as reports or other formats.

SQL*Net—Oracle7 product that facilitates networking between the Oracle database and Oracle clients.

Tablespace—A tablespace is a logical storage unit for segments that is made up of one or more physical data files.

TNS layer (Transparent Network Substrate)—Networking layer provided by SQL*Net that provides a client and a server (nodes) with common application programming interfaces (APIs) allowing a persistent pathway to transmit data between the two nodes.

Trigger—Stored PL/SQL program that executes based on a DML statement (i.e., **INSERT, UPDATE, or DELETE**) being executed.

VARRAY—An Oracle8 collection type that allows for the storage of multiple data values in one column in a single row.

Index

. . . .

Bold page numbers indicate sample exam questions.

CERTIFIED CRAMMER SOCIETY

PHI SLAMMA CRAMMA

A breed apart, a cut above the rest—a true professional. Highly skilled and superbly trained, certified IT professionals are unquestionably the world's most elite computer experts. In an effort to appropriately recognize this privileged crowd, The Coriolis Group is proud to introduce the Certified Crammer Society. If you are a certified IT professional, it is our pleasure to invite you to become a Certified Crammer Society member.

Membership is free to all certified professionals and benefits include a membership kit that contains your official membership card and official Certified Crammer Society blue denim ball cap emblazoned with the Certified Crammer Society crest— proudly displaying the Crammer motto "Phi Slamma Cramma"—and featuring a genuine leather bill. The kit also includes your password to the Certified Crammers-Only Web site containing monthly discreet messages designed to provide you with advance notification about certification testing information, special book excerpts, and inside industry news not found anywhere else; monthly Crammers-Only discounts on selected Coriolis titles; *Ask the Series Editor* Q and A column; cool contests with great prizes; and more.

GUIDELINES FOR MEMBERSHIP

Registration is free to professionals certified in Microsoft, A+, or Oracle DBA. Coming soon: Sun Java, Novell, and Cisco. Send or email your contact information and proof of your certification (test scores, membership card, or official letter) to:

Certified Crammer Society Membership Chairperson
THE CORIOLIS GROUP, LLC
14455 North Hayden Road, Suite 220, Scottsdale, Arizona 85260-6949
Fax: 480.483.0193 • Email: ccs@coriolis.com

APPLICATION

Name:

Address:

Society Alias:

Choose a secret code name to correspond with us
and other Crammer Society members.
Please use no more than eight characters.

Email: